ALSO AVAILABLE FROM CQ PRESS:

Politics in Britain
Bruce F. Norton

Politics in France
Charles Hauss

POLITICS IN

GERMANY

M. Donald Hancock
Vanderbilt University

Henry Krisch
University of Connecticut

Best wishes to good friends & colleagues — stück auf!

Henry

CQ PRESS
A Division of SAGE
Washington, D.C.

CQ Press
2300 N Street, NW, Suite 800
Washington, DC 20037

Phone: 202-729-1900; toll-free, 1-866-4CQ-PRESS (1-866-427-7737)

Web: www.cqpress.com

Cover design: Kimberly Glyder
Composition: MacPS, LLC
Photo Credits:
AP Images: 7 (top and bottom), 31, 53, 66, 81, 133, 147, 168, 179, 201
Wikipedia Commons: 118

♾ The paper used in this publication exceeds the requirements of the American National Standard for Information Sciences—Permanence of Paper for Printed Library Materials, ANSI Z39.48-1992.

Printed and bound in the United States of America

12   11   10   09   08   1   2   3   4   5

Library of Congress Cataloging-in-Publication Data

Hancock, M. Donald.
    Politics in Germany / M. Donald Hancock, Henry Krisch.
        p. cm.
    Includes bibliographical references and index.
    ISBN 978-1-933116-07-5 (alk. paper)
    1. Germany—Politics and government—20th century. 2. Germany—Politics and government—21st century.   I. Krisch, Henry. II. Title.

    JN3971.A58.H35 2008
    320.943—dc22

                                                                2008018708

For Kendra and Erik, my daughter and son,
in gratitude for what they have taught me
about life and love.
M. Donald Hancock

For my daughter Jennifer and my son Daniel,
for all they have meant to me.
Henry Krisch

Contents

8. Organized Interest Groups and Social Movements   136

9. Socioeconomic Policies and Performance   157

10. Germany in Europe and the World   173

11. Germany in the Twenty-First Century   188

Boxes, Maps, Figures, and Tables

Boxes

Maps

Figures

Tables

Preface

In these early years of the twenty-first century, with internal and external armed conflicts raging throughout the "global south" and the rise of new world powers such as China and India demanding increased attention, one may well ask: Why a book on German politics? Is this not just an example of the traditional American academic focus on European states?

We believe there are two compelling answers to this question, one practical, the other philosophical. The practical answer is that Germany is the strongest economic power and most populous nation in the European Union (EU), which itself is a major force in world affairs. It is thus important to know not only how Germany's politics, economic policies, and foreign policy affect the rest of the EU (and Europe in general), but also how Germany compares on each of these dimensions with its neighbors. Moreover, given Germany's current strength and history, it is natural to ask how democratic at home and peaceful abroad today's Germany has become and is likely to remain. This combination of analytical description and comparison is a major feature of our book and the first reason for writing it.

The second reason, the philosophical one that is almost unavoidable for any scholar dealing with modern Germany, is to link present-day Germany—united, peaceful, democratic, and prosperous—with the Germany that preceded 1990. During this period Germans achieved great successes in the sciences and arts, as well as innovative social policy and efficient administration, but they also supported authoritarian rulers and tyrannical dictatorships when their efforts at revolutionary transformation and democratic government fell short. Finally, in their name and with the collaboration of a majority, the crimes of World War II and the Holocaust were perpetrated.

We do not pretend to have an answer to the historical riddle of how Germans could rise to such heights and also sink to such depths; in any case, this is a book on contemporary politics, not one of history. Nevertheless, we could not analyze and describe the Germany of the twenty-first century without being aware of its historical background. Thus an underlying theme of our book becomes: Is Germany today a modern democratic European state like its EU partners, or is it an exceptional case?

In undertaking this assessment, we bring together complementary intellectual experience and perspectives. One of us (Hancock) has written extensively on western Germany, Scandinavia, and the EU; the other (Krisch) on the former Soviet-bloc German Democratic Republic (GDR). Both of us have studied and taught postwar German politics in explicit comparative contexts (West European and the Soviet bloc, respectively). We therefore view modern Germany from the dual perspectives of the former Federal Republic in western Germany and the one-time GDR in the east. We ask, at relevant points, what the legacy of this almost half century of partition and two-state competition has been for Germany today.

Acknowledgments

I (Henry Krisch) thank the staff of the Homer Babbidge Library at the University of Connecticut, particularly Steven Batt, as well as several colleagues in all parts of Germany, for help with sources. For earlier research in Germany, some of which I have used in this book, I thank the staff at the Humboldt University Library in Berlin and the staff at the SAPMO, the Berlin section of the German Federal Archives devoted to the parties and mass organizations of the GDR. I owe a debt to colleagues both here and in Germany for many years of intellectual stimulation and frequent reality checks about the nuances of German politics. I especially owe my collaborator, Don Hancock, for exemplary scholarly collaboration. He made coauthorship—a new form for me—an experience full of plusses and no minuses. I certainly appreciated his grasp of the modernization processes and the political economy of Germany. He would probably agree that his strengths in German affairs and mine dovetailed nicely, a judgment with which we hope our readers will agree. Finally, none of these good things would have happened but for the patient and, where necessary, critical support of my wife, June.

For my part (Donald Hancock), I am deeply indebted in turn to the knowledge and acumen of Henry Krisch. We first met during graduate studies and our initial teaching experiences at Columbia University, and we have maintained a close personal and professional friendship through the years. While our immersion in German and comparative politics diverged for much of that time along the lines of Europe's Cold War division, Germany's reunification and the eastward extension of the EU have brought a convergence of our research interests and deepened our understanding of German politics in its multiple dimensions.

On behalf of both of us I would like to thank Brian Boling, Larry Romans, and Amy Stewart-Mailhoit in the documents section at Vanderbilt University's Jean and Alexander Heard Library for their indefatigable help in tracking down countless sources and references. Students, as always, proved a powerful intellectual stimulus in the course of our research and writing—among them, Boyce Adams, Irek Kusmierczyk, Rodelio Manacsa, and Matthew McGrath. I also wish to acknowledge the assistance and encouragement of a number of Vanderbilt stalwarts: Anja Beck, a visiting scholar from Leipzig at the Center for the Americas; John McCarthy, director of the Max Kade Center for European and German Studies; and fellow political scientists James Booth, Tim Boyd, Florence Faucher-King, Marc Hetherington, Michaela Mattes, and Neal Tate. Friends on both sides of the Atlantic provided us with indispensable insights and understanding of Germany on a personal level of society and politics.

We also wish to thank Elise Frasier and Charisse Kiino, our development and acquisitions editors, respectively, at CQ Press, and Lorna Notsch, our project editor, for their patient understanding of authors' travails and their expert handling of our manuscript. Finally, both of us are grateful for the careful reading of draft chapters by several outside reviewers, including Patrick Altdorfer, University of Pittsburgh; Mary Hampton, Air Command and Staff College; James McAdams, University of Notre Dame; David Patton, Connecticut College; Lori Poloni-Staudinger, Northern Arizona University; Susan Scarrow, University of Houston; Robin E. Taylor; and Helga Welsh, Wake Forest University. They inspired us through their suggestions and constructive criticism.

Introduction

Germany as a Normal Democratic Polity

G ermany has always been and continues to be what Gustav Heinemann—a former president of West Germany and one of the country's most thoughtful leaders—called a "difficult fatherland." Germans, no less than foreign observers, remember Germany's descent into the ruthlessness of the Nazi regime. The magnitude of World War II, the enormity of the Holocaust, and the repercussions of these remain moral blots on the nation's record. Furthermore, for more than forty years there were two German regimes: the Federal Republic of Germany in the west and the German Democratic Republic (GDR) in the east. Each was embedded in mutually hostile military alliances, and Germans died at German hands along a border that divided both the country and its capital.

German unification formally ended the country's postwar division between antagonistic capitalist-democratic and communist states, but it left unresolved a number of important questions about the nation's past and future. If it is true, as some scholars and political leaders have argued, that Germany followed a distinctive path of development, a "special path" (*Sonderweg*) that led from deep historical roots through the Imperial regime and the Weimar Republic into the abyss of national socialism,[1] then one would expect the prosperous and democratic Germany to be a fragile social anomaly occasioned by the Cold War. Conversely, if pre-Hitler Germany was as "normal" in its political, economic, and social arrangements as say, France or Russia, then the rise of a peaceful, democratic, and prosperous united Germany might be seen as a resumption of an interrupted standard European path. As Mary Hampton has observed, this would suggest that unified Germany has once again become a "normal nation."[2] This, of course, raises the question of what such a "normal" path would entail.[3]

1

Related to this line of thought, there are scholars who suggest that the fall of communism in Central and Eastern Europe means that history has resumed where it left off in 1945. So what are the implications of this for Germany in the twenty-first century? Was West Germany's unprecedented affluence and political stability beginning in the early 1950s an anomaly fostered by the imperatives of the Cold War? Will these achievements continue to characterize the economic and political performance of a reunified Germany? To what extent does Germany, in the twenty-first century, face social, political, economic, and international problems comparable to those facing its fellow democratic partners in the European Union? In the chapters that follow, we seek an answer to this question of Germany's destiny by testing German actions and institutions to see whether contemporary Germany is indeed a normal modern democratic European state in its problems as well as in its achievements.

The modern German national state dates only from 1871. It has never been conterminous with German ethnic settlement or German cultural life. Unification poses anew fundamental questions concerning national memories and identity. As Alan Watson provocatively asks: "[W]ho are the Germans now? Do the Germans now constitute a normal nation? Have they begun to rediscover their own identity and patriotism? Or do they remain different and dangerous?"[4] Answers to these questions clearly reveal that German national identity is a complex and changing mosaic consisting of multiple historical, cultural, political, and economic components. The legacy of Germany's postwar division constitutes a profound singularity in comparison with other European nations. Forty-five years of separation between western and eastern Germany, as well as the course and rapidity of German reunification in 1989–1990, decisively shape ongoing efforts by Germans to redefine their identity within the boundaries of a reestablished sovereign national community. In the process, should it not be expected that a unified Germany will adopt a normal European patriotic pride in its achievements even as it also faces normal European problems?

German unification has meant the extension of western German political and social norms and institutions, socioeconomic relations, and ways of life to the former German Democratic Republic. We explore how such institutions and social norms may have been altered by their expansion into a reunified Germany. Such an assessment necessarily encompasses mass values and attitudes, political parties and election outcomes, the welfare state, economic policies and performance, and the conduct of foreign policy. It also includes important questions relating to how the reconstitution of capitalism and the creation of Western-style trade unions and business associations in the former GDR affect industrial relations on a national basis. We also discuss an issue fundamental to eastern German awareness of "what remains of the GDR"—or, perhaps, what should remain?

Such questions underscore the elusiveness of political "normalcy" as Germany approaches its third decade as a reunited nation. While western

German constitutional norms and institutions prevail throughout both parts of the country, deeply rooted psychological cleavages persist among citizens on both sides of the former border. One consequence is that Germany's party system has assumed greater complexity than in the previous "old" Federal Republic because of widespread electoral support for the newly constituted Left Party, which is an amalgamation of the postcommunist Party of Democratic Socialism (PDS) of East Germany and dissident Social Democrats and others of West Germany. At the opposite ideological extreme, radical right movements challenge the dominant political culture in much the same fashion as the National Front in France and the Freedom Party in Austria. The dramatic disclosure at the turn of the century of illegal financial contributions to former chancellor Helmut Kohl and other prominent members of the Christian Democratic Union (CDU) prompted an interim crisis of the party system reminiscent of the implosion of the Socialist and Christian Democratic parties during the early 1990s in Italy.

And these issues matter, because Germany's location in the heart of Europe means that it constitutes an important economic and political link between West and East. As a founding member of the European Coal and Steel Community and the European Economic Community (now the European Union), Germany has steadfastly advocated economic integration and institutionalized political cooperation in Western Europe. The demise of communism in the former Soviet empire offered the Federal Republic a leadership role in extending these principles to the new democracies and market economies of Central and Eastern Europe. Germany's presidency of the EU during the first half of 1999 and again in 2007 underscored its leaders' strong commitment to that community's further "widening" and "deepening."

By virtue of its geographical location and considerable material and human resources, unified Germany confronts a set of newly crucial foreign policy issues. Shall it play a global political role, perhaps as a permanent member of the United Nations Security Council? Or should it seek a more limited, perhaps regional role, particularly within and through the EU? What are the domestic and international political implications of German military involvement in NATO's war against Serbia in 1999 and the ongoing struggle to establish peace in Afghanistan? What political, economic, and military role will Germany play in the expanded European Union and an increasingly globalized world? And finally, what are Germany's special relations with the United States and Russia?

In considering these and related issues, we concentrate on the period since the mid-1980s while drawing on relevant historical antecedents. Conceptually, we utilize multiple principles of comparative analysis in our assessment of politics in Germany: (1) modernization theory, which for us is a shorthand label for interrelated processes of industrialization and postindustrialization, social mobilization, and political development over time; (2) political and popular culture, which we utilize to assess successive tides of value changes, the diffusion of an elite-mass democratic consensus in Germany, and linkages between politics and society as expressed through literature, music, and cinema; (3) constitutionalism, political institutions, parties, and interest groups; and (4) comparative public policy, with attention to both domestic and foreign policy choices and performance.[5]

Because of its turbulent past and contemporary status as one of the most powerful European states, Germany offers a compelling opportunity for such analysis. Having experienced a prolonged period of "modernity gone awry" and more than four decades of national division, what sort of Germany has now emerged in the ever-changing European context? How will Germany's role in the twenty-first century compare with its troubled and problematical one in the twentieth? How do German policies and problems compare with those of its democratic industrial partners? To what extent has unified Germany in fact become a "normal" nation?

We see Germany as the product of multiple political systems in the past giving way to the current democratic constitutional system, a country seeking to subsume in one national community deep historical cleavages of region and religion, the more recent division between East and West, and the current struggle to integrate substantial non-German immigrant minorities, particularly large Turkish and Islamic communities. That is the Germany whose politics is described and analyzed in the chapters that follow.

1

Land, People, Society

Geography, history, and political symbolism loom large over unified Germany. The move of its national government from Bonn on the Rhine to Berlin on the Spree signifies Germany's redefinition of its status as a nation-state and assumption of a new role in European and world affairs. The election of Gerhard Schröder as head of a national Social Democratic–Green coalition in 1998 and the formation of a Christian Democratic–Social Democratic "grand coalition" government in 2005 under Angela Merkel, Germany's first female chancellor, marked the rise to power of a new, younger generation of leaders who—while wholly cognizant of their nation's multiple histories—nonetheless look to the future with measured confidence. The "Berlin republic" has indeed superseded the Bonn and the Weimar republics. It simultaneously retains fundamental political, institutional, and economic attributes of the "old Federal Republic" in the west and imbedded cultural and social features of the former German Democratic Republic (GDR) in the east.

Berlin itself embodies multiple threads of Germany's past, present, and future. While it was the historical center of Prussian and Imperial German militarism and subsequent National Socialist oppression over Germany and eventually most of Europe, Berlin was also a center of German democracy and cultural achievement in the Weimar era, as well as a Western bulwark during the Cold War and (in the east) the capital of the German Democratic Republic. Sobering reminders of the Nazi legacy are manifest in the form of a vast Russian military cemetery in eastern Berlin, street signs depicting Nazi-era anti-Semitic laws lining a residential street in western Berlin, and a newly constructed Holocaust memorial in the center of the city. Classical structures such as the Brandenburg Gate, the state opera house, Humboldt University, and former royal palaces on the boulevard Unter den Linden in the east contrast smartly with the architecturally prize-winning reconstruction of the *Reichstag* building; a new chancellery; the sprawling, reconstructed Lehrter train station; and spiraling skyscrapers in Potsdamer Platz (prewar Germany's equivalent of Times Square and Picadilly Circus). Hitler's bunker remains buried under a construction site in the shadow of Göring's former air force ministry, which was transformed into government offices in "GDR times" and subsequently served as the headquarters of the postunification trusteeship agency for privatization in eastern Germany. Brightly lit postmodern buildings line Friedrichstrasse, once a drab connecting point between East Berlin's major train station and the crossing gate from West Berlin at Checkpoint Charlie. A number of buildings and monuments from GDR times no longer remain.

Unified Germany is the product of centuries of economic, social, and political development. These intertwined processes of system change comprise a complex global process of modernization that has transformed traditionally rural societies into the advanced industrial nations of Western Europe, the Americas, most of the British Commonwealth, and parts of Asia. Germany's own course of modernization proved singular, involving rapid industrialization and social development following the nation's first unification in 1871 but also a torturous course of political change that embraced Imperial authoritarianism, the democratic experiment of the Weimar Republic, Nazi totalitarianism, and postwar variants of communism and Western-style democracy. Following a brief conceptual explication of modernization, this chapter focuses on the material and social basis of Germany's contemporary modernity. Chapter 2 addresses Germany's tortuous political development from 1871, and chapter 3 explores postwar division and unification.

Modernization as Concept and Process

Modernization can be broadly defined as a historical process by which people in a defined territory acquire increased control over nature and society through the application of advanced technology, science, and expanded social cooperation.[1] A necessary prerequisite is the diffusion of collective values that embrace a shared sense of political community and the idea of progress. This revolution in human consciousness was launched by the Age of Enlightenment, in which Continental and American theorists and political activists put forth transformative ideologies of philosophical liberalism and its later rivals on both the conservative right and socialist left. Other variants of collective human consciousness—not all of which are based on the Enlightenment's concepts of economic and political progress—range from patriotism founded in collective historical memories and a shared sense of national purpose, religious community, ethnicity, or a blend of these to xenophobic nationalism, religious messianism, and racism.

Germany's history has many moments worthy of praise and celebration, as this young couple is doing at the 2006 World Cup soccer competition held in Germany. Its history also has many occasions for regret and penance, emotions Chancellor Willy Brandt displayed before the Warsaw Ghetto memorial in Warsaw, Poland, in December 1970.

Historically, modernization measured as active system change began with political development involving the attainment and maintenance of territoriality, the establishment of recognized political authority, the emergence of nation-states as the principal actors in international politics, and the expansion of the concept of "citizenship" and rights of citizens. Modernization subsequently proceeded through closely interrelated processes of economic development and social mobilization. Empirical measures of economic modernization include a long-term continuum from industrialization, which began in the eighteenth century in Britain and the American colonies, to postindustrialization in the latter part of the twentieth century throughout most of Western Europe, North America, and other highly developed regions. This continuum involves, first, the transition from a predominantly agrarian society to one in which most workers are employed in the production and distribution of material goods, and, subsequently, the transformation of such a society into one in which a majority of people are engaged in public or private services; the creation and application of new forms of scientific, technological, and social knowledge; or both. The explosion of a mass entertainment industry—including music, movies, videos, and television—is another manifestation of postindustrial society. (We address specific German manifestations of some of these aspects of "popular culture" in chapter 4.)

Accompanying the emergence of postindustrial societies in Europe, North America, and other economically advanced regions has been the diffusion of what scholar Ronald Inglehart has described as postmaterialist values. In contrast to materialist values, which affirm basic survival needs such as food, shelter, and security, postmaterialist values embrace individual desires to belong to informal groups that extend beyond the biological family and inherited social class, an increased emphasis on work satisfaction, greater aesthetic sensitivity, and a quest for enhanced self-esteem and self-realization.[2] As Inglehart argues:

> The values of Western publics have been shifting from an overwhelming emphasis on material well-being and physical security toward greater emphasis on the quality of life.... Today, an unprecedently large portion of Western populations have been raised under conditions of exceptional economic security. Economic and physical security continue to be valued positively, but their relative priority is lower than in the past.[3]

These value changes have as significant consequences for political and social behavior in contemporary society in Germany as they do elsewhere, as we argue (following Inglehart's lead) in later chapters. To the extent that the GDR, like its fellow Soviet bloc societies, lagged substantially behind Western countries in the postindustrial transition, attitudes in eastern Germany differ in important ways from those in western Germany.

Like political modernization, social mobilization is a multifaceted dimension of modernization. Requisites include urbanization and enhanced communication among citizens through greater individual proximity and the diffusion of new forms of information exchange and consciousness-raising socialization experiences, both of which are provided in part through such media as newspapers and—in the twentieth and twenty-first centuries—radio, television, and the Internet. Equally crucial is the role of education in promoting the acquisition of new individual-mass skills, such as literacy and technical competence with increasingly sophisticated machines ranging from those on the assembly line through mechanized farm equipment and transportation vehicles to today's computer technology. Social mobilization also involves the formation of new types of organizations that integrate workers, farmers, and other groups into industrial and postindustrial society. Examples include trade unions, agrarian cooperatives, political parties, professional interest groups, and grassroots mobilization movements.

Modernization has assumed a vast range of forms over time and around the world. It may be gradual and driven largely by private groups and interests, as was the case in the transition of the United States from an agrarian society to an industrial democracy in the nineteenth and twentieth centuries. It may be coercive and directed by central government power, as was the case in Stalinist Russia and postrevolutionary China and Cuba, or it can assume some combination of these historical patterns. These contrasting patterns and outcomes underscore the relativity of modernity; there is no universal model of economic, social, and political development. Moreover, as Samuel Huntington has persuasively argued, modernization is not a unilinear process; nations and regions may indeed attain new levels of modernizing change, but they also may undergo regressive change in the form of economic recessions, political decay, or both.[4]

Nor is modernization an unmitigated social blessing. Much of its impetus has arisen from warfare, with its resultant physical destruction and immeasurable costs to human lives. Both industrialization and postindustrialization have disrupted the lives of countless people over time, depriving entire occupational groups of their traditional livelihoods and uprooting individuals from family group, residence, and religious moorings. Similarly, the application of advanced scientific and technological knowledge has resulted in devastating unintended consequences, as grimly testified to by the estimated ten thousand birth defects caused by the drug Thalidomide during the 1950s and early 1960s and the Chernobyl nuclear disaster in the Ukraine in 1986.[5]

It is our argument in this book that Germany has undergone a modernizing process in large measure congruent with that of other modern European (and to perhaps a lesser extent, non-European) countries, with the result that its political, social, and economic orders closely resemble theirs. Of course, Germany has had some unique historical experiences—the Hitler era with its Holocaust and postwar occupation and division are obvious examples—but similar observations could be made about many other

European Union (EU) states—Italian fascism, French collaboration, and the very different experiences of European countries during World War II are prominent examples. We will show in subsequent chapters that Germany's postwar development (1945–2008) has made it a standard modernized society.

Physical Geography

Germany's natural and human resources constitute the material and social basis for the nation's historical process of modernization as well as its contemporary status as one of the most important countries in Europe. Its geographical location means that German economic performance and its domestic and foreign policies are fatefully intertwined with those of its neighboring states and the European continent as a whole.

Unified Germany has a clearly defined national territory encompassing 137,735 square miles (356,733 square kilometers), which exceeds the size of both Italy and the United Kingdom but is eclipsed by France.[6] Germany borders on fully nine countries: Denmark in the north; Poland and the Czech Republic to the east; Austria and Switzerland to the south; and France, the Netherlands, Belgium, and Luxembourg to the west. The country consists of three principal geographical regions: a mountainous region bordering Austria in the south, an uplands region stretching across the central part of the country from west to east, and a lowland plain region along the northern seacoasts and the border with Denmark. Climatic conditions vary among these regions depending on elevation and proximity to the warming waters of the North Atlantic. The coldest parts of the country in winter can be found in the Bavarian Alps in the south and parts of eastern and northeastern Germany. Physically, the regions are closely integrated through a vast network of rivers, shipping canals, and highly advanced transportation systems.

Germany's terrain encompasses rugged contrasts ranging from mountains in the south to rolling countryside dotted with farms, picturesque river valleys, lakes, islands, and sweeping beaches on both the north and Baltic seacoasts. Its most important rivers are the Rhine and the Elbe, both of which run from south to north, and the Danube in the south, which extends into Austria and southeastern Europe. The Oder River in the east marks the boundary between unified Germany and Poland.

Forests shroud a large portion of the countryside and are home to mythical tales of heroic adventure and folklore. Much of the most famous German epic poem from medieval times, the *Nibelungenlied,* is based in the Rhine valley,[7] and seven small hills south of Bonn depict the legendary dwarfs of the *Snow White* fable. The forests today constitute favorite excursion sites for Germans of all ages,[8] and in recent decades the protection of these woodlands from the ravages of industrial pollution has become a major rallying cry for the country's vocal environmentalists.

Germany's largest lake is the Bodensee, located in the southwestern part of the country. Its principal islands include Rügen and Usedom off the Baltic coastline and Sylt, Föhr, and Nordstrand on the North Sea. The country's highest mountains are the Zugspitze in the Alpine region bordering Austria, the Feldberg in the Black Forest, and the Schneeberg and Ochsenkopf in Thuringia in eastern Germany.

Because of historical traditions of decentralization and political federalism, no single city dominates Germany in equivalent fashion to London, Paris, or Rome. Berlin is the largest with a population of 3.5 million, followed by Hamburg on the North Sea with 1.7 million, Munich in Bavaria with 1.2 million, Cologne with 958,600, and Frankfurt am Main with 660,800. Other important cities for industrial, commercial, or educational reasons include Düsseldorf on the Rhine, Freiburg in the southwest, Lübeck on the North Sea, Göttingen in the central part of the country, and Magdeburg, Erfurt, Dresden, Leipzig, and Potsdam in eastern Germany. Hamburg and Leipzig are important publishing centers; Frankfurt am Main is the country's financial capital; and Munich, Berlin, and several smaller cities are cultural centers.

Economic Modernization

Germany's natural resources include rich deposits of iron, coal, industrial salt, and arable land tilled mainly on small farms in the west and vast agricultural collectives in the east. Initially a laggard nation compared to earlier economic development in France and Britain, Germany attained industrial "take off" during the latter part of the nineteenth century.[9] Its coal output increased from 26.4 million metric tons in 1870 to 109 million by the turn of the century, while its production of iron ore rose from 2.9 million metric tons to 12.8 million during the same period.[10] Production of both continued to climb until it peaked in 1918 and 1913, respectively. The country's output of crude steel has steadily outpaced that of all of its European neighbors since the mid-nineteenth century. Comparative historical indexes of industrial production to the eve of World War I are depicted in Table 1.1.

An important component of industrialization was a steady increase in railway lines, which significantly facilitated the transport of coal and iron to factories and the shipment of machine goods, consumer products, and agricultural goods to markets. Rail systems also helped promote social mobilization through the mass transportation of people. Germany began developing a national railway system late; in 1835 it had only 6 kilometers of rail line compared to 141 in France, but Germany quickly caught up with its neighbor to the west. The two countries had constructed approximately equal mileage by the end of the 1830s, but (as indicated in Figure 1.1). Germany first edged and then surged ahead in railway construction in subsequent decades.

Table 1.1	Indexes of Industrial Production, 1850–1913				
Year	France	Germany	Italy	Russia	United Kingdom
1850	33.5	9.5	—	—	28
1860	39.1	13	—	—	31.7
1870	40	19	40	11	40.2
1880	49.4	26	42	18	50.3
1890	57.3	40	51	32	63.3
1900	67.7	61	61	63	80.1
1910	81.1	86	95	91	91.5
1913	88.8	91	102	95	93.9
1913	100	100	100	100	100

Source: B.R. Mitchell, *International Historical Statistics: Europe 1750–2000,* 5th ed. (New York: Palgrave Macmillan, 2003), 422–424.
Note: — indicates data unavailable for a country for the time period specified.

Figure 1.1	Length of Railway Line, 1840–1920 (in kilometers)

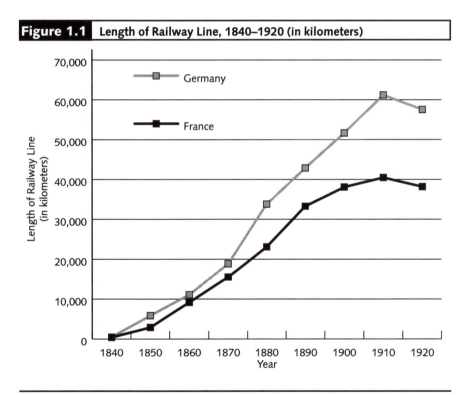

Source: B.R. Mitchell, *International Historical Statistics: Europe 1750-2000,* 5th ed. (New York: Palgrave Macmillan, 2003), 673, 676.

Patterns of industrialization varied across the country from the mid-nineteenth century into the twentieth. A tradition of political liberalism in southwestern Germany fostered a spirit of individual entrepreneurship, which encouraged the development of small workshops and factories that later served as the basis for automobile and electrical industries. In contrast, Prussian and later Imperial German policies in the north deliberately favored the rapid emergence of larger, more centralized enterprises such as those in steel manufacturing, chemicals, and pharmaceuticals. An underlying motive on the part of governing political elites was to enhance the nation's wartime capabilities.[11] Possibly for this reason, Germany was a global innovator in government-funded scientific research; industrial chemistry is a famous example.

Social Modernization

The population living in Germany originated from diverse ethnic tribes— among them Franks, Saxons, Bavarians, Swabians, and Frisians—who gradually coalesced into an identifiable, loosely organized political and cultural community from the eighth century onward on the basis of similar linguistic roots, a common religion (Christianity), and military conquest by the more powerful kingdoms occupying the region. Germans became distinguished from the French in the west, Slavs in the east,[12] and other European nationalities to the north and south by the end of the tenth century, exporting their presence through migration eastward into Central Europe while eventually acquiring a sense of collective identity shaped by language, literature, and shared historical experiences.[13] The Germans did not establish themselves as a recognized nation-state, however, until the proclamation of the Imperial regime in 1871. Even then, discernible regional and linguistic differences persisted within the unified nation and beyond its borders.

Industrialization, which was accompanied by a gradual increase in national wealth and improved sanitation conditions, triggered a steady growth in Germany's population. From an estimated 35.3 million in 1850, the number of Germans grew to approximately 40.8 million in 1870. By the turn of the century, the national population had jumped to 56.1 million—easily outnumbering France's 38.9 million. Within less than ten years Germans numbered 63.7 million compared to 39.4 million French men and women.[14]

A key consequence of both industrialization and increased population growth was accelerated urbanization, which significantly facilitated social mobilization in its broadest dimensions. As indicated in Table 1.2, Berlin experienced the most explosive growth from 1850 through the early 1930s, followed by Hamburg, Cologne, and Munich. Dresden and Frankfurt am Main were close behind.

Industrialization fundamentally altered the structure and composition of the labor force and society at large. The number of gainfully employed workers nearly doubled between 1882 and 1925, from 17.6 million to 32 million. Female employment nearly tripled during the same period,

Table 1.2	Population of Major German Cities, 1850–1931 (in thousands)				
City	1850–1851	1870–1871	1900–1901	1920–1921	1930–1931
Berlin	419	826	1,889	3,801	4,243
Cologne	97	129	373	634	757
Dresden	97	177	396	529	642
Frankfurt	65	91	89	433	566
Hamburg	132	240	706	986	1,129
Munich	110	169	500	631	735

Source: B.R. Mitchell, *International Historical Statistics: Europe 1750–2000*, 5th ed. (New York: Palgrave Macmillan, 2003), 74–75.

increasing from 4.3 million to 11.5 million. By 1925 most women in the workforce were concentrated in agriculture, manufacturing, and services, with the number of females employed in the latter sector exceeding that of men—2.3 million compared to 2.2 million.[15] Germany's transition from a predominantly agrarian society in the nineteenth century to an industrial society in the early twentieth is clearly presented in Table 1.3, which depicts both a steady decline in the percentage of workers employed in agriculture and parallel increases in the percentages of those engaged in manufacturing, commerce, and transportation.

Rapid structural changes in the labor force accentuated deeply rooted socioeconomic cleavages within the German populace. While many citizens benefited materially from the country's industrial revolution, some clearly benefited more than others—among them, industrialists, businesspeople, landed aristocrats (the *Junkers,* concentrated in eastern Germany), civil servants, and property owners in general. Industrial and agricultural workers, in contrast, suffered relative depravation: substandard housing, long work hours, low wages, and wretched working conditions. These socioeconomic distinctions manifested themselves in palpable class distinctions between a small but powerful upper social class, a larger and increasingly affluent middle class, and a largely powerless but growing working class.

Perceptions of exploitation on the part of industrial workers fueled expanding membership in national trade unions and growing electoral support for the Social Democratic Party (SPD) in protest against the privileged status of the socioeconomic and political elites of Imperial Germany.

Table 1.3	Percentage of Workers by Economic Sector, 1882–1925						
Year	Agriculture	Mining	Manufacturing	Construction	Commerce	Transportation	Services
1882	47	3	27	5	5	2	2
1895	40	4	29	7	6	3	11
1907	37	5	29	7	7	4	11
1925	30	4	32	6	10	5	13

Source: Calculated from B.R. Mitchell, *International Historical Statistics: Europe 1750–2000*, 5th ed. (New York: Palgrave Macmillan, 2003), 150.

Paradoxically, both the unions and the SPD served in unanticipated fashion as instruments of vertical integration into the broader fabric of society, in part by providing cultural and educational advancement to their members and securing limited political and economic reforms even as they played their partisan role as advocates of fundamental system change to the advantage of the working class. This dual role proved a fateful bane for the Social Democrats when they first assumed political power in the aftermath of the 1918 "November Revolution" that resulted in the proclamation of Germany's first democratic republic; their verbal commitment to class struggle and revolution cost them middle class electoral support while their de facto commitment to upholding a democratic state and working for slow reforms alienated revolutionary elements (see chapter 2).

Formal education reinforced Germany's social cleavages. Long a European and international bastion of advanced higher education—particularly in the natural sciences and the humanities at such renowned universities as those in Berlin, Königsberg in East Prussia, Halle, Heidelberg, Göttingen, and Bonn—Germany's rigid hierarchical educational system favored the upper and upper middle classes. Only those who progressed beyond elementary school on the basis of rigorous examinations and completed a demanding *Gymnasium* secondary school education were permitted to matriculate into universities. Rarely was this possible for children of the lower middle and working classes, who lacked parental assistance with their academic studies, partly for reasons of cost but perhaps even more due to a rigid class structure. Here Germany in fact resembled other European democratic states. Women were encouraged to pursue careers as teachers, but they were excluded from attending universities until the twentieth century. Rather than contemplate secondary—much less higher—education, many working-class men and women participated instead in apprenticeship programs designed to train them for jobs in industry and commerce.

Another source of social cleavage, albeit one that cut across class and occupational lines, was religion. A stalwart Christian nation during the early Middle Ages, Germany was riven by a north-south religious division in the aftermath of the Protestant Reformation in the sixteenth century.[16] The Thirty Years War of 1618–1648, fought primarily on German soil by contending French, Swedish, and Austrian forces, resulted not only in widespread physical destruction and the loss of countless lives but also in a permanent division between predominantly Protestant regions in the north and east and Catholic regions in the south, southwest, and the Rhineland. Protestants became a majority within the German populace as a whole; in response, Catholics cultivated a strong identity as a beleaguered religious and cultural minority. Jewish Germans formed a small but economically and culturally influential minority.

During the 1870s Catholic political leaders established a party of their own, the *Zentrumspartei* (Center Party), to defend Catholic interests against oppressive measures carried out by the Imperial government in the form of a protracted "cultural struggle" (*Kulturkampf*) instigated from above to promote Protestant hegemony. Simultaneously, a separate Catholic trade union movement was established that competed for allegiance among the nation's industrial workers (see chapter 8).

Regional Diversity

The sixteen states making up today's Federal Republic reflect the nation's traditions of historical and regional diversity as well as East-West economic and political differences. Some of the larger states, including Bavaria and Baden-Württemberg, correspond to previously independent kingdoms. The rest of the state is comprised of postwar territorial amalgamations, former provinces of Prussia, smaller historical kingdoms, and city states. These include North Rhine-Westphalia, Lower Saxony, Hesse, Rhineland-Palatinate, Schleswig-Holstein, the Saarland, and the three city states of Berlin, Hamburg, and Bremen (see Table 1.4). Among the five federal states incorporated from the former German Democratic Republic in 1990, Saxony ranks first in population, followed by Saxony-Anhalt, Brandenburg, Thuringia, and Mecklenburg–Western Pomerania.

The structure of the labor force differs significantly among the states, reflecting regional contrasts in levels of economic and social development. As indicated in Table 1.5, Berlin—with its preponderance of federal, state, and city government services—ranks as Germany's most postindustrialized area; Hamburg follows a close second. Manufacturing dominates in Baden-Württemberg,

Table 1.4 German States by Population and Area, 2005		
State	Population (in millions)	Area (in square kilometers)
North Rhine–Westphalia	18,075	34,083
Bavaria	12,444	35,752
Baden-Württemberg	10,717	35,752
Lower Saxony	8,001	47,620
Hesse	6,098	21,115
Saxony	4,296	18,418
Rhineland-Palatinate	4,041	19,847
Berlin	3,388	892
Schleswig-Holstein	2,829	15,763
Brandenburg	2,568	29,477
Saxony-Anhalt	2,497	20,455
Thuringia	2,355	16,171
Hamburg	1,735	755
Mecklenburg–Western Pomerania	1,720	23,173
Saarland	1,056	2,569
Bremen	663	404

Source: Statistisches Jahrbuch 2006 für die Bundesrepublik Deutschland (Wiesbaden: Statistisches Bundesamt, 2006), 78.

Rhineland-Palatinate, Bavaria, and North Rhine–Westphalia, which are all situated in western Germany; among the eastern states, Saxony-Anhalt and Brandenburg are the most industrialized. Commerce is an important economic sector in Hamburg, Bremen, and Schleswig-Holstein; it is less so in Baden-Württemberg, Thuringia, Bavaria, Saxony, Saxony-Anhalt, Brandenburg, and Rhineland-Palatinate. The highest percentage of workers engaged in agriculture and other primary occupations is concentrated in Mecklenburg–Western Pomerania and Brandenburg, both in eastern Germany. The number of agrarian workers in Bavaria and Lower Saxony exceeds the 2.3 percent average among the ten "old" federal states in the West.

The historical trend toward increased female employment has continued unabated throughout unified Germany. In 2005 women made up 44.9 percent of the workforce, with an overwhelming majority of them engaged in public and private services (82 percent). Male workers, in contrast, are more widely dispersed among manufacturing (29.3 percent), commerce (15.3 percent), public administration (13.2 percent), and construction (10.4 percent).[17] More men than women are classified as "self-employed" (14.2 percent compared to 7.5 percent) and as state "officials" (*Beamte*) (7 percent compared to 5 percent), while women outnumber men as white-collar employees (64.8 percent compared to 41.8 percent).[18]

Table 1.5	Economically Active Population by Occupational Groups and State, 2005 (in rounded percentages)		
State *(Land)*	Agriculture	Manufacturing	Services
Baden-Württemberg	2	33	65
Bavaria	3	29	68
Berlin	—	14	86
Brandenburg	4	22	74
Bremen	—	22	78
Hamburg	—	18	84
Hesse	2	23	75
Mecklenburg– Western Pomerania	4	18	78
Lower Saxony	3	25	72
North Rhine– Westphalia	1	25	73
Rhineland-Palatinate	3	26	71
Saarland	1	29	70
Saxony	2	27	71
Saxony-Anhalt	3	24	73
Schleswig-Holstein	3	20	77
Thuringia	3	29	68

Source: Calculated from the absolute number of workers engaged in each occupational category in *Statistisches Jahrbuch für die Bundesrepublik Deutschland 2006* (Wiesbaden: Statistisches Bundesamt, 2006), 78.

Note: — indicates numbers for specific industry are negligible or inapplicable for specific region.

Social Structures

Social structures diverged markedly in western and eastern Germany from the mid-1940s into the early 1990s, but unification has yielded a national— if not yet fully integrated—community that resembles that of other advanced industrial countries. In comparative perspective, contemporary Germany is one of the most highly developed countries in the world. Its per capita income in 2005 ranked fifth among comparable nations in Europe and North America, as indicated in Table 1.6.

During the past half century Germany has experienced major changes in the ethnic and demographic composition of its population—as well as in the very definition of what it means to be "German." In common with other modern nations, these changes involve some of the most contentious issues in contemporary society:

- Integrating new religious communities and ethnic groups into the new community and re-defining German citizenship.

- Confronting population growth or decline, including contrasts between eastern and western Germany, and the changing age structure of the population with its implications for pensions and the labor force.

We consider Germany's responses to these challenges at appropriate junctures throughout the book, especially in the final chapter. Here we set the demographic stage for German politics and policies.

Table 1.6	Per Capita Income, 2005 (in U.S. dollars)
Country	Per Capita Income
United States	41,789
Canada	34,058
United Kingdom	32,860
Sweden	32,111
Germany	30,777
France	30,266
Italy	28,094

Population, Immigration, Identity

With a population of 82.2 million, Germany is the most populous member of the European Union and the most populous European country after Russia.[19] This total reflects the increase, by about one quarter, of Germany's population as a result of unification. West Germans (and West Berliners) comprise 79.7 percent of the national population—65.7 million compared to 16.6 million in the eastern states (with East Berlin). The relative weight of eastern German influence and involvement in the politics and society of the country is therefore numerically weak, a factor affecting many electoral and legislative calculations. Thus, although eastern German problems and sensibility are important issues, nationwide German institutions, including political parties (aside from the Left Party), have less incentive to respond to eastern than to western German interests.

A unique feature of postwar German population movements has been the migration, often through flight, of East Germans to West Germany. Early postwar waves of such migration, through which the GDR lost many young and skilled people, resulted in strengthened border regimes, especially along the zonal borders in 1951–1952, and finally in the construction of the Berlin Wall in 1961. (The political consequences of this movement in helping to bring about the collapse of the GDR in 1989–1990 are discussed in chapter 3.) However, this east to west migration continued after unification. Such migration of young and technically qualified people reflects the expectations of younger eastern Germans: a 2004 survey found that three quarters of qualified job seekers under the age of thirty would move to western Germany for work.[20]

Finally, in keeping with trends in other modern industrial democracies, Germany's population is projected both to decline and to age. This prospect has potentially serious consequences for labor supply and financing of pensions. A 1998 government report estimated that between 1998 and 2030, the percentage of the population age sixty and older will rise from 20 to 36 percent. The number of persons older than sixty, for every one hundred persons aged twenty to fifty-nine, is projected to double between 1995 and 2040; official projections for the years 2010–2050 point in the same direction.[21] One solution for this quandary is to increase immigration into Germany—a course of action suggested by a report on migration commissioned by the Schröder government. Immigration would not only add absolute numbers to the population, it would also decrease the average age. In the words of a leading economic forecaster, Germans should "either have children or open the borders."[22] Increasing immigration, however, continues to be very controversial, due to a collision between two forces: a sense of German nationality as a fragile construct, and the social and economic reality of an invited and needed foreign labor force.

German national identity arose prior to the creation in 1871 of a German national state, an event that excluded many Germans, especially in Austria, from the new political system. German nationality, therefore, was based on ethnic and cultural criteria. These criteria formed the basis for a 1913 citizenship law, which remained in force, with modifications, until January 2000. The 1913 law defined biological descent as the basis for citizenship (the *ius sanguinis*). This made Germans outside the Federal Republic automatically eligible for German citizenship. For example, East Germans could claim German citizenship by reaching West German territory, or ethnic repatriates (*Aussiedler*) from Russia and parts of Eastern Europe could make this claim after unification.[23]

The attachment to this principle, which has been modified or abandoned in a majority of EU member states, rests on a sense of German-ness as an intrinsic quality. Some Germans, it has been argued, have great difficulty with "contradictions, ambivalence and variety," especially in matters of national identity; opponents of liberalized policies reject an expansive and changing definition of German identity.[24] These conservative notions collided with the economic and social reality of postwar Germany. During the early years of West Germany's economic recovery, the need for labor was satisfied by absorption of ethnic Germans fleeing Eastern Europe and Germans fleeing the GDR. The building of the Berlin Wall in August 1961 marked the end of both of these population flows. Germany—in ways similar although not identical to other north and west European countries—responded by initiating, through government-industry understandings, a policy of recruiting foreign ("guest") workers. These workers were primarily from the Mediterranean countries of Europe (Italy 1955, Spain and Greece 1960, Turkey 1961, Portugal 1964, Yugoslavia 1968, and Morocco 1963 and Tunisia 1965), who arrived in such numbers that the number of resident foreigners (*Ausländer*) rose from 668,000 or 1.2 percent of the population in 1960 to 2.9 million (4.9 percent) in 1970 and to 4.8 million (7.7 percent) on the eve of unification. The millionth guest worker arrived in 1964 and received a free Moped.[25]

This internationalization of the workforce, particularly among blue-collar workers, is present in all of the more prosperous EU countries. In Germany, economic opportunity, a generous welfare state (see chapter 9), and a stable society resulted in an immigrant population of 6,751,000 by 2006, or 8 percent of the German population. Turks accounted for 2 percent of the total population, but just over a quarter of immigrants.[26]

In the recession that followed the oil shocks of 1973–1974, recruitment of labor from outside the EU was banned in Germany, and efforts to encourage voluntary repatriation began. However, resident workers were not forced to leave, and indeed, they gained substantial rights. Guest workers, originally thought of as temporary contract laborers, found that a year's work with satisfactory income and housing allowed them to send for their families; after five years, they could gain permanent residence status. Consequently, the resident foreigner population continued to grow. By the 1990s, many in this population were not workers but family members, the consequence of which was that a growing proportion of people permanently resident in Germany found it extremely difficult to become German citizens and thus participate in the politics of the country.[27]

With the SPD/Greens coalition in power after the 1998 election, reform of citizenship laws became the first major item on the new government's agenda.[28] A compromise law that dropped provisions for dual citizenship was passed in spring 1999 and took effect with the new millennium. Under its provisions children born in Germany of foreign parents automatically acquire German citizenship in most cases. Adults can be naturalized more easily as well, with eight years' residence, "express" commitment to the Basic Law, no record of activity hostile to the constitutional order, "adequate" command of the German language, economic self-sufficiency, and surrender of any other citizenship.

Initial implementation of the law, which is handled at the state level, was mixed and dependent in part on the politics of the government in question. However, further legislation now requires the Constitution Protection Office (*Verfassungsschutz*) to uniformly screen all applicants. The standards applied for testing command of German range from "sufficient for normal social discourse" to writing and reading comprehension exercises. In 2005, 117, 241 persons, more than one quarter of whom had come from Turkey, were naturalized.

The reform of immigration law has complemented legislation that took effect in January 2005 that reformed immigration and asylum regulation.[29] This new law explicitly envisions immigration of persons with useful work skills; changes the scope and status of those seeking asylum; broadens the government's powers to expel individuals suspected of committing acts of terrorism; obliges immigrants to participate in publicly sponsored integration (especially language) education; and adjusts all regulations in these areas to EU standards, taking into account the 2004 expansion of the EU. The law also centralizes administration of these matters in a new cabinet-level federal office for migration and refugees.[30] Such reform clearly makes Germany what so many of its leaders have long denied it to be—a country of immigration.[31]

Germans have long grappled with the issue of granting asylum. In response to the Nazi era, Article 16 of the Basic Law specifically provides that "[p]ersons persecuted for political reasons shall have the right of asylum." After unification, there was a sharp rise in asylum seekers; in 1992, almost half a million arrived. Germany became the EU's most-favored destination in absolute numbers, and third per capita after Sweden and Switzerland.

A strong political reaction, which included street violence against asylum seekers, produced a compromise tightening of constitutional provisions, a change upheld by the Constitutional Court in 1996. Under the amended provisions, asylum may be denied persons who come from an EU country or from a country deemed by German authorities to be "safe," that is, free of human rights abuses.[32] The amendments appear to have had the desired effect. By 1997, the number of asylum seekers had dropped by three quarters; in both 1998 and 1999, fewer than one hundred thousand applicants were registered, and only about 3 percent of applicants were granted asylum. Since 2005, the number of asylum seekers has dropped to fewer than 30,000. In 2006, the largest number were from Iraq. Today, the residence of asylum seekers in public accommodations while their cases are heard continues to provide a flash point for rightist violence, but for the most part, asylum has been reduced to its original intention of providing relief for those in immediate danger.

Religious Communities

Religious affiliations in Germany have undergone significant transformations in recent decades. Historically, the German states were, in law and following, Christian communities. Christian church structures were tied to the state; to this day, the government collects church tithes, or taxes (*Kirchensteuer*), from individual wage earners. Especially in the Imperial period, but also in the postwar West German republic, conflicts regarding the role of churches, particularly the Catholic Church, were an important feature of politics.

Articles 137 and 140 of Germany's Basic Law prohibit an established religion, or "state church," and grant religious groups, including non-theistic ones, the right of free association.[33] The articles also provide for state cooperation with religious organizations in such areas as the church tax, religious instruction, social services, and chaplaincy.

The role of organized religious groups, and of religious sentiment, has been changing in contemporary Germany. Of approximately 73 million adult inhabitants sixteen years of age or older, some 56 million, or three quarters, belong to Christian churches. While in the Bonn era there was a slight preponderance of Catholics, since unification there is a small plurality of Protestants (*Evangelisch,* in German terminology); each denomination numbers somewhat more than 27 million. There are smaller Christian communities as well that reflect the presence of Greeks, Serbs, and Russians in the population.[34] Chief among these are the approximately one million Eastern Orthodox Christians.

A major change in the religious and cultural life of Germany in the twentieth century was the reduction of the Jewish community from more than half a million before the outset of Adolf Hitler's rise to power to less than one hundred thousand at the time of unification in 1990. In recent years, however, there has been a renewed influx of Jews, particularly from the former Soviet Union. The same neighborhoods in eastern Berlin, for example, that had seen major Jewish immigration a century ago, are once again areas of Jewish immigrant settlement. Until 2005, Jewish emigration from the former Soviet Union was regulated by a special law; since then it has been regulated as part of general immigration law.[35] The law now provides that a state government (acting in conjunction with the Federal Interior Ministry) may grant residence status to foreigners from a specified country, or groups of foreigners otherwise defined, for humanitarian reasons or to advance Germany's political interests. In June 2005, the state interior ministers, together with the federal government and Jewish organizations, settled on the formal, especially financial, conditions for such emigration. More stringent rules for proficiency of the German language and for economic prospects ultimately were implemented.[36] Although the new regulations reduced the number of Jewish immigrants from the former Soviet Union, the overall result has been to make the Jewish community in Germany the third largest in Europe, with the greatest percentage increase worldwide. As of 2006, a total of 104 Jewish communities representing 107,794 individual members were organized in 23 regional associations under the umbrella of the Central Council of Jews in Germany. Moreover, thanks to an agreement the government and the Central Council reached in 2003, Jewish religious organizations may also be supported by funds collected on their behalf by the state.[37]

The most striking change in Germany's religious population is the rise of a Muslim community of more than 2.5 million over the past four decades. Unlike Christian and Jewish communities, this Muslim community of mostly Turkish and Kurdish ethnicity does not have the legal standing to have the state collect a church tax. Indeed, to provide religious instruction for Muslim children—in keeping with the German school system's provision of voluntary faith-based instruction—the governments of some German states have designated an Islamic organization to assemble appropriate teaching materials.[38] (For discussion of the further consolidation of Islamic and secular Turkish interest groups, see chapter 8.)

The traditional German system of state-regulated churches—and church support for the state—has begun to unravel in modern Germany. The establishment of the "Church of Witness" (*Bekennende Kirche*) in 1934 as a Protestant group distancing itself from the Nazi regime established a precedent for autonomous religious life. The existence of the Protestant "Church in Socialism" in the GDR, a church that strove to provide a free space within an authoritarian social and political structure, was another important step in this regard.

Finally, the rising number of religiously unaffiliated citizens, along with members of spontaneous and loosely organized groups, have made the mainstream, especially Christian, denominations less important in German life. Yet the old attitude, that the state must regulate religious activity on behalf of the community, is still strongly felt. Religious communities in Germany face a variety of internal and public issues. For the Islamic community, this includes the adaptation of religiously sanctioned social customs to modern secular law; for the Jewish community, this means assimilating immigrants from Russia while representing the community in regard to Holocaust issues. The Christian churches, meanwhile, must deal with issues of relevance in an increasingly secular public; for the Catholic community, there is the additional tension over church teachings regarding clerical celibacy, procreation, and related issues.

Conclusion

Contemporary German society can only be fully understood in the context of the nation's turbulent political history. Economic and social development has proven relatively successful; by the first decade of the twentieth century Germany had been transformed into a modern European industrial nation. In contrast, however, political change proved fatefully flawed with the demise of the Weimar Republic, Germany's first democratic experiment, in 1933, and the rise of Adolf Hitler to power as architect of a totalitarian imperialistic regime.

2

A Turbulent History Is Prologue to the Present

When the major European nations went to war in 1914, Germany was in the mainstream of European political, social, and economic development. For example, its systems of higher education and scientific research were world models. (Indeed, both the American research university and much of modern American social science would be inconceivable without their German precedents.) In a very different field, the German labor movement, and particularly the Social Democratic movement and its party, was the standard against which other revolutionaries measured their progress.

Yet when we (and generations of Germans) think of Germany in the twentieth century, it is the nation's destructive turn to dictatorship, military aggression, and genocide that comes to mind. German politics since 1945 has taken place in the shadow of, and in reaction against, the nation's path in the 1930s and 1940s. What went wrong? The short answer is that Germans, when faced with a lost war, a harsh peace, and economic distress, failed to create democratic civil order.

Imperial Germany's defeat at the hands of British, French, and U.S. forces in November 1918 marked the beginning of an extended period of political and economic uncertainty bordering on intermittent chaos. After Kaiser Wilhelm II abdicated under pressure by German military and political leaders,[1] the Social Democrats hastily proclaimed a democratic republic on November 9 in the teeth of determined ideological opposition by Communists on the left and newly emergent radical movements on the extreme right.[2] The resulting Weimar Republic achieved a semblance of stability during the ensuing ten years, but the Great Depression prompted the

25

beginning of a system crisis in 1929 that culminated in Hitler's rise to power in January 1933.

Germany's rapid progression from authoritarianism to democracy to Nazi totalitarianism within a scant fifteen years proved anything but "normal" in comparison with the success of parliamentary democracies in the United Kingdom, France, and Scandinavia. It was, however, broadly congruent with failed democracies during the interwar period elsewhere, notably in Italy, Greece, Spain, Portugal, and most of Central Europe. By the mid-1930s there was hardly a democratic regime in Europe east of the Rhine except for Czechoslovakia. Moreover, many countries that remained democratic experienced major domestic attacks on their political systems.

It was Germany's power, combined with its political failings, that proved so baneful for Germany itself, Europe, and the world. In this chapter, we recount these developments and show how their outcome in the post-1945 occupation regime laid the groundwork for postwar German politics.

The Weimar Republic

The Weimar Republic drew on multiple political antecedents from Germany's past, including a tradition of federalism, a written constitution, a deeply ingrained respect for law, and core democratic principles and organizations. The latter included manhood suffrage, which was extended in January 1919 to include women as well; competitive national and state elections; and the existence of democratic political parties. The most important among these parties were the majority Social Democrats, the Catholic-based Center Party, and a smaller Progressive Liberal Party. Mass organizations such as trade unions constituted other democratic bulwarks.[3]

Together the Social Democrats, the Center Party, and the Progressive Liberals instituted parliamentary democracy in 1919 to replace the Imperial system's previous concentration of executive power in the hands of a hereditary monarch and an appointed Imperial chancellor.[4] The new head of state became a popularly elected Reich president; day-to-day government authority was vested in the hands of a Reich chancellor and members of a national government who were collectively accountable to a majority of members of the elective lower house (the Reichstag). In what would later prove a fateful decision, democratic leaders at the constituent assembly inserted provisions for the exercise of emergency powers (Article 48) that would enable a government to rule by decree in the absence of support by a parliamentary majority.

From its inception, however, the Weimar Republic was confounded by a punitive peace treaty (the Treaty of Versailles) imposed by the Western Allies in June 1919, attempted Communist revolutions in Berlin and other major cities during the republic's formative years, and an abortive conservative coup in March 1920.[5] The regime was further weakened by a devastating inflationary spiral in 1922 that wiped out the savings of most middle-class citizens. Above all, Weimar democracy was undermined by the persistence of authoritarian attitudes and structures throughout German society and the accompanying absence of positive attitudinal support among public officials, including the judiciary and the military, and many members of the general public.

The onset of the Great Depression in October 1929 provoked a prolonged socioeconomic and political crisis from which the Weimar Republic never recovered. An immediate response in Germany, as elsewhere in the industrialized world, was a sharp jump in unemployment. By March 1930, 2.2 million persons were out of work. Two years later, the number had increased to more than six million.

The Rise of the Nazis to Power

In response to a deteriorating economy and increasingly violent social conflicts, in 1930 President Paul von Hindenburg began utilizing emergency powers under Article 48 of the constitution to name a succession of semi-authoritarian cabinets, all of which failed to ameliorate Germany's deepening crisis. In the election of July 1932, the radical left Communist Party of Germany (KPD) and the radical right National Socialists (NSDAP) gained a negative majority in parliament, paralyzing Germany's fragile system of parliamentary democracy. In response to conservative machinations von Hindenburg wearily agreed in January 1933 to appoint Adolf Hitler as chancellor of a right-wing coalition government in the hope that the Nazi leader would restore political and economic stability, but still be checked by conservative allies.

The National Socialists' rise to power was a consequence of Germany's tortured political history and Hitler's charismatic qualities as an impassioned orator. It is important to remember, however, in the words of historian Fritz Stern, "[T]he rise of National Socialism was neither inevitable nor accidental. It did have deep roots, but the most urgent lesson to remember is that it could have been stopped."[6] The movement was born out of anguish over military defeat in 1918 and sought to mobilize Germans from all socioeconomic backgrounds in a disciplined effort to transcend their historical dualisms in a new unity of state, nation, and race. Hitler exploited the so-called shame of Versailles, middle-class fears of revolutionary socialism, the recurrent economic crises of the 1920s, and traditional forms of religious and cultural anti-Semitism to advance the National Socialists' claim to power. He promised everything the Weimar Republic allegedly failed to provide: decisive leadership, the restoration of German honor, sustained economic growth, full employment, low interest rates, stable prices, domestic law and order, and above all, national unity. Means to these ends included the creation of a strong central power in the state, the transformation of Germany into a racially homogeneous "people's community," and repudiation of the Versailles treaty.[7]

Hitler's success in forging a powerful mass movement based on these principles lay in his unusual ability to command intense personal loyalty.[8] His charisma was characterized by hypnotic intensity, carefully planned theatrics, flattery as appropriate, and threats when necessary. These qualities enabled him to allay the doubts of skeptical critics and, in time, to arouse the loyalty of millions of enthusiastic followers.

Nothing in the Nazis' ideology, leadership, or electoral support preordained their triumph in 1933. Undeniably, defensive class interests played a role in Hitler's successful bid for the chancellorship. Frightened lower-middle-class voters—including many farmers and urban dwellers who felt abandoned by the liberal and conservative parties—contributed most to the groundswell in NSDAP support from July 1930 onward. During this period Hitler also attracted considerable financial contributions from apprehensive Ruhr industrialists who saw in him a tactical ally in their struggle to contain Communist influence. Yet the very rapidity of the Nazi electoral advance between 1928 and 1932, as well as an abrupt decline in support for the party in the election of November 1932, indicates that the movement was a classic example of what has been termed a surge movement. In short, the growth of Nazi strength was the product of Germany's economic crisis and the absence of sufficient political resolve and imagination on the part of the Weimar Republic's governing elites. Hitler and his party might well have suffered the historical irrelevance of their racist-nationalist counterparts in Britain and Scandinavia if republican leaders had been able to devise an effective program to combat the domestic effects of the depression or, failing that, at least to unite in defense of the Weimar system. They did neither, and consequently, the Nazi vision of a national revolution became increasingly plausible to nationalist conspirators and a cynical electorate alike.

The Third Reich

Once in office, Hitler consolidated power in the hands of his party through a comprehensive program of political, economic, and ethnic "coordination" (*Gleichschaltung*). He dissolved the Reichstag and ordered new elections in March 1933. Through a massive propaganda effort and the forceful intimidation of the Communist and Social Democratic parties, the NSDAP succeeded in increasing its share of the popular vote to nearly 44 percent. Claiming a technical parliamentary majority after banning the KPD for allegedly engaging an arsonist to burn down the Reichstag building on the eve of the election, Hitler petitioned parliament for a grant of extraordinary authority to deal with Germany's "national emergency." A majority meekly complied, with only the Social Democrats voting against the so-called Enabling Act of March 23. By transferring all legislative powers to the cabinet, this measure effectively made Hitler dictator. He went on to achieve the ultimate concentration of personal power a year later when von Hindenburg's death enabled him to unite the chancellorship and presidency to become Germany's all-powerful *führer* (leader).

The National Socialists rapidly institutionalized a totalitarian regime. By the end of 1933, they had dissolved all political parties except for the NSDAP and had proclaimed the "insoluble" merger of party and state. Simultaneously, Hitler neutralized the meager influence of the conservatives in his cabinet, eventually replacing them with trusted party aides. Accompanying these steps were the replacement of previously elected and appointed state officials with loyal Nazis and the subordination of the various states to central authority.

Parallel processes of economic and social *Gleichschaltung* included the dissolution of trade unions, the subordination of private capital to central state planning, and the extension of National Socialist control over the mass media and the educational system. Discriminatory racial policies began in 1933 with laws driving Jews out of the civil service and went on to include a lengthening list of persecutory decrees. The campaign reached its first climax with the promulgation of the infamous Nürnberg laws of September 1935, which stripped Jews of their legal and political rights.[9]

A gradual escalation of official harassment against the five hundred thousand Jews in Germany (who made up less than 1 percent of the population) erupted in a violent pogrom during the night of November 9, 1938, the infamous "crystal night" (*Kristallnacht*), a reference to the broken glass of Jewish homes, shops, and synagogues; ninety-one people were killed. From then on, the regime implemented an increasingly blatant policy of anti-Semitism that culminated in the notorious wartime "final solution." Some six million European Jews and many other minorities, such as the Roma, or Gypsies, and regime opponents were to die, either through illness or execution, in Nazi-administered concentration and extermination camps in the ensuing Holocaust.

The domestic effects of the Nazi takeover were highly mixed. Politically, Germany became "united" as never before under clearly recognized national authority. Yet citizen equality was negated through Nazi suppression of parliamentarism, political parties, and individual rights. Socially, Nazi efforts to eliminate all sources of potential opposition destroyed the institutionalized power of the traditional aristocracy. Germany's monarchists and heirs to the *Junker* tradition of paternalistic rule were never again to play a decisive role in national affairs.[10] In terms of its social performance, the Third Reich maintained previously attained levels of mass literacy and technical competence. But public education and intellectual life suffered. The number of secondary and university students declined in comparison with the Weimar period, and the quality of higher education, research, and culture plummeted as a result of the party's imposition of narrow standards of ideological orthodoxy and the emigration or arrest of most leading intellectuals.

The National Socialists achieved their greatest success in the economic sphere. Within three years after Hitler's rise to power, Germany had recovered from the ravaging effects of the depression. Restored productivity brought an end to mass unemployment and falling prices for industrial goods and farm products. Without question, Germany's economic recovery was attributed in part to global factors, including the gradual resumption of international trade from the mid-1930s onward, but it also was stimulated by the central government's expanded powers to direct manpower allocation, investments, prices, and incomes.

World War II and the Occupation Regime

With the attainment of totalitarian political and social control and renewed economic growth, Hitler turned to foreign policy. In quick order, he implemented a calculated strategy to extend Nazi Germany's external influence and boundaries. After a plebiscite, or referendum, the Saarland rejoined the Reich in 1935, after fifteen years under French direction. A year later, Hitler remilitarized the Rhineland in flagrant violation of the Versailles treaty. Simultaneously, he proclaimed a "natural alliance" between Germany and fascist Italy against the Western democracies. In 1938, Germany annexed Austria and, with British and French acquiescence, fatally weakened Czechoslovakia through the Munich Conference of September 1938. Hitler then absorbed the remaining Czech provinces in March 1939. Emboldened by these successes, he demanded that the Free City of Danzig and the Polish Corridor, products of the Versailles settlement, be returned to Germany. This time, however, Britain and France balked.

Determined to restore Germany's eastern boundary by whatever means, Hitler stunned the world by negotiating a ten-year neutrality and nonaggression pact with the Union of Soviet Socialist Republics (USSR) in August 1939. This agreement, which contained a secret protocol providing for the division of Poland and the Baltic states between Germany and Russia, opened the way to military conflict in Europe.[11] Hitler knew that the British and the French would respond to a German attack on Poland with a declaration of war, but there was little that either country could do to assist the Poles in the face of Soviet premier Josef Stalin's pledge to refrain from war with the Third Reich. Thus, Hitler ordered his troops to cross the German-Polish border on September 1.

The resulting six years of total war, aerial bombardments of civilian populations, and mass exterminations belong among the most tragic in human history.[12] The course of the war included Germany's and Russia's joint subjugation of Poland and a separate Russian attack on Finland and the Baltic republics in 1939 and Germany's occupation of most of Western Europe the following year. In June 1941 Hitler revealed the full extent of his ambitions when he launched a full-scale invasion of the Soviet Union. In response, the Soviets entered a military alliance with Britain and the United States.

After two years of Nazi military advances into eastern Europe, the Red Army dramatically turned the tide by halting the German offense in January

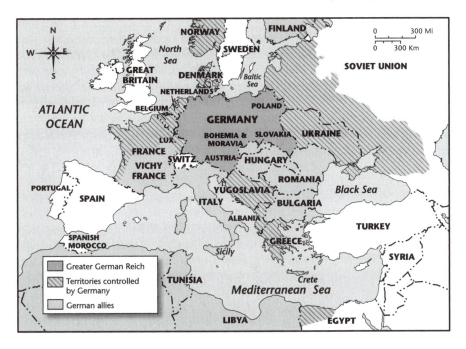

1943 at Stalingrad. Simultaneously, the Anglo-American powers launched a massive counteroffensive against the Axis states in North Africa and Italy. In June 1944, Anglo-American troops staged the largest amphibious operation in history by crossing the English Channel to establish an Allied bridgehead on the northern coast of occupied France. Henceforth, it was only a matter of time until Germany would fall before the joint advance of U.S., British, free French, and Russian forces.

Allied bombs leveled many German cities during World War II, but numerous landmarks have since been rebuilt. The photo on the left shows the statue of German religious reformer Martin Luther standing in front of the ruins of the Frauenkirche, or Church of Our Lady, in Dresden, East Germany, on March 13, 1967, twenty-two years after the church was destroyed in an air raid. The second image shows the statue in front of the restored building on February 9, 2005.

The escalation of Germany's demand for living space into a global war transformed the historical "German question" into an international issue with high political, military, and economic stakes for all the major powers. No longer were Germans free to pursue their historical quest for modernity on their own terms. Instead, Germany increasingly became an object of international politics. As a result, the underlying causes of German political instability and external aggression became of direct relevance for the wartime Allies. Their joint task from 1943 onward was to devise a suitable strategy to ensure that Germany would never again threaten world peace.

As the Allied armies began to press toward the German heartland in a two-front war, their civilian leaders initiated high-level consultations concerning a postwar political settlement in Europe. International security was uppermost in the policy calculations of U.S. president Franklin Roosevelt, British prime minister Winston Churchill, and Stalin. Following a meeting with Churchill in January 1943, President Roosevelt announced that the Allies would seek Germany's unconditional surrender. When Roosevelt, Churchill, and Stalin met for the first time at a conference in Teheran, Iran, in November 1943, the Allies agreed to the political and economic decentralization of Germany through occupation zones and the transfer of at least some German territory to the Soviet Union and Poland.[13]

At a second Big Three summit, held at Yalta in the Soviet Union in February 1945, the wartime leaders concurred on including France as a fourth occupation power. The wartime allies also agreed to nullify the Third Reich's annexations of Austria, Czechoslovakia, and Alsace-Lorraine and to restore Germany's prewar boundaries with its neighboring countries. Supervising the implementation of joint occupation policies would be a four-power Allied Control Council composed of the supreme military commanders of the various occupation zones and located in Berlin. The former German capital, located deep in the heart of the zone assigned the Soviet Union, would similarly be divided into four sectors for occupation purposes.

Germany's Political Eclipse

Following Hitler's suicide in a bunker beneath the rubble of the Reich Chancellery on April 30, 1945, the High Command capitulated unconditionally on May 8–9, 1945, to the Allies. Germany's military defeat was accompanied by a political eclipse unprecedented in modern times. Germany was now occupied by the Soviet Union, the United States, the United Kingdom, and France, and these states assumed sovereign powers over the nation. Moreover, these powers not only divided German territory and the city of Berlin into four occupation zones, they also truncated German territory.

By wartime inter-Allied agreement, the 1938 annexation (*Anschluss*) of Austria to Germany was undone; Germany's prewar borders with Denmark, Belgium, France, and Czechoslovakia were restored; and German territories east of the Oder and western Neisse rivers, including East Prussia and the Free City of Danzig, were assigned "for administration" to Poland or annexed, as in the case of northern East Prussia, by the USSR. French efforts to separate the Saarland from Germany and to weaken or remove German control of the Ruhr industrial district either failed or were in part subsumed by European integration. These territorial structurings would later become permanent in the 1990 "two plus four" treaty that established the framework for German unification.[14]

The Potsdam Conference, July–August 1945

To codify the terms of the occupation regime, as well as to discuss broader issues of war and peace, the new U.S. president, Harry S Truman, traveled to Germany in mid-July 1945 to confer with Soviet and British leaders. The Allied heads of government and their advisers convened on July 17 in the former garrison town of Potsdam on the western outskirts of Berlin in what proved to be the final Big Three summit.

When the leaders affixed their signatures to the official communiqué summarizing the results of the Potsdam Conference on August 2, they seemed to have reached a basic consensus on means to prevent future German aggression. Their joint response to Germany's historical record of external aggression and the rise of national socialism involved a combination of punitive measures and positive reconstruction. The Allies agreed to work toward such objectives as disarmament, denazification, economic and political decentralization, and democratization. The Potsdam accord called for the restoration of local self-government, the licensing of democratic parties, and free competitive elections to regional, provincial, and state administrative bodies as specific steps toward the piecemeal revival of German political activity. Although the Allies did not sanction the immediate creation of a central German government, they did concur that "certain essential German administrative departments, headed by State Secretaries, shall be established, particularly in the fields of finance, transport, communications, foreign trade and industry. Such departments will act under the direction of the Control Council" in Berlin. They further confirmed that Germany would be treated as a single economic unit during the period of occupation, and that occupation officials would pursue common economic policies within their respective zones.[15]

Undermining the apparent East-West consensus on basic political and economic objectives of the occupation was intense disagreement concerning important security and economic issues affecting the Allies themselves. In addition to a protracted dispute over whether to draw Germany's eastern border along the Oder and Neisse rivers or further east, the Allies sharply disagreed over Soviet demands that Germany pay $10 billion in reparations. Of this amount, Stalin proposed that 50 percent should be extracted within two years "by removal of national wealth" from Germany as a whole. The remainder would be paid in the form of annual deliveries in kind over a ten-year period. Truman responded that the Soviet plan was impractical. In the end, Stalin accepted a suggestion by the United States that reparation payments should be calculated in terms of a "statement of percentages" rather than a fixed dollar sum and that Russia could extract the bulk of reparations from its own zone of occupation.[16]

Both decisions proved fateful for the future course of postwar German political development. British and U.S. acceptance of the Oder-Neisse boundary accorded ex post facto sanction to unilateral action within the

Soviet Union's sphere of military presence in Central and Eastern Europe. In turn, Stalin's endorsement of the American formula for extracting reparations on a zonal basis marked a significant retreat from the formal Allied commitment to treat Germany as a single economic unit.

Germany Divided, 1945–1949

The Potsdam Conference proved the final benchmark in international collaboration among the Allies. Initially, swift action was taken to establish central administrative procedures to plan and oversee quadripartite occupation measures. These included the liquidation of Nazi organizations and laws, demilitarization, the trial and punishment of prominent Nazi war criminals, the dismantling of industries for reparation purposes, and the reorganization of the German judicial and educational systems.

In addition, in July 1945 the occupation powers undertook a major move toward the construction of a post-totalitarian political system when they authorized the restoration of semiautonomous states (*Länder*) based on Germany's historical state boundaries. In 1947 the four powers decreed the dissolution of the Prussian state. Soviet officials established five states in the east; the Western Allies initially created twelve. Most of the latter were based on earlier kingdoms and city-states such as Bavaria, Lower Saxony, Bremen, and Hamburg. Two were new constructs, both carved out of former Prussian territory: North Rhine–Westphalia, a large, populous state encompassing the Ruhr industrial base; and Rhineland-Palatinate, a more agrarian state located on the west bank of the Rhine.

In a parallel but less coordinated step to restore political life, the four Allies sanctioned the revival of political parties, trade unions, and other voluntary associations. The Soviet Union acted first by licensing four "antifascist" parties in June 1945. These included the resurrected Communist Party of Germany (KPD), the Social Democrats (SPD), a new Liberal Democratic Party (LPD), and a new Christian Democratic Union (CDU). All four parties were subsequently established on a regional level in the three Western zones as well. A similar pattern characterized the revival of trade union and other group activities. Soviet officials sanctioned the forthright establishment of the Free German Federation of Trade Unions (FDGB) and a farmers' cooperative organization. In contrast, the Western Allies permitted workers, farmers, business associations, and professionals to organize in their own zones only on a decentralized and gradual basis.

Despite initial success by the Allies in coordinating key elements of their occupation policies, zonal autonomy proved to be a fatal flaw in the Potsdam agreement. France was the first to thwart the accord.[17] Apprehensive that the restoration of a national government could lead to the eventual resurgence of German military strength, French officials vetoed U.S. efforts in late 1945 to establish central administrative departments. Similarly, the French military commander blocked other Allied proposals to permit the restoration of national political parties and trade unions. In each case, French officials justified their refusal on the grounds that the Allies should seek prior agreement on measures to prevent future German aggression. As a means to promote its postwar economic recovery, France also unilaterally detached the highly industrialized Saarland on the Franco-German border and incorporated it into its own national economy.[18]

All of this proved of critical significance in the light of divergent Soviet and Western interpretations of the political and economic provisions of the Potsdam agreement. Pursuing a Marxist-inspired strategy to eliminate the economic basis of historic German authoritarianism, Soviet military administrators authorized the expropriation of all banks within their zone and the establishment of new municipally owned ones as early as August 1945. The following month, the Saxon state government implemented a massive land reform in which two million hectares of land that had formerly belonged to the *Junkers* and other large landowners were distributed among 333,000 farmers. Under the authority of the Potsdam agreement to punish war criminals, the Soviet Military Administration then nationalized heavy industry, mines, and all property of the former German government, the Prussian state, and the Nazi Party. These measures were endorsed in a popular referendum held in Saxony in June 1946 that subsequently served as the ideological justification for expropriating virtually all privately owned enterprises throughout the Soviet zone. To ensure that domestic political control over the new collective economic resources would remain safely in the hands of orthodox Marxist-Leninists, the Soviets forced the merger of the east zonal KPD and SPD in April 1946 into a single Socialist Unity Party (SED) under firm Communist control.

In contrast to the sweeping economic and political reforms sponsored by Soviet occupation officials, the Western Allies pursued far less revolutionary objectives. Similar to the Soviets, they utilized the Potsdam accord as the legal basis for prosecuting Nazi war criminals and dismantling heavy and light industry that had been utilized for wartime production. In like manner, they recruited reliable nonfascist leaders to assume leadership positions in political parties, trade unions, industry, and state administrations. Beyond denazification, demilitarization, and economic and political decentralization, however, the Western occupation powers stopped short of sweeping industrial or land reform. Instead, their occupation policies were designed to eliminate Germany's economic war potential and maximize sociopolitical conditions of libertarian democracy.

The absence of common reform policies and central German administrative agencies accentuated the development of fundamental differences between the Soviet zone of occupation and the three Western zones. As Cold War tensions deepened, sessions at the Allied Control Council in Berlin became more and more acrimonious. The Soviets renewed their wartime claim to $10 billion in reparation payments from Germany as a nation, which the United States rejected, while the French continued to press their demands to detach the Ruhr industrial area and integrate the Saarland into the French national economy.

When a four-power foreign ministers' conference held in 1946 in Paris failed to reconcile these policy differences, U.S. officials concluded that the basic difficulty confronting the Allies was the absence of German economic unity. Accordingly, the United States offered to merge its zone of occupation with that of any of the other three. Both France and the Soviet Union balked, but Britain cautiously accepted the offer in late July. Thus the stage was set for a series of strategic moves that would mean the repudiation of the Potsdam facade of four-power government and Germany's division into separate libertarian-capitalist and communist regimes by 1949.

Conclusion

Through their divergent occupation policies, the former wartime allies fundamentally altered the requisites of political modernity in Germany. By dismembering and dividing the former Reich, they undid Germany's first unification of 1871. At the same time, their efforts to demilitarize and democratize Germany resulted in a profound transformation of authority relations and fundamental rights of citizenship. The result of occupation in the Soviet zone was a decisive break with Germany's economic and political past. There, radical occupation reforms and communist dominance resulted in the introduction of a Soviet model of centralized state socialism. The founding of a separate West German Federal Republic, in contrast, offered democratic German leaders an opportunity to achieve what had eluded their ideological forebears of 1848 and 1919: a working democratic order that would command the allegiance of its citizens, sustain domestic political stability, and enable Germany to live in peace with its European neighbors.

3

Germany Divided and Unified

Gerner politics during the twentieth century was dominated to an unusual extent by history and Germans' reactions to that history. The
half century of Germany's foreign occupation, division, and unification forms the immediate chronological background to the contemporary
scene. For more than forty years, German politics were shaped by powerful
external forces of foreign occupation and alliances and by an intense inter-
German competition between the two German states created in the war's aftermath. The end of the Cold War signaled an end to this postwar phase of
German history. In the following chapters, we explore the problems and
prospects of German politics, domestic and foreign, now and in the near future. Here, we first review the course of German division and the country's
unification.

During the Cold War era of German history (1945–1990), three themes
dominated politics in both East and West Germany: the future of the
German national state, German national identity in its historical context,
and the impact on German politics of the international environment.
German politics also was animated by contentious domestic social and economic issues. Indeed, the two German states developed starkly contrasting
socioeconomic systems. From the perspective of the unified Germany of the
twenty-first century, however, with its dominant West German political and
economic systems, that economic and social competition is important for
the part it played in forming German identity.

The Germans dealt with these issues in the framework of two rival states,
each linked to a major Cold War bloc. This "cold civil war" on German territory ended with the collapse of the East German state in 1989, the acquiescence of the Soviet Union to German unification within the Western
alliance a year later, and the unification of Germany as the Federal Republic

of Germany. This proved to be a struggle between two uneven partners. The victorious western Federal Republic was larger, more populous, better endowed with natural resources, and linked to the economically and militarily more powerful ally. Thus the resolution of Germany's problems in the Cold War historical era has led to a united Germany that must cope with a difficult dual heritage (Nazi and communist), as well as with the task of integrating a poorer, smaller, defeated region into the modern German polity.[1]

Competing Regimes

As shown in chapter 2, the erosion of four-power Allied control led to the emergence of competing regimes. The Western Allies established interzonal economic coordination (1946–1948) and a Parliamentary Council (*Parlamentarischer Rat*) to prepare the formation of a government in the Western zones. The Soviet authorities, from 1947 on, established "administrations," which in 1949–1950 became a Soviet Zone government.[2]

In the fall of 1946 the United States and Britain negotiated a series of agreements to establish joint agencies governing finance, agriculture, transportation, and communication. These arrangements were made in close consultation with German administrative officials and were formalized in a two-power agreement signed in December that established "Bizonia." The formation of Bizonia coincided with the revival of German political life throughout the divided nation. Statewide elections were held in June 1946 in the American zone to choose delegates to draft new state constitutions. French, British, and Soviet officials conducted local elections in September, and statewide elections followed in the Soviet zone in October. In each case new local and state government bodies were formed and assumed limited legislative and administrative powers. Hence, the Anglo-American move to merge occupation zones inevitably pointed toward the eventual transfer of political authority back to the Germans. The central question that confounded Allied policy councils at the beginning of 1947 was whether France and the Soviet Union would join in the restoration of German political unity or whether either or both would continue to withhold cooperation.

A significant shift in U.S. foreign policy during 1947 toward a goal of economic self-sufficiency within the joint U.S.-British zones, coupled with U.S. endorsement of French claims to economic union with the Saarland and international controls over coal and steel production in the Ruhr region, laid the basis for a coordinated economic policy in the Western zones of occupation. Underlying American emphasis on German economic recovery was the realization that cooperation on German issues with the Soviet Union was no longer possible. Accordingly, President Harry Truman and his key foreign policy advisers decided by the beginning of 1947 to promote general European recovery as a deterrent against perceived Soviet military and ideological threats to the North Atlantic region. U.S. officials concluded that German productivity must be restored as quickly as possible. To win

European support for this policy, and to aid European recovery in general, Secretary of State George Marshall issued a dramatic invitation at Harvard University in June 1947 to extend U.S. economic assistance to Europe to facilitate its postwar reconstruction. These multiple foreign policy initiatives signaled U.S. determination to promote the rehabilitation of Germany within a broader context of European recovery and cooperation.

The proclamation of the Marshall Plan aid program was accompanied by further measures to encourage German economic self-sufficiency. U.S. and British officials authorized the creation of an Economic Council and an Executive Committee in Bizonia. In July 1947 the Anglo-American powers agreed to increase Bizonia's steel and coal production to 1936 levels. These moves encouraged the French to modify their own German policies, in part because the prospect of U.S. economic assistance drastically diminished the necessity for France to exploit German resources for rebuilding its own economy. Consequently, France agreed to merge its zone of occupation with the American and British zones to form Trizonia, and was invited to participate in a 1948 London tripartite conference on Germany that was held to consider the full scope of German and European recovery. "It was in this indirect way," Roy Willis notes, "that the British, American, and French governments decided to hold what proved to be the most important conference on the future of Germany since the end of the war."[3]

In the significant absence of the Soviet Union, the three Western powers, as well as representatives from Belgium, the Netherlands, and Luxembourg, conferred about Germany's fate through early June 1948. Three crucial decisions emerged that sealed Germany's division and, as an unexpected consequence, prepared the way for West Germany's economic integration into Western Europe:

(1) the formation of a federal West German state that would encompass the American, British, and French occupation zones;

(2) the replacement of the occupation regime by an Occupation Statute that would govern arrangements for achieving a trizonal fusion and codify remaining Allied restrictions on West German sovereignty; and

(3) the creation of an international Authority of the Ruhr (in concert with the West Germans and the Benelux countries) to govern coal and industrial production in the region.

The military governors transmitted the instructions contained in the London Agreements to the minister-presidents of the twelve West German states in early June 1948. Subsequently, a parliamentary council (*Parlamentarischer Rat*), made up of delegates elected by the various state parliaments, convened on September 1 in Bonn to draw up a constitution for the new federal republic. In the crucial preliminary session, the delegates elected Konrad Adenauer—leader of the western branch of the postwar Christian Democratic Union (CDU)—to serve as the council's chair.

The Allied initiatives, coupled with countermoves by the Soviet Union, resulted in a rapid escalation of tension between East and West. On March 20, 1948, the Soviet military governor walked out of the Allied Control Council in Berlin, thereby bringing to an end the remaining semblance of four-power government in Germany. On June 18 the Western powers introduced the *Deutschmark* (DM), thereby implementing a long-overdue currency reform in their zones to stimulate economic growth. The Soviets reacted by introducing a new "east mark" in their zone and sought to extend its use to all of Berlin. When the Western Allies introduced the DM into their sectors of West Berlin, Soviet military officials imposed a blockade on access to the city by highway, train, and canal. The West, led by the United States, responded with an airlift of foodstuffs and essential supplies to sustain the Allied garrisons and the city's beleaguered population.

Soviet intentions in implementing the Berlin blockade apparently were aimed at blocking the establishment of a separate West German state. Soviet officials sought to advance their substitute vision of a centralized all-German government based on the economic and political principles of the Soviet zone through a combination of official denunciations of Western policy and the convocation of a "German People's Congress" (*Deutscher Volkskongress*) in October 1948 in East Berlin. The intent of this congress was to draft a socialist-inspired constitution for a unified German state. The Soviets finally abandoned their efforts, however, in the face of Allied determination to remain in the divided city and progress toward drafting a constitution for the Western zones through the Parliamentary Council in Bonn. On May 5, 1949, the Soviet Union agreed to lift the blockade. Three days later, the Parliamentary Council formally adopted the Basic Law, establishing a legal-institutional framework for the Federal Republic of Germany (*Bundesrepublik Deutschland*).

Similar to the constitution of the Weimar Republic, the Basic Law provided for a liberal capitalist system based on the principles of popular sovereignty, federalism, and constitutional order. Legislative power was vested in a popularly elected lower house (the *Bundestag*) and an appointed upper house (the *Bundesrat*), whose task was to represent the financial, territorial, and administrative interests of the West German states. Highly conscious of the constitutional weaknesses of Germany's first experiment with parliamentary democracy, the framers of the Basic Law provided for a weak, indirectly elected federal president. Most executive authority was concentrated in the hands of a federal chancellor elected by a majority vote of the *Bundestag*, although removal of the chancellor by that body was made difficult. Framers also drew heavily from the American precedent to establish an independent Federal Constitutional Court with sweeping powers of constitutional review.

After the Basic Law won the approval of the Western Allies and the endorsement of all the West German *Länder* except Bavaria, the Parliamentary Council proclaimed its official ratification on May 23.[4] West German national elections followed on August 14, resulting in a narrow Christian Democratic plurality. Konrad Adenauer was elected federal chancellor in early September by a single-vote majority in the newly constituted *Bundestag*. He proceeded to form a coalition government with the Free Democrats and a smaller regional party. On September 21 Adenauer presented his cabinet to the three Allied high commissioners who, on the same day, succeeded the military governors as the highest representatives of the Western powers in Germany. By receiving Adenauer and his cabinet, the American, British, and French commissioners formally recognized the establishment of the Federal Republic as the successor government to the German Reich.

In the Soviet Zone, the German People's Council (*Deutscher Volksrat*)— a body of delegates from the larger and ostensibly all-German "People's Congress"—was transformed in October 1949 into a provisional German People's Chamber (*Volkskammer*), which prepared for elections in October 1950. Elections in East Germany were contested by a single slate "National Front," the original multiparty system of 1945 having been destroyed first by the largely forced amalgamation of the Social Democratic and Communist parties (SPD, KPD) into the Socialist Unity Party of Germany (SED) in 1946, then by the conversion of the Christian Democrats (CDU) and Liberal Democrats (LDPD) into "bloc party" agents of the SED, and finally, by the conversion of the SED in 1948–1949 into a Stalinist ruling "party of a new type."[5] This sealed the transformation of the GDR into a Communist dictatorship on the Soviet and East European model. Delegates to the *Volkskammer* proceeded to elect a president of the GDR and a cabinet. Ministerial positions were distributed among leaders of the various East German political parties, although de facto leadership was vested in the Communist-dominated Socialist Unity Party.

Both German states were presented as provisional. The Federal Republic defined itself as a democratic political framework pending the ability of all Germans to exercise self-determination: its Basic Law lacked the legal status of a full-fledged constitution, and its capital was the quiet Rhenish university town of Bonn. The East German state, for its part, described itself (until 1971), as the germ cell of a new and revolutionary Germany: "the first workers and peasants state on German soil." It proclaimed a revolutionary legitimacy based on breaking with German past and denounced the Federal Republic as an instrument of Western division of Germany.

These divergent developments provided the institutional framework for a half century of German politics. For the Germans this meant that, contrary to general expectations at war's end, Germany's unity and national statehood were endangered. Reactions to this situation dominated German politics in both the East and the West until 1990.[6] Each postwar German state—the western Federal Republic of Germany and the eastern German Democratic Republic—strove to realize German interests by playing a valued role within its respective alliance. As a result of this territorial segregation of German political forces (conservative and moderate in the West;

radical and left-wing in the East), FRG and GDR leaders built polities and societies directly opposed to one another. With the collapse of the Soviet-bloc alliance structure and the dissolution of the GDR, it is the political, economic, and social institutions of the postwar West German republic that shape the unified Germany of today.

The Politics of the Two German States

West Germany, under the leadership of Konrad Adenauer, became a state marked by successful integration into a Western alliance structure seen as the surest path to international rehabilitation. The postwar political-social system consisted of a constitutional republic with elaborate safeguards against political subversion and a market economic system coupled with an extensive social welfare network and substantive participation by the state and labor in economic decisions.[7] The Federal Republic also served as a founding member of the West European integration process, beginning with the creation of the European Coal and Steel Community in 1951–1952 and continuing with the establishment of a more ambitious European Economic Community (today's European Union) in 1957–1958. These factors—constitutional democracy, economic liberalism, extensive social provisions, and European integration—have remained to this day both the main pillars of public policy and the broadly accepted popular consensus underlying German political legitimacy.

Although the emergent West German state did not abjure the goal of a unified Germany—indeed, the Basic Law proclaimed that it was the task of the "entire German people to achieve the unity and freedom of Germany in free self-determination"—it was clearly meant as a defensive refuge against a perceived Soviet and German Communist threat. West German politics thus consisted of balancing the freedom, social welfare, and Western integration of some three quarters of the total German population against the problematical prospects of national unification. The Federal Republic was at once a bulwark against the East, a refuge for freedom and prosperity, and a self-conscious successor state to past German regimes.[8]

The GDR, by deliberate contrast, was designed as a revolutionary break with German history. Its legitimacy rested on its claim of having destroyed the power of the large landowners and major industrialists who had—it was asserted—made possible a reactionary and militarist Germany, of which the Nazi regime represented but the latest and most awful stage.[9] Its political institutions were, after an initial "people's democratic" period, modeled closely on those of the Soviet Union; most important was the role of the SED. The leader of the SED was always the most important political figure in the GDR, within limits set by Soviet power. Walter Ulbricht emerged as sole leader by 1957; he was replaced in 1971 by the second and last GDR leader, Erich Honecker.

In the four decades after their founding, the two German states struggled to shape Germany's future. Building on the foundations noted above, this meant that successive West German governments sought to defeat the GDR in a political civil war. Although the strategies pursued by various Bonn governments differed and were often the subject of intense domestic political dispute, the goal remained the same.

The CDU-led governments of 1949–1966 pursued these goals through a policy of isolating the GDR internationally (the "Hallstein Doctrine," which denied diplomatic ties with Bonn to any state that recognized the GDR), minimizing any direct ties (largely economic) between the two governments, and above all, denying legitimacy, especially symbolic, to the GDR. One example will suffice: no government agency, and most of the press, forbore to use the name GDR; gradually it was used in quotation marks. It was only after 1971 that the name was generally used. Across the dividing line, the GDR engaged in similar practices.

SPD-FDP coalition governments of 1966–1982 under Willy Brandt and Helmut Schmidt, as well as their CDU-led successors under Helmut Kohl, used a policy of "small steps" that led to a hoped for "transformation through close approach" (*Wandel durch Annäherung*). Although differing in policy details and rhetoric, all West German governments after 1971 dealt directly with the GDR leadership, helped the GDR economically, and maintained, in the words of the former West German president Richard von Weizsäcker, that the "German question remains open." It is a sign of the remarkable continuity of this policy that in 1987 GDR leader Erich Honecker made his first and only state visit to West Germany.

The fundamental goal of East German policy was to reshape Germany on the Soviet model of political, economic, and social organization. In the GDR, the party leadership under Walter Ulbricht first established its control of state and society and of Ulbricht's own position. The "leading role" of the party was formally enshrined in the GDR constitution, and "socialist democracy" in government; a centrally planned economy was instituted; and the closest possible military, diplomatic, and foreign trade links with the Soviet Union were introduced into the political system.

Under Ulbricht the GDR maintained a commitment to German unity and to fostering radical political transformation in all of Germany. Under Honecker, the GDR pursued an official policy of distinguishing itself from both West Germany and the notion of a single German nation-state through a policy of rigid separation (*Abgrenzung*). Ironically, it was while striving to establish a separate East German identity that the Communist regime made its strongest claim to Germany's national and cultural heritage. Among the highlights of this policy were the celebration of Berlin's 750th anniversary and the 500th birthday of Martin Luther, and the restoration of such figures as Bismarck and Frederick the Great to historical favor.[10]

The mutually hostile relations between the German states during the early Cold War era were punctuated by an uprising in East Berlin and other cities on and after June 17, 1953,[11] and the building of the Berlin Wall on August 13, 1961.[12] The uprising of June 17 was a major factor in shaping the image each Germany had of the other. To West Germans, it confirmed the repressive and illegitimate character of the GDR regime and came to be seen as the first of a series of blows for freedom from Soviet and local Communist domination. This rebellion would stretch through Poland (1953), Hungary (1956), Czechoslovakia (1968)—and Poland again (with the rise of Solidarity in 1979–1980) until a series of upheavals brought down the structure of Soviet domination in Central and Eastern Europe and put an end to the GDR itself in 1989–1990.

For East German leaders, "1953" remained a source of deep-rooted fear and suspicion of their own people. The population of the GDR was seen as liable to enticement or subversion from contact with the West. While all Communist regimes severely restricted contact with foreigners, the GDR's elaborate efforts to prevent such contacts were based on fear of the continued effect of national and familial ties to West Germany. Moreover, aware that only direct Soviet military action had saved the East German regime in 1953, GDR leaders had an additional reason to stress their ties to the USSR—"learning from the Soviet Union means learning to win"—which was to boomerang as the impact of Gorbachev and his policy of *perestroika* on the East German public grew between 1985 and 1989.

At the end of a decade of existence, the growing economic and political strength of the FRG seriously compromised all efforts at a stable, let alone flourishing, GDR. This was especially true in regard to the drain of population from East to West. Although there was always some traffic in both directions—for example, Hans-Dietrich Genscher, West Germany's foreign minister from 1957 to 1990, had fled from the GDR, whereas Angela Merkel moved with her father (a Protestant minister) in the opposite direction—the bulk of population transfer went from East to West. Social and political pressures on those who continued to profess religious beliefs and were stymied in their professional lives generated the desire to leave; the match of skills and opportunity was often the final motivation. Thus the GDR not only lost population in general between 1949 and 1961, but also young and skilled persons in particular.[13]

The Wall and *Ostpolitik*

The exodus to the West peaked in early 1961, driven largely by resistance to a GDR campaign to collectivize agriculture and the rise in international tension fueled by the threatening rhetoric Soviet leader Nikita Khrushchev used beginning in 1958 in regard to Berlin. Ulbricht and GDR leaders, desperate for control of the East German population, gained explicit approval from the Soviet leadership for a drastic measure to isolate the GDR from its western rival: the Berlin Wall was erected on August 13, 1961. In the twenty-eight years it snaked through the city of Berlin, the wall had paradoxical effects on German politics. On one hand, it dismayed many East Germans, angered West Germans, and was a permanent propaganda liability for the GDR. Yet on the other hand, it made political and social stabilization of the GDR possible by closing the last remaining readily available exit route from the GDR. East Germans, for the most part, adjusted to life within the confines of the Communist system. They strove to achieve what was possible, sometimes pushing to expand the bounds of the permissible, sometimes sinking back into the "niches" of private life, and, especially in the last years of Communist rule, rebelling against the regime's strictures.

At the same time, the wall symbolized the fragility of the East German system. Neither in its relations with the Federal Republic nor with other Western states or with the third world was the GDR able to escape the shadow of the barrier that divided Germans from one another. While in reality GDR border controls differed neither in kind nor quantity from those of other Communist states, it was the wall's symbolic admission that the GDR could not compete in a straightforward comparison with the Federal Republic that damaged East Germany's image abroad and at home. For broad sections of the East German population, party members included, restrictions on travel and on contacts with West Germans were and remained to the end a major source of dissatisfaction.

The relative stabilization of the GDR after 1961 was challenged by the Brandt government. Brandt made ratification of nonaggression treaties completed with Moscow and Warsaw in 1970 dependent on a four-power agreement that would stabilize the situation of West Berlin a year later. By this *neue Ostpolitik* (new Eastern policy), the Brandt government complemented Adenauer's Western orientation and integration with an active policy that gave the Federal Republic an important presence in the Soviet bloc.[14]

These diplomatic successes gave Brandt a decisive electoral victory in 1972 as well as international recognition, including the Nobel Peace Prize. They also led indirectly to the downfall of GDR leader Ulbricht. Confronted with opposition within the SED leadership over domestic policy, Ulbricht became politically vulnerable when he opposed the Soviet détente with Bonn. With Soviet support and approval, he was replaced by the GDR's last leader, Erich Honecker, in May 1971.

Bonn's strengthened position in European affairs also resulted in an arrangement between the German states. The 1972 Basic Treaty (*Grundlagenvertrag*) between East and West Germany was an acknowledgment of two basic realities of the German situation. One was West Germany's economic and political strength, which forced the GDR to negotiate from a weaker position. The other was the need to embed German relations in a framework acceptable to the occupation powers, particularly the Soviet Union and the United States. By terms of the treaty, the two German states recognized each other's jurisdiction over their respective territories, pledged to refrain from the use of force against each other, promised to encourage personal contacts and cooperation in such areas as environmental protection, and established mutual diplomatic ties, albeit through special missions (*ständige Vertre-tungen*) rather than embassies. They agreed to disagree on the questions of citizenship and German nationality.

In addition, West German representatives were able to attach a special "Letter on German Unity" to the treaty protocol in which the Federal Republic gave up its claim to be the sole representative of the German nation on the international level. The GDR consequently obtained universal diplomatic recognition in 1973–1974, and both German states became full members of the United Nations. The treaty also marked a major step toward German freedom of action in world affairs by reducing the constraints on German diplomacy that had arisen from Allied occupation rights.

Two German States, Two Alliances

The mutual relations of the two Germanys outlined up to this point took place within the framework of, and were shaped by, the presence and power of the victors of World War II, especially the United States and the Soviet Union. In the first postwar decades, these powers determined the general structures and details of Germany's domestic life, and external relations and military capabilities were wholly outside either Germany's provenance.

For each of the great powers, its respective German client was an important geographic and economic asset. The inclusion of West Germany in the Marshall Plan and the crushing of the June 1953 uprisings in East Germany each demonstrate how important West and East Germany were. From the two German states' perspective, close and loyal ties to their respective superpowers were major tools to advance German interests.

Thus, West Germany under Adenauer undertook building close ties with France; indeed, the acceptance of the Schuman Plan for the creation of a West European Coal and Steel Community formed the germ of today's European Union. Possibly controversial issues, such as reversion of the Saarland to West Germany, were handled with care, and relations between the two nations generally, especially under French president Charles de Gaulle, became and have remained a major anchor of German policy. At the same time, West Germany never overlooked the importance of its U.S. connection. The United States was the essential security guarantor and most willing of all Western powers to support German unification. Against considerable domestic opposition from those who feared a negative impact on eventual reunification and those who eschewed German military action in the wake of Nazi aggression, Adenauer pushed through German rearmament and NATO membership. In any conflict between so-called Gaullists and Atlanticists for German loyalty, the ties to Washington came first. In fact, in the struggle over NATO plans for missile deployment in the early 1980s, both Schmidt and Kohl supported the U.S. position at considerable domestic political cost.

Despite such actions, U.S. officials were at first suspicious of Brandt's policies. However, the United States came to support détente policy in general. The German drive for unification received indispensable support from both the United States and the Soviet Union in 1989–1990.[15] U.S. support for a unified Germany in NATO was steadfast, despite serious high-level misgivings in many West European capitals. The four-power agreement and "2+4" treaty (the two Germanys, the Soviet Union, France, Great Britain, and the United States) of September 1990 restored full sovereignty to Germany in military and foreign affairs. Germany agreed to accept borders and territory not exceeding the four occupation zones and Berlin, thus formally abjuring the Polish lands beyond the Oder and Neisse rivers.

More surprising than U.S. support for German unification within NATO was Soviet acquiescence to it.[16] For four decades, Soviet policy in Europe rested on the military presence in Germany that was the fruit of the USSR's great victory of 1945. Soviet control of the GDR gave Moscow what its tsarist predecessors had once had: a permanent voice in German affairs, a guarantee against a too-powerful united Germany, and the ability to play two German suitors against one another. The Soviet occupation of eastern Germany had been from the start a source of economic advantage that began with reparations and then grew to include the fruits of a relatively advanced industrial system of the GDR; an opportunity for military pressure in western Europe; and an instrument of Soviet domination of eastern Europe through the Soviet forces in Germany and their supply and support network.

Soviet actions in 1948–1949, 1953, and 1961 showed how important this position was to Soviet leaders. Paralleling Western policy, they promoted the establishment of the GDR; saw to it that the Soviet system was installed there; allowed GDR membership in the Soviet-led military bloc of the Warsaw Pact Organization and economic alliance of the Council for Mutual Economic Assistance (CMEA); and supported the GDR's international ambitions.

Nevertheless, it had always been clear that Soviet leaders would not allow the GDR to obstruct their pursuit of Soviet interests in relations with the United States and the Federal Republic. As early as the Berlin Blockade, as vividly as the tank confrontation at Checkpoint Charlie on Berlin's *Wilhelmstrasse* in 1961, and as recently as incidents in the late 1980s—it was always Soviet policy to uphold the special rights of the occupation powers "for the whole of Germany." Moreover, West Germany's increasing economic, technological, and military importance, along with its central role within European institutions, persuaded the Soviet Union to sometimes place relations with Bonn ahead of the interests of its East German client state. This was the case at the time of Brandt's *Ostpolitik* and proved to be so again in the crisis brought on by the collapse of the GDR.

Weaknesses of the GDR, 1987–1990

The events traced here—from Germany's defeat in 1945 through recovery to reunification in 1990—provide a common historical background for all Germans. But the roughly one quarter of the population in the former GDR has had a second experience of political and social discontinuity. In nearly every aspect of German life, including political attitudes and the political party system, the special experience of East Germans sets them apart from their compatriots to the west. To what extent this has been so, and how much it continues to be, are themselves controversial issues. Here we briefly discuss the impact of the GDR's collapse on Germany and on Germans' historical awareness.

As seen, the GDR enjoyed a period of relative domestic stability after the building of the Berlin Wall. The decade that followed saw a series of reforms aimed at increased economic efficiency. Under Honecker (1971–1989) the GDR regime compromised with the population by providing such social assurance as employment and subsidies for basic commodities and permitting gradual acceptance of Western consumer values. There was a concerted program of housing construction, the use of foreign exchange to import consumer goods, and appeals to pride in the German past. East German officials also formed an arrangement with the Evangelical Protestant Church that allowed the church—"a Church within Socialism"—to expand its welfare activities, undertake educational and cultural programs, and resume the construction of churches.[17] This "unity of social and economic policy" became the chief legitimating force in GDR politics.

The GDR greatly expanded its international presence in these years. As noted previously, the international détente of 1971–1975 brought the GDR general diplomatic recognition, UN membership, and in 1975 full participation in the Helsinki Conference on Cooperation and Security in Europe. The Honecker leadership used these opportunities to advance its position in German affairs by dealing directly with the Federal Republic, as well as by acting as a valuable Soviet surrogate.

In the decade of the 1980s relations between the two German states grew ever closer. Political contacts ranged from ministerial visits to partner-city programs, and contacts between the SED and West German parties, most conspicuously the SPD, increased. There was increased West German economic support for the GDR, ranging from semi-secret West German payments for the release of GDR political prisoners to the billion-*Deutschmark* bank credit guarantee arranged by Bavarian governor and CSU leader Franz-Josef Strauss in late 1987. For its part, the GDR steadily increased the number of its citizens allowed to travel to West Germany, either because they were past retirement age or because of "pressing family concerns,"[18] and eased the conditions for Western visits to the GDR.

The climax of this trend came with Honecker's official visit to the Federal Republic in September 1987. Aside from the personal and symbolic elements—Honecker was able to visit his Saarland childhood home, as well as the birthplaces of Karl Marx and Friedrich Engels—the visit showed West Germany's acceptance of East Germany as an autonomous international entity. Given that the Soviet leaders had forced Honecker to cancel a planned visit to West Germany in 1984, the success of the 1987 visit showed the GDR's greater autonomy within the bloc.

The Rise of Discontent and the End of the GDR, 1987–1990

Yet in the fall of 1989, the Communist regime in the GDR collapsed. A year later the GDR vanished into unification on Western terms.[19] What accounts for the rapid and seemingly unexpected decline of the GDR after 1987?

It is useful in this discussion to distinguish among long- and short-term factors. The former includes the regime's economic shortcomings; its dwindling legitimacy, especially among youth; and the increasing immobility of its leadership. East Germany's worsening economic situation, highlighted by shortages of consumer goods, contributed to the GDR's loss of legitimacy, mocking the explicit bargain proclaimed by Honecker that in the GDR "hard work pays off" in terms of improved living standards.

Many of the regime's domestic opponents strove to improve the system; however, in the last decade of the GDR's existence these opponents increasingly protested the system as such and increased their demands for freedom of emigration. They found logistical support and social backing within the Evangelical Church and sympathy from within lower ranks of the SED.[20] But few could hope that the regime would respond with reforms. The SED's eleventh and last party congress, held in 1986, did not make a single change in an aging leadership. A proposal in 1989 to move the forthcoming twelfth congress up a year, together with hints of a party purge, were widely seen as maneuvers to keep the old leaders in place even longer. When those leaders ostentatiously associated themselves with the repressive Romanian regime and the violent suppression of Chinese dissent on Tiananmen Square in June 1989, the chances for reform seemed small indeed. It was in these circumstances that a series of short-term setbacks lead to the collapse of the GDR.

Reform-minded East Germans looked to Mikhail Gorbachev's programs of domestic reform to alleviate their situation and discovered to their dismay that the very regime that had proclaimed its unfailing loyalty to the USSR ("Learning from the Soviet Union means learning to win!") now declared its independence from Soviet models. So while East Germans chanted "Gorby! Gorby!" at the GDR fortieth anniversary celebrations in October 1989, the regime rejected any applications of *perestroika* or *glasnost* in East Germany itself.

Gorbachev could not help with GDR domestic reform, but he could—and did—transform the GDR's international situation in such a way as to lead to the country's downfall. In the breakup of the international structures that had kept the GDR in existence, the crucial development was the Soviet decision to abandon its commitment to support Communist regimes in Eastern Europe by force. This was a consequence of Gorbachev's commitment to a "common European house," which meant sacrificing Soviet positions in exchange for access to Western economic resources. Superpower agreements on missile reduction and further disarmament steps paved the way for Western willingness to support German reunification and the ability to gain Soviet acceptance of a united Germany's membership in NATO. Consequently, neither Soviet nor West German leaders, each of whom had in different ways and for different motives contributed to the GDR's existence, had an incentive to continue to do so.

Crisis and Response, 1989–1990

The slow disintegration of the GDR exploded into a systemic crisis when Hungary dismantled its frontier barriers to Austria in May 1989.[21] The result was an exodus of East Germans by way of Hungary and Austria to West Germany, especially after September 1989 when the Hungarians officially refused to block their way. Other East Germans entered the premises of West German embassies in Prague and Warsaw and the Permanent Mission in East Berlin to seek exit to the West. The regime's response incorporated the worst alternatives: it denounced those leaving (the official SED daily declared "no one would shed a tear" for them) but then agreed to give exit papers to those in the embassies as long as they left through GDR territory.

The deepening crisis increasingly encompassed those East Germans not willing to leave the country. It also was accompanied by growing activism of the regime's opponents. A series of public demonstrations in 1988–1989, the most significant of which was a challenge to the official returns in municipal elections in May 1989, led to outbursts of political action by late summer that challenged the foundations of the regime.

This wave of street demonstrations engulfed the GDR, especially Leipzig, where a tradition of weekly "peace services" had been established at the city's St. Nicholas Church. Beginning in September, these services were followed by peaceful but massive marches along the main boulevards of the city center during which marchers demanded political and economic changes in the GDR. Under circumstances that remain unclear, authorities failed to implement plans to put down these demonstrations by force. This failure to act marked the regime's loss of control over developments.

Demonstrations spread to other cities, including Berlin, and continued as the regime crumbled. Notable was the demonstration on Berlin's *Alexanderplatz* on November 4, at which leading cultural and political figures called for fundamental reforms. Meanwhile, despite repeated arrests and beatings of demonstrators, it became clear that the regime had lost the chance to suppress these demonstrations. Honecker had been removed from the leadership on October 18; the tenure of his successor, Egon Krenz, would be measured in weeks.

By year's end, the SED itself was in disarray, having been partially reformed and renamed at a special party congress in December. Most of the old party leaders were expelled, some were arrested, and the party's formal leadership role in society was ended by amending Article 1 of the GDR constitution. This article had previously accorded the SED a constitutionally guaranteed leadership role in governing the GDR. By this point the ruling party had been challenged not only by mass demonstrations and church-protected activities, but by organized political forces as well. Chief among these were the Social Democratic Party, reconstituted in August 1989, and a broad coalition of activists united in the New Forum (*Neues Forum*).[22]

The political crisis of the winter of 1989–1990 was resolved temporarily by the establishment of a caretaker government under the leadership of the SED's Hans Modrow, together with a Round Table over which Evangelical Church leaders presided. This caretaker government was divided half and half between organizations that had been social "transmission belts" of the old regime and those that sprang up in late 1989. The Round Table paid special attention to the role of the state security (*Stasi*) and was responsible for the preservation of and access to that organization's files. It commissioned an ultimately abortive reform constitution and forced agreement on early free elections, which were held on March 18, 1990.

West Germany's Role and the International Setting

The rise of popular sentiment favoring reunification in the winter of 1989–1990 was accompanied by the growing intervention of West German political actors in GDR affairs. As *Wir sind das Volk* (We are the people) yielded to *Wir sind ein Volk* (We are one people) the Kohl government's early reactions to the upheavals in the GDR were restrained. Kohl's ten-point program of November 1989 foresaw a lengthy process of improving relations between the German states, but the continuing flight of East Germans and concomitant growing dislocation of GDR life forced a change of policy. With the apparent acceptance by Gorbachev of German self-determination at a January 1990 meeting with Krenz, Bonn's policy swung over to one of rapid reunification.

Thus the March 1990 election in the GDR became in practice a referendum on reunification. Kohl cemented an electoral "Alliance for Germany," of which a revamped East German CDU was the core. Contrary to general expectation in Germany and abroad, a late swing of voter opinion gave the alliance 48 percent of the vote; the once-favored SPD emerged a distant second, and the Party of Democratic Socialism (the PDS, or a renamed SED) was third with just over 16 percent. The party representing the dissident activists of fall 1989 received 3 percent.

When the wall came tumbling down, Berliners from both parts of the formerly divided city cheered. Here, East Germans (backs to camera) flood through the dismantled Berlin Wall into West Berlin at Potsdamer Platz on November 12, 1989.

The GDR government that emerged from the election carried out its mandate to negotiate the terms of reunification. In practice, this amounted to accepting plans worked out in Bonn, with only marginal adjustments. While both German states negotiated with the occupation powers in the "2+4" talks, the GDR was barely involved. As a telling indication of how pressing the economic disruption in the GDR had become, the two German states negotiated an economic and social union prior to political unity. This pact made the West German *Deutschmark* legal tender throughout eastern Germany at politically favorable but economically dubious exchange rates. It also transferred West Germany's system of property ownership, workplace relations, and social insurance to the GDR. The treaty of political unification of August 31, 1990, sealed the de facto union and the political victory of the Federal Republic.

German reunification became feasible with the agreement of the four powers, particularly that of the USSR. Here the direct negotiations between Kohl and Gorbachev, culminating in July 1990, provided the crucial breakthrough.[23] Soviet agreement for a united Germany within NATO was purchased at the price of subsidies for relocation of Soviet forces in Germany; a phased, four-year withdrawal of Soviet troops, although Western forces remained as NATO contingents; and a reduction of overall German armed forces.

Institutional Setting for Reunification

A critical element in the reunification process was the choice of a constitutional framework. One option was to use Article 146 of the Basic Law. According to this article, a new constitution freely adopted by the "entire German nation" would supersede the Basic Law and would have entailed a new formulation of basic principles and goals, as well as possible institutional changes. Proponents of this method, then and now, argued that it would have given the East Germans an equal and legitimating coauthorship of a reunification constitution. Some West Germans favored this procedure precisely to force fundamental changes in the constitutional character of the republic. In fact, given the relative demographic and electoral weights of the two states, and the contents of the Round Table–sponsored GDR draft constitution, the outcome would have been a constitution largely the same as the revised Basic Law.

The method ultimately used was to invoke Article 23, which had been used in 1956 to incorporate the Saarland into the Federal Republic. Under this article, the East German states, reconstituted in September 1990, collectively acceded to the Federal Republic. The political significance of this step was to legitimize the political-constitutional order built in West Germany over four decades as the most suitable framework for a democratic polity for the whole of Germany. It was—and was seen as—confirmation of the political victory of the Federal Republic in the Cold (civil) War that had dominated postwar German life.

Although in general West German institutions and practices were exported to the eastern states, two institutions deserve special note.[24] These are the *Treuhandanstalt,* the holding company charged with privatization of socialized property in the former GDR, and the so-called *Gauck-Behörde,* the agency first headed by an East German dissident pastor, Joachim Gauck, that was charged with safeguarding and making accessible the records of the GDR Ministry for State Security. Both of these institutions were created by the last, noncommunist GDR legislature and carried over into the united Germany.

The *Treuhand* operated under constraints imposed by the terms of the economic and social union of 1990. This meant that it had to follow the principle of restitution of lost property before compensation, which led to years of uncertainty as to property rights for both investors and East German users of property, particularly homes. Moreover, the *Treuhand* was directed to privatize rather than continue to subsidize GDR enterprises. This meant that many businesses were shut down for lack of investors willing to carry enterprises that were no longer competitive in market terms. Even for those enterprises worth saving, there were few if any East Germans with sufficient capital to bid for them. In practice, there was often political intervention by the Federal Republic and East German state governments and the application of some European Union (EU) subsidies to preserve some key plants, including steel and shipbuilding works. Nonetheless, the result of this policy was to severely reduce the industrial capacity of the eastern states. Given that such industrial plants had provided not only employment, but a range of social services and community ties as well, the impact on eastern German society was quite negative.

The *Gauck* authority safeguarded and made available records of great value to scholars. More recently, it has provided closure for the many eastern Germans subjected to the *Stasi*'s secret scrutiny. Ironically, because of the ready availability of *Stasi* files—and their potentially sensational value in political struggles—the *Gauck* program has emphasized the role of the *Stasi* in GDR life, at the expense of a focus on such institutions as the ruling party and the state machinery.

Conclusion

With the legal framework of the two treaties on economic and political arrangements between the German states and the "2+4" treaty between these states and the four occupying powers, Germany regained unity and full sovereignty. Having also agreed on a formal juridical acceptance of Poland's western border, the two Germanys reunited on October 3, which was subsequently proclaimed the German national holiday. The Germans were again masters of their own house, although still linked to NATO and the EU and with carefully friendly relations with Russia.

In the contemporary "Berlin republic," the issues that dominated the divided Germany after 1945 have faded away; Germany's relation to the external framework of the EU on the one hand, and the domestic relations within an increasingly multicultural country on the other, have gained in importance—as they have in most of Germany's EU partners. The current and ever-changing attitudes of Germans toward their country and its history are discussed further in chapter 4.

4

Political and Popular Culture

Germany has long been an exemplary case for the importance of culture in its multiple dimensions: the high culture of literature, art, music, architecture, and language that helps define collective identity and a sense of community in the modern nation-state; the values, beliefs, and patterns of individual and group behavior that comprise contemporary social culture; the particular subset of political values, beliefs, and orientations that constitute political culture; and aesthetics, fads, and shared visual, musical, and other mass experiences associated with popular culture. In this chapter, we concentrate on German political culture, paying special attention to Germans' response to their national identity and their common past. We end with a discussion of politically relevant aspects of literary and popular culture.

Political Culture

Germans born in the second decade of the last century have been subjects of no fewer than six political regimes, seven if they lived in the former GDR.[1] Such a person presumably has internalized attitudes toward politics, society, and culture supportive of each of the very different political systems of modern Germany and has quickly and completely replaced them with new attitudes as circumstances and the demands of rulers changed.[2] Whether or not asking such adaptability of Germans was ever plausible, the strength of contemporary German democracy has been seen as requiring attitudes congruent with a democratic polity, a pluralistic society, and a market economy.[3]

Exploring, measuring, and evaluating such congruence of attitude and regime is the subject of political culture research. The modern study of political culture derives from efforts to explain the collapse of the Weimar Republic's democratic institutions. What can such research tell us about the present and future relationship between democratic stability in Germany and German political culture?

The political culture of the Weimar era has been widely viewed as incongruent with strengthening democracy. Weimar was the "republic without republicans"; those social groups that had supported the authoritarian Second Empire could not (or would not) be won over, and support among intellectual elites was grudging at best. The natural supporters of the republic, especially the working classes, were weakened by competition between Weimar's political mainstay, the Social Democrats, and the increasingly Stalinist German Communists.[4]

The Nazi regime drew support both from supporters of the traditional, authoritarian traditions that had weakened Weimar and from those advocating a strain of social radicalism similar to communist views. Nazi leaders, perhaps with the growth of popular discontent during World War I in mind, paid close attention to the popular mood, especially on economic issues. Despite a fluctuating level of largely economic grumbling, there is little evidence of any substantial loss of regime legitimacy, even as (or perhaps because) Germany's defeat in war approached.[5]

After 1945

When the Second World War ended in 1945, all four occupying powers confronted a population that could not be assumed to hold democratic values. Indeed, suspicion of Germans' popular attitudes was widespread among the first postwar cohort of German political leaders, many of them former exiles. Survey research among the German population began almost at once, with the U.S. military government taking the lead.

Ten years of detailed polling clearly showed how the experiences of the postwar years produced a shift in political attitudes.[6] This research revealed that while relatively few Germans still supported the Nazi leaders in the aftermath of defeat, attitudes congruent with the former regime were still widespread.[7] These included disapproval of political contention, with many Germans regarding social cohesion as more important than individual liberty and identifying the prewar Nazi period (1933–1939) as one of the best periods in German history.

With perhaps surprising rapidity, however, political attitudes in West Germany changed definitively toward congruence with a democratic political system. Substantial majorities came to support the democratic political system, found satisfaction with regime performance, and showed a rising sense of personal political efficacy. These changes were grounded initially in the economic success of the Federal Republic's first decade; however, they survived and were strengthened despite Germany's first postwar recession in the 1960s, a confrontation with the wartime generation's Nazi involvement and the crimes of that regime, and renewed radical attacks on the democratic system in the 1970s. By 1980, a democratic political culture clearly had taken root in West Germany. This culture survived the crisis of reunification in 1989–1990 and has been transplanted successfully into the former East Germany.[8]

This is not to say that there are not fluctuating levels of dissatisfaction with the political system. Such dissatisfaction has produced a slogan and a mindset—in German, *Politikverdrossenheit,* or being fed up with politics. This became the "word of the year" for 1992 after then federal president Richard von Weizsäcker used it to deplore poor governance and the resulting disenchantment. Yet, despite "the usual" recurrent scandals, including a major financial scandal involving the Christian Democratic Union (CDU) in 1991, the level of public concern has not risen to levels significant for broader attitudes.[9]

Attitudes in the Former GDR

While a democratic political culture took root in West Germany in the postwar years, the German Democratic Republic that emerged in the Soviet occupation zone witnessed a very different development. There an authoritarian regime sought to mold the consciousness of the population, especially its younger members, into a political outlook that owed as much to a Soviet model as to German traditions.[10] East German leaders, as a self-selected revolutionary elite, sought to impose their version of a dominant political culture. Among the chief elements of this culture were the legitimacy of a Leninist party-state leadership, subordination of the individual to collective goals, the desirability and superiority of a planned economy, and increasingly, a focus on the GDR as the national home of its people.[11]

This official and pervasive culture came to be opposed by a political culture that found its home in the alternative movements of the 1980s. The gradual erosion of support for the official view is difficult to document directly, given the obstacles surrounding survey research in the GDR. There is, of course, the indirect evidence of mass behavior: the growing pressure for freedom of travel, the rising number of applications to emigrate to the Federal Republic, and the growth of the aforementioned alternative culture. It seems clear that the regime found it difficult to propagate its values within newer generations, particularly as its own policy failures with regard to economic welfare and the national question of German identity undermined its legitimacy.[12]

One of the few pieces of direct evidence of changing attitudes may be found in research into the opinions of young East Germans.[13] This research shows that during the final decade of East Germany's existence there was a marked decline in acceptance of the official ideology, particularly concerning acceptance of the validity of Marxist-Leninist prescriptions, along with a broader shift to personal and material goals.[14] Such changes were not uniform across all groups of young East Germans. For example, strong identification with the principles of Marxism-Leninism in the years 1975–1989 dropped scarcely at all—from 61 percent to 57 percent—among post-secondary students; among apprentices, however, the drop was from 46 percent to 9 percent.[15]

Since Reunification

The collapse of the East German regime in 1989 and the reunification of Germany in 1990 raised anew the issues of political culture and system congruence. Would the former East Germans adopt Western values regarding democratic politics in general and the specific institutions of the German state in particular? The initial euphoria of 1989–1990 suggested, as former chancellor Willy Brandt memorably said, "That which belongs together will now grow together."[16] But would the very different experiences of the East German population, especially since the building of the Berlin Wall in 1961, have resulted in a very different sort of political socialization? The older generation in the "new federal states" would be asked for the second time in a half century to display new political attitudes in support a different political system. Younger eastern Germans would, like the post-1945 generation, be asked to subscribe to a political culture very different from that officially held by their elders.

The East German population was asked to adapt the most in part because the political stabilization of the Federal Republic in western Germany had developed along with economic prosperity. The solidity of this system was a major factor in justifying the extension of its institutions, and it was hoped, its values into the former GDR. After all, it was from the GDR that millions had fled, it was to the West that so many had looked for cultural and lifestyle values, and finally, it was the GDR whose political system had crumbled, not that of the Federal Republic. For these reasons West Germans were not asked to rethink their values; whatever deficiencies the FRG may have had, it was East Germans who faced a reevaluation of their political attitudes.[17]

Pollsters, journalists, scholars, artists, and politicians have been busily taking the eastern Germans' political temperature with the varied tools of their trades in the years since reunification. The result has been a flood of data regarding attitudes and opinions. Moreover, the political behavior of Germans in the eastern states may shed light on their political attitudes. What do these various sources reveal? In the perspective of more than a decade and a half since reunification, three main conclusions stand out:

- East Germans have accepted West German political structures and practices;

- East German attitudes toward politics are highly contingent on regime performance, especially in economic policy; and

- East Germans increasingly feel more like German citizens, albeit like "second class" Germans, and less like East Germans.[18]

For example, a 2004 poll showed that more than 80 percent of respondents thought in looking back that German reunification had been a good thing, with slightly more West Germans than East Germans answering in the negative.[19] In a 2000 poll, 71 percent of East Germans identified themselves as "Germans" rather than as "East Germans."[20] Seven years later, similar polls showed that the proportion of easten Germans judging reunification to have been a good thing had risen to roughly 80 percent. The slightly lower percentage of western Germans of this opinion may result from another finding: given the large monetary transfers from West to East, more than half of western German respondents thought that eastern Germans had been the principal beneficiaries of unification. Only 19 percent of Germans in the eastern part of the country felt the same.[21]

Former East Germans consistently show lower, albeit still positive, levels of trust in political institutions than do former West Germans; further examination relates this discrepancy to economic complaints, particularly feelings of second-class status. A deeper investigation reveals that while roughly 80 percent of East Germans agree when asked if East Germans will be treated as second-class citizens for some time to come, only half of all East Germans felt themselves to be such. When specific East German respondents were asked whether they personally feel slighted, only a quarter agreed.[22] In a similar vein, when asked whether they had been satisfied with what had been officially designated as "the real existing socialism" of the GDR, only a third of respondents agreed.

Moreover, these supportive attitudes are as present, if not more so, among the young than they are among the old. Thus, despite the strong link between low support and economic dissatisfaction, youth attitude studies show that there is indeed broad, if qualified, support for democratic politics. When asked specifically about a range of qualities linked to democratic behavior, such as whether an individual has the right to express views that run counter to those of a majority or whether there could be a viable democracy without opposition, youth respondents in the early 1990s answered with high levels of agreement in both the former East and West Germanys.[23] Trends such as these have held steady throughout the past decade, indicating that, at the very least, Germans in the former GDR have reached a level of democratic acceptance equal to that of West Germans after a similar time period following the war. That this should be so despite greater economic woes is indeed a hopeful sign. A recent follow-up study to earlier surveys shows that while an overwhelming majority of East German youth saw no future in the former GDR, equally few wish a return to it;[24] their critical views of a united Germany are performance-based critiques, particularly with regard to unemployment.[25]

Robert Rohrschneider has described East Germans as "grudging democrats," wanting political democracy but with greater social acceptance and economic improvement than they have received thus far.[26] Voting patterns in eastern Germany tend to support concerns regarding fragile commitment to democratic politics. Party loyalties, except those for the Party of Democratic Socialism ([PDS], now the Left Party), tend to be shallow and voting behavior volatile. As shall be shown to a greater degree in chapter 6, this has led to a dual party system in unified Germany, with eastern Germany maintaining a three-party system dominated by the CDU, SPD (Social Democrats), and Left Party. The Left Party is strong in all five states of the former GDR and in East Berlin; it has, for example, participated in or tolerated governments in three instances. Should this be seen as a weakness of democratic support? Or would it be more meaningful to point to the failure of the Left Party to win any eastern German election? More generally, how much regime-attitude congruence is necessary for long-range political stability? Is incongruence in eastern Germany greater than in some other democracies? Would a "solid East" of Left Party support be more of a problem for regime stability than a Democratic "solid South" was for many decades in the United States?[27]

Contemporary Attitudes and Political Behavior

At present, differences between East and West Germans with regard to political culture are not so great as to threaten the stability of the democratic political system. Although West German attitudes were shaped by the early decades of the Federal Republic, these attitudes, like those of East Germans, have also been influenced by events, sometimes in ways that resonate in contemporary Germany. For example, in what has been called Germany's "Red Decade,"[28] the political and social systems of the Federal Republic were challenged by a generational cohort of disgruntled rebels. (The movement aspect of this alternative scene is discussed further in chapter 8.) From the formation of the CDU/SPD grand coalition cabinet in 1966 and the 1967 death of a Berlin student demonstrator, through a decade of sometimes violent opposition to political and personal orthodoxy, young Germans withdrew their affective support from the Bonn Republic. In this they shared actions and attitudes with young people in such countries as France, Italy, and the United States.

The shifting attitudes of this "1968 generation" seemed to mark a withdrawal of support for the democratic institutions of postwar Germany. Yet paradoxically, the rejection of authoritarian and traditional structures in politics, in the universities, in gender and generational relations, and—especially important for Germany—in a critical approach to dealing with the older generation's Nazi past, strengthened democratic forces in Germany, led to important reforms, and absorbed its advocates into the existing German institutions. Like their counterparts abroad, they did not succeed in overturning the system, and for the most part they made their peace with it.

Somewhat ironically, the call to revolutionize Germany by a "long march through the institutions" resulted in the system absorbing the energies and careers of its opponents; Joschka Fischer's path from street fighter to foreign minister is paradigmatic here. One factor in this shift was the chancellorship of Willy Brandt, with his call to "dare more democracy," another was a revulsion against the increasingly ruthless and counterproductive violence of the movement's radical offshoots, especially the Red Army Faction (RAF). This spasm of violence culminated in the "German autumn" of 1977; the example of a functioning democracy defending itself against violent attack provided a model that was especially relevant three decades later in dealing with twenty-first century terrorism (see chapter 5).

Another legacy of the Bonn Republic, one congruent with attitudes prevalent in the former GDR, was a commitment to a social economy and society. Commitment to a social support network has strong historical roots in Germany (as discussed further in chapter 9) and is often cited as a feature of East German life worth retaining. The commitment of the CDU/CSU to religiously colored social doctrines has meant that attempts to reform the economy and the system of social benefits in the direction of what its critics call global neoliberalism, which is often associated with the United States, has run into strong opposition. Such attitudes are important in explaining the spread of the Left Party as a national political force.[29]

A more general examination of German political culture shows that German attitudes and their relation to stable democratic institutions are more like similar issues in other democracies than special in some German way. For example, consider the well-documented fact that voter turnout has been consistently lower in eastern than in western Germany.[30] This may be due to the fact that eastern voters, for reasons not immediately apparent, regard the electoral act as promising less in serving their interests. Or one may look to the GDR experience or postunification Germany for explanations; one also could consider why turnout varies among regions and groups in many democratic polities.

Looking at recent German political culture, it is noteworthy that the pattern of ranking democratic practices lower than other achievements, first noted in the classic study *The Civic Culture*,[31] may still be present today, as suggested by the data in Table 4.1.[32]

Table 4.1	Question asked: "Of which achievement of our country are you as a German especially proud?" (responses in percentages)		
Trait	Western Germans	Eastern Germans	All Germany
Social peace	47	35	45
Economy	33	33	33
Democracy	32	15	19
Culture	17	25	19
History	10	13	10
None of these	8	15	10

Source: Bundesverband deutscher Banken, "Bilanz für die Zukunft: 50 Jahre Bundesrepublik Deutschland," *Demo/Skopie* no. 5 (July 1999), 15.

Similar results were obtained shortly after reunification, whereby Germans in both East and West were proud of "being German," but a far larger percentage of West Germans also expressed pride in their political system.[33] These findings were part of a study commissioned on the fiftieth anniversary of the Federal Republic. The survey also revealed that a majority of Germans were cool toward but supportive of their polity, affirmed democracy as stable but needing reform, and viewed social peace as a high value. A large majority foresaw Germany as part of federal Europe within fifty years.

Attitudes toward Germany's Basic Law are a good focal point for judging support. For Germany as a whole, more than 80 percent thought that the Basic Law had "proven itself." Broken down between West and East, the numbers are 85 percent and 65 percent, respectively. Among eastern Germans, positive feelings toward the Basic Law seemed linked strongly to age, as indicated in Figure 4.1.

A question concerning the general functioning of the political system revealed that more than 80 percent of both western and eastern Germans thought it was performing well.[34] Yet a nagging sense of economic disadvantage between the two parts of unified Germany remains a potentially troubling factor. A more recent study found that 76 percent of eastern Germans do not think that eastern living standards will soon approximate those in the west. This may have affected eastern Germans' sense of diffuse loyalty to the national polity, as Table 4.2 indicates.[35]

Is German democracy based on a firm stratum of support in principle, or are Germans, in the words of an old cliché dating from the Weimar era, only "fair weather democrats"? The rapid and drastic political changes in the Europe of the twentieth and early twenty-first centuries should caution us

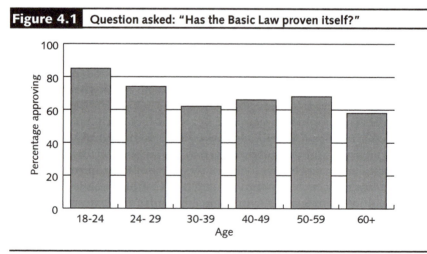

Figure 4.1 Question asked: "Has the Basic Law proven itself?"

Source: Bettina Westle, *Kollektive Identität im vereinten Deutschland* (Opladen: Lesk+ Budrich, 1999), 4–5.

Table 4.2	Question asked: "Do you feel yourself to be a German or a West or East German?" (responses in percentages)					
		1993	1999	2000	2001	2002
West Germans	"German"	80	81	87	81	82
	"West German"	15	15	10	15	13
East Germans	"German"	48	68	71	60	55
	"East German"	51	30	27	37	41

Source: Bundesverband deutscher Banken, inter/esse no. 11 (2002), cited from www.bankenverband.de.

against overestimating the importance of long-range cultural factors. The policy-based support of early postwar West Germans and postunification East Germans suggests that the German political leadership has considerable latitude in governing. For East Germans, as for other post-Communist East Europeans, social and economic events since 1990 are of paramount importance. This gives any German government considerable leeway to take effective action to govern in a way that strengthens democracy.

Although we concentrate in this chapter on the attitudes and experiences of the overwhelming majority of the population that is ethnically German, it is important to bear in mind that there are other groups whose attitudes toward the German polity are shaped by quite different experiences. An important example is the large German-Turkish minority, whose members' attitudes were not shaped by generations of life in Germany; rather, their attitudes continue to be influenced both by their German surroundings and by their continuing Turkish connections. (Consider the analogous situation of many Mexican or Dominican immigrants in the United States.) In an important recent study, Ayhan Kaya showed how the German-Turkish group has become "transmigrants who can practically and symbolically travel back and forth between their countries of destination and origin."[36] This in-between condition is shaped, as Kaya shows, by such factors as readily available travel to Turkey (more than half of German-Turks do so at least once a year) and widely available Turkish and German-Turkish media. Just as Germans in the former GDR can decide whether to identify themselves as "Germans" or "East Germans," German-Turks can see themselves as Turkish, German, both, or neither, as the data summarized in Table 4.3 shows.

Table 4.3	Question asked: "Do you feel affiliated to ..." (responses in percentages)	
	Birthplace in Turkey	Birthplace in Germany
Turkey	55	25
Germany	17.7	35.2
Equal affiliation > both	24.2	37
Equal detachment < both	2.5	2.7

Source: Adapted from Ayhan Kaya, "German-Turkish Transnational Space: A Separate Space of Their Own," German Studies Review, vol. 30, no. 3 (October 2007): 490.

Germany's location in the heart of Europe has long made it the destination of choice for immigrants. Recent influxes of workers from the Middle East and Asia have met with mixed receptions, however, in part because of differences in religion, language, and culture from mainstream German life. Efforts are being made to bridge these gaps: 71-year-old Asiye Cebeci, a native of Turkey, lives in a multicultural eldercare facility in Duisburg, Germany, in which residents take part in a variety of shared activities to expand cultural understanding.

Attitudes toward the Common German Past

Given that Germany's history has been a troubled one, with fluid changes of borders, dramatic cleavages of religion, and abrupt and severe changes of regime, Germans in both parts of the country have had difficulty coming to terms with their individual and collective pasts.[37] German history has been accompanied by a steady drumbeat of puzzled comments on the elusiveness of "Germany" and what it means to be "German." A sixteenth-century humanist complained that "no country ... embraces so many lands under one name"; Goethe and Schiller famously asked, "Germany? But where is it? I don't know how to find such a country." [38]

Germany's past continues to provide fuel for political controversy. The difficulty of coming to terms with the past—in German known as *Vergangenheitsbewältigung*—is compounded by the double task of coping with both Nazi and Communist legacies. No wonder then that many Germans wish to be done with the constant preoccupation with a problematical past. In recent years, this sentiment has ranged from Martin Walser's call for a historical appreciation freed from focus on Auschwitz to former chancellor Kohl's remarks about the "grace of recent birth." [39]

In West Germany dealing with the Nazi past has been a difficult process, one that has undergone several phases and is not yet complete.[40] In the 1950s, the Federal Republic, with denazification behind it and an anti-Communist consensus central to its legitimacy, forbore to search out Nazi sympathizers or officials, especially in the civil service.[41] It was only in the 1960s, particularly through the German trial of perpetrators from Auschwitz beginning in 1963, that a more active reckoning with the past took place. The meaning of the Nazi period in German history is bound to remain, like many historical issues, a contentious one.

The situation for eastern Germans has been quite different. They lived under a regime that explicitly claimed to represent a qualitative break with not only the Nazi era but with the German past in general. These antifascist credentials attracted many adherents to the GDR's side in the early years, and they remained a major source of legitimacy to the very end and into the present. An individual seemingly could come to terms with the Nazi heritage simply by supporting the authorities. For the GDR population at large, the notion that the Nazi horrors were the fault of German capitalists and landowners, and not of the working masses, facilitated a convenient evasion of personal responsibility, since most former property holders had left for the West and the GDR was officially antifascist. Only a few writers and analysts, most notably Christa Wolf in her novel *Model Childhood*, confronted the Nazi pasts of many East Germans.[42]

Dealing with the GDR's past involves yet other complexities. For West Germans, including many of those in the west who had fled the GDR, the failures of the GDR seem self-evident, and the need to master its past superfluous. Just as official antifascism "excused" East Germans, the West's Cold War victory allowed West Germans to brush aside any question of responsibility for developments in the former Soviet Zone or any need to make adjustments in German life to accommodate East German sensibilities.

East Germans obviously face a more complex task. Even those East Germans who opposed many or all aspects of Communist rule may feel that their potential contributions to German life are being ignored by assumptions that the victors have little to learn from the vanquished.[43] Those who invested careers, loyalties, or simply time in maintaining the GDR, along with those who played important roles there, such as party, state, and economic officials, and of course agents of the *Stasi,* clearly had an interest in how their pasts were processed into German life.

The focus of these complaints has come in the call for "respecting the biographies" of East Germans. The Left Party, as the party best in articulating East German resentments, has made this a major demand. But what does this mean in practice? One legitimately may ask that scholarly achievements or even such daily life minutiae as the East German form of the walk-stop traffic sign, the *Ampelmännchen,* be seriously considered for incorporation into German life. It is another matter to ask for "respect" for those wielding power against their Western competitors and, all too often, their own people. Even seemingly neutral achievement, such as sports performances, may be thus tainted.[44]

There have been two main approaches to dealing with the GDR's past: one has been the method of factual inquiry, and the other that of assessing criminal liability. The former was formalized in a special parliamentary commission to explore the GDR heritage;[45] it produced valuable and interesting historical material but not a definitive and consensual judgment on the GDR legacy. The other approach led to a series of trials of former GDR state and party officials.

These trials also have failed to produce such a judgment. Some, especially those of certain senior officials, ended without judgment due to the death or infirmity of the defendants. Others, including those that have sent several former SED leaders to prison, were for the crime of manslaughter arising from use of deadly force against those attempting flight across the Berlin Wall. Aside from the complex legal issues raised by these trials, they have had the unfortunate result of seeming to reduce an oppressive political regime to a handful of criminal actions.[46]

More than a decade after reunification, widespread political fatigue with these issues may be noted. A 1999 survey found that substantial majorities in both parts of Germany favor dropping the subject; indeed, more favored this with respect to the GDR than with respect to the Nazi regime. And a similar shift in perspective regarding the Nazi period may be observed. A well-publicized debate between the novelist Martin Walser and the late head of the Jewish organization in Germany, Ignatz Bubis, as to whether or not Auschwitz should be regarded as the central point of German history was an example of this. Speaking to mark the fiftieth anniversary of the Basic Law, the Social Democratic former Lord Mayor of Hamburg, Klaus von Dohananyi, declared that "Germany is more than Holocaust and [postwar] reconstruction."[47]

In the contemporary "Berlin Republic" the issues that dominated the divided Germany after 1945 have faded away. However, Germany's relation to the external framework of the European Union on the one hand and the domestic relations within an increasingly multicultural country on the other have gained in importance, as they have in most of Germany's European Union (EU) partners. Nowhere is this "normal" sense of history more apparent than in the upsurge of attention paid to German suffering during and after World War II.[48]

An important turning point in how Germans view this part of their past was provided by the then federal president Richard von Weizsäcker in his 1985 speech commemorating the fortieth anniversary of the war's end in Europe. In calling May 8 a day of liberation from tyranny also for Germans, he declared it a "day of remembering" the suffering inflicted on people"; the context makes clear that he included Germans. He also called it "for us Germans, not a day of celebration."[49] It is important to note, however, that von Weizsäcker's bold declaration was met by substantial and multipartisan criticism from those who preferred to emphasize Germany's defeat and saw little positive in the May 8 anniversary.[50]

In recent years, Germans have openly and frequently discussed such hitherto taboo subjects as their own suffering during and after World War II. Two widely recalled episodes of wartime suffering are the expulsion of ethnic Germans from Eastern Europe and Russian territories and the bombing of German cities by American and British aircraft. Wolfgang Thierse, the eastern German Social Democrat who served as presiding officer of the *Bundestag* from 1998 to 2005, asked, "What does it mean that we talk about our own victims more than before? The mourning for victims in the destroyed and bombed cities is not only legitimate but part of a complete memory."[51]

The question of expellees was widely considered in West Germany during the 1950s, when the Adenauer government sought the expellees' political support and refused to accept loss of eastern territory beyond the Oder and Neisse rivers. In later years the issue receded, especially under the impact of Brandt's *Ostpolitik* of improving relations with Poland, Czechoslovakia, and the USSR. Nonetheless, the issue can suddenly resurface to political significance.[52]

A more recent historical issue impacting politics is that of the bombing of German cities. The new attention to this part of the German wartime experience was triggered by several important books, chief among them those of W. G. Sebald and Jörg Friedrich.[53] Sebald argued that, at least in published literature, there has been an inability to confront *German* suffering that an honest accounting of the past requires. He wrote that "when we turn to take a retrospective view, particularly of the years 1930 to 1950, we are always looking and looking away at the same time." Honesty, Sebald concludes, requires Germans to accept that they were victims of a brutal campaign without compelling strategic justification, but that they were not innocent victims. He writes:

> And when we think of the nights when fires raged in Cologne and Hamburg and Dresden, we ought to remember that as early as August 1942, when the vanguard of the Sixth Army had reached the Volga ... [and] the city of Stalingrad, then swollen (like Dresden later) by an influx of refugees, was under assault from twelve hundred bombers, ... that during this raid alone ... forty thousand people lost their lives.[54]

The essayist and novelist Peter Schneider has provided a similarly compelling account of Germans' experiences, including his own memories of fleeing from air bombardment.[55] Responding to the unexpected burst of writing on this subject, he asks, "After all, do we not, the children and grandchildren, still behave at times as though we were traumatized? Do we not walk like sleepwalkers through your rebuilt cities ... do we not now pose before the rest of the world as champions of innocence?" It is very important that Schneider broadens the discussion of German victims by pointing to other examples of "repressed" politically unpopular memories, such as Stalin's deportation of the Volga Germans, the jailing of political opponents of the April 1946 forced merger of the Social Democratic and Communist parties in the Soviet Zone, or the mass rapes of German women by Soviet soldiers.[56] "Like Sebald," he declared, "I belong to the generation that declared war on the Nazi generation ... in 1968. [We] simply banished from ... [our] version of history all stories about Germans that did not fit in with the picture of the 'generation of perpetrators'."

These changes in German attitudes are highlighted in the recent works of the Nobel Prize–winning novelist Günter Grass.[57] Grass's novel *Crabwalk* is not only about a disaster in which thousands of Germans died at Soviet hands, the author also extends his historical memory to encompass Stalinist persecution, Nazi anti-Semitism, current right-radical youth, West German leftist orthodoxy, and the effect of past crimes on the present. The main character, standing between generations, is perhaps a "typical" postwar German born of the disasters of the war, in a lifeboat fleeing the sinking *Gustloff*.[58] Grass begins his novel with the question, "Why only now?" This question took on special poignancy when it was revealed that Grass himself had hidden important elements of his own war-time experiences.[59]

What has changed in Germans' perceptions of their past? Perhaps an answer may be found in the current generation's changed views of German patriotism. Gerhard Schröder, chancellor from 1998 to 2005, may stand as an exemplar of this cohort of Germans born at the end or just after World War II. This generation of German political leaders sees patriotism as a positive and self-evident value in marked contrast to earlier leaders, for whom speaking positively of "the nation," and especially of Germany, was difficult.[60] Former federal president Johannes Rau, a senior Social Democratic leader, declared in an interview that while he is "glad to be a German," he cannot apply the notion of "pride" to his homeland (*Heimat*);[61] citing another former federal president, Gustav Heinemann, Rau said he loved his wife but not the state. Rau is not alone in these thoughts; many of his fellow Germans have found national rituals and symbols difficult.

It is instructive to contrast Rau's attitudes with Schröder's. For example, in an interview in 2001, Schröder declared himself to be "a German patriot, who is proud of his country."[62] In a campaign speech in August 2002, Schröder declared that his government had set off "on our German way." This was widely taken as a hint of Germany's confidence in following its own foreign policy interests, especially with regard to Iraq.[63] For the most part, Schröder was careful to modulate his expressions of patriotism, declaring, for example, that "patriotism is that which I do daily, insofar as I work for my country, for Germany";[64] similarly, he explained that patriotic sentiments are best when they arise spontaneously in the people and not when they are organized for partisan purposes.[65] Indeed, Germans and the world took note that during the soccer World Cup 2006, held in Germany, Germans displayed their flag or its national colors (black-red-gold) on cars, signs, and their faces with apparent joy and little uneasiness.

Such attitudes are not likely to change with the transition to the chancellorship of Angela Merkel, although having grown up in the GDR, she may have more muted feelings about "Germany." In an interview around the time of the 2005 election she seemed to reduce patriotism to community feeling and an instrument for improving economic performance.[66]

Although Germans may be turning to a more self-assertive identity, as recent debates over use of military force (discussed in chapter 10) show, Germany will not be able in the foreseeable future to avoid the consequences of its violent past in the twentieth century any more than other nations. The impact of the past on Germans' sense of nation and self-will remain powerful and problematic. As James Young trenchantly asked, "How does a nation of former perpetrators mourn its victims? How does a divided nation re-unite itself on the bedrock memory of its crimes? Nations do not build themselves on the memory of their crimes but on the memory of their triumphs and martyrdom."[67] Brian Ladd has pointed to the crux of the difficulty with respect to the old and new seat of government, Berlin: "the sandy soil of the German capital conceals traces of a history so fiercely contested that no site, however vacant, is safe from controversy."[68]

Literary and Popular Culture

Alongside the traditional methods and findings of survey research cited above, literature and popular culture provide important insights into political culture as well. From medieval folk tales through Martin Luther's translation of the Latin bible into German in the sixteenth century to the successive regime changes of the twentieth century, literary and other cultural media have expressed, shaped, and often manipulated political consciousness and identity. Such cultural instruments of identity were all the more important in the historical absence of a German national state with its attendant symbols.

Modern illustrations include Bertolt Brecht's didactic use of such dramas as *Mother Courage* and *The Three Penny Opera* to raise critical social awareness among members of his audience. Others are the emphasis of expressionist art, literature, and cinema during the late Imperial and early Weimar eras on the "disjointedness" of the human condition in the face of relentless technological change and bureaucratization and the explicit subjugation of cinema, literature, the news media, and architecture to the totalitarian political objectives of national socialism.

Political elites in the German Democratic Republic utilized similar instruments of political consciousness-raising and control to promote conformist Communist values and regime loyalty from the late 1940s onward, although a number of talented writers and artistic performers were able to thwart official censorship by expressing alternative sociopolitical perspectives. Leading examples are novelist Christa Wolf and screenwriter and author Ulrich Plenzdorf. Both were convinced socialists who gained national and international recognition for their portrayal of East Germans who, in various ways, defied official SED ideology. One of Wolf's best-known novels, *The Quest for Christa T* (*Nachdenken über Christa T*), published in 1968, was initially banned in the GDR because of its emphasis on individual "subjective authenticity" as opposed to party-approved norms of citizen engagement on behalf of communism. Even more subtly subversive was Plenzdorf's 1972 play *The New Sorrows of Young W* (*Die neuen Leiden des jungen W*) about a young apprentice in Berlin smitten by Goethe's classic *Sorrows of Young Werther* and J.D. Salinger's *Catcher in the Rye*. The protagonist dies in an explosion of a machine he has constructed in what could be interpreted as either an industrial accident or (much more convincingly) an act of suicide, an act considered taboo in the eyes of the ruling SED.

A kindred dissenting spirit was songwriter and folk singer Wolf Biermann, who was also critical of orthodox ideology. GDR officials stripped Biermann of his East German citizenship in 1976 while he was on tour in the Federal Republic, an action that provoked vehement protests by Wolf and other German intellectuals. Biermann continued to criticize Stalinist features of the GDR while in West German exile. Since reunification Wolf has remained a prolific writer, while Plenzdorf has become a visiting lecturer at the German Literary Institute in Leipzig.

Postwar Germany boasts two winners of the Nobel Prize for literature. The first, an astute critic of West German society, was Heinrich Böll, most notably in his novel *Billiards at 9:30*. The second is one of western Germany's best-known and controversial authors and social critics, Günter Grass, an especially incisive practitioner of political discourse through historically informed fiction.[69] His *The Tin Drum,* published in 1959, recounts German-Polish relations in pre–World War I East Prussia with great depth and empathy. The narrative begins in 1899 near the Baltic port city of Danzig, which then belonged to Imperial Germany, with the marriage of the maternal German grandmother and Polish grandfather of the novel's chief protagonist, a midget named Oskar. Early passages depict a harmonious relationship between Germans and Poles on the level of ordinary citizens. As Grass wrote of the men who worked the river barges carrying timber from Czarist Russia into East Prussia: "There were neither political disputes, nor knife battles between Germans and Poles, nor any mutiny springing from social grievances."[70] The two nationalities were also bound by a common fear of authority figures: Poles of arrogant Germans, Germans of autocratic Russians. For his thoughtful and revealing insights into social relations of the time, the Polish government has named Grass an honorary citizen of today's Gdansk.

Cinema

From the perspective of most scholars of literary and other expressions of high culture, popular culture occupies a lesser level of intellectual significance. Indeed, popular culture eludes definition: "It is only recently that attention has been turned towards establishing the value of studying popular culture from the condemnation of it." [71] Yet popular culture, which encompasses experiences ranging from "radio, music videos, blockbuster films…, [to] the raciness of Rock 'n Roll in the context of 1950s morals," [72] touches millions of citizens in their everyday lives and hence is eminently worthy of serious attention. German cinema testifies to this importance.

German cinema first gained international recognition during the Weimar Republic with the release of classical productions such as *The Cabinet of Dr. Caligari* (1920), *Nosferatu, the Vampryi* (1922), *Metropolis* (1927), *The Blue Angel,* starring Marlene Dietrich (1930), and *Eine Stadt sucht einen Mörder (Murderers Among Us* (1931).[73] The rise of national socialism brought an abrupt end to German renown and prompted the exile of many of cinema's most talented writers, directors, and actors, most of whom emigrated to the United States.[74]

The slow recovery of an indigenous film industry after 1945 initially proved unremarkable. One exception was the release of a powerful antiwar movie, *Die Brücke (The Bridge)*, in 1961. The story is of a heroic but ultimately fruitless attempt by a group of high school students to defend a bridge leading into their home town against the advance of U.S. troops in the closing days of World War II. After this, West German cinema grew in breadth of technique and scope of themes in the late 1960s and early 1970s with the advent of a number of director-driven productions comparable to those of Ingmar Bergman in Sweden and Peter Bogdanovich in the United States. Almost without exception these German films were more politically polemical than their Swedish and American counterparts. Among the notable architects of a "New German Cinema" were Wim Wenders, Rainer Werner Fassbinder, Werner Herzog, and Volker Schlöndorff, all of whom produced films that "challenged tradition and were often critical of bourgeois society and irreverent in their treatment of German history." [75]

Critical films were also important in shaping GDR popular and political culture. East German filmmakers struggled within political controls to deal with politically and socially sensitive topics. Notable were films of Konrad Wolf, some based on his experiences as a Soviet soldier entering Germany in 1945, including *I was 19*, and tributes to personal self realization such as *Solo Sunny.* East German films that dealt with socially and politically sensitive subjects included *Divided Sky* (flight to the West), *Her Third One* (feminist consciousness), *Bear Ye One Another's Burden* (the growing importance of religious values), and *The Legend of Paul and Paula* (the rise of a youth culture). Some of the most daring were either banned by the regime, notable among them *Trace of Stones* and *Sun Seekers,* or released only after long delays.

Partly because of its overtly ideological content, the New German Cinema in West Germany proved commercially unsuccessful. Movie attendance declined, and American films dominated theatrical releases. It was only after reunification that German cinema achieved a new voice and a rebirth of international recognition. Several recent German films stand out: *Run Lola Run (Lola rennt,* 1998), *Downfall (Untergang,* 2004), and *Lives of Others (Das Leben der Anderen,* 2006). The first of these depicts a frantic run through unified Berlin—presented in three scenarios with different outcomes—by a free-spirited young lady, Lola, as she frantically seeks to find money to save her boyfriend's life. As Barbara Kosta, an astute student of German popular culture, observes:

> *Run Lola Run ...* [says] quite a bit about the new Germany, about its cinematic aspirations and the turn it has taken, and about the image that the new nation wants to project for its own consumption as well as for its international audiences. In addition, the fast-paced editing that defies memory and that locks the spectator into the present ... reflects on contemporary Germany's relationship to history.[76]

Downfall and *Lives of Others* are anything but ahistorical. *Downfall* is a dramatic reenactment of the final days of Hitler and his entourage in the führer's bunker as the Red Army relentlessly approaches the heart of Berlin. It is a poignant reminder of the fate suffered by all Germans—high and low—during the final throes of World War II. *Lives of Others,* a 2007 Academy Award winner for best foreign language film, depicts a complex tale of espionage by a sympathetic *Stasi* officer and the political "betrayal" and love life of an East German playwright in the twilight years of the GDR. The story is compelling, culminating in street scenes from unified Berlin and the playwright's moving accolade to his erstwhile *Stasi* agent.

On a lighter political note, two notable movies capture scenes and lives of ordinary citizens on the eastern side of the Berlin Wall. *Sonnenallee (Sun Boulevard),* released in 1999, is set on the short East Berlin end of a major thoroughfare in the center of the city. Wrongly interpreted by some movie critics as a nostalgic rendition of life in the former GDR, the film is a subtle comedy that depicts the everyday lives and foibles of a group of teenage friends. It is primarily a love story that pokes fun at West and East Germans alike, including pedantic SED officials who censor innocuous musical texts. One of the coauthors of the screenplay, Thomas Brussig, later expanded on the characters and themes of the movie in an eminently readable short novel, *Am kürzeren Ende der Sonnenallee,* published in 2005.[77]

The second film, *Goodbye Lenin* (2003), is a tragicomedy involving efforts by a young East Berliner to protect his ailing mother, an erstwhile supporter of the SED, from learning of German reunification. The mother had lapsed into a lengthy coma after suffering a heart attack just prior to the opening of the Berlin Wall; the doctor warns her children upon the mother's awakening that any shock could cause a second heart attack and possibly her death. The son restores familiar artifacts and visual scenes from GDR times in their apartment with the reluctant support from his sister and the more enthusiastic assistance of a video-savvy friend. His intent is to shield his mother from the knowledge that the SED regime no longer exists. In the process he creates a GDR that might have been—one more humane and democratic than the reality that previously governed their lives.

Important artistic reflections of contemporary Germany's ethnic diversity are the prize-winning films of Fatih Akin, a Hamburg-born son of Turkish parents. In such films as *Im Juli* (*In July*) and *Head On* (*Gegen die Wand*), he chronicles the lives of Germans and Turks in both countries. Akin also is known for his political protest actions against U.S. foreign policy under the George W. Bush administration.

Music

Alongside cinema, rock music also delivers a powerful popular message. The contributors to Sabrina Ramet's edited volume, *Rocking the State,* recount how rock musicians fermented critical consciousness about the shortcomings of communism throughout the former Soviet bloc and thus helped pave the way for the democratic transitions of the 1990s, especially in the former GDR.[78] Young citizens there became increasingly enamored of the music of Western rock bands and singers, much of it anti-authoritarian. Among the most popular were Uriah Heep; Jethro Tull; Chicago; Blood, Sweat, and Tears; Elton John, and the Beatles.

East German authorities were initially critical of such manifestations of Western "decadence" and "subjective individualism" but pragmatically relented in response to grassroots ferment among young people. By the 1980s these officials actually encouraged the formation of rock bands in the GDR whose ostensible purpose was to celebrate socialist achievements. Rock musicians frequently ignored this dictum, inviting censorship and performance *Verbot*. In Ramet's words, rock musicians served in the GDR and throughout Central and Eastern Europe "a bit like prophets.... The archetypal rock star became, symbolically, the muse of revolution." [79] Unification brought the end of most of the East German bands with the diffusion of an all-German entertainment culture, but a few artists and groups have survived and even prospered.[80]

Other Forms of Popular Culture

Popular culture embraces other forms of communication as well. One is a long-standing tradition of political humor, expressed in venues ranging from satirical cabarets in Berlin, Düsseldorf, and other cities to talented comedians who attract extensive appreciative audiences thanks to radio and television. Examples of the latter include Karl Valentin (1882–1946), a creative artist who influenced the dramatic theories and techniques of a young Bertolt Brecht; Loriot, whose clips on YouTube reveal a style of social commentary reminiscent of Monty Python; and Harald Schmidt, a political humorist who hosted a popular late-night talk show modeled after Jay Leno's *The Tonight Show* that was often critical of incumbent politicians. In 1993 Schmidt was named Germany's "Entertainer of the Year" and awarded other prestigious prizes.

Comic books are yet another form of popular culture that command widespread interest. Many are designed strictly for leisure reading, including German versions of such American favorites as *Superman* and the ever-popular *Asterix and Obelix* children's series translated from Latin. A far more serious use of comic books as an educational tool is a new publication about the Holocaust entitled *The Search,* which was introduced in German classrooms on an experimental basis early in 2008.[81] An English-language precedent is Art Spiegelman's *Maus* (1997), which uses a comic book format to chronicle the lives of a Jewish father and his son who survive the atrocities of the Nazi era.[82] *Maus* has been adopted as a textbook in a number of American university courses that deal with the Holocaust.

Conclusion

Survey research and popular culture intersect to reflect a unified Germany affirming a rediscovered national identity, democratic consciousness, and individual accountability. These are central themes of the chapters that follow.

5

Constitutional Principles and Political Institutions

A tradition of federalism and constructive responses to historical experiences shape Germany's formal institutional structures and decision-making procedures. The nation's first unification in 1871 yielded a federal system dominated by Prussia, the largest and most populous state in the empire and its aristocratic–upper bourgeois–military elite. Power was institutionalized under mixed democratic-traditional elites in a more centralized version of federalism established under the Weimar constitution in 1919. Hitler and the National Socialists abolished federalism after coming to power in 1933 in favor of a unitary system of government. This system was summarily dismantled by the four occupation powers in 1945, and one of the last consensual actions of the Allied Control Council was the dissolution of the state of Prussia in 1947 in accordance with the dictates of political decentralization under terms of the Potsdam agreement.

Contemporary Germany builds on the restoration of federal institutions enacted in the three Western zones of occupation during the early postwar era. Eastern Germany similarly reinstated federalism under its 1949 constitution, only to abandon it in 1952 in favor of an SED-dominated unitary political system. A key constitutional and institutional feature of German unification in 1990 was the recreation of five state (*Länder*) governments in the GDR, which collectively joined the Federal Republic according to provisions laid out in Article 23 of the Basic Law.[1] The resulting system combines principles of "classical" parliamentary democracy with elements of institutional decentralization. Post-unification efforts to devise an entirely new constitution, spearheaded primarily by politicians in eastern Germany and members of the Social Democratic Party, failed in the face of conservative determination to maintain the Basic Law throughout all of Germany with relatively minor constitutional revisions.[2] This decision demonstrated how ingrained and legitimate the Basic Law had become in West Germany. The price paid for this, however, was the missed opportunity of giving East Germans a sense of efficacy and a stake in the new (to them) political institutions after unification.

The "founding fathers" of Germany's Basic Law gathered in Bonn in 1948–1949 to draft a new constitution in response to Allied occupation directives to establish a West German state. They drew from the negative experiences of both the Weimar Republic and the Third Reich to construct a more viable democracy.[3] As previously recounted, a central feature of the Weimar constitution was a strong presidency with authority under Article 48 to enact policies by decree, including the right to appoint governments, in the event of a national emergency or parliamentary stalemate. Their historical knowledge of the fateful consequences of Article 48 inspired the delegates to the Parliamentary Council in Bonn to restrict presidential powers in favor of a "chancellorship democracy." Simultaneously, the blatant disregard of individual rights under the National Socialist regime prompted them to elevate fundamental civil rights to the prominent first section of the Basic Law.

The results of constitutional engineering in the Parliamentary Council resemble fundamental parliamentary norms in the older democracies of the United Kingdom and Scandinavia while incorporating features distinctive to Germany. Basic principles include (1) an evolving system of cooperative federalism; (2) the constitutional affirmation of fundamental democratic principles based on the principle of popular sovereignty; (3) a largely ceremonial head of state in the office of a federal president; (4) the concentration of executive power in the hands of an elected federal chancellor and members of a cabinet who are politically accountable on a day-to-day basis to a majority of deputies in the lower house of parliament; (5) a vertical distribution of executive, legislative, and administrative powers between the national government (the *Bund,* or Federation) and the sixteen *Länder* that comprise the expanded Federal Republic; and (6) an independent judiciary capped by a Federal Constitutional Court with the power of judicial review. Other important institutions include the public administration, the military, and the European Union. Transformed also after reunification in 1990, and of growing importance since 9/11, are German security arrangements.

Cooperative Federalism

The Basic Law affirms the primacy of federal over state law while simultaneously providing the legal basis for a system of exclusive national, concurrent, and state jurisdiction not unfamiliar to citizens of tne United States.[4] Article 73 accords the national government exclusive authority over foreign affairs, citizenship, passports, federal railroads and air transport, and postal service and communications. In addition, the article gives the federal government oversight of the legal status of persons employed by the federation and federal corporate bodies under public law, industrial property rights, the police, the defense of democracy and the constitution, and "protection against efforts in the federal territory that, by the use of force or actions in preparation for the use of force, endanger the foreign interests of the Federal Republic of Germany."

The most important spheres of concurrent legislation catalogued in Article 74 of the Basic Law include civil law, criminal law, and court organization and procedures; the registration of persons; laws governing association and assembly; laws relating to residence, including those of non-nationals, weapons, and explosives; refugee and expellee matters, public welfare; and economic policy in such areas as mining, industry, power supply, crafts, trades, commerce, banking, stock exchanges, and private insurance. Other concurrently governed areas are the production and utilization of nuclear energy for peaceful purposes; labor law; the regulation of educational and training grants and the promotion of scientific research; the transfer of land, natural resources, and means of production to public ownership; and road traffic, motor transport, and highway construction.

Under terms of a constitutional amendment adopted in 1969, the national and state governments share legal responsibilities for the "expansion and construction of universities ... [and] improvement of regional economic structures and agriculture." [5] An accompanying amendment also provides that "the Federation and the *Länder* may ... cooperate in educational planning and in the promotion of institutions and projects of scientific research of supranational importance." [6]

The constitutional principle determining whether the federal government or the *Länder* act in matters of concurrent legislation is essentially one of practicality. Article 72 of the Basic Law stipulates that the federal government shall legislate in matters of concurrent jurisdiction under the following conditions: (1) if legislation by a particular state cannot effectively deal with an issue; (2) if "the regulation of a matter by a [state] law might prejudice the interests of other *Länder* or the people as a whole"; or (3) if "the maintenance of legal or economic unity, especially the maintenance of uniformity of living conditions beyond the territory of any one *Land,* necessitates such regulation." As noted later in this chapter, these legislative rules resemble the quasi-federal system of decision making within the European Union (EU).

The individual states exercise jurisdiction in policy areas not explicitly enumerated in the preceding catalogue of exclusive or concurrent legislation. These include public education, ranging from preschool facilities to universities; local police protection; television and radio; and museums, theaters, libraries, and other cultural facilities. The states delegate responsibility for purely local services, including public facilities, hospital care, and local streets and roads, to the country's 13,230 city and county government units. Constitutionally, the latter are guaranteed "the right to regulate on their own responsibility all the affairs of the local community within the limits set by law."[7]

National-state relations have evolved dynamically during the development of the Federal Republic over the past five decades, with a discernible tendency toward the centralization of executive and legislative power at the expense of the state governments. The increased coordination of economic, social, and educational policies under federal aegis has intensified what Germans call *Politikverflechtung,* which can be loosely translated as the political "webbing" of national and state decision making. The *Länder* have nonetheless reclaimed relevance since unification, in large measure because of political assertiveness on the part of government leaders in the five "new federal states" in the East in response to persisting economic and social differences between the two parts of Germany. As Arthur Gunlicks, a close observer of German federalism, argues,

> The *Länder* are important arenas for domestic politics, and ... some of the most controversial issues in Germany are based on policies pursued by *Land* governments. The conflicts that result are usually partisan in nature, but the federal system gives the parties the opportunity to raise issues, challenge opponents and actually implement policies in ways that hardly exist in unitary states.[8]

State-level governance is also important for administrative and political recruitment purposes. An example of the former is the increasing normality of cooperation among and between states, especially in broadcasting, education, and the implementation of new citizenship and immigration legislation. Politically, the federal states prove a "haven" for parties defeated in national elections and as proving grounds for future national leaders. Of the eight different SPD (Social Democratic Party) and CDU/CSU (Christian Democratic Union/Christian Social Union) chancellor candidates since 1983, all but Angela Merkel had been or were at the time of candidacy the prime minister of a state.

Basic Rights

A second basic principle of Germany's constitutional order governs civil liberties. The first section of the Basic Law constitutes the equivalent of a political, social, and economic bill of rights applicable to individuals and groups. These provisions cannot be abolished through constitutional amendment, which reflects a determined effort on the part of delegates to the Parliamentary Council to distance postwar Germany from the Third Reich. They include basic rights familiar in other Western democracies, such as individual liberty, equality before the law, religious freedom, freedom of expression, freedom of assembly, the privacy of personal communication through mail and telecommunication, and freedom from unreasonable searches of one's home.[9]

Some may say that this is taking the concept of keeping government under wraps a little too far; others will simply say that art is in the eye of the beholder. This aerial view shows the "Wrapped Reichstag" project in Berlin on June 23, 1995, completed by artists Christo and Jeanne-Claude.

At the same time, constitutional rights contained in the Basic Law reflect a response to German history while simultaneously incorporating "modern" features of twentieth-century constitutionalism that are absent, for example, in the U.S. Constitution. The first of these concerns the protection of human dignity: "(1) The dignity of man shall be inviolable. To respect and protect it shall be the duty of all state authority. (2) The German people therefore acknowledge inviolable and inalienable human rights as the basis of every community, of peace, and of justice in the world." [10] Several provisions reflect the determination to avert Nazi-era attacks on individual freedom and to encourage active defense of democratic institutions. Thus, Germans cannot be made stateless and may be extradited only in limited circumstances to other EU states or an international tribunal (Article 16). Article 20 defines the Federal Republic as a "democratic and social federal state," one in which all sovereign power emanates from the people." Notable is this article's explicit grant to "all Germans" of the right actively to resist anyone seeking to destroy the democratic order.

Another distinctive provision affirms the constitutional sanctity of marriage and family alongside the legal protection of illegitimate children, who, in the language of the Basic Law, "shall be provided by legislation with the same opportunities for their physical and spiritual development and their place in society as are enjoyed by legitimate children." [11] A fundamental contrast to the American principle of separation of church and state is contained in Article 7, which governs public education: "Religious instruction shall form part of the ordinary curriculum in state and municipal schools."

"Modern" features of the German constitution include freedom of association, including membership in trade unions and professional groups,[12] and the right of individuals to choose a trade, occupation, or profession.[13] The Basic Law also contains a potentially contradictory set of principles pertaining to a constitutional guarantee to own and inherit private property,[14] on the one hand, and the authority of the state to transfer "land, natural resources, and means of production" to public ownership through appropriate legislation and with suitable compensation, on the other.[15] At the time the Basic Law was adopted, these opposing provisions were designed to assuage contrasting ideological preferences on the part of conservatives and the more radical Social Democrats who dominated the proceedings of the Parliamentary Council. In later years, they provided a legal basis for intense conflict between employer groups and trade unions over co-determination legislation.[16]

National-State Institutional Actors

The Basic Law also provides the legal basis for a finely tuned system of executive-legislative relations and federal structures that disperse power among national and regional institutional actors. At the apex of the system is a dual executive consisting of a largely ceremonial federal president and a much more powerful federal chancellor. The president's role corresponds approximately to that performed by hereditary heads of state in northern and western Europe and the Italian president. The federal chancellor, meanwhile, is more secure in office than most counterparts elsewhere in Europe because of a combination of constitutional engineering and the nature of the postwar party system. Legislative power is divided between a directly elected lower house of parliament, the *Bundestag*, and an upper house, the *Bundesrat*, which is composed of delegates appointed by the various state governments. Each of the sixteen states has its own directly elected assembly.

The Federal President

The framers of the Basic Law created the federal presidency to serve as Germany's head of state, a person who would represent the nation to the international community while performing carefully circumscribed domestic political tasks. In the process they deliberately restricted the powers of the office to prevent a possible reoccurrence of presidential rule akin to the Weimar experience. The result is an indirectly elected federal president with limited legal authority.

Germany's president is chosen for a five-year term by a special Federal Assembly, the *Bundesversammlung*, which is made up of the members of the lower house of parliament and an equal number of delegates from the various state parliaments. An incumbent may be reelected once, which means that the maximum term in office is ten years. These constitutional provisions resemble those found in Italy, where a president with limited powers is elected by the two houses of parliament, but contrast sharply with the direct election of the Weimar president and the president of the French Fifth Republic. Indirect elections ensure that the federal president lacks a popular mandate and therefore the institutional authority and political prestige associated with strong heads of state such as the U.S. and French presidents. Federal presidents may be impeached by a two-thirds majority of either the *Bundestag* or the *Bundesrat* if they "willfully violate" the Basic Law or federal statutes.[17] Thus far no impeachment motions have been filed against any incumbent president.

The federal president's most important responsibilities are to nominate a chancellor candidate following national elections to the *Bundestag;* appoint the chancellor if the candidate receives a requisite majority; appoint and dismiss members of the federal cabinet upon the recommendation of the federal chancellor; and, under special conditions, order new national elections. The Basic Law foresees two such contingencies: (1) If an absolute majority of members of the *Bundestag* is unable to agree on the election of a federal chancellor, the president may choose either to appoint the plurality candidate or dissolve the lower house and call a new election; or, (2) if a majority of the lower house rejects a motion of the federal chancellor for a vote of confidence.[18] The three (not identical) occasions when new elections have been held—1972, 1983, and 2005—are discussed in chapter 7. In the latter event, the chancellor may petition the federal president to dissolve the *Bundestag*. If the president concurs, a new election must be held within twenty-one days.

In addition, the president is empowered to appoint and dismiss federal judges, civil servants, and military officers, albeit only on the recommendation of the chancellor and the cabinet. The president also has the right of pardon for civil and criminal offenses and may perform various ceremonial duties. In the latter capacity, the president "shall conclude treaties with foreign states … [and] shall accredit and receive envoys."[19] Actual decisions concerning the conduct of German foreign policy, however, are made at the cabinet level.

Nine men representing three of Germany's mainstream political parties have served as president since the inception of the Federal Republic. Their elections were by no means nonpartisan affairs. Each was selected as the preferred candidate of the dominant party in the governing coalition in the *Bundestag*. They are, in chronological order, Theodor Heuss, a prominent Liberal and respected intellectual (1949–1959); Heinrich Lübke, a Christian Democrat (1959–1969); Gustav Heinemann, a Social Democrat (1969–1974); Walter Scheel, a prominent member of the Free Democratic Party (1974–1979); Karl Carstens, a Christian Democrat (1979–1984); Richard von Weizsäcker, a Christian Democrat (1984–1994); Roman

Herzog, also a Christian Democrat (1994–1999); and Johannes Rau, a Social Democrat (1999–2004). The current federal president is Horst Köhler, a Christian Democrat and former head of the International Monetary Fund. He defeated the first woman to be nominated by a major party, Gesine Schwan of the SPD. Like the election of the federal chancellor, the vote for federal president is also by secret ballot, which may lead to surprises; for example, Köhler "lost" twenty-one CDU/FDP (Free Democratic Party) votes when he was elected in May 2004.

While Germany's presidents lack extensive political power, several of them have utilized the office as a "moral pulpit" to raise citizen consciousness about important public issues. Through his unswerving commitment to democratic values and his demonstrated anti-Nazi record, the first federal president, Theodor Heuss, contributed significantly to the legitimation of the fledgling Federal Republic in the early 1950s. In more recent years, both Richard von Weizsäcker and Roman Herzog spoke to all-German themes during the course and aftermath of German reunification, including the need for West and East Germans to cultivate a shared sense of national identity that transcends their separate postwar histories. Moreover, President von Weizäcker took up permanent residence at the presidential palace, Schloß Bellevue, in Berlin in 1994 in a demonstrative affirmation of his personal commitment to German unity, a precedent that has been continued by his successors.

The Federal Chancellor

Effective executive authority is concentrated in the hands of the federal chancellor and members of the federal cabinet. In key departures from the Weimar experience and established procedures in most other parliamentary systems in Europe, delegates to the Parliamentary Council crafted stringent provisions for the selection of chancellors and their potential dismissal in a conscious effort to preclude rapid executive turnover and any resulting political instability. First, Article 63 of the Basic Law stipulates that a chancellor must be elected "without debate" by a majority of the members of the *Bundestag* "upon the proposal of the federal president." Only in the event that the federal president's nominee fails to obtain a requisite majority may the *Bundestag* elect a chancellor nominated from within its own ranks.[20] Second, Article 67 imposes severe limitations on the capacity of the *Bundestag* to cast a vote of no confidence and thereby oust an incumbent chancellor: "The *Bundestag* can express its lack of confidence in the federal chancellor only by electing a successor with the majority of its members and by requesting the federal president to dismiss the federal chancellor. The federal president must comply with the request and appoint the person elected." Together, these provisions have contributed to an extraordinary record of executive stability in the Federal Republic. Members of the *Bundestag* have acted on Article 67 only twice in an effort to depose a chancellor: in 1972, a motion against Willy Brandt failed by three votes, and in

1982, the *Bundestag* successfully ousted Helmut Schmidt while simultane-ously electing Helmut Kohl as his successor.[21]

The central leadership role accorded the federal chancellor is based on the constitutional maxim that the chancellor "shall determine, and be respon-sible for, the general policy guidelines."[22] Moreover, the chancellor's au-thority is considerably strengthened by a number of extralegal factors. Among them is a status as a prominent leader (if not chair) of the governing party, the strength of parliamentary support, visibility in the public media, and the prestige that accrues from periodic meetings with foreign state offi-cials, including other heads of government in the EU. In addition, a chan-cellor's authority may expand or contract in accordance with less tangible elements of personal leadership style, the degree of political support within a parliamentary faction, and the policy effectiveness of the government.

Once a federal chancellor has been elected by a parliamentary majority and duly appointed by the federal president, the first task is to recommend candidates for the president to appoint as members of the federal govern-ment. Ministerial assignments are typically the object of intense consulta-tions both within the chancellor's own party and between it and any coalition partners. Cabinet seats are generally appointed according to the parliamentary strength and policy priorities of the parties that make up a coalition. The most prestigious assignments are the vice-chancellorship and the ministers of foreign affairs, finance, economics and technology, justice, defense, and the interior. Other cabinet posts include agriculture and forestry; labor and social affairs; family, senior citizens, women, and youth; health; traffic, construction, and housing; protection of the environment and nuclear reactor safety; and economic cooperation and development.

The policy role of federal chancellors assumes diverse forms. As chief ex-ecutive officer, chancellors chair regular meetings of the cabinet to discuss evolving policy guidelines and resolve potential disputes among different ministers. In addition, they act as principal government spokespersons during important plenary sessions of the *Bundestag*. Each federal chancellor delivers an annual keynote address on the state of the union, presents and defends the annual budget, and speaks to particular foreign and domestic is-sues as they arise. Assisting the federal chancellor in day-to-day policy for-mation and evaluation is a staff of lawyers, economists, political scientists, and other experts who serve in the Federal Chancery in the vicinity of the re-modeled Reichstag building in the center of Berlin.

Federal chancellors also perform important leadership tasks within their respective political party. They consult regularly about government and party policy with party stalwarts in the parliamentary caucus and *Länder* organizations and campaign actively in behalf of the party during national and state elections. In recent decades, chancellors and chancellor candidates have also assumed an increased interest in recurrent efforts to elaborate or revise their parties' programs.

Christian Democratic leaders claimed the chancellorship for thirty-six of the first fifty-six years of the Federal Republic. They were Konrad Adenauer (1949–1963), Ludwig Erhard (1963–1966), Kurt-Georg Kiesinger (1966–1969), and Helmut Kohl (1982–1998). In contrast, Social Democrats served as federal chancellor for only twenty years: Willy Brandt (1969–1974), Helmut Schmidt (1974–1982), and Gerhard Schröder (1998–2005). Angela Merkel reclaimed the office for the CDU following the formation of a grand coalition cabinet in November 2005. Each incumbent has displayed individual leadership styles and contributed in different ways to the development of the Federal Republic and its political and economic performance, as recounted throughout this book.

Legislative Institutions

Germany's historical traditions of democratic representation and federalism are institutionalized in a bicameral parliament. The *Bundestag,* or lower house of parliament, directly represents the nation's voters, whereas the *Bundesrat,* or upper house, provides the state governments with a direct voice in the legislative process. Since the creation of the Federal Republic, the two houses have maintained a close, if sometimes contentious, working relationship that reflects a far greater degree of political maturation on the part of their members than their predecessors in previous German regimes.

The *Bundestag*

The historical antecedents of today's *Bundestag* are the national Reichstags of Imperial and Weimar Germany. The former was elected by adult males, which was a progressive concept in Europe in 1871, but it served in a subordinate position to the national government and an appointive upper house that represented the various kingdoms and states that made up the Imperial Reich. The Weimar constitution significantly strengthened the legislative powers of the reconstituted Reichstag, whose members were elected by universal suffrage beginning in 1919. The constitution introduced the principle of parliamentary government and, in marked contrast to the Imperial regime, brought the German military under legislative control, at least in theory. The tragic demise of democracy under national socialism, however, combined with the abolition of all political parties except the NSDAP, reduced the role of the Reichstag to that of a doleful acclamatory body uncritically supportive of the regime.

The restoration of democratic representative institutions in Germany began under careful Allied supervision in 1945 with the recreation of elective local and state assemblies throughout occupied Germany. With the adoption of the Basic Law in western Germany in 1949 and the proclamation of the German Democratic Republic later that year, parallel parliaments were established in the form of the *Bundestag* and *Bundesrat* in the West and a People's Chamber (Volkskammer) in the East. Reunification in 1990 brought the dissolution of the latter and the creation of a larger all-German parliament based on established West German institutional structures.

Today's *Bundestag* consists of deputies elected for four-year terms on the basis of a dual electoral system that combines features of proportional representation and single member representation. (Details of the electoral system are explained in chapter 6.) The German electoral system has served as a model for a number of newer democracies, especially those in Central and Eastern Europe. In its origins, the system reflected the interests of the two major parties (the CDU and the SPD), the preferences of the Western occupation powers, and determined efforts by drafters of the Basic Law to learn from the "lessons" of the Weimar collapse.

Consistent with well-established principles of parliamentary government in Europe and elsewhere, the *Bundestag* serves as the legislative basis of cabinet government. As such, it is unquestionably the more important of the two parliamentary bodies in the Federal Republic. Among its chief functions, as previously recounted, are the election of the federal chancellor following each national election (or between elections if a chancellor resigns[23]) and the constitutional authority under Article 67 of the Basic Law to dismiss an incumbent chancellor by electing a successor by majority vote.

Once federal chancellors assume office, they and their cabinet colleagues become politically accountable for their actions to the *Bundestag*. The *Bundestag* may demand the presence of any member of the federal government and exercises a variety of parliamentary control functions over executive and administrative actions. These include the right to pose "interprellations," that is, formal party queries, about government policy, as well as questions raised by individual deputies during a weekly question hour; the authority to convene special committees of investigation; and the right to designate a military ombudsman, known as the *Wehrbeauftrager,* who has independent power to investigate alleged abuses within Germany's armed forces. In contrast to the British parliamentary system, in which committees exercise little independent authority in relation to the government of the day, but to a lesser degree than committees in the U.S. Congress, *Bundestag* investigative committees exercise considerable power. Recent important *Bundestag* investigations include the probe of CDU party finances in 2000–2001 (see chapter 6) and the handling of a terrorism suspect after 9/11.

Internally, the *Bundestag* consists of a series of leadership groups and standing committees. The chief executive officer is an elected *Bundestag* president who functions as the equivalent of speaker of the house and traditionally represents the largest political faction. He or she is assisted currently by six elected vice presidents who jointly make up the executive committee (*Präsidium*) of the lower house. Only twice has the SPD formed the numerically largest faction and therefore named the *Bundestag* president: Annemarie Renger (1972–1976) and Wolfgang Thierse (1998–2005). Renger and the CDU's Rita Süssmuth (1988–1998) have been the only women to hold this position. In a break with precedent, a majority of the *Bundestag* refused to approve Lothar Bisky, the PDS/Left Party candidate, for the office of *Bundestag* vice president because of his alleged ties to the *Stasi,* the former East German secret police. The Left Party eventually named a replacement, who was duly elected. The *Bundestag* president and vice presidents confer regularly with members of a Council of Elders (*Ältestenrat*), which consists of twenty-nine deputies representing the various parties in approximate proportion to their parliamentary strength, to coordinate general legislative activity and plan the day-to-day parliamentary agenda.

The parties themselves are organized in parliamentary factions (*Fraktionen*) that correspond to the Anglo-American legislative caucus. Each is led by a chair, whose dual task is to help forge party policy and factional unity on pending legislative matters. In addition, each factional chair represents his or her party during floor debates and in consultation with parliamentary officers about such matters as the daily agenda. Members of the parliamentary factions are assigned to various party working groups (*Arbeitskreisen*), each of which corresponds to important areas of national legislation. Among these are working groups on foreign and defense policy, economic policy, social policy, and legal affairs. These internal committees play a crucial role in determining the fate of prospective legislation, as their members are usually experts in their policy fields and can therefore strongly influence the formation of party policy before particular bills are formally debated in parliament. While the *Bundestag* is in session, the various party factions generally meet on at least a weekly basis to consider reports from their working groups, review their legislative strategy, and debate policy or internal questions of general interest.

During plenary sessions *Bundestag* deputies sit from left to right in party groups in an extended semicircle in front of a raised podium that accommodates the presiding officers and government speakers. With 226 members, the CDU/CSU made up the largest faction in the current, sixteenth *Bundestag* (2005–2009). Two CDU deputies have died since 2005, although because they held "excess mandate" seats, they were not replaced. The CDU/CSU faction is followed closely by its grand coalition partner, the SPD, with 222 members. The three opposition parties are the FDP (61), the Left Party (54), and the Greens (51).

The bulk of legislative deliberations, as is true in other representative democracies, occurs within the parliament's elaborate committee structure. During the sixteenth legislative period, the *Bundestag* established twenty-two standing committees, most corresponding to the jurisdiction of cabinet-level ministries. The more important, as measured by their membership, were committees on foreign policy; internal affairs; finance; defense; laws; budgetary matters; economics and technology; agriculture and forestry; labor and social order; the environment; traffic; European Union affairs; culture and the media; and family, senior citizens, women, and youth. Smaller committees included those dealing with electoral verification, sports, and mail and telecommunications. Committee members are appointed on a proportional basis by the president of the *Bundestag* in consultation with the various party factions.

The *Bundesrat*

The *Bundesrat* continues an institutional tradition first established under the Imperial constitution and continued, under the name of Reichsrat, through the Weimar era. Its members are appointed by the various state governments, which are in turn based on elective assemblies in each of the sixteen *Länder*. State elections are held at staggered four- or five-year intervals.

As the institutional representative of the sixteen states in the legislative process, the *Bundesrat* provides an important channel of regional influence in national policy formation. This upper house does not serve as a basis for government formation and accountability comparable to the role performed by the *Bundestag* or the Italian Senate; nonetheless, it provides significant "correctives" to the legislative process. Moreover, because of partisan alignments among its members, it can either facilitate or complicate the task of national policy formation.

The various states are represented in the *Bundesrat* according to their respective populations. Following German reunification in 1990, the number of seats allocated to each of the states was adjusted through constitutional amendment: the smaller states are represented by three deputies, states with more than two million inhabitants are accorded four seats, states with more than six million have five, and states with more than seven million have six.[24] At present, the sixteen states fall into the three, four, or six seat categories, as indicated in Table 5.1. For reasons of population and political arithmetic, states in the western part of Germany clearly dominate the composition of the upper house. Deputies cast their votes as a bloc in accordance with political instructions from their state governments.

In their role as national parliamentarians, *Bundesrat* deputies are constitutionally empowered to act on behalf of the *Länder* in the legislation and administration of the Federation.[25] This means that all government bills must be submitted first to the *Bundesrat* for its opinion. Similarly, the *Bundesrat* has the constitutional power to review all legislation passed by the

Table 5.1	Number of State Seats in the *Bundesrat*	
Three Seats	Four Seats	Six Seats
Bremen	Berlin	Baden-Württemberg
Hamburg	Brandenburg	Bavaria
Mecklenburg– Western Pomeraniaa	Hesse	Lower Saxony
Saarland	Saxony	North Rhine–Westphalia
	Saxony-Anhalt	
	Schleswig-Holstein	
	Rhineland-Palatinate	
	Thüringia	

Source: Compiled by the authors.

Bundestag, and members of the *Bundesrat* may initiate legislation on their own volition. As indicated in the following description of the legislative process, these provisions accord the *Bundesrat* multiple possibilities to create legislative delay, the right of a suspensive veto, and, in the case of constitutional amendments and changes in *Länder* boundaries, the power of absolute veto.

Structurally, the *Bundesrat* is organized on the basis of state delegations rather than party factions. The partisan composition of these delegations mirrors the partisan balance in the respective state parliaments. Each state is represented in standing committees that correspond to the ministries on the federal level and to committees in the *Bundestag.* In plenary sessions, members sit in elevated rows in relation to a podium reserved for the presiding officers in the center of the hall. The *Bundesrat's* chief executive offices include an elected president, whose office rotates in alphabetical order among the sixteen states on an annual basis, and three vice presidents. Its deputies are served by a secretariat of approximately 170 persons whose task is to assist in preparations for and the conduct of plenary and committee meetings.

The direct participation of state representatives in legislative decisions enhances the significance of regional variations in party strength. As long as the parliamentary majority in the *Bundestag* corresponds approximately to the composition of the governments in most of the state parliaments, and hence to the majority in the *Bundesrat,* the two houses of parliament perform their legislative functions with minimum friction. But if one majority prevails in the lower house and another in the *Bundesrat* by virtue of different electoral outcomes on the national and state levels, the result can be a parliamentary stalemate. Throughout Schröder's second term (2002–2005), for example, his governing coalition lacked the thirty-five seats needed for a *Bundesrat* majority.[26]

The Legislative Process

The dual executive, the *Bundestag,* and the *Bundesrat* interact to determine national legislation and legal decrees. The federal government and parliament share legal responsibility for policy deliberation and enactment, although for constitutional and political reasons the federal chancellor and any ministerial colleagues perform the leading role in initiating the majority of federal decisions. Bills may be introduced formally by the federal government, the *Bundesrat,* and the *Bundestag.* Government bills must be submitted first to the *Bundesrat,* which is entitled to state its position on them within six weeks. Conversely, bills initiated by the *Bundesrat* must be referred directly to the federal government. The latter is required to submit such proposals, along with its own views on their relative merits, to the *Bundestag* within three months. A bill originating in the *Bundestag* must be signed by at least 5 percent of its members (thirty-four deputies at present) or by a party faction.

Legislation initiated within the *Bundestag* itself, along with bills submitted by the federal government and the *Bundesrat,* are reviewed by members of the Council of Elders and then submitted to the lower house for a preliminary vote in plenary session. If a bill passes the first reading, it is referred to the appropriate parliamentary committee for detailed deliberation and potential modification. If a committee majority endorses the bill, it is resubmitted to the *Bundestag* for a second and third (final) reading. Proposed measures thus endorsed by the *Bundestag* must then be sent without delay to the *Bundesrat.* If the upper house similarly approves the measure, the legislative process is completed, and the bill is referred to the federal government for the final steps in its formal enactment. If, however, either house rejects a bill, the federal government, the *Bundesrat,* or the *Bundestag* may demand that a joint consultative committee (*Vermittlungsausschuß*), which is made up of an equal number of members from both chambers, be appointed to reconsider the measure. If the consultative committee proposes any changes in a bill, the bill must be resubmitted to both houses for renewed deliberation and a vote.

Once parliament endorses a measure, the bill goes to the federal government for signature by the minister in charge of that particular policy area. From there, a measure is sent to the federal president for a countersignature. A bill becomes law upon publication in the Federal Registry of Laws.

Executive Preeminence

As Table 5.2 indicates, the executive clearly dominates the legislative process. Most bills originate in the federal government, and of those an overwhelming majority have been endorsed in successive legislative sessions. In contrast, only a scant number of measures proposed by members of the *Bundestag* during the same period have been enacted into law.

Underscoring the pivotal policy role of the federal government is a simultaneous increase in the number of legal ordinances (*Rechtsverordnungen*) issued by the chancellor's office and the other ministries. Such decrees have the force of law and require only the consent of the *Bundesrat* before they are enacted (Article 80). They typically take the form of executive elaborations of general statutes previously endorsed by parliament. In recent years the number of legal ordinances has decreased from 1,753 during the thirteenth legislative session (1994–1998) to 968 during the fifteenth session (2002–2005). The majority of ordinances were in the areas of traffic regulations, finances, economics, and agriculture.[27]

Executive preeminence in the Federal Republic is hardly surprising given the constitutional prerogatives of the federal chancellor and the considerable political resources of the parliamentary majority. As in other stable parliamentary regimes in Europe, chancellors can usually rely on the loyalty of the deputies within their own factions and those of any coalition partners to mobilize majority support for the government's legislative agenda. Moreover,

Table 5.2	Legislative Activity, 1990–2006*				
			Legislative Session		
	12th	13th	14th	15th	16th
	1990–1994	1994–1998	1998–2002	2002–2005	2005–2006
Type of activity					
Bills initiated by:					
Federal government	407	443	443	320	180
Bundestag	297	329	328	211	84
Bundesrat	96	151	93	112	52
TOTAL	**800**	**923**	**864**	**643**	**316**
Origins of ratified bills:					
Federal government	345	403	394	281	137
Bundestag	99	102	108	85	21
Bundesrat	28	36	22	17	6
Federal government/					
Bundestag/Bundesrat	50	25	35	17	3
TOTAL	**507**	**566**	**559**	**400**	**167**
Consultative committees convened by:					
Federal government	14	10	10	11	—
Bundestag	—	8	1	1	—
Bundesrat	71	74	66	90	1
TOTAL	**85**	**92**	**77**	**102**	**1**
Enacted as laws:	62	73	63	88	1

Source: Statistisches Jahrbuch 2007 für die Bundesrepublik Deutschland (Wiesbaden: Statistisches Bundesamt, 2007), 106.
*Legislative activity through December 31, 2006.

executive preeminence in Germany corresponds to similar patterns in other modern democracies. Comparable to postwar tendencies in the United States, the United Kingdom, France, and the Scandinavian countries, the German executive has accumulated increased power as a consequence of diverse international and domestic developments. Among these developments are the growing complexity of legislation, recurrent economic and foreign policy crises, and a steady expansion in the role of the economic and social roles of national governments—all of which have encouraged the centralization of executive power as a universal phenomenon.

Public Administration

An important corollary of German federalism is that policy implementation is institutionally fragmented. Historical tendencies toward administrative-bureaucratic centralization, which began with the founding of the German Empire in 1871 and reached their apex under the Nazi regime, were abruptly reversed in 1945 when Allied officials implemented a sweeping program of political and economic decentralization. Facilitating Allied efforts to dismantle the unitary administrative apparatus of the Third Reich was the decision early during the occupation years to dissolve Prussia and establish successor *Länder* in its place, including North Rhine–Westphalia and Lower Saxony in the West and, until 1952 and again after 1990, Brandenburg and Mecklenburg–Western Pomerania in the East.

The result of Allied-sponsored reforms is the emergence of what Guy Peters has described as "(p)robably the most extreme version of ... administrative devolution and administrative federalism" within the Western democracy community.[28] By this, Peters means that most legislation, executive decrees, and court decisions are enforced by *Länder* bureaucrats rather than by federal officials. The principal exceptions include foreign policy, national defense, the railway system, and the post office, all of which are administered by federal agencies. Other policy decisions, ranging from economic management to agriculture and the provisions of social services, are delegated to the states for administration. Empirically documenting this division of labor is the fact that in 1996 only 14 percent of all public administrative officials worked for the national government, compared to 52 percent employed by the *Länder* and 34 percent by local county and city governments. Forty percent of public servants were women, most of whom were employed on either the local or state level.[29] An important consequence of "administrative federalism" is that policy implementation may vary somewhat from *Land* to *Land*. As Peters observes:

> Although the federal ministers must assure that the programs of their ministry are administered properly and uniformly throughout the country, in practice they have few means of enforcing such uniformity. The system allows for considerable autonomy in the *Länder* with respect not only to the organization of their own civil service systems, but also to the manner of executing public policies. The logic behind such a system—from the administrative rather than political point of view—is that different local conditions may require marginally different solutions. Further, different local historical factors and differences in the religious composition of the *Länder* may require variations in the internal procedures of administration.[30]

The Judicial System

Germany's legal system consists of a multi-tiered network of local, state, and federal courts. Local courts (*Amtsgerichte*) serve as the first instance for minor civil disputes and criminal offenses. More important offenses, along with appeals from the local courts, are tried in state courts (*Landgerichte*), which are presided over by a single judge, or in state civil or criminal "chambers" (*Zivil-* or *Strafkammer*), which are more complex structures made up of several judges. The highest court of review on the state level is the

Table 5.3	Types and Number of Local and State Courts by State, 2006					
State	Local courts	State courts	State civil chambers	State criminal chambers	Provincial civil courts	Provincial criminal courts
Baden-Württemberg	108	17	170	251	46	8
Bavaria	72	22	219	190	60	12
Berlin	12	1	73	60	28	5
Brandenburg	25	4	40	30	18	2
Bremen	3	1	15	35	5	2
Hamburg	8	1	33	56	14	6
Hesse	76	9	137	118	35	7
Mecklenburg– Western Pomerania	21	4	29	24	10	4
Lower Saxony	80	11	145	208	50	10
North Rhine–Westphalia	130	19	346	304	119	11
Rhineland-Palatinate	46	8	68	67	25	5
Saarland	10	1	17	12	7	2
Saxony	30	6	67	64	18	3
Saxony-Anhalt	30	6	67	64	18	3
Schleswig-Holstein	27	4	72	90	19	4
Thüringia	23	4	28	31	8	2
Total	**668**	**16**	**1,495**	**1,581**	**473**	**86**

Source: *Statistisches Jahrbuch 2007 für die Bundesrepublik* (Wiesbaden: Statistisches Bundesamt, 2007), 262.

provincial court (*Oberlandesgerichte*), which exercises both civil and criminal jurisdiction. Serving as the final instance for appeals involving ordinary civil and criminal matters is the Federal Court of Justice (*Bundesgerichtshof*) located in Karlsruhe in Baden-Württemberg. In addition, specialized state and federal courts exist to settle disputes involving labor regulations, administrative decrees, social conflicts, and public finance.[31] Important social issues can sometimes land in seemingly apolitical administrative tribunals. An example of this is a series of decisions that reached the highest civil service court, the *Bundesverwaltungsgericht,* concerning whether female Muslim schoolteachers may wear head scarves in the classroom.

The number of local and state courts, by type and each of the *Länder,* is shown in Table 5.3. Presiding over them in 2004 were some 20,395 judges, an overwhelming majority of them (19,931) serving on the local and state levels. Among them were 6,424 women. In 2005, local courts ruled in 1.5 million cases, most of them involving rental or commercial disputes and traffic accidents. That same year, state level courts ruled in 14,224 cases involving criminal appeals and 430,236 civil disputes, while provincial courts processed 14,224 criminal cases.[32]

The Federal Constitutional Court

One of Germany's most important political institutions is the Federal Constitutional Court (*Bundesverfassungsgericht*), which is also located in

Karlsruhe. Adapting the American precedent of a Supreme Court to German conditions, the founding fathers of 1948–1949 established the Federal Constitutional Court as an independent institution with sweeping legal authority as guardian of the postwar democratic order.[33] The court consists of two panels, or senates, each consisting of eight judges. All judges are elected, half by the *Bundestag* and half by the *Bundesrat,* for twelve-year terms. Judges are formally appointed to office by the federal president. Unlike ostensibly nonpartisan Supreme Court justices in the United States, their German counterparts are nominated and supported by the political parties.

Article 93 of the Basic Law empowers the Federal Constitutional Court to pass final judgment on

The constitutionality of federal and state laws;

Disputes "concerning the extent of the rights and duties of a highest federal organ or of other parties concerned who have been vested with rights of their own by [the] Basic Law or by rules of procedure of the highest federal organ";

Legal disputes between the federal government and the states, as well as conflicts between the states; and

"Complaints of unconstitutionality" submitted by individuals, local governments, or associations of local government.

A crucial component linking the court's role to the defense of democracy is found in Article 21, which extends the power of the Federal Constitutional Court to rule on the constitutionality of political parties. While the Basic Law explicitly affirms that "political parties shall participate in the forming of the political will of the people," it simultaneously affirms that "[p]arties that, by reason of their aims or the behavior of their adherents, seek to impair or abolish the free democratic basic order or to endanger the existence of the Federal Republic of Germany, shall be unconstitutional." Article 21 assigns the responsibility of such judgments to the Federal Constitutional Court, which "shall decide on the question of unconstitutionality."

The Federal Constitutional Court has frequently been called on to exercise its sweeping jurisdiction. In a landmark 1958 decision, it upheld the principle of individual freedom of expression under Article 5 of the Basic Law.[34] That same decade the court outlawed both a neo-Nazi Party and the Communist Party of West Germany at the behest of the federal government. During the 1970s, conservative political spokespersons turned to the court to challenge the constitutionality of controversial national legislation, including a state treaty between the Federal Republic and the former German Democratic Republic and a 1976 bill on expanded rights of codetermination, which various employer groups sought to annul through judicial channels. In both of the latter cases, the Federal Constitutional Court ruled in favor of the federal government. Much as in the United States, Germans have turned to the court to adjudicate politically sensitive social issues. Thus, in both 1975 and in 1993, it struck down intricately negotiated liberalizations of the abortion law. It has also been prominent in foreign policy/military decisions, especially in its 1994 ruling permitting "out of [NATO] theater" actions (see chapter 10). Recently, the court ruled unconstitutional a Bavarian school regulation that permitted the display of crucifixes in classrooms as incompatible with the constitution's guarantee of freedom of religion (Article 4 of the Basic Law).[35]

In aggregate terms, the caseload confronting the court has remained relatively constant in recent decades. The number of cases it has reviewed, most of which involve "complaints of unconstitutionality," rose from 5,612 in 2004 to 6,174 in 2006. During the same period the Federal Constitutional Court heard an annual average of 2,720 cases involving constitutional issues. Since 2001, however, the number of appeals to the court has risen dramatically, surpassing 6,000 in 2006. Many cases involve appeals from prison inmates. However, the number of *successful* appeals has remained constant.[36]

The high frequency of legal disputes concerning the constitutional rights of individuals and groups is significant. For one thing, it indicates a growing inclination on the part of Germans, similar to that of Americans and Canadians, to look to the courts for the resolution of civil disputes rather than to the national and state legislatures. For another, continued litigation involving basic rights reveals heightened public awareness of a persisting contradiction in German society between constitutional ideals of human dignity, liberty, and equality, on the one hand, and the realities of socioeconomic inequalities and political dissent, on the other.

The German Military

Historically, one of the most baneful national institutions in Germany was the military. Established as an institutional extension of monarchical power beginning in the seventeenth century, the Prussian army and later the Imperial Reichswehr were "removed completely from the realm of the civilian constitutions."[37] The German military remained in essence a "state within the state" until the adoption of the Weimar constitution in 1919 subjected the Reichswehr to parliamentary oversight and cabinet control (see chapter 2). Even then, the Reichswehr remained an authoritarian and largely unrepentant instrument of force whose leaders engaged in a relentless pursuit of weaponry modernization, the disguised training of hundreds of thousands of "voluntary recruits" through cooperative arrangements with private industry, and secret rearmament and training missions in the Soviet Union with the covert consent of the civilian leadership.[38] Hitler's rise to power in 1933 transformed the already authoritarian Reichswehr into the ruthlessly efficient Wehrmacht of the Third Reich whose mission became the political-military subjugation of much of Europe in World War II.

To their credit, not all of the Wehrmacht's officers uncritically supported Hitler and the Nazi regime. Fearing the consequences of Hitler's imperialistic policies for Germany's domestic future, a number of officers plotted a succession of assassination attempts, none of which succeeded. The most dramatic failure occurred on July 20, 1944, when Colonel Claus von Stauffenberg, a leading member of a national resistance movement, planted a bomb at Hitler's military headquarters near the eastern front. The bomb exploded but only injured Hitler. In the aftermath of the so-called officers' plot, 4,980 officers and civilians were executed.[39]

The Reich's defeat in 1945 brought wholesale disarmament throughout occupied Germany, but the escalating Cold War prompted rearmament in both postwar regimes. A 1950 U.S. proposal that West Germany should contribute to the Western defense effort led, after protracted domestic controversy, to the creation of a German Federal Army, the Bundeswehr, in 1955. The Federal Republic simultaneously joined the North Atlantic Treaty Organization (NATO).[40]

Politically and institutionally, the Bundeswehr differed fundamentally from previous German military establishments. It was placed under firm civilian control, with the minister of defense serving as commander in chief in peacetime.[41] Officers and recruits were trained in democratic principles, including the concept of "inner leadership" (*Innere Führung*), which can be best conceived as responsible personal behavior in carrying out military assignments rather than mindless obedience. A Parliamentary Commissioner for the Armed Forces (*Wehrbeauftragter*) was created to protect the constitutional rights of those serving in the military. Like the precedent-setting office of the ombudsman in Scandinavia, the commissioner is authorized to investigate individual complaints and submits an annual report on his or her findings to the defense committee of the *Bundestag*. In place of a national command structure comparable to that in most other countries, NATO originally assumed direct operational authority over the Bundeswehr's army, naval, and air force components. The federal government, acting through the ministry of the interior, retained autonomous control only over the country's armed border guards (*Grenzschutz*).

The Soviets and East German Communists anticipated Western rearmament initiatives by creating armed paramilitary police units in the GDR beginning in the late 1940s. These units served as the basis for a National People's Army (NVA), which was formally established in January 1956 through an amendment to the GDR's constitution. East Germany simultaneously joined the Soviet-dominated Warsaw Pact security system. Similar to civil-military relations in the Soviet Union, the NVA was established as a political army under the direct control of the ruling Socialist Unity Party (SED).[42] This principle was explicitly codified in the SED's 1963 party program, which proclaimed: "The most important source of the strength of our armed forces is their leadership by the party of the working class. The party seeks to ensure that all members of the armed forces become class-conscious fighters for socialism."[43]

Throughout most of the life span of the GDR, the NVA served as an ideologically conscious, well-trained, well-equipped, and subservient military ally of the Soviet Union. Soviet officials maintained tight and unusual restrictions on East German armed forces. The GDR had no air force and was, indeed, forbidden to engage in research or the manufacture of aircraft. Moreover, the numerical strength of the Group of Soviet Forces in Germany exceeded at all times that of the NVA. Only in the wake of East Germany's deteriorating economy in the mid-1980s and Mikhail Gorbachev's domestic program of economic, political, and social reforms in the Soviet Union did the NVA begin to disintegrate internally. A loss of discipline and unprecedented protest actions by enlisted individuals prompted military leaders to initiate democratic reforms in late 1989, but they proved futile in the larger context of Germany's "rush to unity."[44]

A common uneasiness about a German military force may account for the parallel institution of conscientious objection to military service in both Germanys. The GDR was the only Warsaw Pact member state to allow noncombatant service in "construction battalions." The Federal Republic has allowed alternative "civilian service" (*Zivildienst*) from its outset. According to the Basic Law, conscientious objection is a fundamental right.[45] Germany allows such objection to military service for philosophical and personal as well as strictly religious reasons. About half of those who apply are granted this status. Since unification, the number of those applying for conscientious objector status has ranged between 125,000 and 190,000 annually, with the highest total in 2002; the most recent figure, for 2006, was more than 140,000.[46] The palette of possible alternative service is very broad but generally within the parameters of needed public service, particularly in caring for ill or otherwise impaired individuals. The number of available places is far smaller than the number of those eligible to work. Fewer than half of those applying for this status in 2006 actually performed such service. At the beginning of 2008, 3,518 persons were added to their ranks.

A significant achievement of German unification has been the creation of a cohesive national defense force. This process involved overlapping stages of transformation, beginning with the formal dissolution of the already disintegrating NVA on October 3, 1990, the day of German political unity. All generals and admirals of the former East Germany military as well as officers older than fifty-five years of age were summarily dismissed, and officers assigned from the West took their place. Structurally, the former command structure of the NVA was replaced by a special Eastern Command with headquarters at the former East German defense ministry in an eastern suburb of Berlin. Accompanying these initiatives was the simultaneous necessity to reduce the number of personnel in accordance with an agreement reached earlier in the year between Chancellor Kohl and Soviet president Gorbachev to restrict the size of the all-German Bundeswehr to 370,000 men and women.[47] This of necessity required "painful personnel reductions."[48] A third imperative was the disposal of most East German military equipment and ammunition.[49]

Alongside these measures was the daunting challenge of political reeducation among East German soldiers. Lt. Gen. Jörg Schönberg, former chief of the Bundeswehr's Planning Staff in Bonn, was charged with overseeing the transition of the military in eastern Germany. He set the tone for what this transition would require in his first address to former NVA service personnel on October 4. Schönberg emphatically rejected concepts of "class war, the class mission, class hate, and the conception of the enemy." He called instead on the active participation of East German soldiers, "above all our young conscripts," in achieving "the unity of the nation in the democratic state based on the rule of law."[50]

By mid-decade amalgamation was complete. While for primarily ideological reasons most personnel reductions were borne by former members of the NVA, ultimately some 3,000 East German officers and 7,600 noncommissioned officers were retained in the all-German Bundeswehr.[51] Through its internal structure, the Bundeswehr thus promotes East-West social integration across the former German-German border more than any other institution in the expanded Federal Republic.

As a result of military reforms of 2000–2004, the armed forces have been reduced in size and reorganized into joint-force commands. Out of 250,000 men and women, of which the army accounts for just under half, some 35,000 form a rapid deployment force. An additional 70,000 are designated for peace-keeping and nation-building assignments. The remainder provide support and perform other duties.[52] Like its two predecessors, the core of the national Bundeswehr remains a conscript force based on mandatory nine-month service for men once they reach eighteen years of age, unless they choose alternative civilian service. Women serve in increasing numbers in all branches of the armed forces, including combat units. Recruits from all parts of the country complete their basic training and serve in military units together.[53]

The all-German military retains the constitutional and political characteristics of the earlier West German Bundeswehr. It remains under the civilian control of elected officials in the cabinet and the *Bundestag* but is no longer under the strategic command of NATO. The concept of *Innere Führung* continues to serve as an important instrument of citizenship training in democratic values and individual behavior. Despite the move of other national government agencies to Berlin in 1999, the Bundeswehr's main military headquarters remain in Bonn in part to avoid symbolic associations with historical memories of earlier German military regimes and their lack of constitutional accountability.

Contrary to the trend across Europe and against the advice of several expert commissions, German political leaders, former chancellor Schröder and former president von Weizsäcker prominently among them, have rejected calls for a volunteer military force, praising a general obligation for military service as strengthening the democratic nature of the armed forces. Roughly half of all EU nations and about the same proportion of NATO countries do not have compulsory military service.

German Security Arrangements since 9/11

As in many countries in the years since the attacks of 9/11 and subsequent violent acts in Bali, Madrid, London, and elsewhere, Germany has moved to expand the powers of various security organizations. The German response to these dangers is powerfully conditioned by two historical experiences: the brutal repression of the Nazi period as well as the Communist dictatorship in the GDR, and the effective democratic response to left-wing terrorism in the 1970s, associated with the Red Army Faction (*Rote Armee Fraktion,* or *RAF*). The former has made both German politicians and the public careful about expanding policing powers; the 1970s experience demonstrated that a democratic state could take effective and forceful action in its defense.

Germany's security architecture is strongly marked by the federal devolution of executive authority discussed earlier in this chapter.[54] Thus while the chief agency for fighting "ordinary" crime, the Federal Criminal Office (*Bundeskriminalamt*), possesses impressive data and information dissemination capacity, it has had difficulty in obtaining jurisdiction from the corresponding state offices (*Landeskriminalämter*); it has recently taken over some high-level political and criminal prosecutions. (A proposal by the then SPD Interior minister Otto Schily that would have placed greater powers in the BKA was blocked by the state governments.) The Federal Office for Protection of the Constitution (*Bundesverfassungsschutz*) concentrates on political extremism of left and right and, ever more so, on foreign and especially Islamist extremism. The Federal Border Protection Service (*Bundesgrenzschutz*) formerly guarded the border with the GDR. Since reunification, and with the abolition of border passport controls among most EU states on the basis of the 1990 Schengen accord, it has far fewer borders to guard; it now concentrates on airports and railroad stations and routes. The agency responsible for foreign espionage and counterterrorism is the BND (*Bundesnachrichtendienst*), which in 2006–2007 became a center of controversy over possible involvement in renditions overseen by the Central Intelligence Agency of the United States.

In the aftermath of 9/11, these and other government security agencies received a sizable budgetary increase from the Schröder government for "domestic security." In addition, two legislative initiatives were approved that granted the security and intelligence services new and broader powers. These included expanded authority to monitor both individuals and organizations suspected of security dangers, removal of religious exemption for organizations that could be banned for endangering the constitutional order, criminalization of the planning of terrorist actions abroad from German soil, allowance for collection of biometric data, and greater access to financial records.

Despite broad acceptance of the need for great security powers, criticism of such measures has continued. In a notable setback for authorities, the courts ruled in favor of a coalition of university students suing to block application of a favorite measure of the 1970s: the mining of data for suspicious patterns of activity. Controversy over these questions has become a staple issue of German politics.

Germany in the European Union

Augmenting Germany's domestic constitutional norms and political institutions is the larger community of the European Union. While the Federal Republic commands considerable autonomy as an independent nation-state, it is nonetheless subject to administrative obligations and binding policy decisions under terms of its membership in the EU (explored further in chapter 9). Successive German governments have willingly promoted these fundamental features of the postwar European integration movement.

In 1951, West Germany was a founding member of Europe's first "supranational" organization, the European Coal and Steel Community (ECSC), whose basic purpose was to establish a regional common market with a Franco-German core, for iron, coal, and steel production and sales. Means to these ends included the gradual elimination of domestic tariffs on such products and the erection of a common external tariff in relation to other countries. Institutionally, the founding members of ECSC established an intergovernmental Council of Ministers, a supranational High Authority, a symbolically important but largely powerless European Assembly, and a European Court of Justice. Legislative power was vested in the Council of Ministers, on which each state was accorded one vote and the right of veto over pending decisions. The High Authority was composed of one to two representatives from the member states (depending on population size) who, once approved in office by the council, acted independently of instructions from their home governments to enact certain administrative prerogatives on their own volition. The High Authority was also accorded the exclusive right to propose ECSC legislation to the Council of Ministers. Members of the European Assembly were recruited among the six member parliaments, and judges to the Court of Justice were nominated by their home governments and approved by the council.

The economic success of the ECSC prompted the same six nations (France, Italy, West Germany, and the three Benelux states—Belgium, the Netherlands, and Luxemburg) to embrace a much more ambitious program of regional integration in the form of a European Economic Community (EEC), which was established in 1957–1958 to achieve a common market for industrial and agricultural goods and the free movement of labor among member states. The EEC's decision-making institutions included its own intergovernmental Council of Ministers and a supranational European Commission akin to the ECSC's High Authority. Simultaneously the European Assembly was renamed the European Parliament; henceforth, it served as an advisory body to both the ECSC and the EEC. The European Court of Justice was assigned jurisdiction to settle legal disputes arising under the treaties.

In subsequent decades the European integration movement achieved extraordinary degrees of economic and political "take-off."[55] Key transforming changes included institutional and policy "deepening." The EEC initiated a Common Agricultural Policy (CAP) in 1962, attained a regional customs union in 1968 (eighteen months ahead of schedule), and achieved independent sources of revenue in 1970 when the council agreed to allocate the EEC all duties levied on industrial and agricultural imports as well as a percentage of the value-added tax collected in each of the member states. In 1967 the ECSC's and EEC's institutions were merged, with a single Council of Ministers and European Commission subsequently serving both organizations. During the mid-1970s the council agreed to allow direct elections to the European Parliament (effective in 1979), which enhanced the parliament's legitimacy and visibility. The parliament's decision-making powers were later extended under a succession of treaties. The sum of these outcomes is the emergence of the EU as a political system embracing multilevel governance reminiscent of German federalism

Parallel with these early moves toward intensified economic cooperation and institutional reform, European leaders engaged in a protracted debate concerning EEC enlargement. The United Kingdom—one of the EEC's most important trade partners—had initially resisted joining the integration movement during its formative stage in the 1950s, but concerns about the potential loss of Continental markets prompted British leaders to apply for membership in 1961. French president Charles de Gaulle brusquely rejected the British bid in January 1963, alleging that the United Kingdom was not yet ready to "join Europe." The election of his more moderate successor, Georges Pompidou, in 1969 yielded a more conciliatory response. In December 1969 the EEC heads of government and the French president agreed to instruct the European Commission to begin negotiations with qualified prospective member states. The result was the accession of Britain, Denmark, and Ireland by the beginning of 1973. Greece subsequently joined in 1981, followed by Spain and Portugal in 1986. Austria, Finland, and Sweden became members in January 1995. Ten former Communist nations and two Mediterranean countries joined between 2004 and 2007. Thus, the original community of six has become a political-economic union of twenty-seven member states.[56] Several additional states are potential candidate members for membership in the foreseeable future.[57]

The elevation of Jacques Delors, a French Socialist, as president of the European Commission in 1985 marked the beginning of a new phase of intensified integration. A policy activist by experience and ideological conviction,

Delors helped shepherd a number of "deepening" initiatives through the Council of Ministers that were subsequently enacted by the national parliaments of the member states. These initiatives included a White Paper of 1985 that established a policy blueprint for the attainment of a single European market by the early 1990s; the Single European Act of 1986, which introduced the principle of qualified majority voting in the Council of Ministers; a community commitment to achieve economic and monetary union (EMU) by 1999, accompanied by the introduction of a common currency; and much of the conceptual basis for the 1991 Treaty on European Union, which codified the financial criteria and timetable for achieving EMU while strengthening the decision-making role of the European Parliament in Community policy.

With the implementation of the Treaty on European Union in 1994, the EEC became today's European Union. Macro-level economic and monetary union became a reality on January 1, 1999, for eleven of the EU's fifteen member states. The attainment of EMU brought with it the introduction of the euro for transactions purposes in national accounts, stock markets, investments, trade, and the EU's own budget. Euro bills and coins began to circulate in 2002. As of 2008, fifteen countries had joined the Eurozone.[58]

The Federal Republic has been a key player throughout the course of the European integration movement. In close cooperation particularly with France, Germany has endorsed all of the transforming changes that have elevated the EU to its current status as an increasingly powerful regional economic and political system in world affairs. Moreover, Germany has been in the forefront of EU member states in advocating the eastward expansion of the union to include most of the former Communist countries in Central and Eastern Europe.

Institutionally, German government officials play a highly visible role in the Council of Ministers and the European Council, while one German national serves on the European Commission, out of a total of twenty-seven members. Because of the size of its population, Germany claims the largest number of seats in the European Parliament, counting 99 out of a total of 785 members during the 2004–2009 legislative session. Hence, Germany's weighty institutional presence within the EU, buttressed by its considerable national economic and social resources, allows the Federal Republic a significant voice in trans-European affairs.

Conclusion

On multiple levels of German federalism as well as within the European Union, political institutions obviously "matter" in serving as the targets of democratic elections and the foci of legislative and executive decision making. The key linkages between institutions and the citizen body are Germany's political parties, organized interest groups, and social movements, the objects of the next two chapters.

6

Political Parties in a Democratic Polity

German political life has, in many ways, taken place within and through political parties.[1] Despite recurrent bouts of public hostility toward them, they remain the main link between citizens and the larger polity.[2] Alongside organized interest groups, parties serve as key instruments of political power and influence in all modern polities. Grassroots or popular movements, which are less well organized but typically promote powerful messages on behalf of the disaffected, are also important sources of policy input and potential system change.[3] Political parties, grassroots movements, and organized interest groups are all based in varying degrees in diverse occupational strata, economic self-interest, competing ideologies, religious versus secular beliefs, materialist versus postmaterialist values, and regionalism. This chapter concentrates on political parties—their constitutional basis, financing, socioeconomic and cultural bases, electoral appeals, and development over time. Elections and their outcomes are considered in the following chapter. Organized interest groups and their role in the contemporary German political economy are discussed in chapter 8.

Social Foundations of Political Life

Social structures diverged markedly in western and eastern Germany from the mid-1940s into the early 1990s, but reunification has yielded a national, if not yet fully integrated, community that resembles that of other advanced industrial countries. According to empirical measures of modernity, contemporary Germany is one of the most highly developed countries in the world. Its per capita income in 2004 ranked sixth among comparable nations in Europe and North America, as indicated in Figure 6.1.

Figure 6.1   Per Capita Income, 2004 (in U.S. dollars)

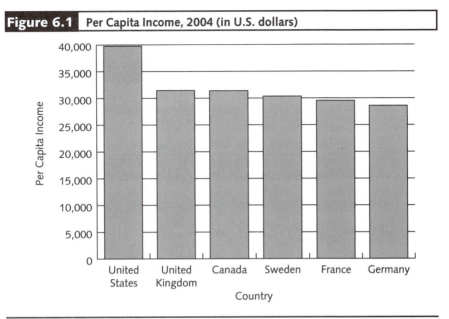

Source: OECD Factbook 2006: Economic, Environmental, and Social Statistics (Paris: OECD, 2006). Available online at http://ocde.p4.sitinternet.com/publications/publications.

A key indicator of Germany's transition to a postindustrial society is change in the composition of the labor force. By 2006 the number of those employed in public and private services had increased to 72.4 percent while the percentage of those engaged in agriculture, forestry, and fishing had fallen to 2.2 percent. Those employed in industry comprised the remaining 25.4 percent.[4] One consequence of these changes is a decline in traditional forms of class voting, as we discuss in the following section.

Religion is another important component of the social foundation of German politics. As shown in chapter 1, a substantial majority of Germans are Christian. Significantly, however, the percentage of Christians within the total population has fallen in tandem with a simultaneous increase in the number of nonaffiliated persons and Muslims. In 1900 fully 98.6 percent of all Germans claimed to be Christian; by mid-2000 the number was 75.8 percent. During the same period, the number of nonreligious Germans increased from 0.2 percent to 17.2 percent. Muslims—not a part of German society in 1900—comprised 4.4 percent of the population in 2000. The number of Jews (1.1 percent in 1900) was dramatically reduced in the course of the Holocaust but has risen to 0.1 percent since reunification. Accompanying these changes has been a shift in the balance between Protestants and Roman Catholics. Whereas in 1900 Protestants outnumbered Catholics by approximately 3:2, by 2000 membership in the two denominations was virtually equal. Projected totals for 2025 indicate basic continuity in most religious groups, except for continuing growth in the number of Muslims (see Table 6.1).

Table 6.1	Religious Adherents in Germany, 1900, 2000, 2025 (in percentages)		
Group	1900	2000	2025 (projected)
Christians	98.5	75.8	73.7
of which Protestant	61.1	37	36.8
of which Roman Catholic	35.7	34.9	34.7
Nonreligious	0.2	17.2	17.6
Muslim	0	4.4	6.2
Jewish	1.1	0.1	0.2
Other	0.2	2.5	2.3

Source: Adapted from David B. Barrett, et al., *World Christian Encyclopedia: A Comparative Survey of Churches and Religions in the Modern World,* 2nd ed. (New York: Oxford University Press, 2001), 299.

Regional Diversity

The regional differentiation in political behavior among the states reflects historically derived patterns of religious and particularist allegiances. Germany north of the Main River is Protestant and votes the Social Democratic Party (SPD), along with parts of southwestern Germany; southern Germany is more heavily Catholic and, along with the lower Rhine area near Cologne, has supported the Christian Democratic Union (CDU) and the Christian Social Union (CSU). It is striking that as of spring 2008, the Left Party has gained seats in four additional states aside from Berlin and the five former East German states, all of which are in northern Germany, suggesting that its electoral base is close to that of the SPD.[5]

For much of postwar Germany's political history, regional frictions, such as those between Prussia and Bavaria, Baden and Württemberg, and local patriotism in the former Hanoverian regions of Lower Saxony, helped shape party allegiances and voting behavior. In the early years of this century, however, and with the exception of the CSU stronghold in Bavaria, almost every German state has seen changes of partisan incumbency.

The employment patterns of the industrial age helped shape partisan allegiances. Social Democrats and, before 1933, Communists were strong in Saxony and the Ruhr industrial area, which is now in North Rhine–Westphalia, and in such urban centers as Hamburg and Berlin. The SPD's postwar strongholds included North Rhine–Westphalia, Hesse, Lower Saxony, Hamburg, Bremen, Brandenburg, and Berlin.

Conservative parties, and especially the CDU after 1945, did well in rural areas and small towns. In the more technology- and service-oriented postmodern economy, however, the states with the highest levels of income and proportion of the national gross domestic product (GDP)—Bavaria and Baden-Württemberg—have supported CDU/CSU candidates, although some of their urban centers, such as Munich and Stuttgart, are dominated by the SPD and, to a lesser extent, the Greens.

"Old Politics" versus "New Politics"

Social class, occupation, and religion constituted the historical basis of what Seymour Martin Lipset and Stein Rokkan termed the "old politics" of social cleavage between Old Left and Old Right political coalitions that emerged out of the transforming ideas of the Enlightenment, industrialization, and the American and French revolutions.[6] Political liberalism became the ideology of middle-class movements, which later became political parties, seeking to achieve constitutionalism and democracy in opposition to privileged and change-resistant groups on the traditional right. Those on the traditional right responded by organizing themselves as Germany's first ideologically self-conscious conservatives. On the left, unions and a spectrum of socialist parties emerged to represent a growing cadre of disenfranchised and politically powerless industrial workers. Catholic and Protestant parties were formed as instruments of social cohesion and political advocacy where religious cleavages were significant. Regional cleavages also served as partial basis for political identity and electoral mobilization. Bavaria, as a large state with a distinctive historical and cultural identity, is a notable example.

"Old politics" dominated the Imperial and Weimar regimes as well as the early years of the Federal Republic and continue to animate political cleavages on many bread and butter issues in contemporary German society. At the same time "new politics" conflicts rooted in postindustrial economic and such social changes as postwar affluence and the maturation of new generations of better educated and informed citizens have taken on immediacy since the mid-1960s. As Russell Dalton observes:

> This *New Politics* dimension [in Germany and other advanced nations] involves conflict over new issues such as environmental quality, alternative lifestyles, minority rights, participation, social equality, and other postmaterial issues. This dimension represents the cleavage between proponents of these issues, the New Left, and citizens who feel threatened by these issues, the New Right.[7]

Contemporary German politics has thus become a complex kaleidoscope involving both "old" and "new" socioeconomic and value cleavages. Class, occupation, region, and, to a lesser extent, religion remain key predictors of electoral choice, but social issues also serve as an important impetus for grassroots organizations and political engagement on the part of citizens and political leaders alike. Muting potentially divisive effects of both "old" and "new" political cleavages, however, is the attainment of a consensual democratic political culture that affirms basic constitutional norms and political practices (discussed in chapter 4).

Political Parties in Historical and Postwar Perspective

Germany's political parties have, in some cases, lengthy histories stretching back to the mid-nineteenth century. Under different names and with varying platforms, these parties largely represented the major class, regional, and religious cleavages in German society.

Until the late twentieth century, party-social links remained strong, giving each party a secure electoral base. An important consequence was the persistence of a conflictual multiparty system that spanned both the Imperial and Weimar regimes (see Table 6.2). The rise of national socialism brought an abrupt end to the multiparty system with the imposition of a single party dictatorship, but after Nazi Germany's unconditional surrender in May 1945 and the advent of the occupation regime competitive parties resurfaced, and while some of these claimed continuity from earlier eras, others were new creations.

Table 6.2	Political Parties in the Imperial and Weimar Eras (on a left-center-right continuum)					
Radical left/ revolutionary	Moderate left/ reformist	Catholic/ reformist	Liberal/ reformist	Liberal/ conservative	Traditional authoritarian	Radical right
		Imperial Germany, 1871–1919				
	SPD, Progressives	Center Party	Constitutional Liberals	National Liberals	Conservatives	
		Weimar Germany, 1919–1933				
KPD	SPD Party	Center Party	Democratic	DVP	NDVP	NSDAP

Source: Compiled by the authors.
Note: KPD = Communist Party of Germany; SPD = Social Democratic Party of Germany; DVP = German People's Party (successor to the National Liberals of the Imperial era); NDVP = National German People's Party (successor to the Conservative Party of the Imperial era); NSDAP = National Socialists.

The Social Democrats

The most consistently democratic and inclusive German party has been the Social Democratic Party of Germany (SPD). Founded in the mid-1870s through an amalgamation of labor and socialist groups, it adopted a seemingly revolutionary Marxist program in 1891. Despite this formal commitment to proletarian revolution, the SPD in practice became a "revisionist" party focused on working within the political system for greater democracy, such as expansion of the suffrage, and for social amelioration. Most of its electoral support was anchored among unionized workers and intellectuals. Under the stress of World War I, the party splintered into several groups.

One of these, representing the overwhelming majority of the old party, took a patriotic if critical stance toward the government; it went on to dominate the immediate postwar and revolutionary regime in 1918–1920.

From among the more radical factions emerged the Communist Party of Germany (KPD). The KPD, like other communist parties, became "Stalinized" in the 1920s and 1930s and had at best a limited, tactical willingness to tolerate democratic politics, as shown by its behavior during the final crisis of the Weimar Republic in 1930–1933.[8]

In postwar Germany, the SPD rejected KPD offers of collaboration and ceased to exit in the Soviet occupation zone, which became the GDR.[9] After early electoral defeats in West Germany, the party formally acknowledged its basically democratic and reformist nature with the adoption of the Bad Godesberg program in 1959.[10] With this step, the SPD abandoned its earlier advocacy of selective nationalization of industry and its equivocal stance toward West German rearmament and participation in the European integration movement. In effect, the SPD became a more moderate "catch-all" party intent on mobilizing as many voters as possible rather than on being dogmatically and ideologically correct. In 1989 and 1998, the Social Democrats "modernized" their program further by incorporating a greater emphasis on international solidarity and security.[11] The SPD has consistently drawn much of its electoral support from among industrial workers, including trade unionists; lower-level white-collar employees; and intellectuals. The post-Godesberg party extended its appeal to many members of the middle class as well.

While it has been in opposition during much of postwar German politics, the SPD has exercised national power during two important intervals. From 1969 until 1982, under Willy Brandt until 1974 and then under Helmut Schmidt, the party fostered domestic social reform and established (see chapter 3) formal ties with the East German regime and détente treaties with the USSR, Poland, and Czechoslovakia through the implementation of its New Eastern Policy. Later, under Gerhard Schröder, the party formed a national coalition with the Greens that governed from 1998 until 2005. The SPD-Green government initiated steps toward controversial economic and social reforms ("Agenda 2010" and "Hartz IV" reforms, discussed in chapter 9) and pursued a more independent German-centered foreign policy for the unified "Berlin Republic" (see chapter 10).

The Greens

The emergence of the Greens (*Die Grünen*) as a state and national force in the 1980s is a prime example of the grassroots mobilization of voters imbued with postmaterialist values and demands for the political system.[12] Tied not to any particular religious, labor, or business groups, the Greens initially presented themselves as an "anti-party" party that affirmed environmental, participatory, feminist, gay-lesbian, and pacifist causes. Under their most prominent leader, Josef (Joschka) Fischer, who served as foreign minister from 1998 to 2005, the Greens at first strove to uphold new and different modes of politics.[13] For example, they separated parliamentary and party position holders and mandated dual-gender party leaderships.

Today the party's principal support comes from younger, better educated, "unconventional" voters, and its advocacy of postmaterialist values positions it slightly to the left of the SPD. Under Fischer's leadership, the so-called realist (*Realo*) wing of the party gradually overcame the fundamentalist (*Fundi*) faction. Perhaps due to their social base, the Greens have had only very limited success in the states of the former GDR.

Post-Communists/The Left

Postcommunists occupy an ideological and electoral space to the left of the more moderate Social Democrats and the Greens. The Communist Party of Germany formed during Germany's transition from the Imperial regime to the Weimar Republic and modeled its principles and many of its early tactics after those of the Communist Party of the Soviet Union. The National Socialists banned the KPD in 1933 and arrested and later executed many of its officials and rank-and-file members. Led by a group of party loyalists who had sought refuge in the Soviet Union during World War II, the KPD reconstituted itself throughout the four occupation zones in 1945; however, it gained political dominance only in the Soviet zone as the Socialist Unity Party of Germany (SED).

East Germany's democratic revolution of 1989–1990 prompted the rise of more moderate leaders; the adoption of a postcommunist, democratic program; and the party's self-reinvention as the Party of Democratic Socialism (PDS).[14] Since unification the PDS has been represented in local and state legislatures in eastern Germany and in the *Bundestag*. In addition, it has tolerated or participated in several state governments in the eastern part of the country. As noted below, since 2005 it has strengthened its position in several former West German states.

During the first postunification decade, the PDS struggled to become more than a regional party of disaffected citizens concentrated in the former GDR, but its inability to become a viable national left-wing force handicapped its leaders' ambition to play such a role. However, it saw an opportunity to overcome this deficit in the rising discontent among Social Democrats and many trade union leaders and members over Chancellor Schröder's economic and social reform policies (see chapter 9). The PDS allied itself with these groups, newly organized in 2005 as the WASG (*die Wahlalternative Arbeit und Soziale Gerechtigkeit*), or the Electoral Alternative for Labor and Social Justice,[15] and the PDS and the WASG worked together in the 2005 *Bundestag* campaign. This electoral collaboration led to a merger consummated, despite some rank-and-file uneasiness in both parties, in June 2007.[16] The star of this process was Oskar Lafontaine. His ascendancy made credible the new party's challenge to the SPD on a national scale, giving it a very well-known if very controversial leader.[17]

The western German potential of the Left Party was highlighted in early 2008 by its electoral victories in three consecutive state elections, in Hesse, Lower Saxony, and Hamburg. (Details are provided in chapter 7.) While local considerations played a part in these particular outcomes, their cumulative impact was to establish the Left Party as part of a national five-party system, at least for the near future.[18]

The Christian Democrats

Among the religiously based parties in Imperial and Weimar Germany, the most important was the Center Party (*Zentrumspartei*), representing the large Catholic minority.[19] Under national socialism the Center "voluntarily" dissolved itself, with a number of party stalwarts such as former lord mayor of Cologne and future chancellor of the Federal Republic Konrad Adenauer retreating into "inner" exile. In 1945 Catholic and Protestant politicians joined hands to form the Christian Democratic Union (CDU) as a "supra-confessional" Christian party designed to transcend historical religious cleavages in Germany. A separate branch of Christian Democracy exists in Bavaria in the form of the Christian Social Union (CSU), which is permanently aligned with the larger CDU in electoral campaigns, parliament, and periodic governments. Both the CDU and the CSU appeal primarily to middle-class voters and social conservatives, especially in Bavaria.

Although the CDU is strongly linked to Catholic voters in historically Catholic regions and has a majority Catholic membership, it has always taken pains to maintain a cross-confessional leadership and public image. From the outset the CDU strongly affirmed Western-style democracy, a socially moderated form of capitalism, anti-communism, and cooperation with the West. As a supra-confessional party, the CDU has striven to represent business, middle-class, and labor interests. A sign of its continuing ties to Catholic social reform doctrines is the party's reluctance to pursue strongly neo-liberal economic policies.

CDU-led coalitions under Konrad Adenauer, who governed as the Federal Republic's first chancellor from 1949 until his retirement in 1963, led West Germany into close political and economic ties with the United States and the countries of Western Europe. By 1957, the Federal Republic had regained most of its sovereignty, established a national defense force (the Bundeswehr), joined NATO, and helped launch the European integration movement. These achievements anticipated by more than a decade the Brandt government's normalization of German relations with Eastern Europe.

The Liberals

Another important player in German coalition politics on both the national and state levels has been the Free Democratic Party (FDP). A postwar merger of the several mutually antagonistic constitutional liberal and national liberal parties of the Imperial and Weimar eras, the FDP has variously embraced a middle course between the two major parties and an ideological position to the right of the Christian Democrats. The party appeals primarily to a solidly upper-middle-class professional voters such as doctors, lawyers, and intellectuals.

A core ideological principle of the party is liberal support of individual rights, including the legal protection of civil liberties. Like the CDU/CSU, the Free Democrats affirm the primacy of private property and a social market economy. But unlike the Christian Democrats, the FDP is avowedly secular in its approach to educational and cultural policy. The party's orientation toward social democracy is similarly ambiguous. While it has generally endorsed SPD social policies, it has strongly resisted early postwar Social Democratic demands for selective nationalization and a more collectivist approach to economic management.

Both a source of strength and weakness is the FDP's highly decentralized organization. The party's founding leaders established this organization as a means to accommodate competing ideological factions (economic conservatives versus social liberals) and regional diversity. Essentially, the party is a federation of state organizations, "each maintaining a degree of well-guarded independence.... The FDP has never sought to be a mass party." [20]

At first a frequent and important coalition partner with the CDU between 1949 and 1965, the FDP later facilitated the first major governmental party change in West Germany by allying with the SPD under Willy Brandt and Helmut Schmidt from 1969 to 1982. It then resumed its role in center-right coalitions under Helmut Kohl (1982–1998) and subsequently has been in opposition on the national level, first to Schröder's Red-Green government (1998–2005) and later the grand coalition of the CDU and SPD (2005–   ).

The Radical Right

A notable difference between the post-1945 party system of the Federal Republic, both before and since unification, and earlier configurations is the absence of a strong authoritarian right-wing movement challenging the democratic order. Of course, this owes something to the ban imposed on Nazi organizations by the occupation powers, but it is noteworthy that extreme rightist parties have not gained entrance into the *Bundestag* in the way that the comparable neo-fascist National Alliance has in Italy and that their presence in state legislatures has usually been of relatively short duration. [21]

Two parties dominate the radical right spectrum of German politics: the National Democratic Party (NPD), which was established in the mid-1960s to affirm "national" values inspired by the Imperial era tradition of authoritarianism, and the *Republikaner* (Republicans), founded in 1983 primarily on an anti-immigration program. Together, the NPD and the Republicans garnered a mere 2 percent of the popular vote in the 2005 *Bundestag* election. Their joint weakness can be attributed to a combination of internal squabbles, leadership incompetence, and to the lessons learned from the excesses of extreme nationalism in the past. [22] The relationship of the NPD to the broader social phenomenon of extreme rightist thought and action is discussed further in chapter 8.

Party Membership and Prospects

German parties have always understood themselves as, and functioned as, mass membership parties. The social bases discussed above provided stable foundations for party loyalty. Thus, one of the most noteworthy recent trends is the steady decline of party membership (see Table 6.3). Among twenty countries surveyed in the late 1990s and early 2000, Germany ranked fifteenth, with a total party membership of 2.93 percent of the electorate.[23] Of the parties currently represented in the Bundestag, only the Greens have gained members since reunification.[24]

Moreover, several of the major parties have an aging membership.[25] More than 40 percent of SPD, CDU, and CSU members are older than forty years of age, whereas the proportion of members younger than twenty-nine years of age is in the single digit range. For the PDS almost 60 percent of its membership is sixty-five years of age or older. (Comparable data for the Left Party were not yet available.) This decline in party memberships has paralleled a slow decline in voter turnout, especially in state, local, and European elections.

These parallel declines have fed into an increasingly volatile electorate. As we note in chapter 7 in our discussion of the 2005 campaign, voters are skeptical that parties will perform as promised; moreover, the old ties of party and social basis have weakened. The slow erosion of working class and organized trade union support for the SPD, which helped produce the demonstrations against Schröder's economic reforms and a sizable defection to the Left Party in the 2005 elections, has coincided with an alienation of "global" sectors of the business class from the more local and traditional

Table 6.3	Party Membership Totals, 1990–2008			
	Year			
Party	1990	1995	2000	2007–2008
CDU	658,411	657,643	616,722	ca. 540,000
CSU	186,198	179,647	178,347	—
SPD	937,697	817,650	734,667	536,655
FDP	178,625	80,431	62,741	ca. 64,000
Greens	41,316	46,410	46,631	44,677 (2006)
PDS/Left Party	280,882	114,940	88,594	71,925

Sources: Oskar Niedermayer, "Entwicklung und Sozialstruktur der Parteimitgliedschaften im ersten Jahrzehnt nach der Vereinigung," *Zeitschrift für Parlamentsfragen,* no. 2 (2001), 435, and ibid, "Parteimitgliedschaften im Jahre 2003," *Zeitschrift für Parlamentsfragen,* no. 2 (2004), 316. For 2004: *Deutscher Bundestag* 16; Wahlperiode, Drucksache 16/1270; party Web sites. For 2006 figures: "Drastischer Mitgliederschwund bei SPD und CDU," *Der Spiegel,* online at www.spiegel.de/politik/deutschland/0.1518.442712.00.html.
Note: — indicates data unavailable for specific party for specific time period.

middle class that formed the basis of CDU support.[26] In this sense the eastern German pattern of weak party identification may be the model for future German politics. While postwar German history has shown the parties' ability to adapt to changing social settings, the older model of a mass party organized in a particular social milieu may no longer serve the polity and may be replaced by a more leadership-centered, media-based, and issue-opportunistic set of parties.

Constitutional Position of Parties

The constitutionally privileged position of political parties owes something to German desires to avoid the weaknesses of the Weimar Republic. The abuse of instruments of direct participation, such as referenda, in the final Weimar years and under the Nazi regime, led the founders of West Germany's political system to seek to channel democratic activism through party organizations. The role that parties play in political life, and the rules under which they operate, are therefore anchored in the German constitutional and legal framework.

The Basic Law states in Article 21 that "parties contribute to forming the political will of the people."[27] While Germany's parties, unlike political parties in the United States or Great Britain, have a formal constitutionally defined role to play, with these opportunities come constraints. Although Article 21 declares that party formation is "free," it immediately stipulates that parties' internal structure must conform to democratic fundamentals, and that parties must make public the source and disbursement of their means and assets.[28] Moreover, a party may be outlawed if its declared goals or the behavior of its followers are found to be harmful to the "free democratic basic order" or the existence of the Federal Republic.

This judgment is left to the Federal Constitutional Court, which, upon application by the federal government, may declare a party unconstitutional. Such judgments were issued twice in the first postwar decade: the neo-Nazi Socialist Reich Party (*Sozialistische Reichspartei, or SRP*) was banned in 1952 and the Communist Party of Germany (KPD) was banned in 1956.[29] During Brandt's new Eastern policies (*neue Ostpolitik*), the government accepted the good faith assurances of a newly founded "German Communist Party" (DKP) that it would be loyal to the Basic Law. Largely for foreign policy reasons, the government thereupon did not pursue legal action against it.

Since then there has been only one application to the court to have a party banned. In the wake of rightist violence in 2000, the Schröder government and both houses of the parliament asked the court to ban the National Democratic Party. Within a year, however, the government's case was seriously compromised when it was revealed that much of the evidence against the NPD had been gathered by paid government agents. In March 2003, the court dismissed the case, and both the federal and Bavarian authorities, which had participated in bringing the case, decided against pursuing the case further.[30]

Party Financing

An important aspect of the quasiconstitutional position of political parties is the system of partial public financing.[31] There is financing because the parties are mandated to perform a public function; it is *partial* because the parties are said to represent groupings of citizens. (The other major sources of revenue are membership dues and political contributions.) The sums are allocated according to how well a party is anchored in German society and thus able to carry out its constitutional functions; this in turn is judged according to three criteria:

- How well the party performed in state, national, and European elections;

- Total membership dues; and

- The sum of contribution.

Parties receiving at least 0.5 percent of the valid votes cast for the party lists in the most recent European or *Bundestag* election (1 percent in a state election) are entitled to funding. Parties that qualify earn €0.70 for each vote cast and €0.38 for every euro received from an individual or corporate entity ("natural person"), up to a limit of €3,300.[32] Because the total amount to be thus expended is fixed by law, currently at €133 million, the amount that parties actually receive may be prorated downward. A party's public funding may also be lessened to ensure that this funding is truly *partial*—that it does not exceed the party's own income from dues and contributions (see Table 6.4).

This system of party financing allows smaller parties, including those that do not reach the 5 percent threshold for *Bundestag* representation, to survive and organize. A number of extreme right-wing parties, of which the NPD is a current example, have benefited from these provisions. Furthermore, this three-fold source of income is not distributed evenly to party

Table 6.4	Sources of Party Finances, 2004 (percentages)		
Party	Public funds	Members' dues	Contributions
CDU	28.8	28.7	18.3
CSU	29.6	25.4	15.8
SPD	27.7	29.73	7.7
FDP	30.7	20.5	29.7
Greens	38.3	21.3	14.3
PDS/Left Party	37.5	44.2	9.5

Source: Adapted from *Deutscher Bundestag* 16; Wahlperiode, Drucksache 16/1270.

organizations at the national level as compared to those at the state and local levels. The former are financed largely through these public subsidies; the latter are financed by dues and donations. This gives party organizations an autonomous source of income, as well as an incentive to recruit members.[33] And while all parties receive income from the three sources listed above, it is notable that the party most directly associated with business interests, the FDP, derives the largest percentage of income from public funds. Conversely, almost half of the PDS/Left Party's income comes from members' dues.

With the funding comes an obligation to report both income and expenditures. Perhaps for this reason, even the major parties receive surprisingly few large (more than €10,000) single-source donations; the CDU, for example, listed only five in 2004 (see Table 6.5). Much as in the United States, some large contributors spread their largesse across the party spectrum: the Deutsche Bank, for example, gave comparable sums to the CDU, the SPD, and the FDP.

The reporting requirements indirectly produced the largest postwar scandal in German politics; the "secret accounts" affair rocked the CDU in 1999–2001.[34] CDU leaders at the national and state levels had conspired to hide large cash contributions through a system of secret and dummy bank accounts in several countries. That this system was organized and supervised over many years by the long-serving "chancellor of unification," Helmut Kohl, seemed truly shocking. The main purpose of this skullduggery seems to have been to strengthen Kohl's personal control over the CDU. After

Table 6.5 Major Contributions by Party, 2004

Party	Single contributions of more than €3,300 each, greater than €100,000	Total of single contributions, each more than €3,300
CDU	Deutsche Bank €325,000 Altana AG €250,000 Südwest Metall €200,000 Verband der chemischen Industrie €112,500 Christoph Kahl €101,400	€4,620,962
CSU	Verband der bayerischen Metall und Elektroindustrie €370,000	€1,164,578
SPD	Deutsche Bank >€100,000 DaimlerChrysler €150,000	€6,060,893
Greens	None	€1,932,853
FDP	Deutsche Bank €100,000 Victor's Bau und Werk €100,000	€1,089,204
PDS/Left Party	None	€617,599

Sources: Adapted from Deutscher Bundestag 16; Wahlperiode, Drucksache 16/1270 and party Web sites.

several probes by both public prosecutors and a commission of the *Bundestag*, the case was settled with the levying of fines against the CDU and several party officials, including Kohl. As part of a plea bargain, Kohl was not required to reveal the names of the contributors to these funds.[35]

This complex affair of intertwined personal, political, and financial scheming had a paradoxical effect on German politics. The immediate political consequences were felt by the CDU and Kohl. The CDU, which had recorded a series of state election victories after its loss in the 1998 national election, suffered a two-year swoon in support. The party also had to pay back €21 million in public funding. Kohl's reputation and influence were permanently overshadowed by his actions, not least of which was his stubborn refusal to give a full accounting.[36] Moreover, because so many senior CDU officials were involved in the scandal, a relatively untried but also untouched figure, Angela Merkel, could become party leader and eventually chancellor of Germany in 2005.

The longer-term consequences of this affair are harder to determine. Certainly, the strong showing by the CDU and CSU in the 2002 national election signaled that the CDU had not suffered lasting damage. Perhaps because no evidence could be found of policy choices influenced by these payments, public anger soon dissipated. That Kohl would have constructed such an elaborate and secret scheme perhaps demonstrates how important it is for a German chancellor to gain control over a party divided along regional, policy, personal, and "level of government" lines.

The Electoral System

The effects of both "old" and "new" politics are filtered through an electoral system that combines the Anglo-American tradition of direct candidate selection and the Continental practice of proportional representation. In *Bundestag* elections, Germany is divided into 299 electoral districts, each of which represents approximately 180,000 voters. Within each state half of the deputies are directly elected by plurality vote in a given constituency; the other half are chosen on the basis of a party's proportional strength in that state.[37] German voters eighteen years of age and older thus cast two ballots: the first is for the direct election of one representative from each of the constituencies, and the second is for the election of delegates drawn from state lists of party candidates.[38] The second ballot is the more important of the two, as the relative percentage of a party's popular support determines the total number of parliamentary seats it is entitled to win in a given state. Seats won by candidates on the first ballot are deducted from the number of seats allocated to parties on the second (proportional) ballot. If, in any given state, the number of seats a party wins on the first ballot exceeds its proportional share of votes on the second, the party is accorded "excess mandates" (*Überhangsmandate*). In 2005, no less than sixteen such seats were added to

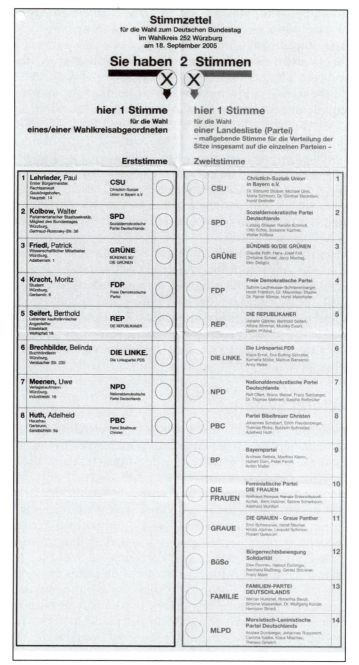

This German ballot has the constituency vote on the left and the party vote on the right, allowing Germans to easily vote a split ticket.

the *Bundestag*. Thanks to the number of excess mandates, the nominal size of the Bundestag thus increased from 598 deputies to 614.

Voters may choose to split their votes between the two ballots, favoring a candidate from one party on the first ballot and another party's list of candidates on the second. This practice of so-called strategic voting allows electors to support two parties at the same time; for example, in the hope that two parties together can garner enough strength to form a coalition. This option can marginally distort electoral outcomes, as discussed in chapter 7.

A second important feature of the German electoral system is the requirement that a party must receive at least 5 percent of the vote on the second ballot to gain proportional representation in the *Bundestag* or a given Landtag. Alternatively, a party can gain representation in the *Bundestag* if its candidates win three constituency seats on the first ballot. If a party wins three seats in this fashion, it will receive as many seats as its percentage of list votes would earn it, even if that is lower than 5 percent. This latter provision has twice (1994, 2002) kept the PDS in the *Bundestag*. (Any candidate getting a plurality of votes cast in a direct district wins that seat.) Except for three special cases in 1972, 1983, and 2005, which are discussed in chapter 7, each *Bundestag* is elected for a four-year term. This holds true for most of the state legislatures as well, although some states have gone to five-year terms.

To understand how these German political parties compete for power through elections and coalition building within the institutional and historical framework described above, we now turn in chapter 7 to consider electoral outcomes and trends.

7

Election Outcomes and Voting Trends

 our election eras characterize postwar German politics: (1) an initial period from 1949 until 1980 in which the Christian Democratic Union (CDU) and the Christian Social Union (CSU), Social Democratic Party (SPD), and Free Democratic Party (FDP) established virtual electoral hegemony in the "old" Federal Republic; (2) the emergence of the Greens as a fourth national party between 1980 and 1990, which triggered the transformation of West Germany's "two and a half party" system into a more fluid multiparty system; (3) the long-term monopolization of power by the Socialist Unity Party (SED) in the former GDR, which abruptly ended with competitive elections in March 1990 that resulted in an electoral victory by anti-communist forces; and (4) a phase of continuing electoral flux in unified Germany that began in the early 1990s and continues into the present. We briefly explore the first of these phases before concentrating on the 2005 *Bundestag* election and its immediate aftermath as a prism for the ongoing transformation of Germany's political parties and the country's multiparty system.

The Emergence of a Two and a Half Party System

Electoral outcomes diverged immediately in 1945 from the country's tortured past and from postwar developments in the Soviet zone of occupation (later the German Democratic Republic, or GDR). In contrast to the highly fragmented and increasingly polarized party systems of the Imperial and Weimar eras, the CDU/CSU, SPD, and FDP swiftly established themselves as dominant mainstream parties during the formative decades of the Federal Republic. As shown in Table 7.1, the three parties increased their aggregate electoral strength in *Bundestag* elections from 72.1 percent in 1949 to fully

Table 7.1	National Elections in West Germany, 1949–1980 (in percentage of party support on the second ballot)					
Year	KPD	SPD	FDP	CDU/CSU	Aggregate CDU/CSU, FDP, SPD Support	Other
1949	5.7	29.2	11.9	31	72.1	22.2
1953	2.3	28.8	9.5	45.2	83.5	14.2
1957	—	31.8	7.7	50.2	89.7	10.3
1961	—	36.3	12.8	45.3	94.4	5.6
1965	—	39.3	9.5	47.6	96.4	3.6
1969	—	42.7	5.8	46.1	94.6	5.4*
1972	—	45.8	8.4	44.9	99.1	0.9
1976	—	42.6	7.9	48.6	99.1	0.9
1980	—	42.9	10.6	44.5	98	2

Source: Forschungsgruppe Wahlen e. V.: *Wahlergebnisse in Deutschland 1946–2006*, 8th ed. (Mannheim: Forschungsgruppe Wahlen, 2006), 102.
*Includes 4.3 percent support for the right-wing National Democratic Party (NPD).
Note: — indicates that data unavailable for a specific party for specific years.

99.1 percent in 1972 and 1976. Their joint support declined only marginally in the 1980 election.

Of the three mainstream parties, the Christian Democrats and the Social Democrats retained a formidable electoral edge over the Free Democrats, but the FDP's support was usually essential to the formation of national coalition governments with one or the other of the dominant parties. The exception was the formation of a CDU/CSU–SPD grand coalition in 1966, which governed until 1969. Aggregate support for the mainstream parties began to ebb toward the end of this phase with the simultaneous advent of the Greens and new splinter parties on the left and right.

A number of factors explain the long-term trend toward the maintenance of a two and a half party system into the early 1980s. Among them were the emergence of an elite–mass democratic political culture; the disappearance or absence of alternative electoral appeals on both the radical right and left, which were reinforced by rulings by the Federal Constitutional Court against anti-democratic parties in 1952 and 1956; and West Germany's unprecedented economic prosperity. The latter achievement facilitated the social integration of millions of expellees and refugees from Central Europe (including the GDR) and subsequently undercut the electoral appeal of such special interest groups as a Refugee Party that enjoyed a temporary surge of support in the 1950s and early 1960s.[1]

Advent of the Greens

Germany's Greens appeared during the early 1980s in tandem with the advent of anti-establishment environmentalist movements in Scandinavia, Britain, France, Italy, and eventually the United States. As previously mentioned, the Greens initially presented themselves as an "anti-party" party in opposition to the policies of the mainstream parties. Specifically, they advocated strict governmental measures to protect the natural environment against, for example, industrial pollution. They were also opposed to the domestic use of atomic energy and the deployment of nuclear weapons on German soil. A distinctive feature of the early West German Green movement was its underground link to youth groups surreptitiously advocating pacifism and social reform under the discreet umbrella of Evangelical Protestant churches in the GDR.

The Greens received a scant 1.5 percent in the 1980 *Bundestag* election, but to the surprise of mainstream party leaders and government officials, the party broke through the 5 percent electoral barrier three years later by garnering 5.6 percent of the vote to win 27 out of 497 seats in the 1983–1987 *Bundestag*. In the 1987 election—the last one confined to the "old" Federal Republic—the Greens confirmed their status as Germany's fourth national party (see Figure 7.1). Their electoral gains were primarily at the expense of the SPD. A counterpart to the West German Greens emerged in 1990 in the GDR in the form of "Alliance 90" (*Bündnis 90*). The two parties eventually merged in January 1993.[2]

The rise of the Greens proved a significant step in the transformation of western Germany's previous two and a half party system into a multiparty system. The party's support grew from 8.4 percent in West Germany in 1987, dropped to 5.1 percent in the all-German election of 1990 (with most of its strength concentrated in the eastern states), reached a peak of 8.7 percent in 2002, and slid slightly to 8.1 percent in 2005.

Figure 7.1	National Elections in West Germany, 1983 and 1987 (in percentage of party support on the second ballot)

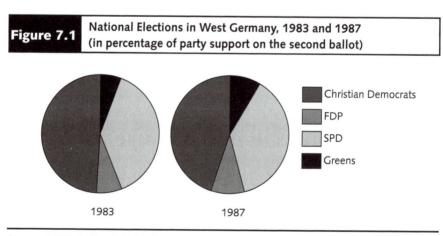

Christian Democrats

FDP

SPD

Greens

1983   1987

Source: *OECD Factbook 2006: Economic, Environmental, and Social Statistics* (Paris: OECD, 2006). Available online at http://ocde.p4.sitinternet.com/publications/publications.

Table 7.2	East German Election Results, March 1990		
Party	Votes	Percentage of popular support	Seats
CDU	4,719,598	40.8	163
SPD	2,525,534	21.9	88
PDS	1,892,381	16.4	66
DSU	727,730	6.3	25
Bündnis 90	336,074	2.9	12
LPD	608,935	5.3	21
DBD	251,226	2.2	9
Grüne	226,935	2	8
DA	106,146	0.9	4
NDPD	44,292	0.4	2
BDF	38,192	0.3	1
VL	20,342	0.2	1

Source: Forschungsgruppe Wahlen e. V.: *Wahlergebnisse in Deutschland 1946–2006,* 8th ed. (Mannheim: Forschungsgruppe Wahlen, 2006), 118.
Note: CDU = Christian Democrats; SPD = Social Democrats; PDS = Party of Democratic Socialism (successor to the Socialist Unity Party, or SED); DSU = German Social Union (the approximate equivalent to the CSU in western Germany); *Bündnis* 90 (Alliance 90); LPD = Liberal Democratic Party of Germany (equivalent to the west German Free Democrats); *Grüne* (Greens); DA = Democratic Departure; NDPD = National Democratic Party of Germany; DBD = Democratic Farmers Party of Germany; BFD = Union of Free Democrats; VL = United Left.

Elections in the GDR

Early local elections in the Soviet zone of occupation were competitive, but the failure of the reconstituted KPD to win major electoral support prompted Soviet and East German Communist leaders to force a merger of the KPD and the zonal SPD in 1946 to create the Socialist Unity Party. The SED was transformed into a Soviet-style ruling party by 1949–1950; it later enjoyed a constitutionally guaranteed leadership role in the GDR. The use of a "unity list" of SED-approved candidates, including those from trade union and farmer organizations as well as SED-controlled "Bloc parties," ensured the SED's monopoly of power during the forty years of the GDR's existence.

Events accompanying Germany's "rush to unity" in 1989–1990 (recounted in chapter 2) spelled an abrupt end to the SED's ascendancy and the existence of the GDR itself. Competitive elections to the East German parliament (the *Volkskammer*) in March 1990 resulted in a resounding victory by pro-democratic parties, with a CDU-led "Alliance for Germany" winning a parliamentary majority (see Table 7.2). The resulting CDU-SPD coalition government negotiated German reunification with the West German government later that year.

Electoral Flux in Unified Germany

Unification in October 1990 established the constitutional and territorial basis for the resumption of free national elections in Germany for the first time since November 1932. Seven parties dominated the campaign: the CDU/CSU, the FDP, the SPD, separate West and East German Greens, and the Party of Democratic Socialism (PDS, a reconstituted SED). For this election only, the Federal Constitutional Court ruled that the 5 percent threshold would apply separately in the eastern and western states. The governing CDU/CSU–FDP parties in the "old" Federal Republic waged a relentlessly upbeat campaign, projecting rapid economic prosperity throughout the eastern states. In contrast, the SPD issued bleak warnings about the unanticipated economic and social costs of unification—but the optimists prevailed. Together, the Christian Democrats and Free Democrats mobilized 54.8 percent of the popular vote to form an all-German coalition government under Chancellor Helmut Kohl. Social Democratic strength fell to its lowest level in decades while the PDS achieved entry into the all-German *Bundestag* with seventeen seats despite its dismal 2.4 percent national support because it surpassed the 5 percent threshold in the eastern states.[3] (See Table 7.3.)

The Christian Democrats and Free Democrats renewed their national mandate four years later, although by a significantly reduced margin of 4.7 percent over the combined SPD/Greens total, as the high costs of unification indeed became palpable in the form of surging unemployment in the east and higher taxes in the west. (See chapter 9.) All three of the opposition parties—the SPD, the Greens, and the PDS—scored small but significant gains. Subsequent elections underscored continuing flux in the multiparty system. Salient trends have included a steady erosion of popular support for the Christian Democrats through the 2005 election, coupled with initial increases in support for the SPD through 1998, for the Greens through 2002, and for the FDP in 2002 and 2005. Another significant trend is a resurgence of strength for the post-communists, primarily in eastern Germany but gradually extending into parts of western Germany as well. Also noteworthy in light of Germany's past is continued public resistance to the electoral appeals of the radical right.

Table 7.3	National Election Results, 1990–2005 (percentages)					
Year	PDS/Left Party	Greens	SPD	FDP	CDU/CSU	Other*
1990	2.4	5.1	33.5	11	43.8	2.4
1994	4.4	7.3	36.4	6.9	41.5	1.9
1998	5.1	6.7	40.9	6.2	35.2	2.1
2002	4	8.6	38.5	7.4	38.5	3
2005	8.7	8.1	34.2	9.8	35.2	3.8

Source: Forschungsgruppe Wahlen e. V.: *Wahlergebnisse in Deutschland 1946–2006,* 8th ed. (Mannheim: Forschungsgruppe Wahlen, 2006), 103.
*Includes support for the radical right (represented by the *Republikaner* (Republicans) and the National Democratic Party (NPD), which together won 1 percent in 2002 and 2.2 in 2005.

Steps toward an Early Election

On the evening of May 6, 2005, on the night of state elections in Germany's most populous state—North Rhine–Westphalia—a political drama began that was to last until the following November. It would mark the end of the SPD-Green government inaugurated in 1998 and the beginning of postwar Germany's second grand coalition (the first being the Kiesinger-Brandt government of 1966–1969). However, the events of these months marked more than a sudden, unexpected transition from one governing coalition to another. At almost every step, they demonstrated important truths about the German electoral, party, and constitutional systems. The unexpected federal election of 2005 can thus serve as a prism reflecting many facets of contemporary German politics.

In the months leading up to that May evening, Chancellor Gerhard Schröder had seen his social and economic reform policies lead to defections from his own party and to a series of state election defeats, which gave the opposition a commanding margin in the upper house, the *Bundesrat*. The North Rhine–Westphalia election returns seem to have convinced him and his advisers that their political weakness in the remaining sixteen months in office would lead both to the defeat of their program and certainly to a loss in the federal election scheduled for 2006.[4] Schröder viewed these developments as calling into question the political basis for his policies, so his decision to call for new elections in 2005 was motivated by a perceived need to buttress his government.

Public opinion polls revealed substantial popular satisfaction with the prospect of early elections. Polls taken in mid-July showed that 75 percent of respondents approved of early elections and a similar majority approved of them *in principle*. Almost three-quarters of respondents accepted Schröder's argument that he lacked a "reliable majority" in the *Bundestag* for his policies.[5] The leaders of the main opposition parties (the CDU/CSU and the FDP) were surprised by the decision but felt confident that, given their electoral successes and poll standings, their anticipated victory would simply come a year early. The PDS and its new leftist ally in the West, the WASG (Electoral Alternative for Labor and Social Justice Party), anticipated that elections born out of discontent with Schröder's policies would yield enough votes to propel their joint electoral list well over the 5 percent hurdle.

Schröder still needed formal authorization from the federal president and the Federal Constitutional Court, since according to the Basic Law the *Bundestag* does not have the right to dissolve itself. A dissolution proposed by the chancellor must be approved by the president; in the last two instances of dissolution, the approval of the Constitutional Court was secured as well. This mistrust of the representative heart of the government is one of the "lessons" of Weimar. In practice, this has meant that a politically deadlocked government, or one that feels it needs a renewed democratic legitimation, must bring about early elections through an elaborate constitutional charade. In this instance, the procedural restrictions, designed to prevent rapid institutional change, were replaced by a presumed political consensus, and Schröder got his early elections.

President Horst Köhler awaited the action of the *Bundestag* in voting on confidence in the chancellor. With the general acceptance of new elections noted above, the government and legislature engaged in a shadow dance of formal actions. The chancellor went through the formalities and scheduled a vote of no confidence for July 1. By prearrangement, the needed majority for a vote of confidence—301 votes of 603 total—was not attained: 151 of 595 deputies voted yes, 296 voted no, and 148 abstained. Thereupon Schröder formally requested that President Köhler dissolve the *Bundestag* and call new elections.[6]

Köhler took three weeks to reach his decision, having meanwhile sent the government a series of questions as to the rationale for elections. As had been widely expected, he approved Schröder's request.[7] His reasoning demonstrated the weight he gave to Schröder's political arguments. The president offered a litany of social and economic problems (some of which, such as too few children [*Wir haben zu wenig Kinder*], would hardly be solved by early elections), and argued that Germany needed a new and forceful government. The 1983 decision of the Constitutional Court, that the president should accept the chancellor's political judgment, barring a plausible alternative interpretation, guided Köhler in his view that the interests of the German people would be best served by new elections.[8]

Not surprisingly, the issue was then appealed to the Federal Constitutional Court. The court announced its decision a scant three weeks before the date (September 18) that President Köhler had set for the elections.[9] By a 7-1 vote, it accepted Schröder's arguments as to his incapacity to govern.[10] Although calls for constitutional revision to give the *Bundestag* a power of self-dissolution were heard in the summer of 2005, political activity on this topic faded away after the election itself.[11]

Seen in this perspective of formality and procedure, the Basic Law was written so as to present obstacles to dissolution of the lower house of the legislature.[12] Indeed, throughout the existence of both the "old" and expanded Federal Republic, only three attempts, including Schröder's, have been made to engineer an early dissolution. The first was arranged in 1972 by Willy Brandt and the second in 1982 by Helmut Kohl. Kohl's initiative was the more controversial and resulted in the important judgment of the Constitutional Court mentioned above. All were political moves designed to strengthen the incumbent executive, and while the circumstances surrounding them were quite different, all relied on the same constitutional foundation.

Brandt's decision was brought about by the crumbling of his narrow parliamentary majority. He had survived a "constructive vote of no confidence," that is, an attempt to replace him as chancellor with CDU leader Rainer

Barzel, by only two votes. From Brandt's perspective, only a new mandate from the electorate could prolong his government and legitimate his new *Ostpolitik;* the opposition, seeing Brandt's weakness, hoped to come to power sooner rather than waiting for the end the government's term in office.

Similarly, Kohl's decision to seek an early dissolution was designed to legitimate and stabilize his newly formed coalition with the FDP. The end of the Schmidt-Genscher (SPD/FDP) government had taken place in the fall of 1982 despite calls for an early dissolution through a successful constructive vote of no confidence. Kohl's election was the result of the defection of the Free Democrats from the governing coalition, despite the party's prior pledge to continue the coalition for a full term. Indeed, the FDP leadership's decision to support Kohl caused a severe internal party crisis; at the decisive meeting of the FDP's *Bundestag* caucus, just under two-thirds of the deputies supported the leadership, and several prominent opponents of this policy later defected to the SPD. Considerable public opposition to a seemingly arbitrary change in government developed. The incumbent federal president, Karl Carstens, gave his approval only with considerable misgivings and after a lengthy study period. The first and thus far only successful use of the constructive vote of no confidence to replace a chancellor showed that this maneuver, while of unimpeachable constitutional legitimacy, no longer corresponded to the public's understanding of its role in legitimating German governments.[13]

Two decades later, the crisis of 2005 illustrated a growing divergence between the formal and informal constitutional order in the Federal Republic, between what Walter Bagehot famously called its "dignified" and "efficient" parts. As we have noted in reference to the Basic Law and Germany's political structures in general, the perceived instability of Weimar's governing institutions led the creators of the Federal Republic to emphasize continuity and stability in important institutions above such alternate values as flexibility and responsiveness. In addition, the decision to arrange an early election in 2005 had political consequences as well as important constitutional impact.[14] Schröder's successful gamble on early elections being approved by political leaders across his party's ideological spectrum, and by substantial majorities in public opinion, meant that, as one observer put it, such a step "is permitted if it is accepted" [*Erlaubt ist, was akzeptiert wird*].[15]

The 2005 Campaign

If the calling of early elections illuminated the changing role of constitutional provisions and institutions in German politics, the brief campaign that followed highlighted both continuing and changing trends in party and electoral affairs. Among those most important for Germany's political future were:

- A strengthened trend toward a more varied and multiple party system and a continuation of the move away from the three-party stability of the 1960–1980 period;

- A growing trend toward a more volatile and less fathomable electorate, which resulted in less reliable polling;

- Continued growth in the importance of nationalized and personalized campaigns, despite the institutional strength of the parties and the continued stated allegiance of voters to them;

- The overwhelming importance of economic issues, especially unemployment, and the widespread despair by voters that neither major (or, for that matter, any minor) party had a promising solution;

- A continuing regional cleavage in electoral preferences between the eastern and western states; and

- A decline in the voting gender gap compared with West German electoral patterns in the 1950s and 1960s.

The campaign's starting point was the deep-seated popular wish for a change in government. Political barometer polls from the previous three federal elections showed these responses to the classic time-for-a-change question, asked a week before each election (see Figure 7.2).[16]

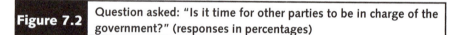

| Figure 7.2 | Question asked: "Is it time for other parties to be in charge of the government?" (responses in percentages) |

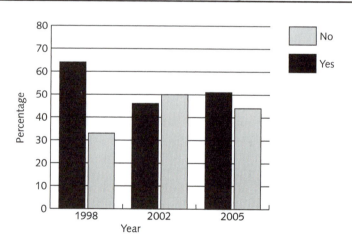

Sources: Mathias Jung and Andrea Wolf, "Der Wählerwille erzwingt die große Koalition," *Aus Politik und Zeitgeschichte* B51–52 (December 19, 2005); Beilage zur Wochenzeitung *Das Parlament:* 3–12; and *Politbarometer* surveys.

Doubts about the CDU's economic program—22 percent of those polled thought neither the CDU nor the SPD would create more jobs[17]—were exacerbated by the party's choice of Angela Merkel as its chancellor candidate and *her* choice for her economic policy adviser.[18] These doubts regarding Merkel's leadership and plans were spotlighted in the one televised debate held just two weeks before the election. There was general agreement that Schröder had "won" the debate; of those who had seen it, the percentage favoring Schröder as chancellor rose from 52 percent to 55 percent.[19] Yet despite such handicaps, Merkel had one great advantage: when voters were asked whether their vote would be based on choice of party or of chancellorship candidate, 70 percent answered "party."[20]

The pivotal issue of job creation, and the effects of the Schröder government's efforts to reform the labor market (see the discussion of economic policies, especially Agenda 2010, in chapter 9), also favored the creation of a party that had a realistic chance to become a nationwide party to the left of the SPD. The PDS had sought for many years, but with little success, to establish a serious political presence in the western states. What made an alliance with the WASG so attractive was that it was different from former West German leftist groupings in that it appealed to social democrats and trade unionists disenchanted with Schröder's policies. In 2002, the PDS dropped just enough below the 5 percent barrier to reduce its parliamentary representation to two members. Now it saw a chance to redress its losses.

The PDS had already announced that its long-time media and political star, Gregor Gysi, would head its ticket in the election. The WASG offered a chance to present another powerful personality—Oskar Lafontaine. Lafontaine had been the SPD chancellorship candidate in 1990, party chair from 1995 to 1999, and finance minister in the first year of Schröder's government, but had become increasingly estranged from his party and from Schröder personally.[21] Reacting to the time pressures of early elections, the PDS and WASG agreed to a joint list of candidates, pending a possible future unification of the parties. Lafontaine and Gysi headed the party lists for North Rhine–Westphalia and Berlin, respectively.[22] A telling example of how far the PDS would go to achieve its long desired breakthrough in the western states is that it agreed to abandon the name it had borne since 1990 and restyle itself as the *Left Party* (*Die Linken*), although it had ten times the party membership of the WASG. As a concession to its own unhappy members, the PDS allowed state-level parties to add "PDS" to the party name.[23] The emergence of the Left Party had an important effect on the electoral outcome, to which we now turn.

Election Outcomes

A decisive feature of the 2005 election was the decrease in the relative share of the vote garnered by the two major parties, CDU/CSU and SPD. Between them they polled only 53.1 percent of *eligible* voters (69.4 percent of votes cast), which was the lowest combined total since the first West German election in 1949. This continued a thirty-year downward trend from the 91.2 percent these parties had reached in 1976.[24] A contributing factor to the CDU's decline was the fact that approximately two out of five voters split their votes, choosing the CDU on the first ballot but supporting the FDP on the second. Ludger Helms has argued that "[t]he basis for this strategic behavior was a widespread fear among supporters of a CDU/CSU–FDP governing coalition that the new government might be a grand coalition (CDU/CSU–SPD) that could be kept at bay only by a strong performance by the FDP."[25]

Accordingly, the sixteenth *Bundestag* elected in 2005 consisted of five firmly established party groups—more than two hundred deputies each for the SPD and CDU/CSU and, for the three parties that form the opposition to the grand coalition: sixty-one seats for the FDP, fifty-four seats for the Left Party/PDS, and fifty-one seats for the Greens.

The 2005 election also revealed a decline in electoral turnout to 77.7 percent, the lowest level in any federal election to date. The increasing volatility of the electorate was also reflected in the shrinking social bases of the major parties. Voters who identified themselves as strongly Catholic voted in fewer numbers for the CDU/CSU than in previous elections, just as workers who are trade union members did in supporting the SPD. Women also voted in fewer numbers for the Christian Democrats than in past elections, dividing their vote with men (each at 35 percent) for the CDU/CSU while according the SPD a slightly higher percentage than men (35 percent and 33 percent, respectively). Women also voted slightly more for the Greens than did men but less than men did for the FDP and the Left/PDS.[26]

The trends described above raised difficult questions for public opinion research and made polling results more questionable. "What is wrong with survey research?" ("*Was ist los mit der Demoskopie?*") cried a high CDU official as the early results came in on election day.[27] Indeed, predictions of a CDU/CSU–FDP victory were reflected in polls from the spring right up to the eve of the election. But the median prediction of the five leading polls turned out to be wrong, especially in the case of the CDU/CSU (see Table 7.4).

Table 7.4 Polling Predictions and Electoral Results (percentages)		
Parties	Median predictions	Actual results
CDU/CSU	41.6	35.2
SPD	33.3	34.3
FDP	7.1	8.1
Greens	7.1	8.1
PDS/Left Party	7.9	8.7
Others	3	3.8

Sources: Polling data from Institut für Demoskopie Allensbach, Emnid, Forsa, Forschungsgruppe Wahlen, GMS, Infratest-dimap; assembled by authors.

Technical issues of survey research aside, the consensus explanation for these discrepancies has been that many voters were cross-pressured by conflicting desires and made up their minds at the last minute.[28] Although most voters wished for a change of government, many lost confidence in Merkel's ability to solve the unemployment problem; moreover, public wrangling within the CDU and CSU leaderships, especially over Merkel's handling of the campaign, allowed many voters to prefer Schröder. Thus Merkel's once overwhelming lead in the polls shrank steadily during the campaign, although not as much as the results revealed. Once again, the campaign itself proved important to the outcome.

If the SPD had retained power in coalition with the Greens by a very small margin in 2002, it now lost the leading role in the government by even less. One key to the small but momentous shift in voter support for the SPD and CDU/CSU between the 2002 and 2005 elections can be found in the relative gains and losses between these parties—what Germans picturesquely call *Wählerwanderung,* or voter migration (see Table 7.5).

These numbers suggest that the SPD would have retained office had the Left Party's vote been roughly equal to the PDS's previous best showing (5.1 percent in 1998). Although in the end its total fell far short of the euphoric predictions of the early summer, the substantial 8.7 percent that the Left Party did achieve cost the SPD dearly. The Left Party received almost two and a quarter million votes more than the PDS had in 2002. Where did these voters come from? Various sources suggest that the Left Party garnered votes in parts of the electorate that had previously been difficult for the PDS to reach, including:

- Unemployed workers in western Germany,

- Voters in thinly settled regions, and

- Voters with low education levels.

In short, the addition of WASG-oriented supporters to those of the PDS allowed the Left Party to broaden its social and geographic base.[29]

Table 7.5	**Voter Migration, 2002–2005 Elections**	
SPD votes lost to ...	CDU/CSU votes lost to ...	CDU/CSU votes gained from ...
Left Party: 970,000 CDU/CSU: 620,000 Greens: 140,000 FDP: 120,000 Others: 140,000 Nonvoters: 370,000	FDP: 1,110,000 Left Party: 290,000 Others: 170,000 Nonvoters: 640,000	SPD: 620,000 Greens: 130,000

Source: Das Parlament, vol. 57, no. 38/39 (September 23, 2005): 3.

Box 7.1

German Parties and Their Political Colors

German political parties (like those in many other European countries) are identified by colors. The practice goes back to the nineteenth century, with the assignment of red and black to revolutionary and reactionary forces—think of Stendhal's
novel *The Red and the Black!* Political observers and headline writers are thus
provided with a convenient color code.

Parties and their...	... colors
CDU/CSU	Black
SPD	Red
FDP	Yellow
Greens	Green
Left Party	Red

The CDU/CSU-FDP coalition under Helmut Kohl (1982–1998) was "black/yel-
low"; the SPD/Green coalition under Schröoder (1998–2005) was "red/green"; a
possible SPD/Green/FDP coalition, which would have the colors red, green, and
yellow is often called a "traffic light" (*Ampel*) coalition. There has been talk recently of a coalition in which the Greens would join the CDU and FDP: black/yel-
low/green recalls a favorite German vacation spot and would be called a Jamaica
coalition.

Who Should Govern?

The 2005 election produced a literally "colorful" outcome (see Box 7.1). Although the SPD gained at least a plurality of votes cast for party lists in
twelve of the sixteen states, the previously governing "red-green" coalition,
with 273 seats, fell short of the 308 seats needed for a majority. However,
the CDU/CSU/FDP "black-yellow" coalition, that had been so widely expected to win an outright majority of seats, only won 287. Polling done just
after the election showed that an astounding 80 percent of respondents said
they were dissatisfied with the results, but an even higher percentage (87 percent) said that, even knowing the outcome, they would not have voted dif-
ferently.[30] Although some very speculative arrangements were then
proposed, such as a "traffic light coalition" of SPD/FDP/Greens, or a "Jamaica coalition" of CDU/CSU–FDP–Greens, in the end, the voters got what
a plurality of 38 percent rather grudgingly preferred over alternative
arrangements: a grand coalition of CDU/CSU and SPD.[31]

The election produced a curious aftermath in the form of a debate over
who would become chancellor. Although the CDU/CSU had four more *Bundestag* seats than the SPD, Schröder argued that, because voters had not
elected a CDU/CSU–FDP coalition, he should have the chance to form a government, even in a grand coalition with the CDU/CSU. Merkel had been

Chancellor Angela Merkel (second from left) of the Christian Democratic Union, the Christian Social Union chair Edmund Stoiber (far left), the chair of the Social Democrats Franz Muente-fering (second from right) and designated chair of that party, Matthias Platzeck (far right).

weakened within her own party by its poor showing in the election, so Schröder hoped to lead a coalition without her. Polling showed that approximately equal numbers thought either Schröder or both should withdraw.[32] After lengthy negotiations, which resulted in the SPD's gaining roughly half of the cabinet positions, Merkel became federal chancellor of a CDU/CSU–SPD government on November 22, 2005.

The election of 2005 and the subsequent formation of a grand coalition suggested to many observers that the German political system, and particularly the parties' role in it, constrained German responses both to long-standing and to new social and economic pressures. These challenges include far-reaching demographic changes, particularly a low birth rate and an aging population; cultural and political challenges resulting from immigrants and their social and cultural integration; and the general global economic challenge subsumed under the catchword "globalization." Divergent policy responses to these challenges exist within both major parties as well as in the Greens and FDP. The extremes of left and right (Left Party and NPD) are in general, to use Charles Maier's term, "territorialist," but they lack influence on national and European policies. That the SPD and CDU/CSU, in particular, have yet to define a clear response to these issues may account for the hesitant and partial policies the grand coalition has advocated.[33] (These and other socioeconomic issues are discussed in greater detail in chapter 9.)

The Future of the German Party System

The central and enduring place of political parties in contemporary German politics naturally raises questions about the future of the party system. So far, the party system has successfully adapted to social and political change, which suggests continued stability; internal and external changes, however, would appear to confront the system with serious and, in part, unprecedented challenges.

As we have seen, the first three decades of the Federal Republic witnessed a progressive consolidation of the party system. The number of parties represented in the *Bundestag* shrank to three, the CDU/CSU, SPD, and FDP. Moreover, aside from the NPD's temporary surge to 4.3 percent in the 1969 election, no other party had come close to clearing the 5 percent hurdle for representation. At its height, this "concentrated" party system saw the major parties, the CDU/CSU and SPD, gain more than nine of every ten votes cast in national elections in the 1970s. In contrast, in the first two elections of the twenty-first century these parties barely attracted 70 percent of the votes. The pattern of "super stability" began to erode with the success of the Greens in electing *Bundestag* deputies in 1983 and has continued into the present with the persistence of a national five-party system. The Greens have been in and out of office and survived their brief eclipse in 1990. The Left Party, which has effectively succeeded the PDS, may have stabilized as a radical (but democratic) force to the left of the SPD comparable to the party of the same name in Sweden.[34]

Furthermore, the nationwide party system of previous decades has been supplemented by a stronger regional emphasis. For example, the Bavarian CSU has established an extraordinary dominance in its home state, while the PDS/Left Party has become an essential element in the political life of the former East Germany. In both federal and state elections, the PDS/Left Party has been one of the three major parties in its region. Just as the CSU has controlled the state government in Bavaria, so the PDS has either participated in or tolerated state governments in Berlin and two of the five eastern German states, or by its presence forced state-level grand coalitions, and all of this with a much smaller electoral presence.[35] Between 1990 and 2005, the PDS/Left Party gained substantial representation in all five state legislatures and in the eastern districts of Berlin. The concentration of the Left's strength in eastern Germany effectively produced two divergent regional party systems; neither the Greens nor the FDP is competitive in eastern German elections.

The formal advent of the Left Party in 2005–2007 was followed by its successful entry into western German politics at the state level. (In this it recapitulated the career of the Greens twenty years earlier.) The Bremen elections in 2007 secured the party's first-ever representation in a western state legislature, when it obtained 8.4 percent of the vote, roughly equal to its vote in the 2005 national election. Ironically, while the Greens made the most impressive gains with 16.4 percent, the fact that Left Party members now served in a western state legislature overshadowed other results. In three state elections held in early 2008 in Hamburg, Lower Saxony, and Hesse, the Left Party increased its presence in the state politics of the old Federal Republic of Germany, winning 6.4 percent in Hamburg, 5.1 percent in Hesse, and 7.1 percent in Lower Saxony, thus gaining seats in all three legislatures.[36]

The most immediate impact of these events was the reaction it evoked within the SPD. Faced with the prospect of a permanent further-left party as a national competitor, SPD leaders became openly divided on how to respond. Some argued against excluding the possibility of a national left-wing coalition perhaps until after the 2013 elections, but most leaders have taken a much harsher line in opposition to the Left Party.[37] Although the new party's immediate prospects have been heightened by its novelty and Lafontaine's leadership, caution regarding the Left Party's future seems advisable.

The Left Party has not reached programmatic agreement on important issues such as a quota for women within the party, the conditions under which it would enter coalition cabinets, integration of minorities, and many others. Working in its favor is the currently fluid state of German voters' party identification and the historically striking weakness of the major parties. Grand coalitions aside, three party coalitions will for some time to come reflect party strengths in the *Bundestag*. This would present SPD and Green leaders with very tempting but difficult choices regarding possible federal or state level governing coalitions with the Left Party (see chapter 11).

From another perspective, however, the German party system has absorbed recent shocks surprisingly well. No significant parties have emerged in western Germany since the advent of the Greens, and thanks to the rapid extension of the party system of the Federal Republic into the GDR in 1989–1990, only the survival of the PDS/Left Party remains as a consequence of that era. The one party that represented the internal GDR opposition, *Bündnis 90* (Alliance 90), merged with the Greens, and little remains of its influence within the merged party. In many of Germany's European neighbors, substantial extreme rightist parties have gained parliamentary influence, which is something Germany has thus far avoided, at least at the federal level. Finally, despite the regional tensions following unification and some political scandals, Germany's party structure has survived.[38]

8

Organized Interest Groups and Social Movements

Organized interest groups in all modern nations constitute a web of representative social structures that complement political parties in that they seek to influence political decisions in multiple policy contexts. By "representative social structures" we mean organizations made up of individuals or groups that share common characteristics such as ownership, occupation, or profession; belief systems such as ideology or religion; and a subnational or transnational identity such as ethnicity or gender.[1] Interest groups differ from political parties in that they do not typically seek public office through electoral competition.[2] Their roles and activities vary among advanced capitalist democracies, ranging from the familiar practice of pressure group lobbying in the United States and Britain[3] to institutionalized participation in what Norwegian social scientist Stein Rokkan once famously described as a "two-tiered system of decision-making" involving both private and public actors,[4] which is discussed below.

Pressure group politics in Anglo-American countries is consistent with a decentralized framework of economic and political pluralism, whereas Rokkan's formulation depicts a tripartite system of shared public and private power characteristic of "democratic corporatism." The latter pattern involves institutionalized structures of policy consultations and corporate bargaining among political officials, business groups, and organized labor alongside the activities of democratically elected governments.[5] Such arrangements are voluntary, which is in fundamental contrast to earlier systems of coercive party-state manipulation of employers and workers under Italian fascism and German national socialism. Democratic corporatism is a central feature of Scandinavian political economy and a recurrent theme in postwar German politics.[6]

Our objective in this chapter is to assess the organizational structures and economic, political, and social behavior of Germany's principal interest groups. We start with those that dominate the labor market and proceed through the media, religious communities, and social movements. In each case we begin with what Gabriel Almond, a leading American scholar of comparative politics, termed a "descriptive census" of the interest groups in question.[7]

Political Framework of Interest Groups

Interest group activity—the formal or informal initiatives of social groups or individuals to influence the political order—has been a constant feature of modern democratic polities. Nevertheless, interest groups and their actions have often suffered from a poor reputation as baleful influences on democracy. In Germany, as in other European states, interest groups have been scorned as "partial," and therefore inimical to the "common" interest. The freely organized representation of socioeconomic interests was contrasted to the formal structures of estates, churches, and similar historically rooted groups. Even after 1945, when the freedom to organize and pressure the government for common purposes was encouraged by the Western occupation forces and explicitly guaranteed in the Basic Law, scholars and publicists continued to warn of the danger of interest group activity.[8]

Critics of interest groups often underestimate the value of the modern "aggregative" function of such activity as a form of participation that provides information, perspectives, and explication of the needs of social sectors. The 1970s law requiring the registration of lobbyists wishing to testify before the *Bundestag* or its committees has generated data showing how changes in society and economy are reflected in the scope and nature of interest group activity (see Figure 8.1). Among economic lobbyists there are more from the tertiary sector, and there has been a notable increase in "movement" lobbyists representing postmaterialist causes.[9]

Origins and Postwar Development of the Trade Union Movement

Germany's labor market is dominated by union and employer associations, with each claiming roots from the nineteenth century. Both groups have long played a prominent part in German politics and in broader social developments. Their principal functions include integration of their members into the broader socioeconomic and political fabric of the nation, direct and indirect support for political parties, negotiation of collective wage agreements, and, in the case of trade unions, "codetermination" in industry

Figure 8.1 Number of Registered Lobbyists, 1972–2007

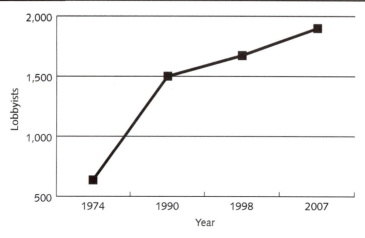

Source: Data compiled from www.bundestag.de/aktuell/archiv/2006/lobbyismus; Martin Se-baldt, "Interest Groups: Continuity and Change of German Lobbyism since 1974," in Ludger Helms, ed., *Institutions and Institutional Change in the Federal Republic of Germany* (New York: St. Martin's Press, 2000), 189.

involving worker representation on company boards. In addition, Germany's trade union and employer associations are members of trans-European organizations that have an influential voice in European Union (EU) economic and social policy discussed below.

Trade unions began to proliferate in the wake of industrialization and the accompanying growth in the number of industrial workers that was recounted in chapter 1. The first unions were associated with the emergent Social Democratic movement of the 1860s and 1870s, but by the end of the century ideological and religious cleavages had spawned separate socialist, Catholic, and liberal associations. The largest among them was the General German Trade Union Association (*Allgemeiner Deutscher Gewerkschaftsbund,* or ADGB). Together with its Catholic and liberal rivals, the AGDB proved a powerful stalwart of democracy and proponent of worker rights during the early years of the Weimar Republic.[10]

The rise of the National Socialists to power brought an abrupt end to interest group autonomy in Germany. Hitler's government banned unions and their right to strike in May 1933 and imposed an institutional merger of labor and private capital in the form of a German Labor Front (*Deutsche Arbeitsfront,* or DAF). For the duration of the Nazi regime, the DAF served as an instrument of Nazi control over the economy and society.

Germany's capitulation and the onset of the occupation regime in 1945 witnessed the reemergence of democratic trade unions but on a different institutional basis than their Weimar precedents. Labor leaders in West

Germany resolved to transcend historical ideological and religious cleavages by forming an ostensibly nonpartisan umbrella organization to represent the interests of organized labor. This ultimately took the form of the German Trade Union Confederation (*Deutscher Gewerkschaftsbund,* or DGB). Established in 1949 this umbrella association represented sixteen (later seventeen) industrial unions with a combined membership of nearly 5.5 million mainly blue-collar workers. Metal workers (*IG Metall*) were by far the largest of the unions, with an initial membership of 2.6 million. Separate organizations were established for salaried employees and public officials.[11]

Beginning as early as 1945, German Communist leaders, under Soviet auspices, saw to the creation of the Free German Trade Union Federation (*Freier Deutscher Gewerkschaftsbund,* or FDGB), a unitary organization that defined itself as a "class organization of the ruling working class in the GDR." [12] Its chair was a member of the SED's (Socialist Unity Party) politburo, and sixty-one union officials were allocated seats in the East German parliament. During most of the German Democratic Republic's existence the FDGB served as a "transmission belt" for SED indoctrination, governance, and provision of social services. At the same time, as the sole permitted voice for workers' interests, the FDGB channeled and represented member complaints and opinions to enterprise management and to the party and state leaders. Within these narrow limits set by the GDR political system, the FDGB did serve classic interest group functions.[13]

Democratization and Germany's rush to reunification prompted the dissolution of the FDGB in September 1990. Many of its members joined West German trade unions within the DGB. Thus trade unions and the DGB itself became all-German institutions.

DGB Programmatic Principles and Labor Market Roles

The DGB identifies itself as "the voice of trade unions in relation to political decision makers, parties and associations .... [Its role] is to coordinate union activities." [14] Programmatically, the federation declares parliamentary democracy "the only form of government that makes freedom and democracy possible. It offers the proper guarantees for the development of free and independent trade unions." The DGB affirms individual civil liberties, active participation by citizens in the political process, gender equality, equality of opportunity (*Chancengleichheit*), and the integration of foreign workers into German society. Its transnational priorities include collective security "to make [another] war in Europe impossible" and support for a more democratic European Union.[15] Officially nonpartisan, in practice the organization has been aligned primarily with the SPD, and to a lesser extent the CDU because of the latter's electoral appeal to Catholic workers.

A DGB core demand throughout the postwar era has been the extension and preservation of rights of worker "voice" in management decisions in private companies. This has taken the form of support for codetermination (*Mitbestimmung*), whereby workers are allocated seats alongside shareholders on company boards. Parity representation was first initiated in the iron, coal, and steel industries in 1947 in the British zone of occupation and later extended to the same economic sectors throughout West Germany through national legislation passed under the first Adenauer government in 1951. A more diluted form of codetermination for remaining industries, in which worker representatives were allocated a third of board seats, was enacted a year later, but a new bill passed under SPD aegis in 1976 introduced near-parity codetermination on the boards of all enterprises that were not a part of the iron, coal, and steel industries.[16]

In exchange for political support for central labor objectives, the DGB and its member unions have pursued a strategy of general wage and strike restraint to bolster Germany's economic growth and stability. The DGB itself does not engage in collective bargaining to determine wages, working hours, and vacation benefits of employees. Instead, that is the responsibility of its member unions. These member unions have traditionally negotiated such bread-and-butter issues with employer associations, typically on a regional or industrywide basis, and such agreements commonly serve as the basis for subsequent agreements negotiated elsewhere.[17] The usually peaceful outcome of negotiations of this sort is Germany's low rate of industrial conflict in comparison with key European neighbors (see Figure 8.2).

Organized labor gained an institutional voice in determining macro-economic policy in 1967 when a grand coalition government of the CDU/CSU

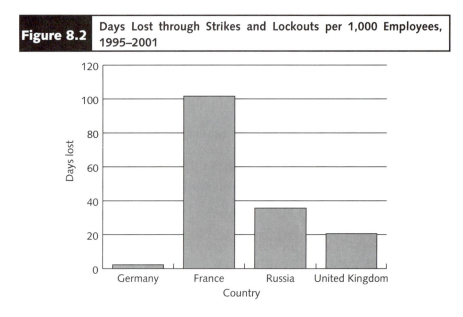

Figure 8.2 Days Lost through Strikes and Lockouts per 1,000 Employees, 1995–2001

Source: *Yearbook of Labour Statistics* (Geneva: International Labour Office, 2005).

and SPD sponsored legislation to establish a "democratic corporatist" policy structure to address the onset of sluggish economic growth and an increase in unemployment. Known as the Law for Promoting Stability and Growth in the Economy, the measure was inspired partly by a British precedent dating from 1962.[18] It created a tripartite consultative process known as concerted action (*konzertierte Aktion*) in which federal officials and representatives of both the DGB and employer associations agreed to meet on a regular basis to discuss measures to exercise wage and price restraint.[19] The sessions contributed to West Germany's economic recovery by the mid-1970s, but they ended on an acrimonious note in 1977 when the DGB withdrew from concerted action in angry response to a move by several employer associations to challenge the constitutionality of the 1976 bill on codetermination. (The Federal Constitutional Court later dismissed the employers' case.)

Union Membership Trends and Institutional Mergers

Dominant organizational developments affecting German trade unionism include, first, slow but steady growth after 1949 followed by an initial post-unification spike in membership; second, a rapid decline in membership since the early 1990s; and, third, institutional mergers during the 1990s and early part of the twenty-first century. As indicated in Figure 8.3, aggregate membership in DGB unions grew from 5.5 million in 1950–1951 to 7.9

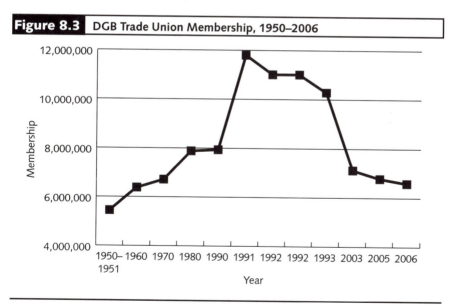

Figure 8.3 DGB Trade Union Membership, 1950–2006

Sources: Data compiled from www.de/dgb/mitgliederzahlen/gesamt1950-1993.htm; www.dgb.de/dgb/mitgliederzahlen/popit?dok=gesamt2005.htm&append=auswahlformular; "Immer weniger Gewerkschaftler im Osten," *Frankfurter Rundschau* online, February 18, 2007; "Nur jeder fünfter Arbeitnehmer in Gewerkschaft," *Frankfurter Rundschau,* December 20, 2006.

million in 1990. Following unification, membership jumped to 11.8 million in 1991, but it has subsequently dwindled to just under 6.8 million.

Principal causes for the shrinkage in union membership include a persistently high rate of unemployment, particularly in eastern Germany, which makes the cost of membership to many individual workers financially prohibitive; and changes in the composition of the labor force and the nature of the workplace. Among the latter are a displacement of hourly wage workers by part-time and self-employed workers, which reflects the rise of a service sector economy in which smaller firms are growing in number. Partly for these reasons, few women and younger employees find union membership an attractive option.[20] It is telling that membership in factory committees (*Betriebsräte*), which were originally established during the early Weimar era as a shop floor instrument of worker representation vis-à-vis company management and were reinstated in 1946, has fallen from representing half of all employees as late as the 1980s to 40 percent a decade later.[21]

Union officials have sought to mitigate the decline in membership through a process of mergers designed to enhance organizational strength. These have resulted in a successive decline in the number of national unions from seventeen in 1978 to thirteen in 1997; nine in 1991, when the union of salaried employees joined a previously independent public service union to form *Ver.di,* the United Services Union);[22] and eight in 2005 (see Table 8.1).

Compared to other developed nations, Germany's trade union density, which is measured by the number of union members as a percentage of the total work force, ranks above that of the United States, Poland, Spain, and

Table 8.1	DGB Union Membership, 2005	
Unions	Membership	Percentage of total
IG Bauen-Agrar-Umwelt		
(Construction, Agriculture, Environment)	391,546	5.8
IG Bergbau, Chemie, Energie		
(Mining, Chemicals, Energy)	748,852	11
Gewerkschaft Erziehung und Wissenschaft		
(Education and Science)	251,586	3.7
IG Metall (Metal Workers)	2.376 225	35.1
Gewerkschaft Nahrung- Genuss-		
Gaststätten (Food and Dining)	216,157	3.2
Gewerkshaft der Polizei (Police)	174,716	2.6
TRANSET (Transportation)	259,955	3.8
Ver.di (United Services Union)	2,359,392	34.8
DGB Total	6,778,429	100
Membership by occupation		
Blue- and white-collar workers	5,868,582	86.6
Public officials	489,506	7.2
Other	420,341	6.2

Source: Data compiled from www.dgb.de/dgb/mitgliederzahlen/popit?dok=gesamt2005. htm&append=auswahlformular.

Japan but is lower than that of a number of other European countries and significantly lower than union density in Scandinavia (see Figure 8.4). German unions nonetheless occupy a pivotal position in the economy, especially in the crucial manufacturing and public services sectors as the principal guardians of labor peace and periodic instigators of strikes.

Overall, however, German reunification has curtailed the political influence of organized labor. In addition to a continuing decline in union membership, the unions have been undermined by a successful strategy pursued by employers to bargain directly with works councils rather than with the unions themselves to achieve more flexible and less costly collective agreements on the enterprise level.[23] In keeping with this, following the 2002 election, then chancellor Gerhard Schröder abolished the Ministry of Labor; appointed a commission headed by the Volkswagen chair, Peter Hartz, to formulate policy proposals affecting labor and social benefits; and proclaimed a new Agenda 2010 reform program that restricted unemployment benefits. Later, in 2003, he abandoned a diluted form of concerted action: the *Bündnis für Arbeit,* or Alliance for Work, which had been established to promote economic growth in eastern Germany. All this was done without

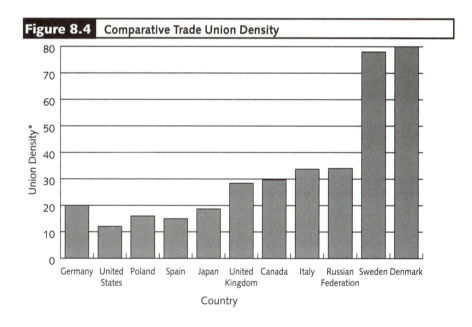

Figure 8.4 | **Comparative Trade Union Density**

Source: Data compiled from www.swivel.com/data.
*Most data are for 2005–2007; however, data for Italy and Russia are from 2001 and 2003, respectively.
Note: Trade union density refers to "union membership as a proportion of the eligible workforce." International Labour Organisation, "Technical Notes: Industrial Relations Indicators," *World Labour Report: Industrial Relations, Democracy and Social Stability, 1997–1998,* 237.

trade union participation.[24] (The economic policy aspects of these developments are discussed in chapter 9.)

Schröder's break with the trade unions led union leaders into ever-more strident opposition—first to the Schröder government in 2003–2005, and subsequently to the current grand coalition cabinet headed by Angela Merkel. Many rank-and-file trade unionists and middle-level union officials have become increasingly friendly to the Left Party, which in turn has energetically wooed them. As a result, the future political strategy of the trade unions is more undetermined than at almost any time in modern German history.[25]

Employer Associations: Origins, Membership, Purpose

The principal interest organization representing private capital is the Federal Union of German Employer Associations (*Bundesvereinigung der Deutschen Arbeitgeberverbände,* or BDA). Firms rather than individuals make up the BDA's membership. Many enterprises are also members of a second employer association, the Federation of German Industry (*Bundesverband der Deutschen Industrie,* or BDI). The two organizations perform complementary functions on behalf of employers. The former is primarily responsible for labor market relations, while the latter seeks to influence economic policy. Public sector employers are represented in the Employers' Association of German *Länder* (*Tarifgemeinschaft Deutscher Länder*) and the Federation of Municipal Employers' Associations (*Vereinigung der kommunalen Arbeitgeberverbände*), both of which perform labor market functions comparable to those of the BDA.

Embryonic employer groups began to emerge during the 1860s in response to the formation of trade unions. A national Association of German Employer Associations was established in 1904, which was officially recognized by the Weimar government in 1916 as a counterpart organization to the trade union confederations. As recounted above, the Hitler regime forced employers and workers into an artificial merger in 1933 in the Nazi-controlled German Labor Front. After occupation officials dissolved the DAF in 1945 and authorized the restoration of socioeconomic pluralism in the Western zones, employer groups formed an organization in 1949 and adopted its current name of Association of Employer Associations in 1950.

The BDA currently consists of fourteen regional organizations, most of which correspond to state boundaries, and fifty-four national associations representing seven economic sectors. Industrial associations dominate BDA membership in terms of size and strategic importance to the economy; among these are associations representing the metal-working, electrical, chemical, printing, and energy industries. Other BDA associations include

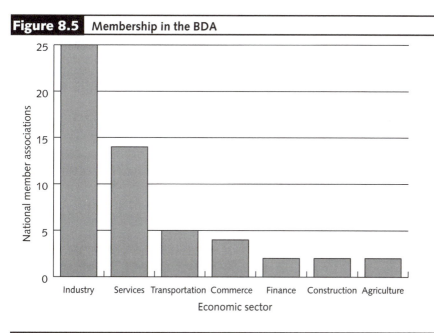

Figure 8.5 Membership in the BDA

Source: Bundesvereinigung der Deutschen Arbeitgeberverbände, "Mitglieder," www.bda-on line.de/www/bdaonline.nsf/id/Mitglieder.

services, transportation, commerce, finance, construction, and agriculture (see Figure 8.5).

The BDA defines its mission as the protection of the "common socio-political concerns" of its member associations.[26] These include collective bargaining responsibilities with unions on the part of its member associations and the confederation's support for measures that promote a "more flexible and transparent labor market" designed to facilitate employment opportunities.[27]

Lobbying alongside the BDA on behalf of business interests is the Federation of German Industry. The BDI is organized in thirty-six national associations representing 100,000 enterprises, including automobile manufacturing, construction, energy, steel, and textiles. The BDI defines itself as the "voice of German industry," an actor in the democratic process, and an institutional link between economics and politics.[28]

The Agricultural Lobby

West German farmers established their own national association in the form of the German Farmers' Union (*Deutscher Bauernverband,* or DBV). Following unification, the DBV extended its organization into the former GDR, and the association currently consists of eighteen state-level associations that in turn represent some five hundred local organizations consisting of individual farmers and cooperatives.[29] DBV representatives lobby public officials on all levels of the German government on behalf of agrarian interests. One of the union's principal targets is the European Union because the EU's Common Agricultural Policy is of central importance for the livelihood of DBV members and their families (see below).

Trans-European Activities

While Germany's economic interest groups devote most of their attention to domestic affairs, they are also active participants in trans-European politics through the European Union. The DGB is one of eighty-two national confederations representing thirty-six countries that belong to the European Trade Union Confederation (ETUC), based in Brussels, Belgium. Founded in 1973, the ETUC seeks to influence European-wide decisions affecting the socioeconomic interests of workers. It does this through its contacts with the EU's Council of Ministers, the European Commission, and the European Parliament.

Both the BDA and BDI are members of Business Europe, a private lobbying association comprised of thirty-nine member associations representing thirty-three countries, most of which are EU member states. The association was established in 2007 as a successor to the *Union des Industries de la Communauté européenne* (UNICE), which had been founded in 1958 to provide an institutional "voice" for private business interests within the territory of the original European Economic Community (EEC). Business Europe utilizes the same institutional channels as the ETUC to promote its claims in the EU economic and social policy process. Business and labor representatives from Germany and other member states also belong to the EU's Economic and Social Committee, which advises the commission, council, and parliament on pending community legislation.

In like fashion, the German Farmers Union belongs to the trans-European Committee of Professional Agricultural Organisations (COPA), which was founded in 1958 in tandem with the creation of the EEC and currently consists of fifty-nine organizations based in the EU's twenty-seven member states. It claims an indirect membership of fifteen million people working in Europe's agricultural sector.[30] Like officials belonging to similar organizations, COPA officials seek to influence community policy through interaction with the European Commission, the Council of Ministers, the European Parliament, and the European Economic and Social Committee.

Religiously Based Interest Groups

As discussed in chapter 1, religious denominations play varied roles in German society and politics. (Data on the size, variety and composition of major religious communities may be found there.) In recent years, various controversies have arisen over religious-secular relations and interactions.

For years, the German government has supported Christian educational facilities through funding and policy. Only recently, however, have similar efforts been made to work with Islamic schools. This class at the Schwabschule, an elementary school in Stuttgart, is part of a pilot program sponsored by the state of Baden-Wuerttemberg to teach Islamic religious classes in German as is already done for Christian denominations.

One example is a controversy regarding participation by the Catholic Church in pregnancy and abortion counseling. Another is an angry and legally abrasive response on the part of German authorities and public opinion from all parts of the ideological and party spectrum toward Scientology. While this controversy, which reached a pinnacle in 1997–1998, seems to have died away, the basic issues of the state's role regarding religious organizations remains.[31]

The expansion of interest group activity may be seen in the organization of Islamic groups so as to represent the interests of this community to government and deal with a range of practical issues at every level. This structured centralization of religious life, not native to the Islamic community, is one that the German authorities also find useful in formulating policies in such areas as religious instruction in schools. Thus both the Islamic and Jewish communities, wishing to influence public policy, have adapted to a "church-like" interest group practice.[32] The Islamic organizations, while they have a large Turkish membership, are religiously based, but there are also ethnic, secular Turkish organizations. In 2007, the Central Council of Muslims in Germany (ZMD) linked with secular, mostly Turkish, political organizations in a Coordinating Council of Muslims in Germany (KRM) to further common causes and policies.[33]

Media

An important avenue for both control of and input to government activity is the decentralized German media. Regulation of media affairs is a matter for state legislation; each state has a press law, although the contents of such laws are generally similar. They include such requirements as assignment of editorial responsibility on mastheads, affording right of reply, and safeguarding the interests of youth. Federal law on the media begins with the Basic Law's Article 5 guarantee of press freedom.[34] For example, journalists may not be compelled to name their sources. The Constitutional Court has affirmed the importance of a free press to the democratic process. Such judicial supervision of media matters can be quite detailed. In a 2007 decision the court voided a decision by the states to lower fees for broadcast reception.[35]

Reflecting the devolution of political and economic power in modern Germany, the press is similarly regional in structure. Very few German newspapers have a national circulation; most reflect both regional and ideological orientations (see Table 8.2). Thus, of the "quality" broadsheets, the *Frankfurter Allgemeine Zeitung* (FAZ) is conservative and regional, the *Süddeutsche Zeitung* (SZ) is Bavarian but slightly left of center, while the tabloid "Taz" (*Tageszeitung*) is insistently countercultural.[36]

Although the Germans remain a nation of newspaper readers, their devotion is flagging in a manner similar to that of the publics in other industrialized democracies. Additionally, doubts as to the efficacy of the press's self-monitoring system, exercised though the Press Council, are increasing.[37]

Table 8.2	Circulation of Major German Daily Newspapers, 2004	
Newspaper	City	Circulation*/ Rank
Bild[+]	Hamburg	3,282,000/1
Süddeutsche Zeitung	Munich	430,000/2
Frankfurter Allgemeine Zeitung	Frankfurt/Main	377,700/3
Cheminitz Freie Presse[++]	Chemnitz	339,700/4
Rheinische Post	Düsseldorf	327,700/5
Mitteldeutsche Zeitung[++]	Halle	276,000/6
BZ[+]	Berlin	227,000/13
Die Welt	Hamburg	202,000/17
Frankfurter Rundschau	Frankfurt/Main	175,000/23
Tageszeitung ('TAZ')[+++]	Munich	153,000/31
Tagesspiegel	Berlin	131,000/46
All newspapers	Germany	21,700,000

Source: Walter J. Schütz, "Deutsche Tagespresse 2004," *Media Perspektiven* online (no. 5, 2005), 205–232, adapted from Table 12, 223.
*Circulation numbers rounded off by authors.
Note: +mass circulation tabloid; ++ in eastern Germany; +++counterculture tabloid

We have noted above that although media affairs are a state responsibility, the federal courts can and do intervene. This is not necessarily an adversarial relationship, however. In recent years, a number of decisions have upheld the security of journalists in the exercise of their professional duties and limited the scope of prosecutorial inquiries into their work.[38]

Postwar Germany's first television network, ARD, is a consortium of states-operated broadcasters. Currently, there are nine such broadcasters that in some cases are operated by two or more states together; although each station does much of its own programming, there are some common productions, particularly the newsprograms *Tagesschau* and *Tagesthemen* (news of the day and themes of the day, respectively). Chancellor Konrad Adenauer's dissatisfaction with ARD coverage led to an attempt to establish a federal broadcaster, but his efforts were thwarted by a 1961 Constitutional Court ruling. As a compromise, the states signed an agreement among themselves to establish a centrally operated second channel, ZDF.[39] (See Table 8.3.)

ARD and ZDF are financed primarily through radio and television users' fees, with the amount determined by an agreement of the states (although as noted above, the public role of these broadcasters allows the courts to set guidelines for adequate support), and the money is apportioned in keeping with each station's viewer total. The special role of public broadcasters is also underlined by an EU decision that certain important events, including World Cup soccer matches involving Germany and the final match, must be shown on public television. Private, commercially financed television has also existed in Germany since the 1980s, and the leading private broadcasters, particularly RTL and SAT1, have achieved large viewer totals.[40]

In gauging the relationship between the media and the political process two issues stand out that are found in other industrial democracies as well. One is the media's image of the electoral process; the second is media treatment of security issues, which in Germany means especially the picture of Islam drawn for Germans in both print and electronic media. As in other

Table 8.3	States and Their Broadcasting Networks
State (*Land*)	Broadcast Network
Baden-Württemberg, Rhineland-Palatinate	Südwestrundfunk (SWR)
Bavaria	Bayerischer Rundfunk (BR)
Berlin, Brandenburg	Radio Berlin Brandenburg (RBB)
Bremen	Radio Bremen (RB)
Hesse	Hessischer Rundfunk (HR)
North–Rhine Westphalia	Westdeutscher Rundfunk (WDR)
Saarland	Saarländischer Rundfunk (SR)
Saxony, Saxony-Anhalt, Thuringia	Mitteldeutscher Rundfunk (MDR)
Schleswig-Holstein, Hamburg, Lower Saxony, Mecklenburg–Western Pomerania	Norddeutscher Rundfunk (NDR)

Sources: Compiled by authors from network Web sites.

countries, the emphasis in campaign coverage on the chancellorship candidates' "horse race" overshadowed treatment of substantive issues. Moreover, a fixation, abetted by clever campaigners, on such relatively peripheral matters as Merkel's choice for economic adviser fueled criticism of whether the media were truly living up to their responsibility to inform the public.[41]

The treatment of Islam-related subjects by the media is important not only insofar as it shapes the German population's perceptions of security issues; it is also vital to the integration of Muslim residents into German society. Therefore, it is disturbing to note that the coverage of Islam-related topics on the major news, talk, and interview programs on ARD and ZDF presents a distorted and rather negative picture.[42] In an analysis of 133 broadcasts that included Islam-related reports, 81 percent of the items presented a negative picture of Islam, with a quarter reporting terrorism and extremism. Of the 19 percent that were neutral or positive, only 8 percent reflected the everyday life of Muslim communities in Germany. Given that German broadcasters receive public input from legislatively mandated advisory councils, and that Muslims are not yet represented on these as Christians and Jews are, perhaps such slanted coverage is not quite so surprising, if no less disappointing.

Social Movements

A notable and encouraging feature of modern German politics has been the prevalence of citizen activism. Unlike the more formal interest groups discussed above, the impact of society on political life has also been mediated by some striking social movements that clearly reflect the changes in political culture discussed in chapter 4. Germany's increasingly "participant" political culture has had its effect on policy outcomes: a striking example discussed in chapter 5 is the routinization of conscientious objection to military service. Other examples include the traditional "Easter marches" against nuclear weapons and nuclear power that date from the 1950s.

Such street protests and marches became part of the political repertoire of younger Germans a decade later, particularly in response to the perceived "undemocratic" nature of the 1966–1969 grand coalition. The rise of the Extra-Parliamentary Opposition (APO) in those years reflected a generational disdain for the political attitudes of the first postwar generation. (The attitudinal dimension of these movements is discussed in chapter 4.) The shift to extraparliamentary street action was sealed by the police shooting of a student, Benno Ohnesorg, during a protest against the visit of the Shah of Iran to Berlin in June 1967.[43]

The protest movements of the 1960s were of course not limited to Germany, although there was a special edge to German generational friction, thanks to the rising chorus of those questioning how their "fathers" had behaved under Hitler. Much like similar movements in France, Italy, and the United States, the street protests eventually branched into reform-minded, so-called postmaterialist politics on the one hand (exemplified in Germany by the rise of the Greens in the 1980s) and violence on the other. In Germany, this violence took the form of the brutal and dogmatic movement of the Red Army Faction (RAF), with its strong third world and pro-Palestinian aspects. (It was later revealed that the movement also benefited from GDR training and financial support.) The string of assassinations and airplane hijackings involving this group climaxed with German commandos storming a hijacked Lufthansa airliner in Mogadishu and the simultaneous suicide of the RAF leaders in their jail cells in Germany.[44]

These decades of such public struggle in West Germany had a belated but important echo in the GDR. As in other East European countries, the East Germans were not in a position to mount a direct political challenge to the regime. They could, however, press the authorities to honor the system's ostensible principles. Using a Soviet sculpture on view at the United Nations of a figure beating swords into ploughshares as their symbol, East Germans increasingly opposed the ongoing militarization of the GDR, and much to the dismay of the regime, an autonomous peace movement arose in the 1980s. Dissent expanded into environmental activism and then broadened further into demands for freedom of travel. (Much of this activity took place under the political shelter and with the logistical support of the Evangelical Church.) These growing and interlocking movements prepared the way for the political movements of 1989–1990, such as the organization New Forum (*Neues Forum*), that played a leading role in the dissolution of the GDR regime.[45]

Social movements in contemporary Germany are by no means uniformly emancipatory and democratic. In many parts of the country a subculture of right-wing extremism has taken root. Although very different in political outlook from the left-wing radicalism of the 1960s and 1970s, these groups' disdain for conventional social values, their distinctive style of music, their clustering in semicommunes, and their distance from the social mainstream all resemble earlier leftist movements.

While there is a political party and an electoral dimension to this movement, its social aspect is notable for an informal, loosely coordinated network of street brawlers; right-wing music clubs and CDs; and random but recurrent violent attacks on foreigners, especially those appearing to be of African or South Asian descent. Like many groups opposed to mainstream society and its values, these right-wing activists have adopted a distinctive dress and style: shaved heads, heavy paratrooper boots with white laces, and leather bomber pilot jackets with various adornments that often feature the double-rune symbol associated with the Nazi SS.

Although these "Baldies" (*Glatzen*) are found in all corners of Germany, they are concentrated in the small towns and rural areas of the former GDR. In some places, these individuals dominate the streets and social spaces to the point that they intimidate local residents and visitors.[46] A newly favored tactic is to join local soccer clubs, as players and as fans. This has resulted in increasing politicization in Germany of behavior common among "soccer hooligans"—mostly young men, often drunk and ready to brawl—who are found throughout Europe.[47]

This rightist extremism has become an almost familiar part of German life, with a recurrent cycle of public and political attention. A "foreigner," whether immigrant, student, asylum seeker, or tourist, will be verbally and then physically attacked, often ending in the victim's death. Witnesses are few or reluctant to come forward; victims cannot, or will not, identify their attackers; and local authorities can be slow to act and often reject "slurs" on their communities that imply the presence of dangerous elements or individuals. When media attention forces state and federal action, leaders denounce these violent episodes, money is set aside for social remediation, public demonstrations such as candlelight vigils are held, and then attention is diverted by some other issue or concern, and the cycle resumes. Authorities often do not prosecute these acts as hate crimes, and aggressive, proactive police work is rare.[48]

One factor contributing to this situation may be a therapeutic approach to violence in which, as one commentator has noted, "one thing was deemed certain, that social problems called for more social workers, more psychologists, more projects, and more benefits" and a new social stratum of professionals to administer, justify, and expand this system.[49] The foreign press often pays critical attention to these events,[50] and serious national publications repeatedly devote whole issues to this theme, but the material is not markedly different from year to year.[51]

That many of these crimes and the general spread of extremist sentiment and behavior take place in the former GDR has an ironic side, as the proportion of "foreigners" to the general population is much lower there than in the western states. While foreign workers, especially from Vietnam and Mozambique, were recruited to the GDR before 1989, they generally lived in segregated communities. Antiforeign sentiment was more often directed against East European "fraternal" allies. This was especially true (and had surreptitious official encouragement) when labor unrest connected with the rise of the Polish Solidarity movement in 1979–1981 led to fuel shortages in the GDR. Indeed, the presence of skinheads in the last years of the GDR was widely known if not officially acknowledged or acted against.[52] Today such right-wing groups still flourish in other former Communist countries. Russia has its skinheads, and violence against minorities, especially Sinti and Roma, is widespread in Eastern Europe.[53]

The question of whether conditions in the former GDR generated eastern German hostility toward foreigners has been widely and hotly debated in recent years. The most authoritative study of the problem was completed by a veteran of longitudinal attitude research among GDR and postunification eastern German youth, Walter Friedrich. He concluded that it is the postunification psychological disorientation and social and economic dislocation in eastern Germany that is responsible for many of the actions of the right-wing extremists.[54] The steady migration of the most ambitious and highly skilled young eastern Germans to more prosperous western parts (analogous to the flight of East Germans noted in chapter 1), has been seen as the leaving behind of those with the least attractive life prospects. (Inasmuch as many right-wing extremists are male, the relatively higher migration of ambitious women to the west may be a factor.) As a result of these trends, a bitter joke circulating in the former GDR is that "DDR" (the German version of GDR) stands for *der doofe Rest* (the stupid remainder).[55]

Although the behavior described here continues to be a problem for the German state and society, it has not disrupted the political system. Indeed right-wing extremists have had less impact on German politics than their counterparts in other European countries both within and outside of the EU.[56] Germany has not had an important right-wing national leader on the order of Haider in Austria or LePen in France. Italy, Denmark, Austria, and Switzerland have had extreme right parties participating in national governments, but no comparable German party has gained *Bundestag* seats nor entered any state government. In part, this may be a matter of no German leader of sufficient talent having yet arisen, and those whom party members have recruited for state legislatures proving ineffective.

The most prominent extreme right party in Germany is the National Democratic Party (NPD). Founded in the 1960s, it nearly entered the *Bundestag* when it won just short of 5 percent of the vote in the 1969 election. Then after a long period of inconsequence, the party regained importance in the first decade after reunification. Since the late 1990s, it has almost doubled its membership and won some important state election victories,[57] including nine seats in Saxony in 2004 with 9.2 percent of the vote and six seats in Mecklenburg–Western Pomerania in 2006 with 7.3 percent. These were also the states in which the NPD did best in the 2005 national elections.

However, although it managed to present party lists in every state and nominate direct mandate candidates in 295 of the 299 constituencies, the NPD did poorly overall in that election (see Table 8.4). And in the first two

Table 8.4	Votes for the NPD in the 2005 National Election
Category	Percentage
Party list vote, nationwide	1.6
Vote in western states and West Berlin	1.1
Vote in eastern states and East Berlin	3.6
Saxony (best result)	4.8
Thuringia	3.7
Mecklenburg–Western Pomerania	3.5
Males, 18–24, nationwide	5.2
Males in eastern states, all ages	4.7

Sources: Interior Ministry data from www.bmi.bund.de/verfassungsbericht/2005_en.pdf; Federal Election Office data from www.bundeswahlleiter.de.

state elections of 2008, in Hesse and Lower Saxony, the NPD received only 0.9 and 1.5 percent of the vote, respectively. Thus, despite its general message against American hegemony and globalization, denial of the Holocaust, and other familiar extreme rightist views, the party remains significant primarily in those areas in which it is also a strong social force.[58]

The Women's Movement

The most consequential movement in Germany in its recent history has been that of women seeking a greater and more autonomous role in political and social life.[59] German feminism has a history reaching back into the nineteenth century, but the half century after the Nazi seizure of power was not kind to feminist ambitions. After the total exclusion of women from positions of influence in the Nazi years, German women faced awesome responsibilities in a wrecked and defeated country that had lost most of its male population in the war and its aftermath. Following a period in which their efforts were essential to reconstruction, women in West Germany returned to domestic life.[60] This retreat from the public sphere was especially notable in political life, in which a female presence in the cabinet was usually limited to a token representative (*Alibi-Frau*) and the percentage of women in the *Bundestag* stagnated at about 10 percent during the first decades of the Federal Republic.[61]

Important changes in the lives of German women have been the result of a loosely organized feminist movement that often has been based in or worked through political parties.[62] The major campaigns of this movement have revolved around equal pay; economic autonomy, such as a married woman having the right to work outside the home without her husband's permission; access to abortion services; and, partly as a tool to achieve these ends, access to political influence.

Some of these and other objectives have been reached, including an antidiscrimination law and the right to serve in combat positions in the armed forces.[63] Others have not, such as equal pay for equal work and a reform of abortion law.[64] It should be noted that in the abortion debate, women led successful efforts to reform the law in 1974 and 1992, only to have the resultant legislation struck down by the Constitutional Court. The latter case was especially interesting because the effort was lead by Rita Süßmuth of the CDU, who was then presiding over the *Bundestag*. Her supporters, from across party lines, included many deputies from the former East Germany, which had had a liberal abortion law since 1972.

Access by German women to greater political power has been facilitated by reform in the way political parties present woman candidates, and by the growing number of female candidates. Here the Greens upon their entry into the *Bundestag* in 1983 promptly lead the way by setting a parity quota of women candidates. (Indeed, the Greens have always had a dual-gender party

Table 8.5	Women as a Percentage of *Bundestag* Members, 1998–2005		
		Session	
Party	14th (1998–2002)	15th (2002–2005)	16th (2005–)
SPD	35.2	37.6	35.6
CDU/CSU	18.2	22.7	20.4
FDP	26.7	24.5	24.6
Greens	58	59.6	43.1
PDS/			
Left Party	59	*	48.1
Total	31.6	32.5	31.8

Source: Melanie Kintz, "Women in the German Bundestag: Recruitment and Legislative Careers," paper prepared for the 31st GSA conference, San Diego, Calif., October 4–7, 2007.
*There were only two directly elected PDS members (both women).

leadership.) Other parties, in varying degrees, hurried to catch up. Some, such as the SPD, PDS, and Left Party, adopted formal quotas; others, such as the CDU, CSU, and FDP have relied on informal arrangements. The result in numerical terms is shown in Table 8.5.

The decisions of party leaderships in Germany have had a powerful effect in this area due to the nature of the electoral system described in the preceding chapters.[65] In the past bias against women has made it more difficult to nominate women in single-member districts than on party lists. The formal steps by the political parties have resulted in an increase in women *Bundestag* members—the current proportion of 31.8 percent is high by German standards. However, at the "top of the greasy pole" (to use

---

Box 8.1

Prominent Women in Modern German Politics

Monika Harms (CDU): first woman to serve as federal attorney general (*Generalbundesanwalt*), 2006–present
Jutta Limbach (SPD): judge on the Constitutional Court, 1993–2001
Ulrike Meinhof: coleader with Andreas Baader of "Baader-Meinhof," a radical leftist terrorist group; committed suicide in custody in 1977
Angela Merkel (CDU): first woman to serve as federal chancellor
Annemarie Renger (SPD): first woman to preside over *Bundestag,* 1972–1976
Gesine Schwan (SPD): university president and first serious woman candidate for the federal presidency (2005)
Alice Schwartzer: feminist; founder and editor of *Emma*; in 1971 initiated public avowal (*"Ich habe abgetrieben"*) by 374 women of having had an illegal abortion
Heide Simonis (SPD): first, and thus far only, woman to serve as prime minister of a German state (Schleswig-Holstein, 1993–2004)
Rita Süssmuth (CDU): cabinet minister, presided over *Bundestag,* 1988–1998

Disraeli's term), no woman has served as federal president; only one woman, Heide Simonis (SPD) of Schleswig-Holstein has served as state prime minister (1993–2004); and only one, Angela Merkel, has held the office of federal chancellor. Women are represented in cabinets, but often as heads of such "soft" ministries as youth, family, or women's affairs. The attitudinal and social barriers to true advancement appear to be more than a matter of formal quotas and parity arrangements.[66]

A Complex Mosaic of Influence

Germany's network of institutionalized associations and social movements reveals a more complex mosaic of group influence in politics than Stein Rokkan anticipated in his concept of the two-tiered decision-making process involving domestic public and private actors discussed at the beginning of this chapter.[67] This is especially true when factoring in Germany's membership in the European Union and the effects of globalization on the nation's economy. Rather than participating solely in a two-tiered domestic system of decision making, German interest groups are embedded in a multilevel system of governance that encompasses national and supranational institutions and actors. This is clearly evident in Germany's socioeconomic policies and performance, explored in the following chapter.

9 Socioeconomic Policies and Performance

G ermany's economic system, that is, its performance in ensuring growth, shared prosperity, and an adequate social welfare net, is of unusual political importance. While Germans face most of the same challenges that confront other industrial democracies, their situation is also unique in three special ways. First, they bear the historical burden of providing an economic basis for strengthening democratic political legitimacy; second, although many comparable countries have economically depressed regions (such as the notoriously underdeveloped Italian *Mezzogiorno* south of Rome), Germans must provide an economic basis for the political reunification of their once divided country; finally, the German economy is expected to be an engine of growth for the entire European Union (EU).

Competing models of advanced industrial society characterize both the "old" Federal Republic and unified Germany. A generic "European Social Model," formulated by the European Trade Union Confederation (ETUC), depicts

> a vision of society that combines sustainable economic growth with ever improving living and working conditions. This implies full employment, good quality jobs, equal opportunities, social protection for all, social inclusion, and involving citizens in the decisions that affect them.[1]

The ETUC's image is essentially a synthesis of Social Democratic and centrist reform principles implemented in Western and parts of Central Europe.[2]

Representatives of private economic interests affirm an implicit European model as well. This model promotes economic growth and job creation through coordinated efforts by governments, private capital, and organized labor to foster entrepreneurship; open new global markets "through bilateral trade and economic agreements"; and "reform European social systems to respond to global challenges."[3] With respect to the latter goal, *Business Europe* asserts: "Globalization requires European labour markets to be more flexible while, at the same time, necessitating new forms of security for workers."[4]

A German Model

Various scholars have formulated a narrower "German model" of advanced industrial society. The basic principles of a *Modell Deutschland* include material prosperity, largely sustained labor peace, codetermination in industry, and a "social market economy."[5] This German model contrasts with more interventionist government policies in France, "coordinated" policy planning and implementation in Sweden, and U.S. and British market-driven capitalism.[6]

A variant of the German model is a "Rhineland model" of capitalism characterized by unprecedented social security and "a civilizing step forward—not only bringing with it a degree of mass affluence, but also political stabilization within a framework of parliamentary democracy following the horrifying excesses of the Third Reich."[7] According to Michel Albert, a French economist and former "czar" of economic planning in France, the Rhineland model is a distinctive German form of "stakeholder" capitalism institutionalized in the form of codetermination on company boards,[8] which he contrasts critically with Anglo-American "shareholder capitalism."[9]

These widely heralded European and German models proved to be bulwarks of postwar German democracy and potent political weapons in the competition with the German Democratic Republic (GDR). By contrast, the current Federal Republic is characterized by fierce political and social conflicts concerning the nature and course of economic life, particularly efforts by the previous Schröder government to promote greater flexibility in the labor market through the pursuit of its "Agenda 2010" and the so-called Hartz IV reforms (discussed below). Broader issues of globalization, including the role of financial speculators and transnational investors—characterized as "locusts" by the first vice chancellor of the CDU/CSU–SPD grand coalition, Franz Müntefering—are characteristic of the current economic outlook.

Whether contemporary Germany continues to constitute a distinctive model of advanced industrial capitalist society is an empirical issue to be decided by measuring the nation's socioeconomic policy and performance within the overlapping contexts of Europeanization and globalization.

Germany's Socioeconomic Polity

Germany's socioeconomic polity rests on three overlapping institutional and policy pillars. The first is a comprehensive welfare state, the second a distinctive style of macro-economic management, and the third integration within the European Union. Together, these pillars constitute the basis of Germany's continued modernization and entry into a "postmodern" world of nations.[10]

The roots of the first of these pillars can be traced to a series of sweeping institutional innovations initiated by Imperial Chancellor Otto von Bismarck during the 1880s.[11] These included the introduction of sickness insurance in 1883, workers' compensation for industrial accidents in 1884, and old-age pensions in 1889. Bismarck's initiatives were motivated primarily by his desire to woo German workers away from the Social Democrats and other reformist parties of the era rather than by any ideological commitment to social welfarism per se, but his achievements served as inspirations to later generations of reformers throughout Europe and beyond to sponsor the creation of welfare states in their own countries. As a leading German scholar observed: "Historians both inside and outside Germany rank the social legislation of the 1880s as a decisive turning-point in modern social history."[12]

Many scholars eschew a comprehensive definition of welfare states on the grounds that historical and contemporary variants are country specific. As Timothy Tilton, a political scientist at Indiana University, asserts in a collection of essays on the future of welfare systems: "The search for a generally-accepted definition of *the* welfare state may well prove fruitless no matter how inclusively it is cast."[13] The reason, he submits, is that different welfare states have different objectives, including

> to dampen radical potentials, to shore up domestic manufacturers, ensure minimum standards of civilized life, or institute rough equality of living standards ... [This] is not an incidental consideration, but a clear indication of the radically different conceptions of "welfare" or "well-being" embodied in the different manifestations of welfare states.[14]

A minimalist definition is offered by A. Briggs, who asserts that common characteristics of modern welfare states include an interventionist role of the government in modifying

> the play of market forces in at least three directions—first, by providing individuals and families a minimum income irrespective of the market value of their work or property, second, by narrowing the extent of insecurity by enabling individuals and families to meet certain social contingencies (for example, sickness, old age and unemployment) ... and third, by ensuring that all citizens without distinction of status or class are offered the best standards available in relation to a certain agreed range of social services.[15]

The German welfare state is a case in point. It evolved through successive stages of regime change in response to different ideological agendas coupled with the universal demands of modernization.[16] Social entitlements were expanded under Social Democratic aegis in the 1920s to include white-collar employees and unemployment insurance. The National Socialists extended these entitlements to include health care and retirement benefits in a calculated effort to mobilize mass support for their totalitarian system, and under democratic governance in the Federal Republic these entitlements were retained.

A major innovation of the West German system was Chancellor Konrad Adenauer's success in initiating a new pension system in 1957. Financed by shared employer and employee contributions, it would provide an adequate standard of living beyond retirement.[17] West German authorities also reinstated a Weimar-era Federal Labor Agency (*Bundesagentur für Arbeit*), whose purpose is to provide information exchange between employers and prospective workers about job opportunities and to dispense unemployment funds.

East German authorities constructed a Communist variant of social security that was inspired by the Soviet experience. This system included universal retirement pensions, free medical care, state-subsidized housing, trade-union-sponsored vacations, and workplace childcare facilities. GDR policy in the Erich Honecker era after 1971 turned from an emphasis on the "classic" Soviet model of investment in capital goods to the provision of such social benefits as housing and subsidized food programs. German reunification brought an extension of West German practices throughout the former GDR. This meant the retention of universal retirement and medical entitlements but the elimination of subsidized vacations and numerous childcare facilities, much to the detriment of working parents (especially women).[18]

Administrative Arrangements

The Federal Labor Agency is a prime example of a distinctive German institutional approach to welfare disbursement. While it is federally funded, the agency is legally a semipublic body governed by representatives of private capital, organized labor, and various professional organizations. The same governing principle applies to most other welfare-dispensing agencies. As David Conradt notes: "These institutions assume functions performed by national governments in centralized systems such as Great Britain and France. In Germany, they lessen the total political load carried by the national government, but they also reduce its strength."[19] They do so by shifting control over important financial and social resources from political actors to ostensibly nonpartisan administrative agencies.

Measures of Commitment to Public Welfare

Germany's contemporary welfare system is a synthesis of Bismarckian principles of minimum standards of social insurance and postwar Christian Democratic–Social Democratic measures to promote greater individual and collective security in collaboration with representatives of private capital. As a close student of German labor market politics has observed: "Both major German parties have been committed to expansive social protection and to politics promoting job security and codetermination ... in enterprise." Their common goal has been to institutionalize a social partnership between private capital and labor to avoid the class conflict that characterized the Imperial and Weimar systems.[20] Critics of the German approach have disparaged it as "corporatist-conservative," in contrast to more egalitarian welfare policies pursued in Scandinavia.[21]

Specifically, the German system is characterized by universal welfare entitlements that are qualified by income-based group exceptions. In descending order, the most important of these include pensions, health insurance, unemployment benefits, child support payments, and welfare assistance to lower-income workers and families (see Table 9.1). With the exception of retirement benefits and child support payments, the German welfare system basically excludes wealthier groups from universal coverage. High-level civil servants and professionals such as doctors and lawyers generally enroll in privately funded health care programs that offer more comprehensive care than the basic insurance programs.[22] Welfare entitlements are paid out of a combination of general tax revenue, joint contributions by employers and employees, and private contributions.

Table 9.1	Government Social Welfare Expenditures, 1995–2005 (as percentages of the annual "Social Budget")				
			Year		
Expenditure category	1995	2000	2002	2004	2005
General retirement benefits	43	42.9	42.7	42.7	45.2
Health insurance	28.1	26.4	26.2	25.2	27.1
Unemployment payments	8	7.3	7.7	8.6	5.1
Child support	1.9	5.0	5.3	5.2	5.5
Social assistance	6	4.6	4.5	4.7	3.8
Youth programs	3.9	3.6	3.7	3.7	3.9
Nursing home support	1.2	3.3	3.2	3.2	3.4
Short-term pensions	3.1	2.8	2.7	2.7	2.8
Accident insurance	2.9	2.6	2.8	2.6	2.7
Housing assistance	0.7	0.7	0.8	0.9	0.2
Assistance to asylum seekers	0.6	0.4	0.3	0.2	0.2
Aid to World War II victims	0.6	0.3	0.5	0.2	0.1

Source: Calculated by the authors from annual expenditures in millions of euros reported in *Statistisches Jahrbuch 2007 für die Bundesrepublik Deutschland* (Wiesbaden: Statistisches Bundesamt, 2007).

As Table 9.1 indicates, expenditures in most categories have remained relatively constant over the ten-year period shown. Only child support and public assistance to nursing homes have noticeably increased since 1995. Government aid to World War II victims has steadily declined as the pool of qualified recipients has grown smaller. A decrease in unemployment payments is linked to efforts initiated in 2001 by the Schröder government to limit the number of citizens on long-term assistance (see below).

A key measure of a nation's social well-being is its investment in health care services. Germany stands out as having one of the highest physician-patient ratios among its principal trading partners. Germany also spends a higher percentage of its total gross domestic product (GDP) on health care compared to its trading partners; only the United States spends more. The country is second to Britain in the percentage of total public spending on health care and ranks third (tied with the United States) behind the Netherlands and Belgium in the health worker density index, which includes the total number of physicians, nurses, and midwives per one thousand persons (see Table 9.2).

Social well-being cannot be measured in economic terms alone, however. A 2007 survey of adults in Australia, Canada, Germany, the Netherlands, New Zealand, the United Kingdom, and the United States found significant differences in the subjective assessment of health care provision experienced by respondents. Germans were second to Americans in reporting dissatisfaction with various aspects of the treatment they had received at doctors' offices and in hospitals. For example, 27 percent of Germans responded that the national health care system should be "completely rebuilt," compared to 34 percent of Americans who held the same viewpoint. Only 9 percent of the Dutch respondents held an equally negative view.[23] In short, material quantity does not necessarily ensure experienced quality of service.

Table 9.2	Comparative Health Care Expenditures and Service, 1990–2004						
	Total % of GDP	Public % of GDP	% of total	Out-of-pocket % of private	Per capita in U.S. dollars	Physicians per 1,000 people		Health worker density index
Country	2003	2003	2003	2003	Year 2003	1990	1997–2004	2000–2003
Germany	11.1	8.7	78.2	47.9	3,204	3.1	3.4	13.2
France	10.1	7.7	76.3	42.2	2,981	2.6	3.4	10.2
Italy	8.4	6.3	75.1	83.3	2,139	4.7	4.2	10.5
United Kingdom	8	6.9	85.7	76.7	2,428	1.4	2.2	—
Netherlands	9.8	6.1	62.4	20.8	3,088	2.5	3.1	16.7
Belgium	9.4	6.3	67.2	66.6	2,796	3.3	3.9	15.6
United States	15.2	6.8	44.6	24.3	5,711	2.4	2.3	13.2
Europe EMU	9.6	7.1	74.1	57.6	2,552	3.1	3.9	12.2

Source: The World Development Indicators 10 Years (Washington, D.C.: World Bank, 2006), 100–102.

The Welfare System in Transition

The German welfare system proved largely successful into the 1970s. It helped sustain a German (or Rhineland) model of capitalism and democracy that compared quite favorably to the "British sickness" of the early postwar era that was characterized by sluggish economic performance and recurrent labor unrest and to erratic French and Italian socioeconomic performance. Gradually, however, a combination of factors converged to pose serious challenges to its continued efficacy. Among these were the successive oil price "shocks" of the 1970s and early 1980s that prompted an economic slowdown accompanied by rapid inflation. Just as the international crisis of stagflation began to subside, major demographic challenges in the form of an aging German population and a declining birth rate were exposed. Together these pose serious financial challenges to the welfare state.[24] Rising unemployment and the unexpectedly high costs of German reunification have further strained the system at the very time that "deepening" of the European Union has imposed new constraints on domestic policy options. The German welfare state is indeed at a turning point.[25]

Germany's Social Market Economy

The material foundation of welfare provisions and democratic stability is a well-functioning economic system. Successive economic crises fatally weakened the Weimar Republic and led to its ultimate demise. A comparable argument can be made about underlying reasons for the collapse of the Soviet Union and the Communist regimes throughout Eastern Europe in 1991.

Postwar West Germany proved fortunate from a historical and comparative perspective. Despite extensive wartime damage to factories, infrastructure, and housing, the infusion of funds from the Marshall Plan helped the Germans begin the arduous task of economic reconstruction utilizing the latest technology. The entry of a veritable army of women into the workforce to help clear the rubble of bombed out buildings (hence their name, *Trümmerfrauen*, or rubble women) and the spontaneous reappearance of Weimar-era works councils further facilitated the reconstruction effort. Not long after, the introduction of codetermination in key industries in the British zone of occupation in 1947 set the stage for a sustained period of labor-management cooperation in industrial relations.

Political and policy factors also proved decisive. The creation of a trizonal economic government in the Western zones of occupation in 1948 under the directorship of Ludwig Erhard, an economist who brought to the job prior experience in industry and democratic politics, established an institutional framework for economic decision making that encompassed the entire territory of the future Federal Republic. Erhard's policy views were strongly influenced by liberal economic and social principles formulated during the war by such scholars as Alexander Rüstow, a Weimar-era official in the Economics Ministry and adviser to prominent democratic politicians.

Rüstow left Nazi Germany in 1933 to teach in Turkey, where he published studies critical of authoritarianism of both the left and the right.[26] Other theorists who specifically addressed a "new liberal" economic alternative to authoritarianism included Walter Eucken, an economist at the University of Freiburg associated with the resistance movement during the Nazi era, and Andreas Müller-Armack, an economist and sociologist who later served as head of the social economics department in the first economics ministry of the Federal Republic.

Erhard appropriated from such writings the concept of a social market economy (*soziale Marktwirtschaft*). Its basic principles included a combination of private ownership of property, government measures to promote competition, comprehensive welfare provisions, and social partnership between capital and labor. In effect, the social market economy sought to balance market forces and social justice.[27] As Chancellor Adenauer's minister of economics from 1949 to 1963 and Germany's second federal chancellor from 1963 to 1966, Erhard oversaw the implementation of these principles as the official economic policy of the fledging Federal Republic. In its early years West Germany's social market economy proved a resounding success.

Patterns of Economic Performance: The Early Years

Economic reconstruction, the implementation of social market economic policies, and a surge in global demand for steel in the wake of the Korean War combined to prompt an "economic miracle" in West Germany that was characterized by unprecedented national prosperity and virtually full employment. Further encouraging a rapid increase in production was the launch of the European integration movement with the creation of the European Coal and Steel Community in 1951–1952 and the European Economic Community in 1957–1958, both of which facilitated intra-European trade by eliminating national tariffs and other restrictions on trade and the movement of workers. West Germany's annual growth rate of 7.9 percent during the 1950s easily outpaced that of other leading OECD (Organisation for Economic Co-operation and Development) countries, including Britain and France (see Table 9.3).

Table 9.3	**Average Annual Economic Growth Rate in Germany and Other Leading OECD Countries, 1950–1984**			
	Time Period			
Country	1950–1960	1960–1970	1960–1970	1974–1984
Germany	7.9	4.9	4.6	1.9
France	4.4	5.9	5.8	2.1
Italy	6.1	5.6	4.9	2.5
Sweden	3.4	4.6	3.1	1.6
United Kingdom	2.8	2.9	2.5	1.5
United States	3.3	4.2	3.5	3

Sources: World Bank, *World Tables 1976* (Baltimore: Johns Hopkins Press for the World Bank, 1976), 398; and OECD, *Economic Outlook No. 69* (Paris: OECD, 2001), 205.

Modification of Social Market Economic Principles

All good things must come to an end, and beginning in the mid-1960s, Germany's growth rate began to slow. The rate of growth declined still further during the 1970s and early 1980s. The country's faltering economic performance had a number of political and economic consequences, beginning with Erhard's forced retirement in 1966 and the formation of the first grand coalition government that year under the leadership of CDU federal chancellor Kurt-Georg Kiesinger and SPD vice chancellor and foreign minister Willy Brandt.

One of the major policy innovations of the CDU-SPD government was the introduction in 1967 of "concerted action" (*konzertierte Aktion*), a tripartite system of economic policy consultation involving meetings between high-level government officials and representatives of private capital and organized labor.[28] Its purpose was to promote economic growth and stability in response to the prevailing economic slump and increased unemployment. Concerted action thus partially transformed social market principles by institutionalizing policy coordination among the country's principal economic actors.

Under the vigorous leadership of SPD economics minister Karl Schiller concerted action helped stimulate economic recovery during the lifespan of the grand coalition. Consensus on basic macro-economic policy goals began to erode on the eve of the 1969 election, however, and the subsequent formation of an SPD-FDP coalition government under Brandt reduced employer incentives to cooperate in the sessions. Organized labor signaled its own erosion of support when several enterprises challenged the constitutionality of a new codetermination bill passed in 1976. A year later the Confederation of German Trade Unions (*Deutscher Gewerkschaftsbund,* or DGB) angrily withdrew from concerted action, thus ending the practice altogether.[29] It was replaced by a less formalized system of bilateral consultations between government leaders and representatives of business and labor groups that prevailed during the remaining years of the SPD-FDP coalition government.

Political Context and Economic Performance

The restoration of Christian Democratic executive leadership under Helmut Kohl in 1982 heralded a qualified return to social market principles with the declared purpose of stimulating an economic *Wende* (change of direction). The CDU/CSU–FDP government was initially able to deliver on its promise, presiding over a healthy average annual growth rate of 3 percent through 1992, which was higher than those of most other leading OECD countries. Even better, this rate was accompanied by an average unemployment rate of 5.8 percent.

Reunification in 1990 fundamentally altered the national economy: first, it initiated a sweeping process of privatization in the former GDR; second, it triggered an initial phase of rapid economic expansion quickly followed by a nationwide economic slowdown and the advent of long-term structural unemployment that was especially pronounced in eastern Germany. Even among employed workers, East German wages lagged behind those of West Germans—averaging 73 percent of the latter well into the twenty-first century.[30]

Growth slowed after 1993 to an annual average of 1.5 percent through the remainder of the decade while unemployment rose to an unprecedented postwar level of 8.4 percent. These negative economic trends proved a major factor in the defeat of the Christian Democrats and Free Democrats in the 1998 election and the formation of a SPD-Green (Red-Green) coalition (discussed in chapter 7). (See Table 9.4 for German and comparative data on successive phases of economic performance from the early 1980s through 2005.)

Agenda 2010 and the Hartz Reforms

Chancellor Schröder's government inherited daunting economic challenges when it assumed office in the fall of 1998. Due to a combination of weak international performance exacerbated by economic crises in Russia and Asia and consumer timidity at home, the annual growth rate slowed still further and unemployment levels continued to climb. In parallel efforts to trim welfare expenses associated with an aging population and the high cost of unemployment benefits, in 2003 the government initiated legislation to cap retirement pensions and introduced a series of reforms under the rubric "Agenda 2010."[31] The declared goal of Agenda 2010 was to modernize both the welfare state and the labor market.

On the supply side of Agenda 2010 was a 25 percent cut in individual income taxes. Simultaneously, new regulatory policies—known collectively as the Hartz Reforms—were enacted that were intended to reduce public expenditures while introducing greater flexibility to the labor market. The reforms were named after Peter Hartz, a human resource executive at the Volkswagen automobile firm who was appointed chair of a fifteen-member "Commission for Modern Services" in February 2002. The commission's assignment was to advise the government and parliament on means to reduce the cost of welfare provisions while encouraging job creation. Four laws based on the commission's recommendations were ultimately enacted between 2003 and 2005.

Key provisions of the Hartz bills included the introduction of job centers within the regional offices of the national Agency for Labor to facilitate worker placement, increased support for vocational training, and sharply reduced payments to unemployed persons, which perhaps not surprisingly

Table 9.4	Indicators of Economic Performance in Germany and Other Leading OECD Countries, 1982–2005

Annual Growth Rate: percentage change of real GDP from previous year

| | | Time period | |
Country	1982–1992	1982–1992	2000–2005
Germany	3	1.5	1.1
France	2.3	1.7	1.9
Italy	2.5	1.8	1.2
Sweden	1.9	2.5	2.7
United Kingdom	2.5	3.1	2.7
United States	3.3	3.7	2.6

Standardized Unemployment Rates

| | | Time period | |
Country	1988–1992	1993–1999	2000–2005
Germany	5.8	8.4	8.5
France	9.1	11.2	9.2
Italy	9.1	10.9	8.7
Sweden	2.8	8.8	5.8
United Kingdom	8.2	7.8	5
United States	6.1	5.4	5.2

Average Inflation Rates

| | | Time period | |
Country	1982–1992	1993–1999	2000–2005
Germany	—	1	1.6
France	—	1.5	2
Italy	—	3.4	2.5
Sweden	6.7	1.5	1.4
United Kingdom	5.1	2.1	1.3
United States	3.8	2.5	2.4

Source: Percentages calculated by the authors from OECD, Economic Outlook 81 (June 2007): 239, 252, 256.
Note: — indicates data unavailable for specific country for specific time period.

proved controversial. Instead of individuals receiving between 53 and 67 percent of net salary for an indefinite period as they did under the pre-2005 system, jobless persons now receive only twelve months of full employment pay followed by a much lower level of unemployment benefits (known as *Arbeitslosenggeld II*). To be even eligible for the lower amount, unemployed persons first have to deplete their life insurance and savings reserves. These changes were clearly designed to discourage citizens from relying on the state for long-term unemployment assistance and to seek at least part-time jobs instead.

The *Bundestag* endorsed the Hartz bills with the support of the Christian Democrats but with divided ranks among the governing Social Democrats. By initiating the reforms, Chancellor Schröder underscored his ideological stance as a more conservative SPD leader than his predecessors and, in the process, alienated many leftist Social Democrats and trade unionists. Herein lies much of the explanation for Oskar Lafontaine's new popularity and increased electoral support for the Left Party, as recounted in chapters 6 and 7.

Economic Performance after 2005

Rank-and-file opposition to the Hartz Reforms contributed to the erosion of SPD strength in the September 2005 election and the party's loss of the chancellorship, but once implemented these reforms did help stimulate an incipient economic recovery. By the end of Chancellor Angela Merkel's second year in office, annual economic growth had surged to 3 percent (compared to 0.8 percent in 2004), and the unemployment rate dropped from 9.5 percent to 8.4 percent. During the same period Germany sustained one of the lowest inflation rates among leading OECD countries: 1.8 percent in 2006, compared to 3.2 percent in the United States, 2.3 percent in the United Kingdom, 2.2 percent in Italy, and 1.9 percent in France.[32] (In chapter 11, we consider whether these favorable trends are likely to continue in the foreseeable future.)

Life in the fast lane, courtesy of carmaker BMW, one of Germany's many exports. The company's logo, recognized around the world, is seen here on the corporate headquarters in Munich.

Global and European Trade

Germany's socioeconomic performance is deeply embedded in multinational factors of trade, human resources, and the policies and politics of the European Union. Economic policy, and with it the viability of the welfare state, is both domestic and foreign. Germany is the leading European powerhouse with respect to global trade, and its central role is as the most important economic "locomotive" within the EU. As Table 9.5 indicates, German exports and imports are second only to those of the United States among OECD countries—eclipsing even those of Japan.

The bulk of Germany's trade is with its European neighbors. As shown in Table 9.6, France is the country's leading trading partner, followed by the United Kingdom, Italy, and the Netherlands. Trade with Spain and Switzerland is also significant. A noteworthy trend is a gradual increase in both exports to and imports from the Russian Federation. The United States is Germany's largest export/import market outside of Europe.

Table 9.5	Shares in World Trade by Leading OECD Countries, 1992–2007

Exports (as a percentage of world trade)

	Time Period	
Country	1992–1999	2000–2007
Germany	9.3	8.9
France	5.6	4.6
Italy	4.5	3.8
United Kingdom	5.4	4.9
Japan	7.3	5.4
United States	13.6	11.4

Imports (as a percentage of world trade)

Germany	9.2	8
France	5.3	4.6
Italy	4	3.7
United Kingdom	5.6	5.5
Japan	6.1	4.8
United States	15.5	16.6

Source: Calculated by the authors from OECD, *Economic Outlook* 81 (June 2007): 283.

Table 9.6	German Trade, 2003–2006			

Exports (as a percentage of exports to the world)

Region/Country	2003	Year 2004	2005	2006
Europe as a whole	74	74	74	74

Within Europe (in rank order of percentage exports)

France	14	14	14	13
United Kingdom	11	11	10	10
Italy	10	9	9	9
Netherlands	9	9	8	8
Austria	7	7	7	7
Spain	7	7	7	6
Switzerland	5	5	5	5
Russia	2	3	3	4

Other Important Markets (as a percentage of total exports to the world)

United States	9	9	9	9
China	3	3	3	3

Imports (as a percentage of total imports from the world)

Region/Country	2003	Year 2004	2005	2006
Europe as a whole	72	71	71	71

Within Europe (in rank order of percentage imports)

France	13	13	12	12
Netherlands	11	11	12	12
Italy	9	9	8	8
United Kingdom	8	8	9	8
Austria	6	6	6	6
Spain	6	6	6	6
Switzerland	5	5	5	5
Russia	4	4	5	6

Other Important Markets (as a percentage of total imports from the world)

United States	7	7	7	7
China	5	6	7	7

Source: Calculated by the authors from euro amounts published in *Statistisches Jahrbuch 2007 für die Bundesrepublik Deutschland 2007* (Wiesbaden: Statistisches Bundesamt, 2007), 471–473.

Immigration and Its Discontents

An accompanying aspect of Germany's pivotal role in the world and European economy is the internationalization of its workforce, particularly among blue-collar workers. A key measure is an ongoing tide of immigration, rooted historically in West Germany's earlier reliance on guest workers (*Gastarbeiter*) from southern European countries and Turkey and—in more recent decades—the appeal of the country's economic prosperity and political stability. Immigrants presently number 1.7 million workers and their families and constitute 9 percent of the country's population. A majority of the immigrants are fellow Europeans (79.3 percent in 2004), dominated by Turks (26.3 percent) who comprise a conspicuous force in the labor market. Other important foreign groups include Asians (12.3 percent), Serbs (5.7 percent), Poles (4.3 percent), and Africans (4.1 percent).[33]

The immigrant tide has created discernible strains in German society, just as it has in other European countries. Much public concern about immigration has focused on cultural-religious differences between the majority Christian population and a growing Muslim minority. These differences have prompted vicious attacks by skinheads and other "white supremacists" against aliens and a spirited national debate on immigration reform that has included measures to ease citizenship requirements as a partial means to offset the country's declining birth rate.[34]

Police and judicial officials have become more vigilant in identifying and detaining potential terrorists among immigrants and their German sympathizers. After authorities determined that three of the hijackers involved in the 9/11 attacks in the United States had been members of a terrorist cell in Hamburg, intelligence officials launched a determined effort to track and apprehend potential suspects. In 2006 police thwarted an attempted bomb plot on a German train, and in September 2007 three men were arrested in southern Germany and charged with assembling car bombs intended for detonation at a U.S. air base. One of the suspects was a Turkish immigrant; the others were German nationals who had converted to Islam and attended jihad training camps in Pakistan.

Europeanization of Socioeconomic Policies

Within the broader fabric of economic and social internationalization, the European Union commands an especially crucial place in German affairs. As we have recounted in previous chapters, West Germany was a cofounder of the postwar integration movement and a key political architect of its successive permutations—from the original European Coal and Steel Community through the European Economic Community to today's European Union. Unified Germany, alongside France and in shifting coalitions with other member states, plays a central leadership role in formulating EU policies ranging from a common agricultural market to an integrated market and Economic and Monetary Union (EMU). The free movement of goods, persons, and investments within the framework of a "deepening" and "broadening" EU has proved a major stimulus to economic growth and prosperity throughout the community.

EU membership also imposes constraints and policy obligations. Representatives of Germany's Federal Bank (*Bundesbank*) help shape the EU's macroeconomic and monetary policies through their membership on the board of the Central European Bank in Frankfurt, but Germany no longer exercises sovereign control over either of these important policy arenas. Nor does it mint its own currency, now that the German Mark—along with the French franc, the Italian lira, and other national currencies—has given way to the euro.[35]

Coupled with EMU one of the most significant consequences of the integrated regional market is a general policy shift within the EU away from Keynesian economic principles, with their emphasis on countercyclical policies instigated by governments to promote economic growth and stability (in the tradition of concerted action during the 1960s and 1970s), toward neo-liberal policies dominated by market forces. The European Commission epitomizes this approach with its explicit mandate to encourage competition through antitrust measures and restrictions on state subsidies to targeted industries and economic sectors.[36]

The loss of Germany's autonomous capacity to pursue independent macro-economic and monetary policies is a partial explanation for the government's inability to respond more effectively to sluggish growth, increased unemployment, and financial threats to the welfare state. The government can no longer act to implement autonomous social market economic policies. The same constraints apply, of course, to other member states in the EU. Recognizing common economic and social imperatives, EU member states launched an ambitious community action program in 2000 known as the Lisbon strategy,[37] the basic goal of which is to stimulate Europeanwide growth through job creation and investment in regional development (including eastern Germany). The target date for achieving this objective is 2010. Germany's Agenda 2010 is a direct derivative of the EU initiative.

Conclusion

What remains, then, of the postwar German model? The short answer is, "very little"; the crucial exceptions being democratic stability and relative labor peace.[38] A European social model is equally tenuous under conditions of sluggish growth and persisting high unemployment, and for the time being, Germany's welfare state remains a national construct. The EU has affirmed a common social charter and social protocol (the latter attached to the Treaty on European Union of 1992), but most welfare expenditures are the prerogative and responsibility of each member state. Nonetheless, the pragmatic necessity to harmonize welfare benefits across national borders, especially given the increased internationalization of the labor force, points toward at least the partial convergence of Europe's welfare systems in the future.[39] Globalization and Europeanization also characterize German foreign policy. Unlike integration within the single market or membership in the EMU, however, foreign policy remains an object of governmental and intergovernmental action.

10 Germany in Europe and the World

For a century following the formation of a German nation-state in the mid-nineteenth century, it was common (especially in Germany itself) to stress the leading role of foreign affairs in shaping public policy. With some important qualifications noted below, we maintain that domestic policy has driven German governments in the six decades since World War II. Whether this is likely to continue in the early twenty-first century will be considered later in this chapter and in the one following.[1]

Foreign Policy in Contemporary German Politics

This relatively greater importance of domestic policy is reflected in popular attitudes toward foreign policy issues. For many years the pollsters for the *Politbarometer* reports have asked Germans to name the two most important issues of the day, and foreign policy questions are never among the first two named by at least 10 percent of the respondents. Often, they are not found among the top ten issues named, period. In the same polls Germans are asked to rank public figures (on a scale of plus or minus 5); the last two foreign ministers (Joschka Fischer, 1998–2005; Frank–Walter Steinmeier since 2005) have always ranked either first or, less often, second. Inasmuch as all other figures named, including chancellors, experience large rises and falls in esteem, and given the lack of interest by responders toward foreign policy issues, we conclude that the favorable reception the foreign ministers receive lies in lack of public concern with their work. (Steinmeier did slip behind Chancellor Angela Merkel after a controversy arose about his work as former chancellor Schröder's aide on a terrorism case.)[2]

Personalities are well and good, but as is widely recognized, budget priorities reflect the "true" values of a community, and when it comes to spending *Deutschmark* or euros, Germans prefer to spend them on domestic projects. Thus, for example, while the rate of inflation grew at 4 percent between 1990 and 2001, budgeting for defense shrank from €32 billion to less than €23 billion; development aid to other countries dropped in the same period from €4.3 billion to €3.6 billion. Only the smallest of the three foreign policy budgets, that of the Foreign Ministry, grew slightly from €1.8 billion to €2 billion. The appropriations for these three foreign policy ministries, taken as a percentage of the total federal expenditures, dropped from 21.5 percent in 1990 to just over 12 percent in 2003.[3] In 2005–2006, German military expenditures constituted 1.5 percent of the gross domestic product, compared to 4.1 percent in the United States, 2.6 percent in the United Kingdom, 2.4 percent in France, and 2 for the European Union (EU).[4]

German Foreign Policy before Unification

The main objective of German foreign policy in both East and West between 1949 and German reunification in 1990 was to restore Germany's status as a sovereign nation-state. In Helga Haftendorn's words: "In 1945 Germany was defeated and destroyed, occupied and divided.... How could Germany grow from a 'twice-bound' state ... into a well-respected member of the international community?"[5] Thus German "foreign" policy aimed at securing the agreement or at least the acquiescence of outside powers (essentially the four occupation powers) to the establishment of full German sovereignty and unification of German territories into a single national-state.[6]

The main steps along this road are associated with three dynamic political leaders, three chancellors whose initiatives marked qualitative changes in Germany's international status. The first of these, Konrad Adenauer, brought West Germany into economic and military coalitions with other Western countries through the Schuman Plan. This then led to the creation of the European Coal and Steel Community in 1952, NATO membership in 1955, and the Rome treaties in 1957 that established the European Economic Community, the forerunner of today's EU. Second, Willy Brandt improved relations with the Soviet Union and East Europe, secured an international settlement of the Berlin issue (1971), advanced reconciliation with Poland (1970), established relations with the GDR (1972–1973), and helped bring both Germanys into the United Nations (1973). Finally, Helmut Kohl (1989–1990) took advantage of an unexpectedly favorable international constellation to manage the peaceful reunification of Germany.[7]

Germany's Role in Europe and the World since 1990

It was during the first dozen years or so after reunification that German leaders and the public were confronted with questions of a different foreign policy orientation for a Germany that had achieved the goals of the postwar half century.[8] This search for a more relevant foreign policy is often described as a contrast between two Germanys: one a "civilian," the other a "national," power. The former would continue being committed to multi-lateral institutions and supranational regimes and devoted to policies reflecting its normative commitment to peace and democracy; the latter would seek to maximize its state interests in the same ways and with the same means, including use of force, as did other states.[9] In fact, Germany, especially during the chancellorship of Gerhard Schröder, managed to pursue both perspectives; the "civilian" model was not abandoned, but it was adapted to pursue new aims with new methods.[10] The latter included ever more frequent deployment of German armed forces abroad in pursuit of both national and multilateral goals.[11]

It is noteworthy that the transition from Schröder to Merkel has produced only small changes of emphasis in German foreign policy, although not surprising in light of her grand coalition government, whose foreign minister was Schröder's close foreign policy adviser.[12] As we note below, Merkel has taken an active role in foreign affairs; her public standing in these matters is higher than in domestic policy. She has sought to smooth relations with the United States, despite continued policy disputes, including clashes over troop deployment to Afghanistan, detainment of individuals by the United States at Guantanamo Bay, and climate change. At the same time she has publicly distanced Germany from such aspects of Russian policy as the treatment of dissidents and pressuring NATO (North Atlantic Treaty Organization) and EU allies while maintaining close ties on such essential matters as energy policy. During Germany's term as EU leader in the first six months of 2007, Merkel obtained substantial progress on basic EU reform, albeit at the interim price of worsened German-Polish relations.

German Military Deployments as a Foreign Policy Tool

The most striking foreign policy consequence of German reunification and full sovereignty has been the more frequent and controversial deployment of German military forces "out of [the European] area" (see Table 10.1). The chronicle of German military deployments abroad over the past decade has been marked by several political trajectories. First is the gradual shift from humanitarian help through peacekeeping to peace enforcing; second, there has been a change from constitutional challenge to acceptance through rulings of the Federal Constitutional Court; finally, an initial public acceptance, especially of humanitarian aid as an expression of Germany's responsibility for a better world, has been overshadowed both by outright political opposition (especially from the Left Party) and growing doubts as to costs, attainable goals, and collateral involvements.[13]

Total German deployments over approximately the past decade number some eighteen episodes; as of spring 2008, eleven were still in operation. They

Table 10.1	German Military Deployments Abroad ("out of [NATO] area")		
Operation/ auspices	Dates	Goal	Details
UN	1992–1993	Cambodia aid	Medical personnel
UN	1992–1994	Stabilize Somalia	1,800 soldiers
UN weapons inspections	1992–1996	Help UNSCOM in Iraq	German helicopter support
NATO	1993–1995	Bosnia	Air missions
NATO and UN	1995–	Post-"Dayton" peacekeeping	Ground forces
NATO air war	1999	Kosovo	Air forces in combat
NATO	2000–	Kosovo peacekeeping	Ground forces
UN/NATO; antiterrorism	2001	"Enduring Freedom" (OEF)	Naval forces, Horn of Africa
NATO/UN	2001–	OEF/ISAF	Afghanistan antiterrorism, nation-building
UNIFIL (UN)	2006–	Arms interdiction after Lebanon war	Naval forces
Various*	1993–	EU and UN support missions	Small numbers, time limits

Sources: Mary Elise Sarotte, *German Military Reform and European Security* [Adelphi Paper 340] (London: Oxford University Press, 2001), 9–11; and Federal Defense Ministry at www.einsatz.bundeswehr.de.
*Small missions to Georgia, Eritrea, East Timor, DR Congo, and Macedonia

range in substance from medical personnel sent to Cambodia in 1992 to current combat operations in Afghanistan. In scope they vary from one or two persons to the almost three thousand in Afghanistan, where Germans form the largest single NATO contingent. Lastly, German forces have been deployed under auspices that range from the United Nations (UN) to the CCSE (Conference on Cooperation and Security in Europe) to the EU and NATO.[14]

This expansive international presence must be seen as part of Germany's search for an appropriate international role, and is the military aspect of the country's search (especially under Schröder) for a permanent UN Security Council seat.[15] Germans remember the accusations made during the 1991 Gulf War that their powerful, united country had limited its role in repelling aggression to mere "checkbook diplomacy." In this context, the Gulf War acted as a sort of catharsis, because Germany was confronted with a question of obligations, both narrowly to the United States and NATO and broadly to the international community. Germany, after having striven for a half century to show how harmless it was, faced requests to act militarily.[16] The Kohl government, politically unsure of public reaction and concerned over a constitutional challenge to military involvement, helped only with money and materiel, but this set the stage for further debates, leading up to a crucial 1994 Constitutional Court decision.[17]

This court decision was brought about by the increasing pressure Germany faced to participate in a variety of peace-keeping actions; a crisis over the constitutional justification for such actions was unavoidable. In 1993, the Constitutional Court ruled by a narrow 5-3 margin that AWACS (radar reconnaissance aircraft) deployment over the Adriatic Sea to help enforce a UN-sanctioned arms embargo in the war in Bosnia had been sanctioned by a UN resolution. Subsequently, both the SPD (Social Democratic Party), which was then in opposition, and the FDP (Free Democratic Party), then in the government, argued that a two-year mission (1992–1994) in Somalia and a naval blockade of the former Yugoslavia were unconstitutional on the grounds that such actions did not constitute the type of defensive steps authorized under Article 87a of the Basic Law. In any case, party members argued, these actions stretched the intent of German membership in such multilateral pacts as NATO (provided for in Article 59 of the Basic Law) so far as to require specific constitutional sanction.

In a historic June 1994 decision, the court ruled that Germany may "assign ... armed forces" to missions undertaken by the UN, NATO, and the European Union. The court drew no distinction between peace-enforcement and peace-keeping missions, and for this reason, it declared the Bosnian and Adriatic missions constitutional. Similar future actions were suitable provided the government sought *Bundestag* approval. (A formal arrangement requiring *Bundestag* action was passed in 2004; previously, the government and the *Bundestag* agreed informally to hold such debates and votes.)[18]

The most dramatic and precedent-setting example of this process came in November 2001. Chancellor Schröder asked the *Bundestag* to approve German military intervention in Afghanistan as part the NATO commitment to aid the United States in its response to the attacks of September 11. In this the Schröder/Fischer government faced strong opposition from members of the coalition's SPD and Green parliamentarians. Although the government had relied on opposition votes to pass its resolution in a previous instance involving a brief peace-keeping mission in Macedonia, Schröder deemed this venture too important not to be supported by a "chancellor majority." He therefore linked approval of this deployment to a vote of confidence in his government, at the time only the fourth such gesture in the history of the Federal Republic In the vote on November 16, 2001, the government triumphed by a margin of 336-226, two votes over the needed absolute majority of 334. (This meant that at least four coalition legislators had voted against the government.)[19]

Even in discussions concerning humanitarian military actions,[20] critical voices are increasingly heard.[21] The very fact that some of these actions that were supposed to be of short or at least limited duration have continued without an end in sight has increased public disquiet about them. Critics call for criteria with which to evaluate the effectiveness of such actions, their cost, and their duration. Opponents may be silenced momentarily by media images of suffering, but they eventually counter that the immediate urge to action is not accompanied by a calculation of effectiveness.[22]

One of the most politically sensitive deployments of German forces abroad was a naval mission to the Lebanese coast following the Israeli-Lebanese (Hezbollah) conflict in the summer of 2006.[23] Although this was a peace-keeping operation involving the inspection of ships to enforce a UN arms embargo, the possibility of combat with Israeli forces in the area and concerns of ever-expanding German involvement in military deployments produced a heated political debate. In light of a UN Security Council mandate and express Israeli acquiescence in German participation in the UN's Lebanese operations (United Nations Interim Force in Lebanon, or UNIFIL), the *Bundestag* approved German participation by a vote of 442-152, with five abstentions. Those who opposed the action included all the Left Party deputies, most of the FDP, thirty-two Social Democrats, and six Greens. Although the mandate of this mission originally was scheduled to expire at the end of August 2007, the government has secured extensions of the mission.

The deployment of forces to Afghanistan most starkly confronts Germans with the reality that military diplomacy involves both killing and dying. Indeed, the country's military commitment to NATO-led security forces in Afghanistan has given rise to growing uneasiness among both the general public and portions of the political leadership. Part of the problem is the blurring of the distinction between bringing stability to the country (peace keeping and nation building) through an international security assistance force (ISAF) and fighting Taliban and al-Qaida remnants as part of the U.S.-led "Enduring Freedom" (OEF) campaign against terrorism. (German naval forces stationed off the Horn of Africa also assist in "Enduring Freedom.")

Until 2007, Germany had resisted taking a more active combat role in the region for any reason. Then in March of that year, the government obtained *Bundestag* approval to have German "Tornado" reconnaissance jets fly support missions in the southern provinces. A Left Party challenge before the Constitutional Court was rejected in July 2007 on the grounds that German actions in Afghanistan contributed to defense of the North Atlantic area and therefore were consistent with the 1955 law on German NATO accession.[24]

Outside of the air support missions, most of the roughly three thousand German troops in the country are working on infrastructure projects in the relatively trouble-free northern provinces, where casualties have been relatively low. Despite complaints from fellow NATO members (especially Canada and the Netherlands) that Germany was shirking its due share of risk in the dangerous areas of southern Afghanistan, the German government has, as of spring 2008, refused to send combat troops there. In this the current grand coalition government has continued Schröder's policies, even at the cost of public rows with the United States at NATO meetings in February and April 2008 and the subsequent annual Munich security conference.[25]

A German medic with the International Security Assistance Force speaks to Afghan girls at a free medical camp in the outskirts of Kabul, Afghanistan, April 2, 2008. Germany's allies have urged the country to increase its military deployments in various trouble zones, but to date the German government has met these demands with considerable restraint.

The ISAF commitment, last renewed in October 2007, has faced mounting questions about its utility as a result of lack of progress in Afghanistan as well as German casualties inflicted by suicide bombers.[26] These objections currently come mostly from Left Party members, Greens, and some SPD political figures, but they reflect longer-range skepticism, much of it along party lines. November 2006 polling showed that only 57 percent of those polled approved of military commitments to secure peace; 69 percent wished to see a reduction in such initiatives. As the accompanying Table 10.2 shows, supporters of the Greens most favored German peace-keeping actions, Left Party supporters supported them the least. The relatively low levels of SPD support are especially striking, given the prominent role played in these policies by the SPD foreign minister Frank-Walter Steinmeier.[27]

Further, a poll commissioned in August 2007 by the weekly *Die Zeit*, found that 62 percent of those polled thought that the Afghan intervention was on the whole wrong (34 percent said it was correct); older respondents, women, eastern Germans, and those with low levels of education tended to hold such negative views.[28] In fairness, it should be added that some objections to an open-ended ISAF commitment have been based on inadequate support by many NATO states as well as the ill-defined goals of the mission. Indeed, critics more attuned to a "realistic" critique of intervention have

Table 10.2	Support for German Military Peacekeeping, 2006			
	Percent support for military peacekeeping in principle		Percent support to reduce number of German commitments abroad	
Party	Yes	No	Yes	No
Greens	81	17	59	39
CDU	65	32	62	37
FDP	63	36	72	27
SPD	51	41	71	27
Left Party	39	59	83	17
All	57	39	69	29

Source: Adapted from Infratest dimap poll, ARD Deutschland TREND November 2006, www.infratest-dimap.de/?id39&aid=143.

pointed to the lack of clarity as to the immediate aims of German and other NATO forces. Are they to implement the Afghan government's desires? Shall they undertake an antinarcotic campaign to reduce burgeoning poppy production and reduce the heroin trade that has exploded in the country? Any plausible course of action—here as in other arenas of intervention—will produce winners appreciative of German actions as well as losers hostile to the outcome.[29] Amid a rising clamor to end the German military presence in Afghanistan, plans to reorganize and redefine the mission there are unlikely to sway much of the public. A German withdrawal from the country, however, aside from its effect on Afghanistan, would also harm Germany's NATO ties, particularly to NATO countries, such as Canada and the Netherlands, that have combat units there.[30]

Germany and Its International Partners

Even in this current era of global commitment, much of Germany's foreign policy remains directed toward the United States, Russia, and the EU. Although all three relationships have undergone some turbulent and controversial moments, the underlying policies have remained largely the same. Germany sees its role in the world, aside from the international responsibility for peacekeeping discussed above, as developing within a European framework. With this view in mind, it wishes to maintain good economic relations with Russia, especially in energy trade and hopes to have a special role in shaping the EU's long-term relationship with that country. And despite some loud disputes, German economic, political, and security ties to the United States remain strong. These policy continuities, however, tend to overshadow changing attitudes at the mass opinion level; thus whether Germany's policies in these areas will have the same direction a decade or more from now is uncertain.

Germany and the United States

As the immediate postwar period gave way in 1946–1947 to the long Cold War era that ended in 1990, Germany and the United States formed a community of mutual interests, one in which the American partner, thanks to its occupation status and overwhelmingly greater resources, was dominant. For Germany, this connection helped bring about German unification and restoration of sovereignty; not surprisingly, German leaders were careful never to stray too far from U.S. views and interests. Therefore, some of the recent outbursts of mutual bad feeling and U.S. (and German) criticisms of recent German leaders must be understood against this background of expected German "reliability."[31]

In truth, German-U.S. relations have not always been smooth, despite the two countries' strong mutual interests: Chancellor Konrad Adenauer questioned President John Kennedy's policies and strengthened German ties to France as a result; Richard Nixon and Henry Kissinger deeply mistrusted Willy Brandt and his *Ostpolitik*; German recognition of Croatian and Slovene independence in 1992 aroused concern in the George H. W. Bush administration.[32] Disagreements over a range of issues, including climate change, international justice, and strategic plans, have arisen since 1990 and indeed have continued under Merkel's grand coalition government and are probably more noticeable without the dampening public effect of Soviet pressure.[33]

The great divide between the two countries came over the invasion of Iraq in 2003. Chancellor Schröder, aware of overwhelming German opposition to the invasion, took a stance alongside that of the Chirac government in France that was adamantly opposed to U.S. policy.[34] Schröder declared that even in the event of Security Council approval, Germany would not support an Iraq invasion.[35] That these statements came during the bitterly contested election campaign of 2002, and that they were widely seen (especially in Washington) as an electoral ploy on Schröder's part, plunged the relationship to new low levels.[36] In reality, the depth of German public opposition to the war caused Schröder's opponent, Edmund Stoiber, leader of the Christian Social Union (CSU), to avoid clear support for the U.S. position; other opposition leaders, while decrying Schröder's style, joined his stance against the war.[37] Berlin-Washington relations have become calmer under Merkel, although she and senior members of her government, as noted above, have disagreed in public with U.S. policy on a variety of issues.

Despite such policy disagreements, U.S.-German relations have remained constant in several important areas, including security cooperation and foreign trade, and Germany had never distanced itself from post-9/11 antiterrorism policies. The extent of German cooperation in intelligence activities, while not clearly revealed, seems to be considerable. Moreover, over the past decade, Germany's trade with its American partner has remained steady. (For the economic importance of German foreign trade, see chapter 9.) In

2006, the United States was Germany's third largest export market and fourth largest source of imports. It may be significant for foreign policy in the near future that German exports to Russia increased by 128 percent in 2001–2006 but only 15 percent to the United States.[38]

As with relations between and among many countries, the various disputes over policy and persons that have roiled U.S.-German relations in recent years will presumably settle into a more normal pattern of pursuit of national goals on both sides.[39] Among the reasons for current rocky German-U.S. relations may be longstanding cultural attitudes, which Germany's independent standing in world affairs have allowed to surface, or perhaps the personality and policies of President George W. Bush. What is fairly certain is that a Germany that has become more of an autonomous actor in world affairs will find issues on which it will not agree with Washington.[40]

Given the global power discrepancy between the United States and Germany, it is not surprising that Germans have more detailed and intense attitudes toward the United States than Americans have toward Germany.[41] German approval of the United States dropped between 2000 and 2007 from 78 percent to 30 percent.[42] (Notably, in 2006, 66 percent of Germans had favorable views of *Americans*.) Among NATO nations, German views of the United States are more negative than those in, among others, Britain, Canada, France, Poland, and Spain. Germans believe that oil and world power are driving forces behind the Iraq War, of which they are very conscious—98 percent say that they have heard of Abu Ghraib, which is more than in, for example, France, Great Britain, and Spain.

This intensity of negative feeling raises questions regarding its possible long-term underlying basis. Among many educated Germans, such issues as climate change, the death penalty, gun control, and multilateral approaches to foreign policy, among others, have arisen as topics of discussion and scrutiny, and differing views on these issues across populations seem to deepen a gulf of outlook between the countries. A 2007 article in *Der Spiegel* described how American university exchange students—in this case mostly in Baden-Württemberg—are subjected to hostility and scorn. At the very least these students are questioned sharply on both U.S. foreign policy and American cultural characteristics, such as gun ownership or the death penalty; and hostility to the Bush administration among German students seems almost universal.[43]

But is all of this necessarily not normal? It might well be argued that it was the close, taken-for-granted parallels in German and U.S. attitudes that were abnormal, products of the Cold War. Divergences and frictions, within a broad alliance, may be considered the norm in most international relation scenarios.[44] Moreover, critical German views of the United States, its politics and social values, have surfaced before; the current period of tense relations may well be succeeded by one of closer ties.[45] To the extent that these tensions are due to German reluctance to support military action, this may be seen as an ironic triumph of U.S. occupation and alliance policy. Half a century ago, who would have been unhappy with the prospect of a peaceful, nonaggressive Germany?

Germany and Russia

German-Russian relations have a much longer and more intense and detailed history than the relations with the United States. Periods of warm relations between Russia and various German states have mingled with those of intense hostility, the latter reaching their high point during World War II. German power has at times exceeded Russia's; at other times, as during the half century after Word War II, Russian (or Soviet) power extended deep into Germany.[46] As Angela Stent points out, before Germany's attack in 1941, the country had more to offer the Soviet Union (and did, as at Rapallo, or in the Hitler-Stalin pact) than the Soviet Union had to offer Germany.

After 1945 and until 1990 both eastern and western Germans needed Soviet support for their own aims and could therefore be manipulated by Soviet diplomacy. Their bi- and multilateral relations were central for the Soviet Union and the two German states. As noted earlier in the text, the Soviet leadership in 1989–1991 failed in its efforts to partially disengage from Central Europe without having to accept a unified Germany into NATO. In the ensuing decade, Germany held a strong economic and political bargaining position with Russia.

Under the multilateral arrangements for German reunification, Germany extended substantial material help to the Soviet Union for the return of Soviet troops to their homeland, including construction of housing. German investment, cultural ties, and scholarly cooperation strengthened German ties to Russia that reflect the absence of any strategic (territorial, global, military) disputes.[47] Peaceful relations are also underscored by the important trade ties between the two countries.[48] German exports to Russia are more than double that of the next highest trade partner, while Germany is the second largest customer of Russian exports. In a pattern that resembles former Soviet-German ties, Russia imports primarily industrial machinery and exports raw materials.[49]

Germany, like much of the EU, is heavily dependent on Russian oil and natural gas imports: Russia accounts for roughly 40 percent of German natural gas imports and more than a third of oil imports. As Vladimir Milov points out, "Germany is the main European energy partner of Russia, and it is widely perceived that Russia and Germany have a 'special energy relationship' of a much better quality than those between Russia and the European Union."[50] Russian oil and gas fields in western Siberia, together with pipeline networks dating from the Soviet era, make Russia the most economically viable source of German energy. Under Schröder, Germany and Russia agreed to build an undersea pipeline in the Baltic to deliver oil and gas directly to German terminals.[51] This relationship of mutual dependence (Russian foreign exchange earnings are heavily dependent on energy sales abroad) has led Germany to seek a long-term "energy partnership." Although Russian reserves are not likely to expand, and Germany will seek to diversify its sources, Russia remains a major long-term energy supplier. Here the issue of German energy relations is linked to Germany's more general political relations with Russia.[52]

Ongoing relations, however, also will be shaped in the near and middle-term future by EU ties to Russia, and Russia's political development and foreign policy. For historical and political reasons, German leaders have envisioned Germany as a bridge builder between Russia and the EU. Seeing no difficult bilateral issues, this seemed a natural role. Along those lines, the current coalition agreement sees it as Germany's place to aid Russia's modernization and help shape Russian acceptance of Western values.[53]

This prospect of close and harmonious German-Russian ties has been clouded by the rise of other issues and by a difference of outlook between Merkel and Steinmeier.[54] Merkel's cooler relations reflect differences between the CDU (Christian Democratic Union) and the SPD, as well as her East German background. Steinmeier has a more pro-Russia (described as *Wandel durch Verflechtung*—"change through integration") policy than Merkel. The frustrations resulting from these differences and emotions over disputes with Russian president Vladimir Putin erupted at a May 2007 EU-Russia summit in Samara, Russia. Rather than arranging EU-Russia cooperation, the participants instead were faced with a crackdown on Russian dissidents seeking to reach the city, a Polish-Russian trade dispute, and suspicion both of Russian domestic policies and pressure on its "near abroad" neighbors.[55]

Germany's intention to be a leader in bringing Russia into multilateral cooperation with the West is further complicated by differing attitudes within the EU itself. Older, West European members support such efforts for reasons similar to Germany's, whereas newer, especially Central and East European, members are suspicious of Russia's intentions. Thus, German-Russian cooperation arouses fears and is used politically in Poland, with which Germany also seeks good relations.[56]

Finally, it is worth noting that closer relations with Russia, and support for the project of bringing Russia into closer relations with Europe, do not enjoy mass support in Germany and perhaps not in Russia either. A majority of Germans (58 percent) thought that excessive dependence on Russian energy was a matter for concern, while 62 percent of Germans polled had a generally unfavorable view of Russia.[57] Moreover, a 2007 poll in Russia, commissioned by the EU, found that a plurality of Russians polled (45 percent) thought that the EU represented a potential threat for Russia. Large numbers did not see Russia as a European society or thought that Western democracy was suitable for the country.[58]

Germany and the EU

For more than half a century, German leaders have steered their country's foreign relations through a multilateral, European channel.[59] This approach has allowed Germany to advance its national interests in a nonthreatening manner, and German leaders have taken care not to get too far ahead of other European community partners. A classic example was the Kohl government's acquiescence in French plans for a common currency in exchange for French acceptance of German reunification. Indeed, Franco-German cooperation has always been the driving force behind European integration, despite inevitable personal and policy disputes between Paris and Berlin.[60] This was all the more so due to repeated British hesitation about a European commitment, which deprived Germany of a European counterweight to France.[61]

Throughout the slow and halting process that has led to the current European Union, Germany has been a proponent of further integration.[62] For example, it has supported successive expansions of the community, the establishment of a central bank and a common currency, and the elaboration of common foreign and security policies. In 2007, the German government was a leader in breaking the logjam in EU development arising from the French and Dutch rejections in 2005 of a proposed EU constitution (discussed further, below).

For the most part, German leaders have worked on the European project knowing that they had broad if not always intense popular support. Overall, Germans do support transfer of responsibility for important functions to European institutions (see Tables 10.3 and 10.4). These include crime and terrorism, the environment, energy, immigration, and defense and foreign affairs.[63] In their positive attitudes towards the European project, Germans are close to median European views.[64]

This congruence between German and European objectives does not mean that there are no points of friction. Germany is a major contributor to EU redistribution programs, and a weaker German economy hampers German performance in this area.[65] Germany also did not abide by economic criteria for euro membership during an economic slowdown in the early years of the twenty-first century. Lastly, German reluctance to spend on foreign and defense projects, noted earlier in this chapter, constrains the EU's ability to develop a common security and defense policy.[66]

Although some analysts have seen this as indicating a more "contingent" Europeanism, the German record of commitment and leadership seems largely intact.[67] This is illustrated by Germany's role in early 2007 in promoting an agreement to break the EU's constitutional deadlock. In lengthy, difficult, and often personally contentious negotiations, Chancellor Merkel—who headed the European Council under terms of the EU's rotating presidency during the first half of the year—secured a compromise on

Table 10.3	German Attitudes toward the EU, 2007 (in percentages)

EU membership brings Germans ...	advantages: 27	disadvantages: 28	some of both: 47
EU unification is proceeding ...	too quickly: 46	too slowly: 10	right pace: 39
EU influence on German affairs ...	too much: 41	too little: 12	right amount: 36
Is there a "European culture"?	yes: 37	no: 60	n/a
Proud to be a European?	yes: 74	no: 22	n/a
Support a European constitution?	yes: 47	no: 14	don't know: 38

Sources: Politbarometer findings on occasion of the fiftieth anniversary of the Treaty of Rome. Repräsentative Umfrage KW-11, March 2, 2007; and Politbarometer KW 13, March 3, 2007, 3.

Table 10.4	German Attitudes in EU Context (percentage in agreement)

Issue	EU average	Germany (West)	Germany (East)	All Germany	Poland	France
EU protects from negative effects of globalization	42	45	32	—	—	—
EU enables citizens to benefit from globalization	50	55	44	—	—	—
More trust in national parliament	43	—	—	51	15	—
More trust in EU parliament	56	—	—	58	60	—
Approve EU enlargement	49	—	—	34	—	32

Sources: European Commission, Eurobarometer 67 (Spring 2007) [German and English language versions], National Report: Germany.
Note: — indicates specific data not available

a weighted voting system and several other contentious issues, including designation of an EU "foreign minister." [68]

This episode showed both the possibilities and limitations of Germany's EU role.[69] As the most populous and economically vital EU member, Germany was expected to take a lead in solving these questions. On the other hand, acts of German leadership laid it open to charges of ambition to dominate the union and favor larger states for its own advantage. Germany's achievements at the 2007 Brussels summit were real; yet they aroused hostility among other member states, particularly from the Polish government then in office. After the subsequent Polish elections, which saw that government defeated, Polish-German relations have improved. Given Poles' awareness of their history, however, any intensification of Russian-German relations may be grounds for Polish suspicion.

Despite such difficulties, it seems likely that Germany will continue on its EU path. It was once a truism for analysts of Germany's role in Europe that she was too small to easily dominate Europe and too large to be ignored by it. These recent developments suggest that by working through the EU,

Germany has found a constructive place as a "middle power" in a Europe that no longer dominates the world.

Conclusion

Throughout the current decade, the question of Germany's fundamental foreign policy orientation and the linked issue of German popular attitudes toward foreign affairs has been a source of concern both for Germans and international observers. In the chapter that follows, we consider how Germans will continue to see the world and their place in it, and what foreign policies may result.

11 Germany in the Twenty-First Century

In the preceding chapters we have argued that Germany experienced a course of economic, social, and political modernization similar to—but at the same time different from—that of other nation-states. The country's political development diverged markedly from historical patterns of democratization in Britain, France, and Scandinavia, with this divergence culminating in the horrendous detour of the Nazi era. Postwar division between antagonistic regimes further underscored German singularity as a modern nation. In contrast, political, economic, and social convergence since reunification—however incompletely achieved—reveal a democratically stable Germany that has emerged in the eyes of many Continental citizens as the acknowledged leader of Europe.[1]

Our concluding argument is that Germany has embraced "normality" in domestic politics and—with qualifications—its conduct of foreign policy. If the "German model" of Rhineland capitalism has ebbed in recent decades, the German experience nonetheless sheds light on a number of common features of contemporary society. In this chapter, we explore core domestic and international issues central to German politics in the twenty-first century. These include East German assimilation into the national socioeconomic system; challenges to Germany's welfare economy; the changing party system; ethnic integration, especially of Turks and other Muslims; Germany's search for an appropriate foreign policy role as a "middle power"; and the emergence of the European Union as a new kind of "postmodern" political system.

East German Assimilation

The difficult assimilation of eastern Germany into the national German political economy reflects the delayed modernization of approximately a fifth of the country's population and resources. Unified Germany is typical of other modernizing societies, inasmuch as uneven development is common in many of them.[2] Rainer Geissler has argued that the GDR lagged behind the Federal Republic in several important aspects of modernization.[3] These included:

- A deficit in productive and subjective well-being

- Excessive concentration of political power

- Weakness of the tertiary (service) sector of the economy

- Lack of social differentiation coupled with excessive egalitarianism ("leveling"), particularly with respect to the reward structure

The delayed modernization of the GDR has important consequences for Germany's future. First, it points to still existing economic deficits in eastern Germany—deficits that persist despite extensive fiscal transfers by the federal government for economic reconstruction in the former GDR (*Aufbau Ost*), in addition to EU regional development funds.[4] On a micro level, workers in the former East Germany continue to earn less per hour than their counterparts in western Germany. Wage differentials in the two parts of the country have declined since reunification, but in 2006 eastern Germans still received only 72.2 percent of western wages. Female workers were slightly privileged compared to male workers, earning the equivalent of 79.2 percent of wages in the west compared to 71.7 percent on the part of east German men.[5]

Demographic projections indicate that by mid-century the population in the eastern states will decline by 31 percent compared to only 14 percent in the west, and that the proportion of elderly compared to those of working age (those between twenty and sixty-five years of age) will by mid-century reach 47 percent in the east compared to 52 percent in the west.[6] This worrisome conjunction of economic and demographic trends has produced widespread flight from many regions of the former GDR. A case in point is the state of Saxony-Anhalt, which has lost a fifth of its population of 2.9 million since 1990 through the migration of younger workers (especially women) to western Germany.[7] One consequence is that enterprising Polish firms now find tempting low-cost opportunities for locating factories on the German side of the border.[8]

Germany's east-west differential social reality is accompanied by divergent attitudes toward the divided postwar past, as we discussed in chapter 4. While many Germans, including those who fled the GDR, harbor negative feelings toward the former East German state,[9] contemporary developments (discussed below) have strengthened social and economic attitudes that have remained strong in the eastern states and indeed have spread across Germany. The historical record of Germany and many other countries, including the United States, suggests that consciousness of the divisions of 1949–1990 will recede as time passes, in part because it was always a more artificial division than, for example, that deriving from the Protestant Reformation. But history shows that it will not disappear entirely. A century after Prussia absorbed the former kingdom of Hanover, local political parties were still able to mobilize lingering resentment.

It is clear by now that the expectation that Germans, east and west, would speedily become one people was illusory. Mitchell Ash is one of the many who have pointed out that rapid unification in 1990 was possible only because both East and West Germans blinded themselves to the difficulty behind the slogan "We are one people" (*Wir sind ein Volk*). Most did not realize, or chose not to see, just how economically disadvantaged the GDR had become, how difficult economic and social unification would prove, and how different the two Germanys had become.[10]

This perhaps should not be so surprising, since Germans consistently rate their own economic conditions as better than the economy as a whole, even when the economy is on the upswing. More noteworthy is the widespread sense that conflicts in German society are growing in intensity. Developments in today's Germany that are feeding these concerns include the international banking and liquidity crisis of 2008 (and beyond) and the still-unfolding money laundering scandal involving prominent German business leaders and their Liechtenstein bank accounts.[11] Recent polling shows that despite a strengthening economy in early 2008 (discussed in this chapter, below), more than three-quarters of respondents believe that they have not profited from Germany's increased prosperity. This negative percentage is lower for those earning more, but it still represents the view of 62 percent of those whose monthly income exceeds €3,000. And there is a growing conviction that German society is increasingly unjust and conflicted: in March and April 2008, fully two-thirds of those polled thought Germany was an unjust society (see Table 11.1).[12]

Table 11.1	Percentage of Germans Who Believe that Conflicts between Social Groups Are Strong/Very Strong
Conflicts among …	Percentage
Poor and rich	81
Foreigners and Germans	64
Employers and employees	63
East and West Germans	42
Young and old	38
Women and men	19

Source: Forschungsgruppe Wahlen e. V.: *Politbarometer*, April 1, 2008, KW 14.

Germany's Welfare Economy

Economic performance clearly affects domestic society and politics. As re-counted in chapter 9, Germany's economy began to rebound in the after-math of the Hartz reforms of 2003–2004 and the formation of the grand coalition in 2005. By 2006 the Organisation for Economic Cooperation and Development (OECD) had proclaimed Germany well on the way toward a "genuine recovery" from its earlier slump.[13] The recovery was led by expan-sion of exports, but it was also fueled by an increase in consumer confidence and spending.

This turnabout enabled Germany to outperform most of its principal trading partners. Its growth rate of 1.7 percent as of mid-2008 was hardly robust in comparison with early postwar patterns, but it marginally ex-ceeded that of the euro zone and Britain, and its annual inflation rate was lower than that of the euro zone, the United States, and Britain. The number of unemployed workers remained high by European and U.S. standards, al-though the rate had declined by early 2008 compared with the preceding de-cade.[14] As a result of the country's improved economic performance, two-thirds of Germans polled in an October 2007 *Eurobarometer* survey considered Germany's situation at that time to be "good" or "very good," compared to fewer than half of the respondents (47 percent) expressing a positive assessment of their own country's economic situation in other EU member states. Predictably, western Germans were more optimistic than eastern Germans in assessing their personal economic prospects.[15]

At the same time destabilizing international conditions pose serious chal-lenges to the German economy. The onset of a worldwide credit crisis and a burgeoning increase in the cost of fuel during the latter half of this decade mirrored worsening conditions in the United States and threatened growth, especially on the EU's southern and northern peripheries. By early 2008 housing prices had fallen precipitously in Spain and Ireland and had begun to slide in Britain as well. In the short run, the German economy was rela-tively well insulated from such trends, and earlier labor market reforms helped German firms remain competitive on the world market despite a surge in the price of exports because of the growing value of the euro in re-lation to the U.S. dollar.[16] Future prospects, however, inevitably remain un-certain.

German economic conditions could worsen, in the eyes of domestic critics, because of policy initiatives and omissions under the grand coalition. Chancellor Angela Merkel's government agreed in April 2008 to increase benefits for some twenty million retirees, a program that will be phased in by the end of 2012 at the cost of some twelve billion euros ($19 billion). Younger Christian Democrats strenuously opposed the decision because it fails to address what they consider a necessary overhaul of the pension system as a whole at a time of increased life expectancy and a declining birthrate.[17] Deepening political tensions between the Christian Democrats and the Social Democrats caused the grand coalition to postpone consideration of fundamental changes in welfare entitlements or a projected rollback of some of the Hartz reforms (as advocated by many dissident Social Democrats and Left Party leaders) until after the scheduled national election in 2009. With both of the major parties beginning to position themselves ideologically for the campaign, some senior Christian Democrats proclaimed that the grand coalition government "has run its course." [18]

The Changing Party System

What lies ahead for the German party system and the institutional structures it dominates? As we noted in chapters 6 and 7, the once stable—indeed, seemingly immobile—"two and a half" party system (CDU-CSU, SPD, FDP) has been steadily dissolving over the past quarter century. This process began with the emergence of the Greens as a participant in national politics in the 1980s, then reunification brought the Left Party (PDS), a "post-Communist" party on the East European model, into the *Bundestag*.

More recent social and economic developments have produced what has been rightly termed a five-party system characterized by erosion of party social bases, which has led to greater reliance on electoral tactics, media campaigns, and shifting allegiances. This new system has also seen declining voter share for the two major parties, and more fluid interparty relations, which has translated into a greater likelihood of lengthier coalition building negotiations after elections. Reviewing the internal party conflicts, disputes over political partners, and rejection of party leaders that have increasingly characterized German politics, one analyst has written of "a little bit society" whose members are not solid partisans of an ideology or party, but rather favor "a little bit" of this or that political program. In short, he declares, "German society has produced the politics that truly reflects it." [19]

Current turmoil centers on the SPD, and is seen as such in public opinion, which is not to say that it will not seize other parties in the future. As of spring 2008, the SPD faced several difficult challenges. Its participation in the grand coalition had brought it less credit with the public than similar participation had the CDU, and its current leader, Kurt Beck, is viewed with increasing mistrust both within the party and by the general public. [20] Most important perhaps is that the question of the SPD's relationship to the Left Party, particularly in regard to state-level coalition governments, divides the party along increasingly bitter lines.

As long as the PDS was strong only in the eastern states, the SPD's two-level approach of coalitions in eastern states but never at the national level worked out well for both sides. But the Left Party, with its evident strength in some western states (see chapter 7), has begun to pose a national challenge on the very issues central to traditional Social Democratic appeal: wages and working conditions, social welfare, and job growth. When Gerhard Schröder moved the SPD toward a more individualistic and less assured social system, those in the party and trade unions who could not accept such changes were a natural reservoir of voters for the Left Party.

Turmoil has also surrounded Beck, a venerable stalwart of SPD politics in his home state of Rhineland-Palatinate, who was elected SPD chair in May 2006 following the resignation of the previous party leader for medical reasons. The party's third national chair since the 2005 *Bundestag* election, neither he nor his immediate predecessors established a clear and convincing programmatic line on social issues. Nor has he sought to reduce German military deployments abroad, despite mounting opposition. With his standing in sharp decline by spring 2008, factions within the SPD had begun fighting over the party's program and leadership with increasing force.

All of this conflict is framed by attitudes toward the Left Party. A recent poll of potential voters revealed, for example, that the party garnered 30 percent support in the eastern states but only 8 percent in the more populous west. When asked whether they could imagine themselves voting for the Left Party, 27 percent of Germans nationally said yes (15 percent maybe, 12 percent surely Responses to this same question in the western states were only 23 percent affirmative (14 percent maybe, 9 percent surely); in the eastern states the corresponding figures were 46 percent, with 18 percent maybe and 28 percent surely. Moreover, although 61 percent responded that they thought the SPD would govern nationally with the Left Party, only 29 percent thought such a government would "be like any other." An astonishing 50 percent asserted that they would not want to live in a country in which the Left Party shared government responsibility.[21]

A good way to understand these conflicting assessments is to consider statements of principle made by Michael Naumann, the SPD mayor (governor) candidate in the February 2008 state election in Hamburg, and by Klaus Wowereit, the lord mayor of Berlin. Although the SPD ran second in Hamburg, under Naumann it increased its vote by 4 percent from the previous election while the CDU lost 7 percent. Shortly before the election, Beck mused publicly about the possibility of an SPD-Green minority government in Hesse tolerated by the Left Party, a reversal of his previous position; Naumann blamed Beck's speculation about such an outcome for costing the SPD votes in Hamburg. The heart of Naumann's argument lay in his assertion that the central significance of the SPD for voters and party members is in its unwavering antifascism and anticommunism. "[The SPD] has always been the party of freedom," he declared.[22] He went on to characterize the Left Party as one open to dogmatic communist candidates and advancing demagogic solutions to domestic and foreign problems.[23] In unusually blunt public language, he charged that "everyone" in the party knew that Wowereit was angling to become chancellor in 2013 with Left Party support. Naumann recommended that the party "win back the trust of the center of society," and defended the Schröder government's economic program, asserting that "Minijobs or part-time work are better than no employment at all."[24]

Wowereit, for his part, has opposed "any stigmatization" of the Left Party and has declared that treating it as part of Germany's five-party constellation is just "a piece of normality."[25] He downplayed the Left Party's recent successes, reminding his interviewers that the CDU had allied itself with former GDR satellite parties and dismissing the Left's populism. Moreover, just as Naumann admitted the need for greater social benefits during the current changes in the economy, so Wowereit declared, "[H]e who can work, and has a chance to work, must go to work—or else." He would not take all responsibility from citizens, who must show individual responsibility for their actions. Lastly, Wowerweit declared that in social affairs, Germany needed to rid itself of the notion that the state is there to provide everything to its citizens.[26]

As head of an SPD–Left Party government in Berlin since 2001, Wowereit has seen his party gain strength against its governing partner. (This also happened in Mecklenburg–Western Pomerania.) The struggle within the SPD is less about whether to cooperate with the Left Party, than it is about how and on what issues. Until now the SPD has pursued economic and foreign policies at the national level that are opposed by its rival. The likeliest candidates for party leadership (at least in 2009) are unlikely to give ground here. Indeed, it is questionable to what extent the supposed "move to the left" (*Linksruck*) represented by the Left Party is in fact a social and political reality.[27] Some Social Democrats advocate a traditional welfare and interventionist economic policy, but skeptics emphasize improvement in the economic conditions of workers in recent years and point out that left-leaning parties have lost some four million votes in nine state elections since 2005.

What is apparent in the debate over the SPD's relations with the Left Party on the national and state levels is the emergence of a new patchwork pattern of politics (*"Patchworks sind die Regel"*) in place of the traditional left-right political dichotomy. On the most important political issues— family, technology, education, integration, and environmental policies— cross-party and indeed cross-outlook political "mosaics" have become the rule. This emerging pattern of looser political constellations affects other parties as well. A sign of this is the emergence of a first-ever CDU-Green coalition government in Hamburg.[28]

Ethnic Integration

In the near term, the most fateful and problematical domestic issue confronting Germany is that of ethnic (especially but not exclusively, Islamic) integration.[29] Sizable ethnic minority communities concentrated in urban centers often do not share language, religious affiliation, or social customs, particularly in regard to gender roles and family structure, with most of the ethnic German majority. This, in turn, affects economic and social policy, the potential staffing of political parties, and—most important—

the very definition of what it means to be "German" in terms of behavior and attitudes.

These issues are present in practically all European countries, and are familiar to North Americans as well. What is an especial German difficulty is the longstanding conviction that Germany is not a country of immigration, despite much historical and certainly more recent evidence to the contrary. Only in the past few years have German governments begun to respond to the need for active policies of integration for a multiethnic Germany. These initiatives have evoked a lively response from a variety of ethnic groups and individuals; Germany today is experiencing an open-ended and intense public conversation on the contours of a new Germany.

Speaking in October 2006 in a *Bundestag* debate on these issues, Interior Minister Wolfgang Schäuble (CDU) declared that the majority of Muslims living in Germany arrived decades ago, with their customs and traditions, their religion and their culture.[30] Many of them, he said, quoting the German-Turkish filmmaker Fatih Akin, had "forgotten to go home."[31] By now, he continued, "Islam is part of Germany and part of Europe, part of our present and part of our future. Muslims are welcome in Germany, where they should develop their talents and contribute to society." Tellingly, however, when Schäuble moved on to enumerate the barriers to integration of these communities, he referred only to attitudes and actions of the minority but not of the majority. For example, he listed such matters as the nature of religious instruction, training of imams, wearing of the Islamic head scarf (*hijab*), the role of women and girls including the issue of so-called honor killings, and the threats of Islamic terrorism.[32]

But what adjustments might be required of the larger community? Faruk Sen, a leading scholar of the Turkish community in Germany, asks why only Turkish (or Muslim) behavior is considered an obstacle to integration.[33] What about the higher than average unemployment rate found in immigrant communities, the virtual political disenfranchisement prior to the reform of citizenship laws, and the educational disadvantages faced by immigrant children in many urban centers? Turkish parents complain, for example, that in the highly stratified German school system, school administrators are much more likely to recommend that their children enter a nonacademic track.[34]

Such contrasts point to the continuing problem of whether Germany's goal should be multicultural, parallel societies; an integrated German community; or political and economic integration with cultural and perhaps social autonomy.[35] Some immigrants do not fit into German society, yet there are Germans who clearly do not envision the prospect of an integrated Turkish and Muslin community. As Simon Green points out, German authorities, backed by the courts, have regularly ruled that teachers are to be religiously "neutral" in classrooms, and as such may not wear a *hijab*. However, nothing untoward is seen in Christian teachers wearing large crosses or crucifixes or with Jewish teachers wearing skullcaps. Very public and visible strife has been caused by plans to build mosques of a size or in a location found obtrusive by other groups. Such disputes have been especially un-friendly in Munich and Cologne, as local dignitaries, including Joachim Car-dinal Meissner, the Archbishop of Cologne, have confessed to "an uneasy feeling" about the presence of a large mosque in their communities. The spokesperson for a German Islamic organization countered: "The 120 thou-sand Muslims of Cologne do not have a single place they can point to with pride as the symbol of our faith."[36]

Germans may be unsure of their views on integration, but Turks, both secular and observant, and other Muslims in Germany are by no means united in their beliefs either. (The varying standpoints of Turkish and Is-lamist groups are touched on in chapter 8.) A clear case in point is the recent public dispute between and among secular and religious Turkish and Muslim women over the wearing of the *hijab*. One view is represented by Ekin Deligöz, a Green Party member of the *Bundestag,* who denounced the compulsory wearing of the *hijab* as a "symbol of oppression." She called on Turkish women to "live in today, in Germany; you live here, so take off the *hijab*."[37] Other Turkish-German women prominent in public affairs rallied to her side. Lale Akgün, an SPD member of the *Bundestag,* asked why a Turkish man could stroll about in a Western style suit while his wife had to wear a *hijab* and long coat.[38] Of course, some women prefer wearing the *hijab,* but still object to men dictating women's dress.[39]

For its part, the government has been slow to respond, convening several "Islam conferences" between government officials and representatives of various groups of Muslims living in Germany. These conferences have had some successes, such as the institutionalization of Islamic religious instruc-tion in public schools alongside classes in Christianity and Judaism,[40] but they have also aroused opposition from within the Islamic community in Germany by seeming to empower some very conservative organizations.[41] In addition, the government did itself no favors when family affairs minister Ursula von der Leyen (CDU) justified holding a "values in education" con-ference limited to only Christian leaders by arguing that German society is based on Christian values and that only by acknowledging that heritage could Germans be open to other values.[42] Chancellor Merkel herself does not enjoy a positive reputation among Turks in Germany. More than three-quarters of those polled stated they did not find her claimed desire to be chancellor of Turks living in Germany plausible.[43]

What might the future of this tangled relationship be? Will a relatively harmonious German society result? While these are unanswerable ques-tions, not the least because so much depends on the actions of Germans, their Turkish neighbors, and the government, we may venture a modest guess at a likely outcome.

For one thing, these difficult issues stand a better chance of being resolved than might previously have been the case, thanks to the demographic stability of Germany over the past several years. The latest available figures from 2005 show that the net population increase through immigration was only about ninety thousand people. Indeed, the number of Germans emigrating—with the United States and Switzerland as their favored destinations—was the highest since 1950. Moreover, the number of immigrants from Turkey was actually lower than the number from Russia.[44] That the friction between ethnic groups is more a matter of unaccustomed multiculturalarity than of an "immigrant tide" becomes clear if we recall some basic demographic data: noncitizen immigrants make up only 8 percent of Germany's population; Turks may make up a quarter of the foreign population (*Ausländer*), but they constitute only 2 percent of the total population.

What this means is that there will be time for second, third, and subsequent generations of Germans of Turkish origin or background to become sufficiently integrated into German life. As one young Turkish German declared, "The either-or times are past."[45] Younger Turkish Germans are more likely to accept German-Turkish intermarriage, and to believe that Islam and democracy are compatible while still wishing to maintain elements of Turkish culture in their lives. They may often be made to feel that they are unwanted in Germany, but their reaction to this behavior by members of the majority population is less negative for men than for women, younger than for older, and less for those who have become citizens than for those who are still classified as visiting workers. These younger Turkish Germans tend to value the democratic political and social culture they enjoy in Germany and are often impatient with the inability of the general German population to understand that they are German born, are German in speech and culture, and feel only vague emotional ties to Turkey. Their views are not universal among Turkish Germans, but they are widespread enough to suggest that, in a pattern familiar to immigrant populations in many countries, there will gradually develop a common society and polity for both groups, even while some ties of religion and family tradition continue to separate them. In short, Germany remade in this image will be a more varied and cosmopolitan society, with an integrated but not totally assimilated Turkish constituency. Already the *döner kebab* has become Germany's favorite snack food. It's a small start, but it's a start nonetheless.

Normalcy in German Foreign Policy

Both achievements and continuing socioeconomic and political problems underscore the extent to which the Federal Republic has attained "normalcy" in domestic affairs in contrast to previous regimes. Western-style democracy and respect for law are firmly entrenched in the unified nation. The challenges of regional disparities and ethnic-cultural integration are global phenomena and are by no means restricted to Germany. Similarly, flux in the multiparty system resembles ongoing changes in a number of Germany's European neighbors, most notably Italy and France. That contemporary Germans confront such issues in a largely peaceful fashion expresses a degree of normality absent in the historical clashes of dogmatic ideologies and armed political opponents.

Normalcy also extends to the conduct of German foreign policy, albeit in special ways. Prior to reunification, as Mary Hampton observes, both the West and East German regimes were at best semisovereign states and therefore constrained in foreign policy choices by their principal political mentors (the United States and the former Soviet Union, respectively) and their regional alliance systems (NATO and the Warsaw Pact). Because of these factors it has been only since 1990 that Germany has begun "the process of defining its identity as a state and a nation."[46]

In chapter 10, we described how Germany has found suitable vehicles through NATO and the EU to realize a foreign policy that safeguards German economic and security interests without alarming the world. While Germany understandably claims the right in the twenty-first century to advocate policies commensurate with its economic, political, and security importance (especially within Europe), the current global distribution of power sharply restricts its potential to achieve great power status.[47]

As we have noted, German foreign policy under Merkel and her SPD foreign minister, Frank-Walter Steinmeier, has not deviated in substance from that of the Schröder/Fischer years. In its relations with the United States, the current government has been careful to avoid provocative rhetoric, something made easier by the fading of U.S. pressure to support the Iraq War. Nonetheless, Germany has not hesitated to oppose specific U.S. initiatives, including rejecting a fast start toward NATO membership for Ukraine and Georgia.[48] Relations with Russia have remained much the same in substance as in the past, although Germany was quick to recognize the independence of Kosovo in 2008 despite Russian opposition. Relations with China have cooled, thanks to Merkel's formal reception of the Dalai Lama and her possible absence from the opening ceremonies of the Beijing Summer Olympics.

During the past decade and a half, the most striking change in German foreign policy has been a rise in military deployments abroad. The flashpoint for both elite and popular discontent about this continues to be the presence of German forces in Afghanistan with the attendant possibility that they will be drawn inexorably into active combat in the southern and eastern regions of that country. Germans may well wonder how it is that, in Charles Maier's words, "[a]n alliance founded in 1949 to protect Western Europeans from invasion now finds itself patrolling Afghanistan at the behest of its major organizer."[49] The weak public support for the Afghan deployment has extended into many segments of political and press opinion. At the very least, critics argue, Germany must elaborate a strategy for effective intervention and persuade NATO to adopt it. Clearly the German government cannot unilaterally withdraw from what is now a NATO project, but it is difficult to imagine German officials accommodating a deeper involvement.[50]

Doubts on this subject do not signify some general German withdrawal from foreign concerns or hostility toward other countries. When asked whether a named country would be a trustworthy partner, most Germans had quite positive views (see Table 11.2). Germans are not indifferent to foreign policy issues, but they do seem to have absorbed a palette of values that can be summed up in the notion of a "civilian state." Bundled in this notion are a reluctance to see military force as an essential element of personal or societal security, a detachment from ideas and emotions of military glory, and a focus on economic and social improvement as the state's primary task. Nor do Germans see the EU as a substitute military great power in which their country can (or should) participate. Far from following a *Sonderweg,* Germans have in this respect become mainstream Europeans.[51]

This European commitment to a civilian state may be seen in a number of related developments. For example, the European response to post-9/11 terrorist threats, while vigorous and determined, has emphasized a criminal justice and police approach rather than a "war on terror." Despite the expectation by scholars and politicians that the end of the Cold War would lead European countries, most worrisomely Germany, to resume the use of force to obtain power, the institutions and attitudes of the civilian EU have been maintained; the failure of the EU to demonstrate the will or spend the large sums of money required to build up a credible EU global military presence serves to underscore this point.[52]

Will such attitudes and policies survive, both in Germany and in the widening EU? Recent international crises, from Kosovo to Iraq, demonstrate continued European dependence on U.S. military power, which makes continued European and German commitment to NATO likely.[53] And while no one can predict such outcomes, it is nonetheless clear that the attitudes we have been describing have become deeply rooted in Germany and much of Europe. As James Sheehan notes,

> In the light of Europe's history over the past hundred years, is it surprising that most Europeans do not want to pay the price of heroism, risk what they have built, sacrifice their personal accomplishments?

Table 11.2	Question asked: "Is [named country] a Trustworthy Partner for Germany?" (change from 2007 in parentheses)
Country	Percentage answering "yes"
France	90 (+4)
Great Britain	86 (+17)
Italy	76 (+11)
Japan	67 (+7)
United States	53 (+21)
Poland	49 (+14)
Russia	35 (+11)
China	15 (n/a)

Source: Polling results are derived from an *Infratest dimap* poll for the TV network ARD as reported in *Frankfurter Rundschau* online, March 11, 2008.

Europeans know, on a way few Americans can, what war is really like.[54]

Certainly Germans exhibit little appetite for military ventures, even as many recognize the necessity of some military actions. A telling illustration of this fact is the controversy in spring 2008 over the restoration of a German medal for heroism in combat, now that Germans are again engaged in dangerous deployments. The traditional honor—the Iron Cross, designed by the famous architect and artist Karl Friedrich Schinkel in 1813—seems tainted by the Hitler regime's use of it. The symbol is still widely used to identify German military equipment, but the government seems for now to have decided against reviving it for use in recognizing individual heroism.[55]

These sentiments are strong in Germany, but are not unusual in today's Europe. Whereas every major European city has monuments to heroes of past battles, few have been built in recent decades. As James Sheehan points out,

> When was the last time a European city built a monument to a military hero, or named a street after a battle? In Berlin, the Defense Ministry faces a street named for a leader of the naval mutiny in 1918 and is flanked by one named for Claus von Stauffenberg, a martyr of the German resistance to Hitler ... the newest monuments in the German capital are dedicated to war's victims, not its heroes.[56]

Germany in a Postmodern Europe

The European Union is a powerful context for conducting German foreign policy. While national self-interest has come to motivate the German government's policy choices more clearly since 1990, the EU's principle of shared sovereignty and common activities accords institutional and resource dimensions to "normality" that transcend the historical nation-state. Robert Cooper, a former British diplomat appointed director-general for EU external and politico-military affairs in 2002, classifies the sum of these dimensions as an unprecedented form of "postmodern" politics that contrasts fundamentally with those of premodern and modern states.[57] Together, these three types of systems constitute a trajectory of the modernization process as applied to international relations theory and practice.

According to Cooper's typology, a premodern system is characterized by the absence of key attributes essential to political modernity: defined territoriality, recognized central authority, and a sense of national identity. Premodern systems may also be riven by Hobbesian-like conditions of tribal, religious, or civil conflict. The examples Cooper cites include Afghanistan, Somalia, and Liberia.[58] In contrast, modern systems such as the United States, Russia, and China embody these requisites of modernity, although some modern countries may still manifest social conflicts akin to those in

Signs like this one at the German-Polish border in Ahlbeck in northern Germany will soon become little more than souvenirs for many Europeans. As of December 21, 2007, citizens of nine of the newest EU member nations have been able to travel passport-free to most other countries in the bloc, including Germany.

premodern systems.[59] A defining feature of modern systems, in Cooper's view, is the state's monopoly of military power and its willingness—or at least its ability—to utilize force against other states as an instrument of foreign policy.[60] Finally, a postmodern system is one characterized by less emphasis on national territoriality among its component parts, a partial merger of domestic and foreign affairs, and the subordination of the "legitimate monopoly on force that is the essence of statehood … to international—but self-imposed—constraints."[61] The European Union is the prime empirical example of such a system.

The most important attributes of the EU as a postmodern system include the regionalization of agricultural policy; the free movement of goods, finances, and people; and joint macroeconomic policies and a common currency within the euro zone. While member states retain such essential attributes of national sovereignty as the power of taxation and self-defense, they are nonetheless subject to European law and binding decisions by community institutions such as the European Council, the Council of Ministers, the Commission, and the European Parliament. The Reform (Lisbon) Treaty of 2007, once fully implemented, will provide for additional instruments of community power in the form of a European president and European commissioner for foreign affairs who will serve as the EU's de facto foreign minister.

The EU's Common Foreign and Security Policy (CFSP), which formally dates from the Treaty on European Union of 1992, constitutes an important adjunct to the national pursuit of foreign policy by Germany and other member states. Its primary mission is to provide implementation services and humanitarian aid in regions of conflict such as Kosovo. NATO remains charged with the primary responsibility for ensuring European security, but the EU has undertaken preliminary steps to provide its own joint security resources with its adoption of a common European Security and Defense Policy (ESDP) and the creation of some fifteen EU battle groups composed of 1,500 soldiers each. Together, the battle groups constitute the nucleus of a standing European army that can be deployed on combat missions in Europe and globally under the authority of the European Council. By 2007 Germany was the lead nation in two of the groups, one headquartered in Potsdam, the other in Paris.

Cooper's depiction of the EU as the world's first postmodern system does not mean it constitutes a new regional nation-state. As practitioners and students of the EU adamantly emphasize, the community is a sometimes untidy and confusing amalgamation of intergovernmental, supranational, and transnational institutions and policies. Nonetheless, its shared resources and common policies, with respect to both domestic and foreign affairs, expand the very meaning of normalcy to include a collective dimension that has already partially transformed international politics, and Germany has been and continues to be an integral part of that system and process.

Afterword

As Germans proceed to grapple with foreign and domestic problems of the twenty-first century, the dramatic events of the Cold War era recede ever further in the consciousness of later generations. We may think of modern German history as unusually memorable, but young Germans seem to have the same ability to learn as little about their country's past as their peers in other Western democracies. In one Brandenburg survey, every third secondary school pupil thought Brandt and Adenauer had been GDR politicians, and more than half could not say in what year the Berlin Wall was built; an equal percentage agreed with the statement "The GDR was not a dictatorship." A parallel survey in North Rhine–Westphalia discovered that pupils there believed, among other things, that the Western Allies had built the Berlin Wall. When Roger Cohen visited a secondary school in Berlin, the most prevalent attitude toward Germany's past was mild indifference.[62] And all this is despite (or because?) of decades of intensive pedagogical campaigns to acquaint German pupils with their history. Whether such developments will help or hinder Germans to deal with the problems of today and of the immediate future we cannot say.

Notes

Introduction Notes

1. See, for example, George Mosse, *The Crisis of German Ideology: Intellectual Origins of the Third Reich* (New York: Grosset and Dunlap, 1964).
2. Mary Hampton, "The Past, Present, and the Perhaps: Is Germany a 'Normal' Power?" Review essay published in *Security Studies* online publication, 01 (December 2000).
3. The authors are sympathetic to the view of such scholars as Mary Fulbrook, who rightly asks what the essential hallmarks of a "normal" European development are. See Mary Fulbrook, *The Divided Nation: A History of Germany 1918–1990* (New York: Oxford University Press, 1992), 4–6.
4. Alan Watson, *The Germans: Who Are They Now?* (Chicago: Edition Q, 1992), 13.
5. In chapters 2 and 5 Hancock incorporates updated and expanded portions of his earlier assessment of German political development and federalism originally published in *West Germany: The Politics of Democratic Corporatism* (Chatham, N.J.: Chatham House Publishers, 1989).

Chapter 1 Notes

1. This definition of modernization is derived from Dankwart A. Rustow, *A World of Nations* (Washington, D.C.: Brookings Institution, 1967), 35; and C. E. Black, *The Dynamics of Modernization* (New York: Harper and Row, 1966), 7.

2. Inglehart first advanced this argument in "The Silent Revolution in Europe: Intergenerational Change in Post-Industrial Societies," *American Political Science Review* 65 (1971): 991–1017 and *The Silent Revolution: Changing Values and Political Styles Among Western Publics* (Princeton, N.J.: Princeton University Press, 1977). He has elaborated his analysis of postmaterialist values on the basis of extensive survey research in Ronald Inglehart, *Culture Shift in Advanced Industrial Society* (Princeton, N.J.: Princeton University Press, 1990) and *Modernization and Postmodernization: Cultural, Economic, and Political Change in 43 Societies* (Princeton, N.J.: Princeton University Press, 1997).

3. Inglehart, *Culture Shift,* 5.

4. Samuel Huntington, *Political Order in Changing Societies* (New Haven, Conn.: Yale University Press, 1962).

5. Thalidomide was developed by a German pharmaceutical company and sold in a number of countries to alleviate symptoms of insomnia and morning sickness among pregnant women. Only about half of the infants afflicted with birth defects associated with the drug survived childhood. Thalidomide was subsequently banned for use during pregnancy. The Chernobyl disaster involved the release of fission material and radiation fuel into the atmosphere, affecting not only workers at the poorly designed nuclear plant but also residents throughout much of the Ukraine and the rest of Europe. The high rate of nuclear fallout resulted in an increase in the number of thyroid cancers among those most directly affected.

6. Italy is 116,333 square miles (301,302 square kilometers), England is 50,363 square miles (130,439 square kilometers), and France is 210,026 square miles (543,965 square kilometers).

7. The *Nibelungenlied*—which consists of a mixture of early Germanic and Nordic mythology—inspired Richard Wagner's soaring operatic opus, *Der Ring des Nibelungen (The Ring of the Nibelungen).*

8. A classical presentation of the forest's role in German aesthetic and political imagination may be found in Simon Schama's work, *Landscape and Memory* (New York: Knopf, 1995).

9. Economic "take off," defined as the onset of sustained growth, is associated with W. W. Rostow, *The Stages of Economic Growth: A Non-Communist Manifesto,* 3rd ed. (Cambridge, England, and New York: Cambridge University Press, 1990).

10. B.R. Mitchell, *International Historical Statistics: Europe 1750–2000,* 5th ed. (New York: Palgrave Macmillan, 2003), 430–431, 454.

11. A classical assessment of the role of the Prussian and Imperial states in promoting rapid industrialization, in part for military purposes, is Thorsten Veblen, *Imperial Germany and the Industrial Revolution*

(Ann Arbor: University of Michigan Press Ann Arbor Paperbacks, 1966). Veblen's book was first published in 1915.

12. There remains to this day a Slavic ethnic minority people, known as the Sorbs (Sorben in German), who live in the forested area south east of Berlin. They have (and had in the GDR) limited social and linguistic rights. See Peter Barker, *The Sorbian Minority and the German State since 1945* (Lewiston N.Y.: E. Mellen Press, 2000).

13. During the Protestant Reformation in the sixteenth century, Martin Luther helped establish the basis for a common Germanic language ("high German" or *Hochdeutsch*) through his translation of the Bible from Latin into German. Hochdeutsch became the preferred language of educated Germans and eventually the linguistic norm of the nation as a whole, although it has never fully supplanted local and regional dialects.

14. Mitchell, *International Historical Statistics,* 80–82.

15. Ibid, 150.

16. A catalytic event was Martin Luther's defiant proclamation in 1517 of ninety-five theses against alleged church abuses, which helped spark the Protestant Reformation in Germany and elsewhere in Central and Northern Europe.

17. Mitchell, *International Historical Statistics*, 82.

18. Ibid.

19. Within Western and Central Europe, France is second with a population of approximately 64 million, followed by the United Kingdom (approximately 60 million), Italy (57.2 million), and Poland (38.7 million). Population data in this section are taken from the reports of the Federal Office for Statistics (*Statistisches Bundesamt Deutschland*) at www.destatis.de. See also Bundesinstitut für Bevölkerungsforschung, at www.bib-demographie.de.

20. A three-month survey, conducted in January-March 2004, found that 84 percent of eastern Germans saw this out-migration as a threat to the future of their part of the country. The readiness to seek jobs in western parts of Germany was greatest in those areas closest to the old East-West border. The numbers obscure the growing trend of eastern commuters to western jobs. See "Abwanderung gefährdet Ostdeutschland," ZDF online, March 26, 2004.

21. "Der Migrationsbericht 1999," *Der Tagesspiegel,* December 18, 1999; Die Beauftragte der Bundesregierung für Ausländerfragen, *Migrationsbericht 1999,* Berlin, 1999; Phillip L. Martin, "Germany: Migration Policies for the 21st Century," Policy Paper #50 (Institute on Global Conflict and Cooperation, University of California at Irvine, April 1999). See also the interview with Walter Link, who chaired the *Bundestag*'s "Enquete-Kommission 'Demographischer Wandel'," in "Trotz der Brisanz herrschte weitgehend

Übereinstimmung" (Beilage zur Wochenzietung *Das Parliament*) 48, nos. 43–44 (October 16–23, 1998): 2.

22. "Deutschland braucht mehr Zuwanderer," *Der Tagesspiegel,* January 6, 2000; Klaus J. Bade, "Verordnete Einwanderung ist kein Allheilmittel," *Frankfurter Rundschau,* January 12, 2000; "Migrationsbericht 1999": 45–47.

23. Ironically, the 1913 law did not define German nationality as such (until the Nazi era, each German state granted citizenship separately) and did not ban dual citizenship—a central issue in contemporary debates. See Erich Röper, "Die doppelte Staatsangehörigkeit als traditionelles Rechtsinstitut" (Beilage zur Wochenzietung *Das Parliament*) 50, no. 6 (February 1999): 16.

24. Beate Winkler, "Den Deutschen darf nichts 'fremd' sein," *Die Zeit,* August 23, 1996. See also Robert Leicht, "Aus Knechten Bürger machen," *Die Zeit,* July 5, 1996. "Jenseits von Schuld und Sühne," *Der Spiegel,* 48, 1998 (title story).

25. Ralf E. Ulrich, "The Reform of German Immigration Law," (Occasional Paper, 1990) American Institute for Contemporary German Studies.

26. See Statistisches Bundesamt, *Statistisches Jahrbuch 2007,* www.destatis.de.

27. A recent analysis of the unintended process by which guest workers became immigrants and residents is Triadafilos Triadafilopoulos and Karen Schönwälder, "How the Federal Republic Became an Immigration Country," *German Politics & Society* 24, no. 3 (Autumn 2006): 1–19.

28. Convenient summaries of the legal provisons are in "Nationality Law," Bonn: Inter-Nationes Legal Texts, October 1999. For an exposition and defense of the law by the sponsoring cabinet member, Interior Minister Otto Schilly (SPD), see his statements, "Was heisst eigentlich 'Nation'?" (Beilage zur Wochenzietung *Das Parliament*) 50, nos. 21–22 (May 1999): 16, and "Wir bilden ein 'Bündnis der Vernunft'" (Beilage zur Wochenzietung *Das Parliament*) 50, no. 13 (March 1999): 14.

29. The text and additional information about the law are available at www.bundesregierung.de/Webs/Breg/DE/Bundesregierung/BeauftragtefuerIntegration/Zuwanderungsrecht/zuwanderungsrecht.html; Thomas Kröter, "Zuwanderungsreform als 'historisch' gelobt," *Frankfurter Rundschau* online, June 18, 2004.

30. This is the federal office for migration, integration and refugees, headed by a state secretary, the *Beauftragte für Migration, Flüchtlinge und Integration.* Merkel upgraded this office in 2005 by placing it in the Federal Chancellery.

31. The new language requirements now apply also to so-called *Spätaussiedler,* ethnic Germans from Russia and Eastern Europe. Persons

of German descent, living abroad, have automatic claim to citizenship. The Kohl government had already taken steps to limit this immigration, both by economic aid to "German" communities abroad and by limiting automatic repatriation to those who had suffered due to their German nationality, resulting in a decline in new arrivals.

32. Alan Cowell, "German Court Upholds Law to Limit Refugees," *New York Times,* May 18, 1996.

33. Bundeszentrale für politische Bildung, *Grundgesetz für die Bundesrepublik Deutschland/Stand: November 1994* (Bonn: Bundeszentrale für politische Bildung, 1994), 87–88. The Basic Law is now also available online at www.bpb.de.

34. Statistisches Bundesamt Deutschland, "Bevölkerung," 1998, www.destatis.de; Evangelische Kirche in Deutschland ("Protestant Church in Germany"); "Christentum und politische Kultur"; "Kirchensteuer 1998." The Web site for the Evangelkical Church is www.ekd.de; the Catholic Bishops Conference is at www.dbk.de.

35. See "Jüdische Zuwanderer aus der ehemaligen Sowjetunion," *Migrationsbericht des Bundesamtes für Migration und Flüchtlinge im Auftrag der Bundesregierung (Migrationsbericht 2005),* Section 2.4, 49–52. The relevant section is paragraph 23. Source online at *BMI: Zuwanderungsrecht in Deutschland,* www.zuwanderung.de.

36. These rules no longer apply to Jewish persons from the Baltic states, now that those states are EU members; the rules on language and economic status do not apply to those certified to be victims of Nazi persecution.

37. For this agreement, see "Schröder und Spiegel zeichnen Staatsvertrag," *Frankfurter Rundschau* online, January 28, 2003. Data on numbers of Jews from the Web site of the Central Council, www.zentralratdjuden.de/en. In 2006, the first rabbis to graduate from a seminary in Germany since 1942 were ordained. "Erste jüdische Geistliche seit 1942 in Deutschland ausgebildet," *Frankfurter Rundschau* online, September 15, 2006. There are about 50,000 reform Jews and an undetermined number of nonobservant Jews.

38. Die Bundesbeauftragte der Bundesregierung für Ausländerfragen, "Islamunterricht ist Beitrag zur Integration," press release, Berlin, November 17, 1999. See also Roger Cohen, "Long Dispute Ends as Berlin Court Backs Islamic School Lessons," *New York Times,* November 6, 1998; "Islamische Föderation will Religionsunterricht erteilen," *Der Tagesspiegel,* May 6, 1997; "Allahs Einzug ins Klassenzimmer," *Süddeutsche Zeitung,* November 6, 1998. A more recent study is Bassam Tibi, "Europeanizing Islam or the Islamization of Europe: Political Democracy vs. Cultural Differences," in Timothy A. Byrnes and Peter J. Katzenstein, eds., *Religion in an Expanding Europe* (Cambridge: Cambridge University Press, 2006), 204–224. Tibi notes (ibid, 215–216) that different German Muslim

interest groups have ties to different foreign governments, particularly to Turkey and Saudi Arabia. See also Jytte Klausen, *The Islamic Challenge: Politics and Religion in Western Europe* (Oxford: Oxford University Press, 2005).

Chapter 2 Notes

1. In the face of a deteriorating military situation on the western front and revolutionary upheavals throughout Germany, members of the military High Command and the last Imperial chancellor, Prince Max von Baden, urged the kaiser to abdicate. He did so on November 9 and promptly left for lifetime exile in the Netherlands, where he died in 1940.

2. Radical right-wingers included roving bands of disgruntled wartime veterans and racist-nationalist political movements. One of the latter was the German Workers Party, founded in Munich in 1918. Adolf Hitler became its leader and transformed it into the National Socialist German Workers Party, or NSDAP, that is, the Nazi party.

3. Useful historical accounts of the Weimar Republic include Richard J. Evans, *The Coming of the Third Reich* (New York: Penguin, 2004); Heinrich August Winkler, *Germany: The Long Road West* (translated by Alexander J. Sager) (New York: Oxford University Press, 2006); Erich Eycke, *A History of the Weimar Republic* (translated by Harlan P. Hanson and Robert G.L.Waite) (Cambridge: Harvard University Press, 1962–1963); John R.P. McKenzie, *Weimar Germany, 1918–1933* (Totowa, N.J.: Rowman and Littlefield, 1971).

4. Together, the three democratic parties won a resounding majority of 83.7 percent in elections to a constituent assembly held in January 1919 to draw up a new constitution. Because of street violence and the threat of revolution in Berlin, the delegates met in the more tranquil provincial city of Weimar that was renowned for its literary and humanistic traditions. Both the constituent assembly and Germany's first democratic republic assumed the name Weimar.

5. Under the Versailles Treaty Germany was forced to cede all of its overseas colonies and portions of its own territory to the newly reconstituted state of Poland in the east and the provinces of Alsace-Lorraine to France in the west; accept responsibility for causing World War I; pay long-term monetary reparations to the Western allies to cover the direct and indirect costs of the war; and limit its military to 100,000 men. The United States Senate refused to ratify the treaty.

6. For the Stern quote, see his speech at the Leo Beck Institute in New York on November 14, 2004, at www.lbi.org/fritzstern.html. The literature on Hitler and the National Socialist movement is voluminous. Standard references include Ian Kershaw's masterful

Hitler, 2nd ed. (Harlow, England, and New York: Longman, 2001) (along with numerous other studies by Kershaw); Karl Dietrich Bracher, *The German Dictatorship* (London: Penguin Books, 1973); Alan Bullock, *Hitler: A Study in Tyranny* (New York: Harper and Row, 1964); Carl J. Friedrich and Zbigniew Brzezinski, *Totalitarian Dictatorship and Autocracy,* 2d ed. rev. (Cambridge, Mass.: Harvard University Press, 1965); Hitler's own *Mein Kampf* (Boston: Houghton Mifflin, 1943); Franz Neumann, *Behemoth: The Structure and Practice of National Socialism* (New York: Free Press, 1942. Unfortunately available only in German is an excellent study by Karl Bracher, *Die Auflösung der Weimarer Republik: Eine Studie zum Problem des Machtverfalls in der Demokratie* (Stuttgart: Ring Verlag, 1957).

7. These demands were codified in a twenty-five-point NSADAP party program drawn up by Hitler and published in February 1920. For a summary, see www.hitler.org/writings/programme/

8. A particularly compelling account of Hitler's hypnotic effect on others can be found in Albert Speer's memoirs, *Inside the Third Reich* (New York: Macmillan, 1970), 15–16.

9. Cornelia Essner, *Die Nürnberger Gesetze oder die Verwaltung des Rassenwahns, 1933–1945* (Paderborn: F. Schöningh, 2002).

10. See Ralf Dahrendorf, *Society and Democracy in Germany* (translation of *Gesellschaft und Demokratie in Deutschland*), 1st U.S. ed. (Garden City, N.Y.: Doubleday, 1967).

11. For details see Anthony Read and David Fisher, *The Deadly Embrace: Hitler, Stalin, and the Nazi-Soviet Pact, 1939–1949* (New York: Norton, 1988) and John Kolasky, *Partners in Tyranny: The Nazi-Soviet Nonaggression Pact, August 23, 1939* (Toronto: Mackenzie Institute, 1990).

12. Standard histories of World War II include Winston Churchill's multivolume *The Second World War* (New York: Time, Inc., 1959), and Liddell Hart, *History of the Second World War* (New York: Da Capo Press, 1999). Other noteworthy sources are Dwight D. Eisenhower's wartime memoirs, *Crusade in Europe* (Garden City, N.Y.: Doubleday, 1948) and A.J.P. Taylor, *The Origins of the Second World War* (New York: Fawcett, 1961, 1968). Taylor's account has generated considerable controversy because of his argument that the responsibility for the outbreak of World War II can be attributed to all of the super powers rather than Nazi Germany alone.

13. A diplomatic history of prewar and wartime big power summits is Lloyd Gardner, *Spheres of Influence: The Great Powers Partition Europe, from Munich to Yalta* (Chicago: I.R. Dee, 1993).

14. The so-called two + four settlement (formally, the Treaty of 12 September 1990 on the Final Settlement with Respect to Germany) provided in Article 1 that the "united Germany shall comprise the

territories of the Federal Republic of Germany, the German Democratic Republic and the whole of Berlin." See *The Unification of Germany in 1990: A Documentation* (Bonn: Press and Information Office of the Federal Government, 1991), 99.

15. U.S. Department of State, *Foreign Relations of the United States: Diplomatic Papers, The Conference of Berlin (The Potsdam Conference), 1945,* vol. 2 (Washington, D.C.: Government Printing Office, 1960).

16. Ibid.

17. F. Roy Willis, *The French in Germany 1945–1949* (Stanford: Stanford University Press, 1962), 51.

18. The French subsequently agreed to the unification of the Saarland and West Germany in the context of European economic integration from the early 1950s onward.

Chapter 3 Notes

1. Henry Krisch, "The Changing Politics of German National Identity," in Peter H. Merkl, ed., *The Federal Republic of Germany at Fifty* (London: Macmillan, 1999), 33–42. The GDR's economic disadvantage relative to West Germany was due to policy choices after 1947 and not primarily to the relative economic endowment of the two states. For a recent treatment, see Christoph Buchheim, "Kriegsfolgen und Wirtschaftswachstum in der SBZ/DDR," *Geschichte und Gesellschaft* 25, no. 4 (1999): 55–80.

2. Norman M. Naimark, *The Russians in Germany: A History of the Soviet Zone of Occupation, 1945–1949* (Cambridge: Harvard University Press, 1995).

3. F. Roy Willis, *The French in Germany 1945–1949* (Stanford: Stanford University Press, 1962), 51.

4. A majority of the members of the Bavarian state parliament voted against the Basic Law because it provided for a more centralized form of government than they would have wished. Nonetheless, the Bavarian Landtag endorsed the Basic Law as binding on the state. An excellent account of the Bavarian debate can be found in Peter H. Merkl, *The Origin of the West German Republic* (New York: Oxford University Press, 1963), 148–161.

5. Henry Krisch, *German Politics under Soviet Occupation* (New York: Columbia University Press, 1974). Krisch reviewed differing interpretations of this event in "Original Sin or Working Class Unity? Conflicting Interpretations of the Formation of the SED," in Peter Barker, ed., *The GDR and Its History: Rückblick und Revision* (Amsterdam: Editions Rodopi, 2000), 145–157.

6. A good account is David F. Patton, *Cold War Politics in Postwar Germany* (New York: St. Martin's, 1999).

7. Peter Glotz, "German Democracy at Fifty: Historical Retrospective and Political Outlook," Research paper, Center for the Study of Democracy, University of California at Irvine. The Bonn Republic, writes Glotz, was a success marked by constructive international integration, a social market economy, and a commitment by all political forces to a limited state with the rule of law.

8. See Gert–Joachim Glaessner, *Demokratie und Politik in Deutschland* (Opladen: Leske + Budrich, 1999).

9. Glaessner op cit., ch. 2; Mary Fulbrook, *Anatomy of a Dictatorship. Inside the GDR 1949–1989* (Oxford: Oxford University Press, 1999); Henry Krisch, *The German Democratic Republic: The Search for Identity* (Boulder: Westview Press, 1985). Fulbrook has recently told this story from a societal perspective in Mary Fulbrook, *The People's State: East German Society from Hitler to Honecker* (New Haven: Yale University Press, 2005).

10. By 1988, the authorities allowed Volker Braun's "Die Preussen kommen!" [The Prussians Are Coming] to be produced—a decade after it was written.

11. A thorough work is Manfred Hagen, *DDR—Juni '53* (Stuttgart: Franz Steiner Verlag, 1992). A recent German retrospective is Rolf Hochhuth, "Der ehrensvollste Tag unserer Geschichte" (Beilage zur Wochenzietung *Das Parlament*) 47, no. 28 (July 4, 1997): 17.

12. Frederick Taylor, *The Berlin Wall: A World Divided, 1961–1989* (New York: Harper Collins, 2006).

13. Rainer Münz and Ralf Ulrich, "Too Many foreigners? Demographic Developments, Changing patterns of Migration and the Absorption of Immigrants: The Case of Germany, 1945–1994." Working Paper 11, Center for German and European Studies, Georgetown University, March 1995.

14. A. James McAdams, *Germany Divided. From the Wall to Unification* (Princeton: Princeton University Press, 1993). See also his earlier *East Germany and Détente* (Cambridge: Cambridge University Press, 1985).

15. Philip Zelikow and Condoleezza Rice, *Germany Unified and Europe Transformed* (Cambridge: Harvard University Press, 1997 [1995]).

16. A detailed analytical study is Hannes Adomeit, *Imperial Overstretch: Germany in Soviet Policy from Stalin to Gorbachev* (Baden-Baden: Nomos Verlag, 1998).

17. Robert F. Goeckel, *The Lutheran Church and the East German State* (Ithaca, N.Y.: Cornell University Press, 1990); Jeffrey Koppstein, *The Politics of Economic Decline in East Germany, 1945–1989* (Chapel Hill: University of North Carolina Press, 1997).

18. McAdams (*Germany Divided,* 167) gives these suggestive figures: in 1986, the regime allowed over a half million East Germans under retirement age to visit the West, under a relaxed interpretation of

"pressing family matters." In 1987, this figure rose to 1.2 million! If one adds in retirees, McAdams suggests, one may have had between a fifth and a quarter of the East German population in the West in 1987 alone.

19. Charles S. Maier, *Dissolution. The Crisis of Communism and the End of East Germany* (Princeton: Princeton University Press, 1997) is the best account in English. For two vivid, if differing, eye witness accounts, see Robert Darnton, *Berlin Journal, 1989–1990* (New York: Norton, 1991), and Peter Marcuse, *Missing Marx. A Personal and Political Journal of a Year in East Germany, 1989–1990* (New York: Monthly Review Press, 1991). See also Laurence H. McFalls, *Communism's Collapse, Democacy's Demise?* (New York: New York University Press, 1995) and M. Donald Hancock and Helga A. Welsh, eds., *German Unification: Process and Outcomes* (Boulder, Colo.: Westview Press, 1994). For a cultural analysis of many works in German, a good introduction is Gert-Joachim Glaessner, *Der schwierige Weg zur Demokratie: Vom Ende der DDR zur deutschen Einheit* (Opladen: Westdeutscher Verlag, 1991).

20. There is an enormous literature in German on this and related topics. In English, see John Torpey, *Intellectuals, Socialism and Dissent* (Minneapolis: University of Minnesota Press, 1995), and Christian Joppke, *East German Dissidents and the Revolution of 1989* (New York: New York University Press, 1995).

21. An account is Konrad H. Jarousch, *The Rush to German Unity* (New York: Oxford University Press, 1994).

22. For the role of Neues Forum, especially in the crucial events in Leipzig 1989, see Neues Forum Leipzig, *Jetzt oder nie— Demokratie, Leipziger Herbst 1989* (Munich: C. Bertelsmann Verlag, 1991).

23. Zelikow and Rice, op cit. A German government insider's account is Horst Teltschick, *329 Tage: Innenansichten der Einigung* (Berlin: Siedler Verlag bei Goldmann, 1991).

24. Thomas A. Baylis, "Leadership Change in Eastern Germany: From Colonization to Integration?" in Peter H. Merkl, ed., *The Federal Republic of Germany at Forty-Five* (New York: New York University Press, 1995), 243–64; see also a later perspective in ibid, "East German Leadership after Unification: The Search for Voice," in Peter H. Merkl, ed., *The Federal Republic of Germany at Fifty* (London: Macmillan, 1999), 135–146.

Chapter 4 Notes

1. These include Imperial Germany, the Weimar Republic, Nazi Germany, the occupation regime, the Federal Republic in the West, the German Democratic Republic in the East, and unified Germany.

2. The literature on political culture is enormous. Basic texts include Gabriel A. Almond and Sidney P. Verba, *The Civic Culture* (Princeton: Princeton University Press, 1963) and ibid, eds., *The Civic Culture Revisited* (Boston: Little, Brown, 1980), including and especially David Conradt, "Changing German Political Culture," 212–272. Gabriel Almond offered an insightful retrospective in his 1995 lecture in the Research Colloquia series at the University of California, Irvine, "The Civic Culture: Prehistory, Retrospect and Prospect," which is available at the Center for the Study of Democracy homepage. See also David Laitin, "The Civic Culture at 30," *American Political Science Review* 89, no. 1 (1995): 168–174. Among the many important more recent writings on this subject, noteworthy contributions include Harry Eckstein, "A Culturalist Theory of Political Change," *American Political Science Review* 82, no. 3 (1988): 789–804; and Ronald Inglehart, "The Renaissance of Political Culture," ibid, 82, no. 1 (1988): 203–230. A recent example is Russell J. Dalton, "Citizen Attitudes and Political Behavior," *Comparative Political Studies* 33, no. 67 (2000): 912–940.

3. A landmark application of the political culture concept to politics in the Federal Republic was Kendall L. Baker, Russell J. Dalton, and Kai Hildebrandt, *Germany Transformed: Political Culture and the New Politics* (Cambridge: Harvard University Press, 1981). Over the years, the political culture approach was assimilated to German political science; see, for example, Bettina Westle, *Kollektive Identität im vereinten Deutschland* (Opladen: Lesk + Budrich, 1999), and ibid, "*Demokratie und Sozialismus: Politische Ordnungsvorstellungen im vereinten Deutschland zwischen Ideologie, Protest und Nostalgie,*" *KZfSS,* [*Kölner Zeitschrift für Soziologie und Sozialpsychologie*] 4 (1994): 571–596. See also Robert Rohrschneider, *Learning Democracy. Democratic and Economic Values in Unified Germany* (Oxford: Oxford University Press, 1999), ch. 2.

4. A classic study is that of Peter Gay, *Weimar Culture: The Outsider as Insider* (New York: Harper and Row, 1968).

5. See, for example, Ian Kershaw, *Hitler 1936–1945: Nemesis* (New York: W. W. Norton, 2000), 746.

6. A readily available source for these data is the summary (with data) published in two volumes by Richard and Anna Merritt. See Anna J. Merritt and Richard L. Merritt, eds., *Public Opinion in Occupied Germany: The OMGUS Surveys, 1945–1949* (Urbana: University of Illinois Press, 1970), and ibid, *Public Opinion in Semisovereign Germany: The HICOG Surveys, 1949–1955* (Urbana: University of Illinois Press, 1980).

7. Merritt and Merritt op cit., [OMGUS surveys], 31–33.

8. A useful summary is Kendall L. Baker, Russell J. Dalton and Kai Hildebrandt, *Germany Transformed: Political Culture and the New*

Politics (Cambridge: Harvard University Press, 1981). See especially chap. 1, "The Changing Political Culture."

9. In the monthly *Politbarometer* surveys of the Forschungsgruppe Wahlen for 2005—a year with higher than usual levels of concern—the percentage of respondents who, when asked to name the two most pressing issues of the day, named *"Politikverdruss/Affären"* hovered near 10 percent. For a German analysis, see Martin und Sylvia Greiffenhagen, *Ein schwieriges Vaterland: Zur politischen Kultur im vereinigten Deutschland* (Munich: Paul List Verlag, 1993), especially 174–188 "Politikverdrossenheit: Parteien unter Druck."

10. Richard J. Evans, "Zwei deutsche Diktaturen im 20. Jahrhundert?" *Aus Politik und Zeitgeschichte* (Beilage zur Wochenzeitung *Das Parlament*) nos. 1–2 (January 3, 2005): 3–9.

11. These issues are examined in Henry Krisch, "Changing Political Culture and Political Stability in the German Democratic Republic," *Studies in Comparative Communism* 14, no. 1 (1986): 41–53.

12. Catherine Epstein, *The Last Revolutionaries: German Communists and Their Century* (Cambridge: Harvard University Press, 2003) especially ch. 8.

13. This work was done at the Institute for Youth Research in Leipzig under its long-time director, Walter Friedrich. The institute avoided the general crackdown on survey work because of its director's personal ties to the head of the official youth organization (FDJ), Egon Krenz, who later became a powerful leader of the ruling party.

14. Almost none of this work could be published before 1989. Fortunately, the institute specialized in longitudinal studies, which were continued after 1989, thus giving us an insight into change from pre-1989 opinions. See, for example, Walter Friedrich/Peter Förster/Harry Müller, "Ostdeutsche Jugend 1992," *Utopie kreativ* 21/22 (1992): 114–125, and Peter Förster and Walter Friedrich, "Jugendliche in den neuen Bundesländern," *Aus Politik und Zeitgeschichte* (Beilage zur Wochenzeitung *Das Parlament*) B19 (1996): 18–29. They write that a change in values and attitudes among youth could be observed already in GDR times (ibid, 20).

15. Ibid, 27

16. The quote is "what belongs together now grows together" ["jetzt wächst zusammen, was zusammen gehört]. He is supposed to have said this—and many people swear they heard it—at a rally on November 10, 1989, in front of the Schöneberger Rathaus (then West Berlin's city hall.) But did he say it? Although many media and some scholarly sources say that he did, we have found different versions of his actual speech. In the version from the SPD files in the German Historical Museum (DHM) in Berlin, these words are missing; see *Ansprache des SPD-Ehrenvorsitzenden Willy Brandt vor dem*

Schöneberger Rathaus in Berlin am 10 November 1989, www.dhm.de/lemo/html/dokumente/DieDeutscheEinheit_rede-Brandt1989/index.html. However, in a chronology (2+4 Chronik), published by Weidenfeld, (www.2plus4.de) the words do appear.

17. A useful discussion is Mary Fulbrook, *Interpretations of the Two Germanies,* 2nd ed. (New York: St Martin's Press, 2000), 74.

18. Samples of important recent work include a special issue of the journal *Berliner Debatte Initial* 11, no. 5/6 (2000), "Demokratie in Gefahr? Politische Kultur in Osteuropa," with contributions especially by Robert Rohrschneider and Detlef Pollack/Jan Wielgohs; David P. Conradt, "Political Culture in Unified Germany: Will the Bonn Republic Survive and Thrive in Berlin? *German Studies Review* 21, no. 1 (1998): 83–104; Ursula Hoffman-Lange, "Politische Grundorientierungen," in Ursula Hoffman-Lange, ed., *Jugend und Demokratie in Deutschland* (Opladen: Lesk + Budrich, 1995), 159–194; Detlef Pollack, "Wirtschaftlicher, sozialer und mentaler Wandel in Ostdeutschland: Eine Bilanz nach zehn Jahren," Aus Politik und Zeitgeschichte (Beilage zur Wochenzeitung *Das Parlament*) B40/2000 (2000): 13–21; and Thomas Gensicke, "Auf dem Weg der Integration: Die neuen Bundesbürger nach der Einheit," *Deutschland Archiv* 34, no. 3 (2001): 398–410.

19. "*Deutsche Einheit,*" a special poll in the *Politbarometer* series conducted by Forschungsgruppe Wahlen (September 2004), 1–4.

20. Gensicke, op cit. 400.

21. Forschungsgruppe Wahlen, op cit., September 2007.

22. Pollack, op cit., 17–18.

23. Hoffman-Lange, op cit., Table 5.4 on 174.

24. Peter Förster, "Die 30-Jährigen in den neuen Bundesländern: Keine Zukunft im Osten!" *Deutschland Archiv* 34 no. 1 (2004): 23–32.

25. This seems to have remained constant from the first surveys soon after unification until today. See Westle, *Kollektive Identität,* 196–197.

26. Rohrschneider, op cit. 62.

27. Detlef Pollack/Jan Wielgohs, "Politische Kultur und demokratische Konsolidierung. Kritische Anfragen an das Konzept der politischen Kulturforschung zu postsozialistischen Gesellschaften," *Berliner Debatte Initial* 11, no. 5/6 (2000): 65–75.

28. The broader organizational setting for these changing political ideas is discussed further in chapter 8. The role of radical ideas is analyzed in Paul Hockenos, *Joschka Fischer and the Making of the Berlin Republic: An Alternative History of Postwar Germany* (Oxford: Oxford University Press, 2008), especially Part II, "The Red Decade," 53–128. See also Tony Judt, *Postwar: A History of Europe since 1945* (New York: Penguin Books, 2005), 390–452.

29. For the argument that it was this notion of a social economy and state that underlay the democratic stability of the Federal Republic, see Klaus Hartung, "Der neue deutsche Weg," *Die Zeit* online, October 9, 2003, no. 42. Hartung writes, "The social state (*Sozialstaat*) not only represents a founding myth of the Federal Republic: it was its core." He points to seminal legislation of the Adenauer years that provided, among other benefits, help for refugees, equalization of social obligations, ands similar measures to heal the social wounds left by the war. The task ahead, as he sees it, is to move from a "social nation" to a more individualistic "citizen nation."

30. Rolf Becker, "Political Efficacy and Voter Turnout in East and West Germany," *German Politics* 13, no. 2 (2004): 317–340.

31. Almond and Verba, op cit.

32. Bundesverband deutscher Banken, "Bilanz für die Zukunft: 50 Jahre Bundesrepublik Deutschland," *Demo/Skopie* no. 5 (1999): 15.

33. Westle, *Kollektive Identität,* 195.

34. Ibid, 4–5.

35. Bundesverband deutscher Banken, *inter/esse* 11 (2002), cited in www.bankenverband.de.

36. Ayhan Kaya, "German-Turkish Transnational Space: A Separate Space of Their Own," *German Studies Review* 30, no. 3 (October 2007): 483–502.

37. Americans may be reminded of debates over "Confederate identity." The literature on German wrestling with the past is enormous. Scholarly treatments in the broader East European context include Helga A. Welsh, "Dealing with the Communist Past: Central and East European Experiences after 1990," *Europe–Asia Studies* 48, no. 3 (1996): 413–428, and Dieter Segert, "The State, the Stasi and the People," *Journal of Communist Studies* 9, no. 3 (September 1993): 202–215. Several aspects of this complex set of issues are thoughtfully discussed by Mary Fulbrook in *German National Identity after the Holocaust* (Malden, Mass.: Blackwell, 1999). German writings on the subject include Christoph Klessmann, "Das Problem der doppelten 'Vergangenheitsbewältigung'," *Neue Gesellschaft/Frankfurter Hefte* 39, no. 12 (December 1991): 1099–1105; Klaus Sühl, ed., *Vergangenheitsbewältigung 1945–1989. Ein unmöglicher Versuch?* (Berlin: Verlag Volk und Welt, 1994); Christoph Kleßmann, Hans Misselwitz, and Günter Wichert, eds., *Deutsche Vergangenheiten—eine gemeinsame Herausforderung* (Berlin: Ch. Links Verlag, 1999).

38. These and other similar quotations are taken from an essay by James J. Sheehan, which has lost none of its analytical power for having been published almost a decade before German unification. See James J. Sheehan, "What is German History? Reflections on the Role

of the Nation in German History and Historiography," *Journal of Modern History* 53 (March 1981): 1–23.

39. Martin Walser's speech objecting to what he saw as an instrumentalization of the Holocaust for current political ends produced a voluminous polemical exchange in the media.

40. Examples are the slow and difficult negotiations over payments for Nazi-era slave laborers, and the decade-long struggle over a Holocaust memorial in the center of Berlin.

41. Official policy here reflected popular attitudes. The percentage of Germans who chose the "peacetime" Third Reich (1933–1939) as the "best period in German history" was still as high as 42 percent in 1951; by 1970 it had declined to only 5 percent. From surveys cited in Baker, Dalton, and Hildebrandt, *Germany Transformed*, 92.

42. Christa Wolf, *Kindheitsmuster* (Berlin and Weimar: Aufbau Verlag, 1976), published in English as *A Model Childhood* (New York: Farrar, Strauss and Giroux, 1980.) First-person accounts of former Nazis who lived in the GDR may be found in Lutz Niethammer, *Die volkseigene Erfahrung* (Berlin: Rowohlt, 1991). The retrospective view of an East German dissident is Konrad Weiss, "Gebrochener, nicht 'verordneter' Antifaschismus" (Beilage zur Wochenzietung *Das Parliament*) 46, no. 20 (May 10, 1996): 15.

43. Hence the choice as "non-word of the year" some time after unification: *Besserwessi*; a pun on the words for Westerner and Know-It-All.

44. Alan Cowell, "Former East Germans Confront Lurid Steroids Legacy," *New York Times*, April 5, 1998; and Alan Maimon, "One Tale of Doping and Birth Defects," *New York Times*, February 6, 2000.

45. Literally, the "history and consequences of the SED dictatorship in Germany," a somewhat question-begging and politicized title; *Deutscher Bundestag, 12. Wahlperiode, Enquete-Kommission, Aufarbeitung von Geschichte und Folgen der SED-Diktatur in Deutschland*, 18 vols. (Baden–Baden: Nomos Verlag, 1995). See Jennifer A. Yoder, "Truth without Reconciliation: An Appraisal of the Enquete Commission on the SED Dictatorship in Germany," *German Politics* 8, no. 3 (December 1999): 59–80.

46. For a thoughtful analysis of this process, see Peter E. Quint, "Judging the Past: The Prosecution of East German Border Guards and the GDR Chain of Command," *Review of Politics* 6, no. 2 (Spring 1999): 303–329. See also Anne Sa'adeh, *Germany's Second Chance. Truth, Justice, Democratization* (Cambridge: Harvard University Press, 1998), especially chs. 3 and 4. Sa'adeh places the post-1989 developments both in a comparative and in German post-1945 perspective. The highest ranking GDR figure to be jailed is Egon Krenz, who briefly succeeded Honecker as SED chief (October–

December 1999). Roger Cohen, "Verdict in Berlin Wall Deaths Is Upheld," *New York Times,* November 9, 1999, and Karl-Heinz Baum, "*Der letzte* SED-Chef muss in Haft," *Frankfurter Rundschau,* November 9, 1999). Border guards at lower levels had previously been convicted; among others tried were, prominently, judges and lawyers convicted of bending GDR law for political purposes. A recent example is "Ehemalige Staatsanwältin der DDR verurteilt," *Frankfurter Rundschau,* February 3, 2000.

47. Matthias Arning, "Von Dohnanyi mag einfach nicht mehr ständig über Auschwitz reden," *Frankfurter Rundschau,* May 27, 2000.

48. A recent scholarly survey of this question is Helmut Schmidt, ed., *A Nation of Victims? Representations of German Wartime Suffering from 1945 to the Present* (Amsterdam: Rodolpi, 2007). As the various contributors to this work make clear, the issue of *German* suffering in the Nazi era has been a problematical and politically charged one since the 1950s.

49. This speech is accessible as an appendix to von Weizsäcker's memoirs [Richard von Weizsäcker, *From Weimar to the Wall: My Life in German Politics* (New York: Broadway Books, 1999); the quote is on page 381.] The German original may be found, *inter alia,* in ibid, *Von Deutschland aus* (München: Deutscher Taschenbuch Verlag, 1987), 9–36.

50. For the text of a declaration published by a group of conservative publicists and politicians, see Reuter Textline/Reuter German News Service, "*Neuer Streit Um Gedenken Nach Aufruf Konservativer,*" April 7, 1995; Norbert Seitz, "Bemuehter Umgang. 50 Jahre 8. Mai - eine deutsche Pathologie," *Süddeutsche Zeitung,* April 15, 1995; a review of the literature is in Enrico Syring, "*Der immer noch umstrittene Jahrestag [der 8. Mai 1945 in Forschung und Literatur]*" (Beilage zur Wochenzietung *Das Parliament*) 45, no. 35 (August 25, 1995): 13–15.

51. Richard Bernstein, "German War Commemoration Ceremonies Stress Responsibility for Europe's 'Mass Graveyard'," *New York Times,* May 9, 2005.

52. For a thorough scholarly analysis, see Philipp Ther and Ana Siljak, *Redrawing Nations: Ethnic Cleansing in East–Central Europe, 1944–1948* (Lanham, Md.: Rowman and Littlefield, 2001).

53. W. G. Sebald, *On the Natural History of Destruction* (New York: Random House, 2003); Jorg Friedrich, *Der Brand* (Munich: Propyläen Verlag, 2002) Hans Erich Nossack, *The End: Hamburg 1943* (Chicago: University of Chicago Press, 2005). The Internet discussion list H-German has archived a wide-ranging discussion of these and other works on the subject. See especially the contribution of Charles Maier, H-Net: Humanities and Social Sciences Online [H-German Forum], posting of November 12, 2003.

54. Sebald, op cit., 104.

55. Peter Schneider, "The Germans are Breaking an Old Taboo," *New York Times,* January 18, 2003.

56. On this latter subject, the best account is in Norman Naimark, *The Russians in Germany* (Cambridge: Harvard University Press, 1995), ch. 2: "Soviet soldiers, German Women, and the Problem of Rape."

57. Günter Grass, *Im Krebsgang* (Göttingen: Steidel Verlag 2002); in English: Günter Grass, *Crabwalk,* translated from the German by Krishna Winston (Orlando, Fla.: Harcourt, 2002).

58. For an interesting critique that places the Grass novel and discussion of it in a larger context, see Robert G. Moeller, "Sinking Ships, the Lost *Heimat,* and Broken Taboos: Günter Grass and the Politics of Memory in Contemporary Germany," *Contemporary European History* 12, no. 2 (2003): 147–181.

59. Grass's admission, in his memoirs *Peeling the Onion,* that he had served in a Waffen–SS unit in the closing weeks of world War II—a fact hitherto unrevealed—produced a storm of controversy and commentary in Germany as well as other countries, including Poland. For an introduction to the issues in English, see Alan Riding, "Günter Grass under Siege after Revealing SS Past," *New York Times,* August 18, 2006.

60. In part this is a generational difference. Gerhard Schröder, for example, was less than a year old when the war ended. For him, as for many of his age cohorts around the world (think of Madeline Albright!), details about his family's past reached him many years later. See Roger Cohen, "Schröder, Like Germany, Is Looking Harder at the Past," *New York Times,* July 2, 2001.

61. "Ich liebe Menschen! Bundespräsident Johannes Rau über richtigen und falschen Nationalstolz," [interview] in *Der Spiegel,* no. 13 (2001), jttp:www/spiegel.de/spiegel/O.15128.124580.00.html.

62. Roger Cohen, "Schröder Joins Debate, Taking Side of Pride in Germany," *New York Times,* March 20, 2001. Cohen remarks that "... Germans are tired of seeing their history reduced to the 12 Nazi years."

63. Werner Reutter, "Germany on the Road to 'Normalcy': Policies and Politics of the Red-Green Federal Government, 1998–2002," in Werner Reutter, *Germany on the Road to 'Normalcy': Policies and Politics of the Red-Green Federal Government, 1998–2002* (New York: Palgrave MacMillan, 2004), For Schröder's speech at an election rally in Hanover on August 5, 2002, see http://berlin.spd. de/servlet/PB/show/1017816/btw2002_0805schroeder_rede.pdf. On this occasion he said, "It is true that we have set forth on our way, our German way (*unseren deutschen Weg*)..." and later, discussing the danger of an Iraq war, he declared that light-hearted war

plans [*Spielerei mit Krieg*] would receive no support from his government. He charged that Kohl had evaded these difficult choices by refraining from military action but helping to finance them. But now, he continued, "this Germany, our Germany is a self confident [*selbstbewusstes*] country...."

64. Interview with *Die Welt,* December 4, 2004, cited in *Deutschland Nachrichten* (German Information Center Web site), December 13, 2004.

65. Interview with *Die Zeit,* November 28, 2002, cited in *Deutschland Nachrichten* (German Information Center Web site), December 4, 2002.

66. "*Das ich Frau bin, spielt keine Rolle,*" [interview with Angela Merkel] *Cicero* (October 2005), www.cicero.de/839.php/ausgabe=10/2005.

67. James E. Young, "Berlin's Holocaust Memorial," *German Politics & Society* 17, no. 3 (Fall 1999): 56.

68. Brian Ladd, *The Ghosts of Berlin: Confronting German History in an Urban Landscape* (Chicago and London: University of Chicago Press, 1997), 233.

69. Grass often presented himself as the political "conscience" of postwar Germany through his sharp criticism of prominent officials and government policies. Grass is a prolific writer and winner of the Nobel Prize for literature in 1999. For many German and foreign commentators, his reputation suddenly became tarnished in the fall of 2006 when he publicly admitted with the publication of his autobiography, *Häuten der Zwiebel (Peeling the Onion)* that he had served in the infamous Waffen SS as a teenager during the last stages of World War II. When asked by a German journalist why he had not revealed this episode earlier, Grass replied: "My silence during all the years is one of the reasons I've written this book. It finally had to come out." "*Warum ich nach sechzig Jahren mein Schweigen breche,*" interview published in the *Frankfurter Allgemeine Zeitung,* August 12, 2006.

70. Günter Grass, *The Tin Drum,* trans. Ralph Manheim (New York: Vintage Books, 1964), 31.

71. www.ucalgary.ca/applied history/tutor/popculture. Accessed May 20, 2007.

72. Ibid.

73. A young Peter Lorre starred in *Murderers Among Us,* which is the story of a child murderer and his pursuers.

74. Among them were Lorre and Dietrich, both of whom sought political refuge in the United States and went on to achieve international stardom in English-language cinema.

75. For an introduction to and survey of East German cinema, see Sean Allan and John Sandford, *DEFA-East German Cinema 1946–1992* (New York: Berghahn Books, 1999), and Daniela Berghahn, *Hollywood behind the Wall: The Cinema of East Germany* (Manchester: Manchester University Press, 2005).

76. Barbara Kosta, "Tom Tykwer's *Run Lola Run* and the Usual Suspects: The Avant-Garde, Popular Culture, and History," in Agnes C. Mueller, ed., *German Pop Culture* (Ann Arbor: University of Michigan Press, 2004), 166–167.

77. Thomas Brussig, *Am kürzeren Ende der Sonnenallee* (Frankfurt am Main: Fischer Taschenbuch Verlag, 2005).

78. Sabrina Petra Ramet, ed., *Rocking the State: Rock Music and Politics in Eastern Europe and Russia* (San Francisco: Westview Press, 1994).

79. Ibid, 2.

80. Among them is *Silly*, a rock band established in 1978.

81. *New York Times,* February 27, 2008. The *Times* article observes: "Among other things, the book shows how far comics have come as a cultural medium taken seriously [in Germany], but also that the Holocaust has come a long way too, as a topic to be freshly considered by a new generation of German teenagers."

82. Art Spiegelman, *Maus: A Survivor's Tale* (New York: Random House, 1986).

Chapter 5 Notes

1. Article 23 (the text of which has subsequently been deleted from the constitution) proclaimed that "This Basic Law is currently valid in the territory of the states of Baden, Bavaria, Bremen, greater Berlin, Hamburg, Hesse, Lower Saxony, North Rhine–Westphalia, Rhineland-Palatinate, Schleswig-Holstein, Württemberg-Baden, and Württemberg-Hohenzollern. It will be enacted in other parts of Germany upon their admission to the Federal Republic."

2. See Peter H. Merkl, *German Unification in the European Context* (University Park: Pennsylvania State University Press, 1993), especially 226–230.

3. The terms "Basic Law" and constitution are used interchangeably in this book. Delegates to the Parliamentary Council chose the former terminology to underscore the transitional nature of their efforts pending German unification and the adoption of an all-German constitution. In practice, the Basic Law (as amended) has become the all-German constitution.

4. Article 31 asserts categorically: "Federal law shall override Land law...."

5. Article 91a.

6. Article 91b.
7. Article 28.
8. Arthur B. Gunlicks, "Fifty Years of German Federalism: An Overview and Some Current Developments," in Peter H. Merkl, ed., *The Federal Republic of Germany at Fifty: The End of a Century of Turmoil* (London: Macmillan Press, 1999), 200.
9. The enumeration of these individual rights is contained in Articles 2, 3, 4, 5, 8, 10, and 13, respectively.
10. Article 1 of the Basic Law.
11. Article 6.
12. Article 9.
13. Article 12.
14. Article 14.
15. Article 15.
16. See chapter 7.
17. Article 61.
18. Article 68.
19. Article 59.
20. The fourth paragraph of Article 63 anticipates further contingencies for the election of a federal chancellor, which thus far have not occurred: "If no candidate has been elected (within 14 days), a new ballot shall take place without delay, in which the person obtaining the largest number of votes shall be elected. If the person elected has obtained the votes of the majority of the members of the *Bundestag,* the federal president must appoint him within 7 days of the election. If the person elected did not obtain such a majority, the federal president must within 7 days either appoint him or dissolve parliament."
21. See chapter 7.
22. Article 65.
23. This has occurred once, when Ludwig Erhard stepped down in 1966 after he lost support within his own Christian Democratic faction. The *Bundestag* elected Kurt Georg Kiesinger as his successor as part of the formation of the first Grand Coaliton cabinet.
24. Article 51.
25. Article 50.
26. For the continuing evolution of German federalism, see Arthur B. Gunlicks, *The Länder and German Federalism* (Manchester: Manchester University Press, 2003), 203, and Gunlick, "German Federalism and Recent Reform Efforts," *German Law Journal* 6 (2005): 1283, at www.germanlawjournal.com/pdf/Vol06No10/PDF_Vol_06_No_10_12831296_SI_Articles_Gunlicks.pdf. See also Stephen J. Silvia, "The *Bundesrat,* Interest Groups, and Gridlock: German Federalism at the End of the Twentieth Century," in Carl Lankowski, ed.,

Breakdown, Breakup, Breakthrough: Germany's Difficult Passage to Modernity (New York: Berghahn Books, 1999), 121–136.

27. *Statistisches Jahrbuch 2007 für die Bundesrepublik Deutschland* (Wiesbaden: Statistisches Bundesamt, 2007), 106.

28. B. Guy Peters, *The Politics of Bureaucracy* (New York: Longman 1978), 111.

29. Percentages calculated from *Statistisches Jahrbuch 1998 für die Bundesrepublik Deutschland,* 516.

30. Peters, *Politics of Bureaucracy,* 111–112.

31. For a discussion of the tendency to settle issues of social integration through litigation, see Michael Naumann, "Das Kreuz mit dem Tuch," *Die Zeit 57,* no. 20 (July 11, 2002): 1.

32. *Statistisches Jahrbuch 2007 für die Bundesrepublik Deutschland,* 263–264.

33. Georg Vanberg, *The Politics of Constitutional Review in Germany* (Cambridge: Cambridge University Press, 2005), 1–3. Vanberg has called the Court "the most notable and powerful such court in the world. Unlike the U.S. Supreme Court, for example, it need not wait for a court case to reach it before making constitutional judgments; both individuals and other parts of the federal government may bring such cases directly to the court.

34. *Lüth* case of January 15, 1958.

35. Classroom Crucifix Case of May 16, 1995. A useful compilation of Federal Constitutional Court case law in English translation is Bundesverfassungsgericht, *Decisions of the Bundesverfassungsgericht— Federal Constitutional Court—Federal Republic of Germany* (Baden-Baden: Nomos Verlagsgesellschaft, 1998).

36. "Immer mehr Bürger beschweren sich in Karlsruhe," *Frankfurter Rundschau* online, March 3, 2007. An analysis of recent developments is Ludger Helms, "The Federal Constitutional Court: Institutionalizing Judicial Review in a Semisovereign Democracy," in Ludger Helms, ed., *Institutions and Institutional Change in the Federal Republic of Germany* (New York: St Martin's Press, 2000), 84–104. See also Rupert Scholz, "Fünfzig Jahre Bundesverfassungsgericht," *Aus Politik und Zeitgeschichte* (Beilage zur Wochenzeitung *Das Parlament*) B 37/38 (September 7, 2001): 6–15.

37. Koppel S. Pinson, *Modern Germany: Its History and Civilization* (New York: Macmillan, 1954), 162. The most authoritative source on the history of the Germany military prior to 1945 remains Gordon A. Craig, *The Politics of the Prussian Army, 1640–1945* (New York: Oxford University Press, 1967).

38. Pinson, *Modern Germany,* 435–436.

39. See Michael C. Thomsett, *The German Opposition to Hitler: The Resistance, the Underground, and Assassination Plots, 1938–1945*

(Jefferson, N.C.: McFarland and Company, 1997); Jürgen Schmädeke and Peter Steinbach, eds., *Der Widerstand gegen den Nationalsozialismus: Die deutsche Gesellschaft und der Widerstand gegen Hitler* (Munich: Piper, 1985); and Klemens von Klemperer, *German Resistance against Hitler: The Search for Allies Abroad* (Oxford: Oxford University Press/Clarendon Press, 1984).

40. This move was accompanied by an amendment to Article 73 of the Basic Law, which extended the federal government's exclusive jurisdiction to include "the defense as well as the protection of the civilian population."

41. Article 65a, adopted in March 1956. In the event of war, the federal chancellor would assume command.

42. Thomas M. Foster, *NVA: Die Armee der Sowjetzone*, 3rd ed. (Cologne: Markus-Verlag, 1967).

43. Cited in Jörg Schönbohm, *Two Armies and One Fatherland*, translated from the German by Peter and Elfi Johnson (Providence, R.I.: Berghahn Books, 1996), 32.

44. An informative assessment of the NVA's efforts at transformation followed by pending collapse is Dale R. Herspring, *Requiem for an Army: The Demise of the East German Military* (Lanham, Md.: Rowman and Littlefield, 1998).

45. Chapter 1, Article 4, paragraph 3 states: "No one shall be forced against his [or now also her] conscience to perform armed military service." The law regulating civilian service came into force after the introduction of conscription in 1956.

46. Data for this section drawn from the Web site of the Federal Office for Civilian Service (*Bundesamt für Zivildienst*), at www.zivildienst.de.

47. Prior to unification the Bundeswehr had numbered 500,000 and the NVA 175,000.

48. Herspring, 149.

49. Herspring, 155–158. Herspring reports that most NVA equipment was destroyed but some was sold or given away abroad. The Bundeswehr retained only some of it for itself, notably a fleet of MiG-29s.

50. Schönbohm, 51.

51. Schönbohm, 206.

52. See data at www.bundeswehr.de; Stephen Szabo, "The German Defense White Paper," *AICGS Advisor,* December 7, 2006.

53. The latter option is available to conscientious objectors under Article 4 of the Basic Law (freedom of religion).

54. For this section generally, see the Web sites of the various security agencies and also Alexander Weinlein, "Gebraucht wird der lange Atem" (Beilage zur Wochenzietung *Das Parliament*) 52, nos. 15–16 (April 12–19, 2002): 6, and Eckart Wertebach, "Deutsche

Sicherheitsstrukturen im 21. Jahrhundert," *Aus Politik und Zeitgeschichte* (Beilage zur Wochenzeitung *Das Parlament*) B 44 (October 25, 2004): 5–13.

55. As in chapter 1, we attribute the concept of "take-off" to W.W. Rostow, *The Stages of Economic Growth,* op cit.

56. Post-Communist members include Poland, the Czech Republic, Slovakia, Hungary, Slovenia, Bulgaria, Romania, and the three Baltic republics (Estonia, Latvia, and Lithuania). The Mediterranean island countries of Malta and (Greek) Cyprus also joined in 2004.

57. They include Croatia and possibly Turkey.

58. The United Kingdom and Denmark negotiated the treaty right to opt out of EMU, whereas Sweden chose for domestic political reasons not to join. Greece did not initially meet the requisite economic criteria for EMU membership but later qualified. As of 2008, the newest members of the eurozone include Slovenia, Malta, and Cyprus.

Chapter 6 Notes

1. Excellent introductions to this topic include Gerald Braunthal, *Parties and Politics in Modern Germany* (Boulder, Colo.: Westview Press, 1996); Thomas Saalfeld, "The German Party System: Continuity and Change," *German Politics* 7, no. 3 (2002): 99–130; and Bernhard Wessels, "The German Party System: Developments after Unification," in Werner Reutter, ed., *Germany on the Road to "Normalcy": Policies and Politics of the Red-Green National Government, 1988–2002* (New York: Palgrave Macmillan, 2004), 47–65. A highly informative comparison of linkages between citizens and political parties is Russell J. Dalton, *Citizen Politics: Public Opinion and Political Parties in Advanced Industrial Democracies,* 4th ed. (Washington, D.C.: CQ Press, 2006).

2. It is notable that the upsurge of dissatisfaction in the 1990s with both parties and politics generally—linked to the catch words *Politikverdrossenheit* and *Parteienverdrossenheit* (roughly, the state of being fed up with politics and parties), which received wide publicity through their use by the then federal president Richard von Weizsäcker—seemed to ebb as quickly as it had flooded. This is not to say that there are no long-range problems regarding party effectiveness and electoral turnout. See Stefan Immerfall, "Strukturwandel und Strukturschwächen der deutschen Mitgliederparteien," *Aus Politik und Zeitgeschichte* (Beilage zur Wochenzietung *Das Parliament*) 1–2 (January 2, 1998): 3–4.

3. For an early and still highly informative assessment of the emergence of grassroots movements in Germany, see Jutta Helm, "Citizen Lobbies in West Germany," in Peter H. Merkl, ed., *Western European*

Party Systems (New York and London: Free Press, Collier Macmillan Publishers, 1980), 576–596.

4. *Statistisches Jahrbuch für die Bundesrepublik Deutschland 2007* (Wiesbaden: Statistisches Bundesamt, 2007), 72.

5. See the map in Jörg Schindler, "Die rote Truppe ist bunt," *Frankfurter Rundschau* online, February 28, 2008.

6. Seymour Martin Lipset and Stein Rokkan, eds., *Party Systems and Voter Alignments* (New York: Free Press, 1967).

7. Dalton, op cit.

8. One study of the SPD from its origins to the end of the Schröder government in 2005 is Heinrich Potthoff and Susanne Miller, *The Social Democratic Party of Germany 1848–2005* (Bonn: J.H.W. Dietz Nachf, 2006). The modern CDU under Kohl's leadership as party chair and chancellor for more than thirty years is covered in Clay Clemens and William E. Patterson, ed., *The Kohl Chancellorship* (London: Frank Cass, 1998).

9. An account of the largely forced SPD-KPD unification in the Soviet zone in April 1946, based on interviews and archival materials, is Henry Krisch, *German Politics under Soviet Occupation* (New York: Columbia University Press, 1974).

10. The program was named after the city on the Rhine south of Bonn where the party congress met.

11. Vorstand der SPD, *Grundsatzprogramm der Sozialdemokratischen Partei Deutschlands,* adopted at a party congress in Berlin on December 20, 1989, and revised at a party congress in Leipzig on April 17, 1998 (Braunschweig: Braunschweig Druck GmbH, 1999).

12. For two early but still valuable studies of the Greens in particular, and the larger radical setting in which the party arose, see E. Gene Frankland and Donald Schoonmaker, *Between Protest and Power: The Green Party in Germany* (Boulder, Colo.: Westview Press, 1992) and Andrei S. Markovits and Philip S. Gorski, *The German Left: Red, Green and Beyond* (New York: Oxford University Press, 1993).

13. An informative biography of Fischer's political evolution from an antisystem protester in his youth to national statesman is Paul Berman, *Power and the Idealists: Or the Passion of Joschka Fischer and Its Aftermath* (Brooklyn, N.Y.: Soft Skull Press, 2005). Fischer's political career is placed in a larger movement context in Hockenos, op cit., 158–185, 199–216.

14. There is an extraordinarily voluminous literature on the PDS, produced in several languages both by scholars and such party leaders as Gregor Gysi and Lothar Bisky. Some useful titles include Dan Hough, *The Fall and Rise of the PDS in Eastern Germany* (Birmingham, UK: Birmingham University Press, 2001); Heinrich Bortfeldt, *Von der SED zur PDS: Wandlung zur Demokratie?* (Bonn:

Bouvier, 1992), which is a semi-insider's account of the PDS's transition from being the ruling party in the former GDR to a struggling postcommunist party in unified Germany; Henry Krisch, "The Party of Democratic Socialism: Left and East," in Russell J. Dalton, ed., *Germans Divided: The 1994 Bundestag Election and the Evolution of the German Party System* (Oxford: Berg, 1996), 109–132, which is an analysis of the PDS's early straddle between its eastern German base and becoming a nationwide left wing force.

15. WASG was a loose collection of (mostly western German) left-wing opponents of Schröder's economic and social policies, including some defectors from the SPD.

16. Basic documents from the unity party congress, including speeches by Lafontaine, Gysi, and Bisky, can be found at: http://die linke.de/partei/organe/parteitage/gruendungspartteig.

17. Lafontaine had, after all, been the SPD's chancellorship candidate in 1990, SPD chair (1995–1999), and for a time (1988–1989) finance minister in the first Schröder cabinet. His commitment to left-wing politics is exemplified by his slogan in his June 2007 congress speech: "Freedom through socialism."

18. Hubert Kleinert, "Warum Deutschland umdenken muss," *Der Spiegel*, February 25, 2008, at www.spiegel.de/politik/deutsch land/0.1518.537472.00.html.

19. A number of smaller Protestant parties existed as well.

20. www.germanculture.com.ua/library/facts/bl_fdp.htm.

21. The NPD's total of 4.9 percent in 1969 came the closest.

22. For a perceptive assessment of the German case with other countries, see Peter H. Merkl and Leonard Weinberg, eds., *Right-Wing Extremism in the Twenty-First Century* (Portland, Ore.: Frank Cass Publishers, 2003).

23. Peter Mair and Ingrid van Biezen, "Party Membership in Twenty European Democracies, 1980–2000," *Party Politics* 7, no. 1 (2001): 5–21. Austria ranked first with 17.66 percent. The mean for the twenty countries was 4.99.

24. This may have been due in part to the Greens' merger with the eastern German Bündnis '90.

25. Oskar Niedermayer "Parteimitgliedschaften im Jahre 2003," *Zeitschrift für Parlamentsfragen*, no. 2 (2004): 320; data from respective party Web sites.

26. Franz Walter, "Bürgertum koppelt sich von Union ab," *Der Spiegel* online, July 9, 2006. For the SPD see Thomas Koch and Wolfgang Schröder, "Auf dem Kurs zu einer Nichtarbeitnehmer-Partei?" *Frankfurter Rundschau* online, January 10, 2002.

27. *Grundgesetz für die Bundesrepublik Deutschland* (Bonn: Bundeszentrale für politische Bildung, 2001), 22.

28. Parties are further and narrowly defined in the national law on parties as "unions of citizens who seek to influence the formation of political attitudes (*politische Willensbildung*) on a national or state level and who seek to participate in popular representation in the *Bundestag* or in a Landtag, and who do so continuously or for a longer time." Moreover, such groups must satisfy detailed criteria set out in the law. The would-be party's seriousness (*Ernsthaftigkeit*) in seeking to reach these goals are judged by the scope and stability (*Umfang und Festigkeit*) of a party's organization, the size of the membership, and its public presence. See the Web site of the federal election commissioner: www.bundeswahlleiter.de.

29. Braunthal, op cit, 102–104.

30. Six of the sitting judges would have had to favor continuing the case, but three of the seven judges voted to dismiss. For a discussion of this case against the background of the NPD's history, see Eckhard Jesse, "Das Auf und Ab der NPD," *Aus Politik und Zeitgeschichte* (Beilage zur Wochenzeitung *Das Parlament*) no. 42 (October 17, 2005): 31–38, and Lars Flemming, "Das Scheitern der Antständigen" (Beilage zur Wochenzietung *Das Parliament*) 55, no. 45 (November 7, 2005): 7.

31. For details of the current system, which has been in effect since a 1994 ruling of the Constitutional Court, see a summary of the system (in English) at www.bundestag.de/htdocs_e/datab/finance/finance_l.html. See also the federal election commissioner: (*Bundeswahlleiter*) at www.bundeswahlleiter.de/wahlen/abc/d/ts2.htm# Staatliche.

32. To qualify to receive such funding, parties must file annual financial statements of income and expenditure with the *Bundestag*.

33. Saalfeld, op cit., 122–123, especially Table 7, 123.

34. Clay Clemens, "A Few Bad Apples or a Spoiled Barrel? The CDU Party Finances Scandal Five Years Later," *German Politics and Society* 23, no. 2 (2005): 72–87, and Clay Clemens, "A Legacy Reassessed: Helmut Kohl and the German Party Finance Affair," *German Politics* 9, no. 2 (August 2000): 25–50. An early but useful chronology of the scandal's unraveling is "Der Fall Kiep und die CDU—eine Chronologie," *Der Spiegel* 49 (November 29, 1999).

35. Clemens, "A Few Bad Apples ...," 78–79.

36. Ibid, "Kohl and the Fall from Grace," www.aicgs.org/topics/Germany2000/clemens.shtml; Roger Cohen, "Kohl, a Stubborn Statesman, May Be Wrecking His Party," *New York Times,* January 12, 2000.

37. www.germanculture.com.ua/library/facts/bl_electoral system.htm, "Electoral System of Germany."

38. Ludger Helms, "The German Federal Election, September 2005," *Electoral Studies* 26 (2007): 225.

Chapter 7 Notes

1. The Refugee Party, officially known as the Association of Refugees and Dispossessed (BHE), was founded in January 1950 to represent the economic and social needs of the nine to eleven million ethnic Germans who had resettled in West Germany from East Prussia and Poland, the Sudentenland in Czechoslovakia, and the Soviet zone/GDR. The party scored initial successes in state elections in Schleswig-Holstein, Hesse, Lower Saxony, and Bavaria. Twenty-seven deputies were elected to the *Bundestag* in the 1953 national election, and the party joined the government as a junior coalition partner in the second Adenauer cabinet (1953–1957). As expellees and refugees became increasingly integrated in West German society, the party's electoral fortunes began to wane and it failed to surmount the 5 percent threshold for *Bundestag* representation in the 1957 election. The BHE was subsequently dissolved and most of its former supporters migrated to the CDU/CSU. For a discussion of the party's ideological appeal and heterogeneous clientele, see Richard Hiscocks, *Democracy in Western Germany* (New York: Oxford University Press, 1957).

2. Although the Bündnis 90 did include an environmental group, their chief link with the Greens was the reluctance of both groups to rush into reunification. Indeed, the Greens, unlike all the other West German parties, did not establish an "eastern branch" for the 1990 GDR elections and extended their party to the East only after reunification had taken place.

3. Because the Greens had not formed an all-German party before the elections, they were nearly shut out of the *Bundestag*: the only-West German Greens failed to clear the 5 percent hurdle, but their East German allies, the *Bündnis 90* did.

4. We do not yet have a detailed insider account of the decision making process involved here, unlike the 1982 change documented in Klaus Bölling, *Die letzten 30 Tage des Kanzlers Helmut Schmidt: Ein Tagebuch* (Hamburg: Rowohlt Taschenbuch Verlag, 1982). For 2005, see "Bundestag wird im Herbst neu gewählt," *Frankfurter Rundschau,* online, May 23, 2005; Claus Christian Mahlzahn, "Selbstmord aus Angst vor dem Tod," *Der Spiegel* online, May 23, 2005. The decision to seek early elections seems to have been taken without serious consultation with Deputy Chancellor and Foreign Minister Joschka Fischer, the leader of the Greens party coalition partner.

5. Forschungsgruppe Wahlen, *Politbarometer* KW 27 (July 1, 2005) and KW 29 (July 11, 2005).

6. Thomas Kröter, "Bundestag stimmt für Neuwahl," *Frankurter Rundschau* online, July 2, 2005. The vote was 151 yes, 296 no, 148 abstentions. While 105 SPD deputies voted for Schröder, enough

(140) abstained for him to lose. It was perhaps a sign of how little the Greens had been consulted that only eight of their number (including Fischer) abstained as planned, while 46 defiantly voted yes.

7. See his formal statement, under the heading "Jetzt haben Sie es in der Hand" (Beilage zur Wochenzietung *Das Parliament*) 55, nos. 30–31 (July 25/August 1, 2005): 17, and "Die Fernsehansprache des Bundespräsidenten—Die Erklärung des Budeskanzlers," *Frankfurter Allgemeine Zeitung,* July 23, 2005, 2. Köhler explained his view of this process in an interview, "Und dann entscheide Ich," *Die Zeit,* 23 (2005).

8. Ibid. See also Richard Bernstein, "German President Dissolves Parliament and Calls Early Elections," *New York Times,* July 22, 2005.

9. "Klagen abgewiesen," *Frankfurter Rundschau* online, August 25, 2005; "Beurteilungsspielraum des Bundeskanzlers bestätigt," and "Sieg für den 'Deutschlandachter'," both in (Beilage zur Wochenzietung *Das Parliament*) 55, nos. 34–35 (August 22/29, 2005): 17.

10. The text is available in German at the court's Web site: www.bundesverfassungsgericht.de/entsdcheidungen/es20050825_2bve000405. html, which includes the dissenting opinion of Judge Hans-Joachim Jentsch. In his dissent, Jentsch pointed out that neither Schröder nor Köhler had pointed to specific legislation that had been blocked.

11. The presiding judge of the court, Hans-Jürgen Papier, who had voted with the majority, called for allowing the *Bundestag* to dissolve itself by a super-majority vote.

12. Article 68 provides that, should a chancellor not receive a requested vote of confidence of a majority of *Bundestag* members (the so-called Chancellor majority), he may ask the president to dissolve the *Bundestag*; the president then has twenty-one days to comply. If during that period the *Bundestag* elects another of its members as chancellor, the proposed dissolution lapses. See *Grundgesetz für die Bundesrepublik Deutschland* (Bonn: Bundeszentrale für politische Bildung, 2001), 41.

13. The political and constitutional background of this issue, as displayed in both the Brandt and Kohl episodes, is explored in Jörg Kürschner, "Neuwahlen nur nach Vertrauensfrage" (Beilage zur Wochenzietung *Das Parliament*) 55, no. 22 (May 30, 2005): 19.

14. For an overview of the campaign and its outcome see Erich Langenbacher, ed., *Launching the Grand Coalition: The 2005 Bundestag Elections and the Future of German Politics* (New York: Berghahn Books, 2006). See also Hans Rattinger and Marie Juhasz, *Die Bundestagswahl 2005. Neue Machtkonstellation trotz Stabilität der politischen Lage* (Munich: Hanns-Seidel-Stiftung and Akademie für Politik und Zeitgeschehen, 2006).

15. Richard Meng, "Mit der Sensation rückt Müntefering zuletzt heraus: Neuwahl," *Frankurter Rundschau* online, December 28, 2005.

16. Mathias Jung, Andrea Wolf, op cit.: 6.

17. Ibid, 5.

18. TV news regarding Kirchhof showed two tendencies as the summer wore on: one, that it was more often mentioned, and that the mentions were increasingly negative. See Frank Brettschneider, „Bundestags Wahlkampf und Medienberichterstattung," *Aus Politik und Zeitgeschichte* (Beilage zur Wochenzeitung *Das Parlament*) B51–52 (December 19, 2005): 19–26, especially Table 5, 25.

19. Forschungsgruppe Wahlen, *Politbarometer,* "Umfrage zum TV-duell vom 04.09.2005," 2; Richard Meng, "Wahklkampf kommt nach Duell in Fahrt," *Frankfurter Rundschau* online, September 6, 2005.

20. Forschungsgruppe Wahlen, *Politbarometer,* September 1, 2005, KW 5.

21. Schröder described the Left Party as having a "rage to regulate" and relying on wishful thinking. Along with Müntefering, he accused Lafontaine and Gysi (although not by name) of having irresponsibly resigned from important positions. "Schröder und die Left Party," *Süddeutsche Zeitung* online, July 5, 2005.

22. A complete list of candidates for both the Länder and the electoral districts may be found in *Das Parlament* 55, no. 36 (September 5, 2005): 13–25.

23. For the often tortuous negotiations to form a joint electoral ticket see, among numerous accounts, "Der PDS-Bundesvorsitzende sieht eine historische Chance," (interview by Robert Roßmann), *Süddeutsche Zeitung* online, June 1, 2005, at http://sozialisten.de/sozialisten/pressespiegel/view_html?zid=27572&bs=1&n=0; "Left Party—aber nur mit PDS," *Neues Deutschland* online, June 24, 2005; "Die Left Party—Aufbruch für eine Politik für soziale Gerechtigkeit, Frieden und Demokratie in Deutschland," online at http://sozialisten.de/sozialisten/nachrichten/view_html?zid=27997&bs=1&n=0.

24. Mathias Jung and Andrea Wolf, "Der Wählerwille erzwingt die große Koalition," *Aus Politik und Zeitgeschichte* (Beilage zur Wochenzeitung *Das Parlament*) B51–52 (December 19, 2005): 3–12. One apparent effect of Merkel's candidacy was to even out the gender-specific attraction of the SPD and CDU/CSU. Female voters moved to the latter, while males moved to the former. See data in www.destatis.de/presse/deutsch/pk/2006/wahlstat_2005b.htm; link to Wahlbeteiligung nach Geschlecht und Altersgruppen seit 1983. Karl-Rudolf Korte makes the interesting point that, as a result of this trend, the grand coalition of 1966 was based on 86.9 percent of the two-party vote, whereas the coalition of 2005 only represents 69.4 percent. Karl-Rudolf Korte, "Was entschied die Bundestagswahl 2005?" *Aus Politik und Zeitgeschichte* (Beilage zur Wochenzeitung *Das Parlament*) B51–52 (December 19, 2005): 12–18.

25. Ludger Helms, "The German Federal Election, September 2005," *Electoral Studies* 26 (2007): 226, citing data published by the Forschungsgruppe Wahlen.

26. Mary Hampton, "Obstacles and Opportunities: The Changing Role of German Women in National Elections (Or Kinder, Kueche, Kirchen ... und Kanzleramt)." Unpublished manuscript on the 2005 election.

27. Matthias Dobrinski, "Die zittrige Hand des Wählers," *Süddeutsche Zeitung* online, September 19, 2005.

28. Ibid; Jeannette Godar, "Das Wahlvolk wird immer wankelmütiger" (Beilage zur Wochenzietung *Das Parliament*) 55, nos. 28–29 (November 11, 2005): 11.

29. Harald Schoen/Jürgen W. Falter, "Die Linkspartei und ihre Wähler," *Aus Politik und Zeitgeschichte* (Beilage zur Wochenzietung *Das Parliament*) B51–52 (December 19, 2005): 33–40. Thanks to Lafontaine's prominence, the Left Party received an astounding 18.5 percent of the vote in the Saarland, an increase of 17.1 percent over 2002.

30. FGW, *Politbarometer* September 3, 2005, KW 38.

31. "Rot-Schwarz, Schwarz-Rot, Jamaika oder Ampel," *Süddeutsche Zeitung* online, September 19, 2005.

32. "Kanzlerstreit soll am Sonntag enden," *Frankfurter Rundschau* online, October 6, 2005, citing recent polls.

33. Dürr (ibid., 34–38) refers to two political camps of "inertia and movement" (*Beharrung und Bewegung*), and Charles Maier speaks of "territorialists and globalists" (Charles S. Maier, "Territorialisten und Globalisten. Die beiden neuen 'Parteien' in den heutigen Demokratien," *Transit—Europäische Revue* 14 (1997). Salved points to the ability of parties to shape their systemic environment to aid their survival in the wake of unification, but leaves open the question of their response to newer challenges. See also Bernhard Wessels, "The German Party System: Developments after Unification," in Werner Reutter, ed., *Germany on the Road to "Normalcy": Policies and Politics of the Red-Green Federal Government, 1988–2002* (New York: Palgrave Macmillan, 2004), 7.

34. The equivalent Swedish party calls itself *Vänstern* (the Left). Like the German Left Party, the Swedish Left is a democratic party that evolved out of an earlier communist party (albeit several decades sooner than its German equivalent). The Swedish Left has never joined a formal coalition with the far larger Social Democratic Party but has generally supported its policies in parliament and government. See M. Donald Hancock, "Sweden," in Hancock et al., *Politics in Europe,* 4th ed. (Washington D.C., CQ Press, 2007), 393–449. Also see Eric S. Einhorn and John Logue, *Modern Welfare States: Scandinavian Politics and Policy in the Global Age,* 2nd ed. (Westport, Conn.: Praeger, 2003).

35. Moreover, fringe parties have had surprising, albeit often transitory, successes at the state level, as in Hamburg, Brandenburg, Saxony-Anhalt, and Saxony.

36. See the analyses of Franz Walter, "Die neue alte Linke," *Der Spiegel* online, May 14, 2007, at www.spiegel.de/politik/deutschland/0,15 18,482717.00.html, and "Die Schwache der Großen," *Frankfurter Rundschau* online, May 14, 2007.

37. Prominent among them is Klaus Wowereit, the lord mayor of Berlin and since 2001 the head of an SPD-PDS coalition government.

38. Tobias Dürr, "Bewegung und Beharrung: Deutschlands künftiges Parteiensystem," *Aus Politik und Zeitgeschichte* (Beilage zur Wochenzeitung *Das Parlament*) 32–33 (August 8, 2005): 31–38.

Chapter 8 Notes

1. By emphasizing *organized* groups, we avoid the vagueness that plagued earlier generations of group theorists who mused about the existence of "potential" or "latent" interest groups. See, for example, David Truman, *The Governmental Process: Political Interests and Public Opinion* (New York: Alfred A. Knopf, 1962). Also see Mancur Olson, *The Logic of Collective Action: Public Goods and the Theory of Groups* (Cambridge: Harvard University Press, 1965). More recent studies of interest groups include G. David Garson, *Group Theories of Politics* 61, Sage Library of Social Research (Beverly Hills, Calif.: Sage Publications, 1978); Gene M. Grossman and Elhanan Helpman, *Special Interest Politics* (Cambridge: MIT Press, 2001); and Amy Gutmann, *Identity in Democracy,* especially ch. 2, "The Value of Voluntary Groups" (Princeton and Oxford: Princeton University Press, 2003).

2. If an interest group does seek public office, it in effect becomes a political party. An example is the short-lived Refugee Party in western Germany noted in the preceding chapter.

3. For a contemporary assessment of British interest groups, see Bruce F. Norton, "Pressure Groups," ch. 6 in *Politics in Britain* (Washington, D.C.: CQ Press, 2007). Noteworthy studies of interest groups in U.S. politics include E. E. Schattschneider, *The Semisovereign People: A Realist's View of Democracy* (Fort Worth, Texas: Harcourt Brace Jovanoich College Publishers, 1960, 1975) and Kevin M. Esterling, *The Political Economy of Expertise: Information and Efficiency in American National Politics* (Ann Arbor: University of Michigan Press, 2004).

4. Stein Rokkan, "Norway: Numerical Democracy and Corporate Pluralism," in Robert A. Dahl, ed., *Political Oppositions in Western Democracies* (New Haven, Conn.: Yale University Press, 1966), 107.

5. Philippe Schmitter and Gerhard Lehmbruch, eds., *Trends toward Corporatist Intermediation* (Beverly Hills, Calif.: Sage Publications, 1979) and Gerhard Lehmbruch and Philippe Schmitter, eds., *Patterns of Corporatist Policy-Making* (Beverly Hills, Calif.: Sage Publications, 1982).

6. M. Donald Hancock, *West Germany: The Politics of Democratic Corporatism* (Chatham, N.J.: Chatham House, 1989). In a later study, Hancock and his collaborators contrasted democratic corporatism with pluralism and étatism as alternative forms of government-group interactions in Hancock, John Logue, and Bernd Schiller, eds., *Managing Modern Capitalism: Industrial Renewal and Workplace Democracy in the United States and Western Europe* (Westport, Conn.: Greenwood-Praeger, 1992).

7. By "descriptive census," Almond meant an inventory of interest groups, their membership, resources, and activities. See Gabriel Almond, "A Comparative Study of Interest Groups and the Political Process," *American Political Science Review* 52 (March 1958): 270–282. Reprinted in Harry Eckstein and David E. Apter, eds., *Comparative Politics: A Reader* (New York: Free Press of Glencoe, 1963), 397–408.

8. Martin Sebaldt, "Interest Groups: Continuity and Change of German Lobbyism since 1974," in Ludger Helms, ed., *Institutions and Institutional Change in the Federal Republic of Germany* (New York: St. Martin's Press, 2000), 188–204. Article 9, section 1, of the Basic Law guarantees "all Germans" the right to form societies and organizations (*Vereine und Gesellschaften*) and Article 9, section 3, explicitly exempts labor struggles from the purview of emergency legislation.

9. Sebaldt, op cit., 195–196. Sebaldt shows that the major activity of these lobbyists is to work with government ministries on the details of regulations designed to flesh out the general clauses in legislation. In 2007, thirteen of some 1,900 lobbyists represent human rights causes.

10. In March 1920 the unions staged a general strike that defeated an attempted right-wing coup (the *Kapp Putsch*). During the Weimar era the unions were active participants in the creation and administration of elective "works councils" established on the enterprise level.

11. They are the German Union of Salaried Employees (*Deutsche Angestelltengewerkschaft*) and the Federal Association of Free Professions (*Bundesverband der freien Berufe*), respectively.

12. Chronik-Gollsar, "Freier Deutscher Gewerkscaftsbund (FDGB)," www.chronikderwende.de.

13. For a broader view of the dynamics of worker-leadership relations in the GDR see Jeffrey Kopstein, *The Politics of Economic Decline in*

East Germany: 1945–1989 (Chapel Hill: University of North Carolina Press, 1997), especially ch. 6.

14. DGB, "Die Aufgaben von DGB und Gewerkschaften," www.dgb.de/dgb/aufgaben/aufgaben.htm.

15. DGB, "Grundsatzprogramm," www.dgb.de/dbg/grundsatzprog/anforderungen.

16. The 1976 bill achieved "near" rather than complete parity codetermination because board chairs (whose appointment must be approved by shareholders) are allowed a double vote in the event of a tie between worker and shareholder representatives on the board.

17. The DGB reported that in 2007 such agreements were in force in 250 branches of industry. DGB, "So funktioniert das Tarifsystem," www.dgb.de/dgb/Tarifsystem.html.

18. The earlier British measure was initiated by a Conservative government in an effort to deal with a persisting "English sickness" characterized by sluggish economic growth and labor unrest. The bill established a National Economic and Development Council comprised of representatives of the government, employer associations, and trade unions.

19. The classic depiction of how industry and labor jointly came to dominate industrial policy is in Peter J. Katzenstein, *Policy and Politics in West Germany: The Growth of a Semi-Sovereign State* (Philadelphia: Temple University Press, 1987). This perspective was applied by M. Donald Hancock in *West Germany: The Politics of Democratic Corporatism* (Chatham N.J.: Chatham House, 1989).

20. Wolfgang Streeck, "Die Gewerkschaften im Bündnis für Arbeit," in Jörg and Hans-Joachim Sperling, eds., *Umbrüche und Kontinuitäten: Perspektiven nationaler und internationaler Arbeitsbeziehungen* (Munich: Rainer Hampp Verlag, 2001), 271.

21. Klaudia Prevezanos, "Stepping Forward: German Trade Unions Prepare for the Future," AICGS *Issues* Report (2001). According to Prevezanos, only eight of fifty companies listed by the German equivalent of NASDQ had such committees. See also Lothar Funk, "Der neue Strukturwandel: Herausforderung und Chance für die Gewerkschaften," op cit. (note 3), 14–22.

22. By 2007 *Ver.di,* with nearly three million members, claimed to be the largest union in the world.

23. Wolfgang Schroeder, "Der neue Arbeitsmarkt und der Wandel der Gewerkschaften," *Aus Politik und Zeitgeschichte* (Beilage zur Wochenzeitung *Das Parlament*) B47–48 (November 17, 2003): 6–13.

24. Wolfgang Streeck, "Industrial Relations: From State Weakness as Strength to State Weakness as Weakness. Welfare Corporatism and the Private Use of Public Interest," in Simon Green and William E.

Patterson, ed., *Governance in Contemporary Germany: The Semi-Sovereign State Revisited* (Cambridge: Cambridge University Press, 2005), 138–164. Streeck (158–162) makes clear the interplay between political and economic events and the political weakening of the trade unions.

25. Compare the hostile reaction accorded both Chancellor Merkel (CDU) and then Vice Chancellor Franz Müntefering (SPD) with the applause for Left Party cochair Oskar Lafontaine at the DGB's 2006 National Congress. "DGB geht auf Konfrontationskurs zur großen Koalition," *Frankfurter Rundschau* online, May 26, 2006.

26. Bundesvereinigung der Deutschen Arbeitgeberverbände, "Name, Sitz, Geschäftsjahr und Zweck," www.bda-online.de/www/bdaoline.nsf/id.

27. Bundesvereinigung der Deutschen Arbeitgeberverbände, "Arbeitsmarkt," ibid.

28. BDI, "Unser Mandat," www.bdi-online.de/de/bdi/72.htm.

29. www.bauernverband.de/index.php?redid=152876.

30. An additional twenty-eight partner organizations from nonmember states, including Iceland, Norway, Switzerland, and Turkey, also belong to COPA.

31. See "Scientology wird bundesweit observiert," *Süddeutsche Zeitung,* June 7, 1997; "Germany to Put Scientology under Surveillance," *New York Times,* June 7, 1997. The recent efforts of Scientology member Tom Cruise to film in Berlin about the 20th of July plot against Hitler, with Cruise himself playing the role of Stauffenberg, has reignited hard feelings. See "Plot Thickens in a Tom Cruise Film, Long before the Cameras Begin to Roll," *New York Times* online, June 30, 2007.

32. For the founding in 2007 of the Coordination Council of Muslims in Germany (KRM), see the interview with its German-born (and Muslim convert) chair, Ayyub Axel Köhler, "Wir vertreten einen Mainstream-Islam," *Die Zeit* online, no. 17 (April 19, 2007). Köhler is also a prominent leader of the older Islamic Council of Germany. For an example of official German pressure to have an Islamic negotiating partner, see the urging of the interior minister, Wolfgang Schäuble, "Wer spricht für die Muslime?" *Frankfurter Rundschau* online, May 2, 2007.

33. For listings of the wide variety of Turkish organizations, both Muslim and secular, with some tied to authorities in Turkey and others not, see Frank Jessen, "Türkische religiöse und politische Organisationen in Deutschland III," *Zukunftsforum Politik Broschürenreihe,* no. 72, Sankt Augustin: Konrad-Adenauer-Stiftung e.V. March 2006, and Canan Atilgan, "Türkische politische Organisationen in der Bundesrepublik Deutschland," Sankt Augustin:

Konrad-Adenauer-Stiftung e.V., n.d. [Materialien für die Arbeit vor Ort Nr. 9].

34. "Freedom of the press … shall be guaranteed. There shall be no censorship." For this text, see the Basic Law online at www.bpb.de.

35. Although the decision was reached on a very narrow legal basis, it was justified in part by the need to safeguard the public broadcasters' freedom. See "21 Cent zu wenig," *Frankfurter Rundschau* online, September 24, 2007.

36. Germans can also read a number of important monthly and weekly journals, including the weekly *Die Zeit,* founded under British license in 1946; the lively new monthly *Cicero;* and other "serious" journals. Additionally, there are two major newsweeklies, *Der Spiegel* (also an early British-zone licensee) and *Focus.* The courts' rebuff of the 1962 attempt, under Adenauer and his then defense minister, Franz-Josef Strauss, to pressure the *Spiegel* away from covering a scandal within the government led to a landmark case and a decision that firmly underlined the importance and special status of press freedom.

37. Achim Baum, "Pressefreiheit durch Selbstkontrolle," *Aus Politik und Zeitgeschichte* (Beilage zur Wochenzeitung *Das Parlament*) no. 38 (September 18, 2006): 6–10.

38. Johanna Metz, "Journalisten im Visier des Staates" (Beilage zur Wochenzietung *Das Parliament*) 56, no. 4 (January 23, 2006): 3, and "Ein offensichtlicher Versuch der Einschüchterung," ibid (interview with Michael Konken, head of the Union of German Journalists).

39. ZDF, based in Mainz, has a governing board that includes some *Bundestag* members; three representatives of the government; and various business, religious, cultural and other organizations, in addition to representatives of the states.

40. Barbara Sichtermann, "Television in Germany," Goethe-Institute, USA-Knowledge-The Press/Radio/TV, at www.goethe.de/ins/us/lp/wis/pre/en14668.htm.

41. Ralf Hohlfeld, "Bundestagswahlkampf 2005 in den Nachrichtensendungen," *Aus Politik und Zeitgeschichte* (Beilage zur Wochenzeitung *Das Parlament*) no. 38 (September 18, 2006): 11–17.

42. Kai Hafez/Carola Richter, "Das Islambild von ARD und ZDF," *Aus Politik und Zeitgeschichte* (Beilage zur Wochenzeitung *Das Parlament*) nos. 26–27 (June 25, 2007): 40–46. Details on the research underlying this article can be found at www.kommunikation swissenschaft-erfurt.de; a press summary is at "ARD- und ZDF- Programm 'stärkt Islam-Angst'," *Frankfurter Rundschau* online, February 3, 2007.

43. Of the leaders and participants in the student and youth revolts of the decade roughly from the mid-1960s to the mid-1970s, one, Rudi

Dutschke, who was shot by a neo-Nazi in 1968 (he remained politically active after a partial recovery and died in 1979), has had a street named after him in Berlin; one of those he influenced to join Green politics, Joschka Fischer, became German foreign minister from 1998 to 2005. For an account of these "alternative" aspects of postwar German politics, focusing on the career of Joschka Fischer, see Paul Hockenos, *Joschka Fischer and the Making of the Berlin Republic* (Oxford: Oxford University Press, 2008).

44. For an excellent account that places these movements and events in both historical and comparative perspective, see Tony Judt, *Postwar: A History of Europe since 1945* (New York: Penguin Books, 2005), op cit., ch. 12 "The Spectre of Revolution."

45. The voluminous writings on GDR dissent and its social manifestation include John C. Torpey, *Intellectuals, Socialism and Dissent: The East German Opposition and Its Legacy* (Minneapolis: University of Minnesota Press, 1995); Christiane Olivo, *Creating a Democratic Civil Society in Eastern Germany* (New York: Palgrave, 2001); Mary Fulbrook, *Anatomy of a Dictatorship: Inside the GDR 1949–1989* (Oxford: Oxford University Press, 1995); and Henry Krisch, *The German Democratic Republic: The Search for Identity* (Boulder, Colo.: Westview Press, 1985).

46. Even the happy experience of hosting the 2006 World Cup soccer championships was marred by a warning issued by Schröder's former press spokesperson that advised foreign guests to avoid certain small towns in Brandenburg. (Indeed, an Afro-German group issued a list of "no-go" areas.) See "Lebensgefahr für Schwarze WM-Gäste in Brandenburg?" *Frankfurter Rundschau* online, May 17, 2006.

47. "Wie Neonazis den Sport unterwandern," *Frankfurter Rundschau* online, February 12, 2008, and "öfters Pöbeleien beim Fußball," ibid, October 13, 2006. For a detailed analysis of the travails of one eastern German soccer club, see "Kehrseite des Sommermärchens" (Beilage zur Wochenzietung *Das Parliament*) 53, no. 13 (March 26, 2007): 3. As part of its anti-American, anti-globalization rhetoric, the NPD organized a rally to greet the Iranian team at the World Cup.

48. For a chronicle of violence against foreigners in eastern Germany between June 2000 and August 2007, see "Ausländerfeindliche Gewalt in Ostdeutschland," *Süddeutsche Zeitung* online, August 21, 2007. Some trials do end in severe sentences, including the maximum penalty of life in prison, for violent acts. See Roger Cohen, "Neo-Nazi Youths Sentenced in Beating of Immigrant," *New York Times* online, August 31, 2000. A telling sign of the constant, if low grade, virulence of these phenomena is the recurrent alarm in journals and

newspapers. Two examples of the range in time and detail of these are Markus Wehner, "Der Jugendklub als 'national befreite Zone,'" *Frankfurter Allgemeine Zeitung,* September 26, 1998, 9; and Achim Zons, "Angekommen am Anfang," *Süddeutsche Zeitung,* August 23, 2007, 2.

49. Klaus Hartung, "Der neue Deutsche Weg," *Die Zeit,* no. 42 (October 9, 2003).

50. Some examples are Alan Cowell, "Neo-Nazis Carving Out Fiefs in Eastern Germany," *New York Times* online, February 8, 1998; "Far-Right Surge Alarms Mainstream Germany," ibid, September 19, 2004, and Richard Bernstein, "Germany's Far Right Tries to Put on a Normal Face," ibid, March 14, 2006.

51. A striking example of this is the semi-official political weekly *Das Parlament* and its scholarly essay insert *Aus Politik und Zeitgeschichte.* Entire issues of the former were devoted to the subject of right-wing extremism in September 2000 and again in November 2005; the latter had theme issues on this topic in September 2000, October 2000, November 2001, and September 2007. In reviewing these materials, it is to be noted that neither the diagnoses nor the prescriptions change much from issue to issue or from year to year.

52. One of us (Krisch) observed a post-performance theater discussion in East Berlin in 1988 during which audience members declared that of course there were skinheads in the GDR, and not just silly imitators of Western trends. Secret studies of these trends, including opinion surveys among youth, subsequently were commissioned by high party leaders.

53. For a survey of this subject, see the special issue of *Das Parlament* 55, no. 45 (November 7, 2005) on right-wing extremism in Europe. For Eastern Europe, see Michael Minkernberg, "Nationalistische Rhetorik ist kein Randphänomen," ibid, 8; and Dieter Segert, "Die Gefahr des Allparteienpopulismus," ibid. An earlier study was Hans-George Betz, "The New Politics of Resentment: Radical Right Wing Populist Parties in Western Europe," *Comparative Politics* 25, no. 4 (1993): 413–427.

54. Walter Friedrich, "Ist der Rechtsextremismus im Ostern ein Produkt der autoritären DDR?" *Aus Politik und Zeitgeschichte* (Beilage zur Wochenzeitung *Das Parlament*) B46 (November 9, 2001): 16–23. Official figures for 2006 showed that the four states with the highest number of violent crimes with a right extreme background were eastern states (counting Berlin).

55. Bernhard Honigfort, "Frau=schlau=weg," *Frankfurter Rundschau* online, May 31, 2007.

56. This is not to say that other European countries have not also had right-wing violence. EU statistics show that Germany trails six EU countries in percentage increase in right-wing violence between 2000

and 2006. During this period, the number of racist attacks in Germany increased 5.3 percent compared to increases of 70.9 percent in Denmark, 45.1 percent in Slovakia, 27.3 percent in Scotland, 27.1 percent in France, 21.2 percent in Ireland, and 8.4 percent in Finland. Smaller percentage increases were reported in England and Wales (4.2 percent) and Poland (2.3 percent), while the number of racist attacks declined by 4.4 percent in the Czech Republic, 2.3 percent in Sweden, and .2 percent in Austria. Statistics from "Assessing Trends in Officially Recorded Racist Violence and Crime, 2007," in *European Union: Racist Violence: Essential Information,*" published by EUMC (European Monitoring Centre on Racism and Xenophobia) and available online at www.fra.europa.eu/factsheets.

57. NPD data and other details of the party from www.bmi.bund.de/verfassungsbericht/2005_en.pdf.

58. In Saxony and Mecklenburg–Western Pomerania, the NPD obtained 14.4 and 16.3 percent, respectively. Felix Lee, "Bis zu 16 Prozent in den Hochburgen im Osten" (Beilage zur Wochenzietung *Das Parliament*) 55, no. 45 (November 7, 2005): 6.

59. There is a coordinating body of women's organizations that does lobbying and educational work. The very breadth of its membership, however, precludes focused campaigns; on the other hand, it does encompass, for example, both Christian and Muslim women's organizations. For the Council of German Women (*Deutscher Frauenrat*), see its Web site at www.frauenrat.de.

60. The iconic postwar woman—analogous in some ways to America's "Rosie the Riveter"—was the "rubble woman" (*Trümmerfrau*) whose heavy labor cleared the streets of bombed German cities.

61. Birgit Meyer, "Much Ado about Nothing? Political Representation Policies and the Influence of Women Parliamentarians in Germany," *Review of Policy Research* 20, no. 3 (2003): 401–422.

62. We will not consider the situation of women in the GDR here. For a combination of necessity (for labor) and ideology, East German women were a major portion of the labor force. Their political representation, however, was extremely limited; for example, there were never any women who were full members of the SED Politburo. One notable exception was Margot Honecker, wife of former head of state Erich Honecker, who served as the GDR's education minister from 1963 until 1989. An unrepentant Communist, Margot chose political exile in Chile in 1992 rather than face German charges of crimes against humanity. In economic administrations as well, women were usually found in lower levels of management and in "feminine" lines of work such as the textile industry. For a comparison of the East and West situations, as well as a pre-and postunification perspective, see Eva Kolinsky, "Women and Politics in

Western Germany," in Marilyn Rueschemeyer, ed., *Women in the Politics of Postcommunist Eastern Europe* (Armonk, N.Y.: M.E. Sharpe, 1994), 63–86; and Marilyn Rueschemeyer, "Women in the Politics of Eastern Germany," ibid, 87–116.

63. "Eile bei Gleichstellungsgesetz," *Frankfurter Rundschau* online, May 11, 2006; "Ende einer 'heilen Männerwelt'," ibid, January 3, 2001.

64. "Frauen verdienen ein Viertel weniger," ibid, March 8, 2007. On the question of how effective women have been in the legislatures, see Birgit Meyer, op cit., 410–417.

65. A comparative study of the effects of electoral systems on gender representation is Richard Vengroff, Lucy Creevey, and Henry Krisch, "Electoral System Effects on Gender Representation: The Case of Mixed Systems," *Japanese Journal of Political Science* 1, no. 2 (2000): 197–227, especially regarding Germany at 209–210, 214–215.

66. Joanna McKay, "Woman MPs and the Socio-Environmental Preconditions for Political Participation in the Federal Republic," *German Politics* 16, no. 3 (September 2007): 379–390, and more informally, Tissy Bruns, "Ende der Schattenspiele" (Beilage zur Wochenzietung *Das Parliament*) 57, no. 7 (February 12, 2007): 4.

67. Rokkan, "Norway: Numerical Democracy and Corporate Pluralism," op cit.

Chapter 9 Notes

1. European Trade Union Confederation, "What is the 'European Social Model' or 'Social Europe'?" www.etuc.org/a/111. The ETUC critically contrasts this concept with the American model, "where small numbers of individuals have benefited at the expense of the majority." Ibid.

2. Leading examples of an institutionalized European Social Market include Germany, Scandinavia, and Slovenia, with the latter exemplifying a well-developed system of decentralized worker ownership of firms.

3. *Business Europe*, "About Us: Mission and Priorities," www.businesseurope.eu/ (November 2007).

4. Ibid.

5. M. Donald Hancock, *West Germany: The Politics of Democratic Corporatism* (New York: Chatham House, 1989). See also Peter J. Katzenstein, *Policy and Politics in West Germany: The Growth of a Semisovereign State* (Philadelphia: Temple University Press, 1987); and Katzenstein, ed., *Industry and Politics in West Germany: Toward the Third Republic* (New York: Cornell University Press, 1989).

6. See Andrew Schonfeld, *Modern Capitalism: The Changing Balance of Public and Private Capital* (New York: Oxford University Press, 1965), and M. Donald Hancock, John Logue, and Bernt Schiller, eds., *Managing Modern Capitalism: Industrial Renewal and Workplace Democracy in the United States and Western Europe* (New York: Greenwood Press, 1991).

7. Peter Wahl, "The End of 'Rhineland Capitalism': Germany at the Crossroads," *Red Pepper Magazine,* www.redpepper.org.uk.

8. See the discussion of codetermination in chapter 8.

9. Michel Albert, *Capitalisme contre capitalisme* (Paris: Editions du Seuil, 1991). Published in English as *Capitalism vs. Capitalism: How America's Obsession with Individual Achievement and Short-Term Profit Has Led It to the Brink of Collapse* (New York: Thunder's Mouth Press, 1993). Cited in Chris Caldwell, "Europe's 'Social Market': Two, three, many capitalisms," *Hoover Policy Review* (October and November 2001).

10. Robert Cooper develops the concept of a "post-modern world," which he contrasts with "pre-modern" and "modern" states in *The Breaking of Nations: Order and Chaos in the Twenty-First Century* (London: Atlantic Books, 2003). We return to Germany's place in a postmodern system of European nations in chapter 11.

11. Peter Flora and Arnold J. Heidenheimer, eds., *The Development of Welfare States in Europe and America* (New Brunswick, N.J: Transaction Books, 1981), 18.

12. W. M. Mommsen, ed., *The Emergence of the Welfare State in Britain and Germany 1850–1950* (London: Croom Helm on behalf of the German Historical Institute, 1981), 71.

13. Timothy A. Tilton, "Perspectives on the Welfare State," in Norman Furniss, ed., *Futures for the Welfare State* (Bloomington: Indiana University Press, 1986), 14. In an earlier coauthored study, Furniss and Tilton provided a useful typology of the "British social security state," the Swedish "social welfare state," and the American "positive state." Regrettably, they did not include Germany in their analysis. See Norman Furniss and Timothy Tilton, *The Case for the Welfare State: From Social Security to Social Equality* (Bloomington: Indiana University Press, 1977).

14. Tilton, op cit., 15.

15. A. Briggs, "The Welfare State in Historical Perspective," *European Journal of Sociology* 2 (1961): 221–258. Quoted in Mel Cousins, *European Welfare States: Comparative Perspectives* (Beverly Hills, Calif.: Sage Publications, 2005), 6.

16. See "Modernization, Democratization, and the Development of Welfare States in Western Europe," in Flora and Heidenheimer, op cit.

17. Current Affairs, "German Welfare State at a Turning Point," Deutsche Welle, August 15, 2004, www.de-world.de/English/0,3367, 1430_A,00.html.

18. See Eva Kolinsky, *Women in Contemporary Germany: Life, Work, and Politics,* 2nd revised ed. (Providence, R.I.: Berg, 1993). Kolinsky notes that a larger percentage of East German women than men became unemployed following reunification, and retired women experienced greater poverty (280–285). She concludes: "[S]ociety after unification has brought more problems than opportunities: material hardship and social uncertainties in place of the system of state provisions and life-style allocations in the past." Such hardships may be generation-specific, however. Kolinsky observes further that "Younger women seem poised to play a full part in rebuilding the working environment, gaining new skills and receiving fairer rewards than the GDR was willing to extend" (286).

19. David Conradt, "How Is Power Used?" in his section on "Germany" in M. Donald Hancock et al., *Politics in Europe,* 4th ed. (Washington, D.C.: CQ Press, 2007), 253. Conradt cites Peter J. Katzenstein, *Policy and Politics in West Germany* (Philadelphia: Temple University Press, 1987).

20. Patricia Dismore, "Country Case Studies and Links. Germany," www.pitt.edu/~heinisch/ca_germ.html.

21. See, for example, Gerhard Bäcker, Walter Hanesch, and Peter Krause, eds., *Combating Poverty in Europe and Germany* (Hampshire, UK: Ashgate Publishing, 2003).

22. Paul Spicker, *The Welfare State: A General Theory* (Beverly Hills, Calif.: Sage Publications, 2000), 145.

23. Cathy Schoen et al., Web Exclusive, "Toward Higher-Performance Health Systems: Adults' Health Care Experiences in Seven Countries, 2007," *Health Affairs* 26, no. 6 (2007): w717–w734. "2007 by Project HOPE," http://content.healthaffairs.org/Most_Read_ 1.php.

24. According to Ministry of Family statistics, 30 percent of working women are childless. Germany's average birth rate of 1.37 children per woman compares with 1.9 percent in France, 1.81 in Norway, and 1.75 in Sweden. This decline has prompted efforts by the federal government to encourage women to have more children through a variety of financial and workplace incentives.

25. Current Affairs, "German Welfare State at a Turning Point," op cit.

26. Rüstow returned to Germany in 1949 and was named a professor of economic and social science at the University of Heidelberg. He later served as the first chair of the German Association of Political Science.

27. Michael Rösch, "The German Social Market Economy and its Transformations." Rösch notes: "Another aim of the Social Market

Economy was to create and develop an economic order which could be accepted by any ideology so that all forces in society could be focused on the common task of assuring the basic living condition and then the rebuilding of the economy," http://tiss.zdv.uni-tuebingen.de/webroot/sp/spsba01_W98_1/germany1b.htm.

28. Concerted action was modeled on a National Economic Development Council (NEDC) introduced by the Conservative government in Britain in 1962. Made up of representatives of the government, private business, and trade unions, NEDC was designed to coordinate measures to combat Britain's then-prevailing "economic disease." See Bruce F. Norton, *Politics in Britain* (Washington, D.C.: CQ Press, 2007), 133–134.

29. Hancock provides a detailed account of "The Rise and Fall of Concerted Action" in his *West Germany: The Politics of Democratic Corporatism* (Chatham, N.J.: Chatham House Publishers, 1989), 135–138.

30. *Statistiches Jahrbuch für die Bundesrepublik 2007* (Wiesbaden: Statistisches Bundesamt, 2007), 523.

31. The freeze on pension benefits was coupled with a requirement for retired persons to pay for their own nursing insurance. The legislation was bitterly denounced by trade unions and left-wing Social Democrats and opposed by the Christian Democratic faction in parliament, at the time still in opposition, on the grounds that it "was not the right solution." Current Affairs, "German Parliament Freezes Pensions," *Deutsche Welle,* November 6, 2003, www.de/de/article/0,2144,1023585,00.html. The 2003 legislation was preceded by cost-cutting reforms enacted in 2001. See Winfried Schmähl, "Paradigm Shift in German Pension Policy: Measures Aiming at a New Public-Private Mix and Their Effects," in Martin Rein and Winfried Schmähl, eds., *Rethinking the Welfare State: The Political Economy of Pension Reform* (Cheltenham, U.K: Edward Elgar, 2003).

32. OECD, *Economic Outlook* 81 (June 2006), 256.

33. *Statistisches Jahrbuch für die Bundesrepublik Deutschland 2005* (Wiesbaden: Statistisches Bundesamt, 2005), 48.

34. "Germany recognizes its face is changing," *International Herald Tribune,* May 6, 2006.

35. As of January 1, 2008, fifteen members of the EU had joined EMU and adopted the euro. They include Germany; France; the three Benelux countries of Belgium, the Netherlands, and Luxemburg; Austria; Italy; Spain; Portugal; Greece; Finland; Ireland; Slovenia; Malta; and southern Cyprus.

36. A blatant exception to the competitive regional market for goods and services (including investments) is the EU's Common Agricultural Policy, which relies heavily on subsidies to farmers.

37. A comprehensive summary and preliminary evaluation of the Lisbon Strategy can be found in Commission of the European Communities, *Communication from the Commission to the Spring European Council: Implementing the Renewed Lisbon Strategy for Growth and Jobs* (Brussels: Commission of the European Communities, December 2006).

38. Events often belie generalizations. An example is a spate of strikes instigated by the railroad union in late 2007 to press for higher wages.

39. See Denis Bouget, "Convergence in the Social Welfare Systems in Europe: From Goal to Reality," in Peter Tayor-Goodby, ed., *Making a European Welfare State? Convergences and Conflicts over European Social Policy* (Malden, Mass.: Blackwell Publishing, 2004).

Chapter 10 Notes

1. General overviews include Helga Haftendorn, *Coming of Age: German Foreign Policy since 1945* (Lanham, Md.: Rowman and Littlefield, 2006); Timothy Garton Ash, *In Europe's Name: Germany and the Divided Continent* (New York: Random House, 1993); Thomas Banchoff, *The German Problem Transformed: Institutions, Politics and Foreign Policy, 1945–1995* (Ann Arbor: University of Michigan Press, 1999); David F. Patton, *Cold War Politics in Postwar Germany* (New York: St. Martin's Press, 1999).

2. *Politbarometer* reports issues by the Forschungsgruppe Wahlen.

3. Gunther Heilmann, "Agenda 2020: Krise und Perspektive deutscher Außenpolitik," *Internationale Politik,* no. 9 (2003): 39–50. Germany currently spends 1.4 percent of GDP on defense, less than either Great Britain or France and below the NATO's target of two percent. Stephen Szabo, "The German Defense White Paper," *AICGS Advisor,* December 7, 2006. Germans continued to oppose greater defense spending, even when they approved of a more active German role in world affairs. See the compendium of survey data in Gunther Hellmann und Sebastian Enskat, "Umfragedaten zu deutscher Aussenpolitik und Deutschlands Rolle in der Welt seit 1990," *Eine Dokumentation Stand,* January 25, 2004, in 2004_Umfragen.pdf at www.das-parlament.de/2004/11/Beilage/oo5.html.

4. www.cia.go/library/publications/the-world-factbook/fields/2034.html.

5. Haftendorn, op cit., 1–2.

6. Inasmuch as contemporary German foreign policy continues that of the (West) German Federal Republic, we will not consider GDR foreign policy in any detail here. As indicated in chapter 3, the two Germanys had similar goals regarding national unification until at least 1961, if not 1970. Thereafter, the GDR leadership stressed the exis-

tence of two German states and generally spoke of national unity as a distant goal. Especially in the 1980s, the GDR tied itself closely to many aspects of the German national heritage. At no time did the GDR achieve as much autonomy from Soviet leadership as West German leaders had attained quite early on. A good point of comparison here is the freedom of the Brandt government to pursue *Ostpolitik,* with visits to Moscow, Warsaw, and Erfurt in the GDR, while as late as 1984, the Soviet leaders blocked Honecker from visiting West Germany. Useful works on GDR foreign policy include A. James McAdams, *Germany Divided: From the Wall to Reunification* (Princeton, N.J.: Princeton University Press, 1993), Patton op cit., note 1, and Eberhard Schulz et al., *GDR Foreign Policy* (White Plains, N.Y.: M. E. Sharpe, 1982). An insightful view of the Soviet-GDR dynamic at a time of particular crisis is Hope M. Harrison, *Driving the Soviets Up the Wall: Soviet-East German Relations, 1953–1961* (Princeton, N.J.: Princeton University Press, 2003).

7. A thorough account, both an insider's tale and historical analysis, is Philip Zelikow and Condoleezza Rice, *Germany Unified and Europe Transformed: A Study in Statecraft* (Cambridge: Harvard University Press 1997). For an account in German by Kohl's chief adviser, see Horst Teltschik, *329 Tage: Innenansichten der Einigung* (Berlin: Siedler, 1991).

8. For a recent historical overview of these developments, focused on Germany but including a broader European framework, see James Sheehan, *Where Have All the Soldiers Gone? The Transformation of Modern Europe* (Boston: Houghton Mifflin, 2008), especially ch. 8, "The Rise of the Civilian State."

9. As James Sperling (among others) has pointed out, "Germany's 'European' and 'democratic' commitments were both a normative stance as well as a tactical advantage in Germany's effort to rejoin the world order as a 'normal' state." James Sperling, "The Foreign Policy of the Berlin Republic: The Very Model of a Post-Modern Major Power? A Review Essay," *German Politics* 12, no. 3 (December 2003): 1–34.

10. An observer of Schröder-Fischer foreign policy has noted that to secure SPD and Green approval for important qualitative changes in German policy toward military action, such steps had to be sold as a humanitarian rather than as a *Realpolitik* measure; Fischer defended intervention in Kosovo in 1999 by declaring that "never again Auschwitz" nowadays must mean "beware of the origins" (of crimes against humanity). Gregor Schöllgen, "Deutsche Außenpolitik in der Ära Schröder," *Aus Politik und Zeitgeschichte* (Beilage zur Wochenzeitung *Das Parlament*) 20, nos. 32–33 (August 8, 2005): 3.

11. August Pradetto has pointed out that foreign policy was not a central issue for the Schröder government when it came into office in 1998. However, circumstances forced it to modify its expectations. This applies especially to the commitment of German forces in Afghanistan, Kosovo, and particularly after 9/11, in war on terrorism areas. See August Pradetto, "From 'Tamed' to 'Normal' Power: A New Paradigm in German Foreign and Security Policy?" in Werner Reutter, ed., *Germany on the Road to "Normalcy": Policies and Politics of the Red-Green Federal Government 1988–2002* (New York: Palgrave Macmillan, 2004), 209–234. Pradetto notes that while Germany remained committed to multilateralism and a strongly institutional orientation (UN, NATO, OSCE, EU, etc), it was able to work through these institutions for new national goals.

12. See, for example, Schröder's op-ed piece in fall 2003 (Gerhard Schröder, "Germany Will Share the Burden in Iraq," *New York Times,* September 19, 2003) and most commentaries on Merkel's policies, as for example, Richard Bernstein, "New German Leader, Same Ties to U.S.," *New York Times,* October 14, 2005.

13. The strategic rationale for this policy was clearly enunciated in the government's *White Paper 2006 on German Security Policy and the Future of the Bundeswehr;* an English-language version can be found at www.bmvg.de/portal/a/bmvg. See also Stephen Szabo, "The German Defense White Paper," *AICGS Advisor,* December 7, 2006. Especially relevant for the deployment of German forces abroad is the White Paper's redefinition of German security objectives away from a territorial defense to "international conflict prevention and crisis management, to include the fight against international terrorism." (White Paper 2006, op cit., 9.) The headline writers' shorthand for this is "Germany's defense line begins at the Hindu Kush."

14. Mary Elise Sarotte, *German Military Reform and European Security* (London: Oxford University Press, 2001), 9-11 [Adelphi Paper 340]. Data was also drawn from German government sources; see www.einsatz.bundeswehr.de, and author's tabulations. In 2000, German forces accounted for the second largest NATO contingent in Kosovo, and a German general commanded KFOR.

15. In the 2001 debate over the Afghan deployment, Schröder explicitly linked such actions to "a united and sovereign Germany accepting its greater responsibility in the world." See his speech in the *Bundestag* as reported in *Das Parlament* 50, nos. 48–49 (November 23/30, 2001): 11.

16. Kerry Longhurst, *Germany and the Use of Force: The Evolution of German Security Policy, 1990–2003* (Manchester, UK: Manchester University Press, 2004), 56–57.

17. Longhurst (ibid, 63–64) is especially good on the political party wrangling on these issues.

18. Longhurst (ibid, 64) is surely correct in her assessment: "In mapping the trajectory of change in Germany's post–Cold War security policy, the Constitutional Court's decision of 12 July 1994 is of central significance." See also *Focus on Germany* (New York: German Information Center, 1994).

19. Longhurst, ibid, 84–88. See Schröder's speech (note 15).

20. That is, in addition to the positions espoused by political parties.

21. Herfried Münkler, "Militärinterventionen in aller Welt," *Frankfurter Allgemeine Zeitung,* October 9, 2006, 8. In Münkler's pungent phrasing, "Der Imperativ, etwas tun müssen, Überlagert die überlegung, was man tun kann." ("The imperative to do *something* obscures the issue of what one *can* do.")

22. As Matthias Geis has put it, Germany, having gained full sovereignty at unification, finds that as an "internationally embedded middle power," it has difficulty refusing appeals for German military contributions, whether these come "from the USA, the UN or even just from CNN." See Matthias Geis, "Die Armee, die nicht verweigern darf," *Die Zeit* online, no. 31 (July 27, 2006).

23. Alexander Weinlein, "Marsch in die historische Mission" (Beilage zur Wochenzietung *Das Parliament*) 56, no. 3 (September 25, 2006): 1. Geis (op cit.) sees this mission as breaking the "last geo-historical taboo" for German military action.

24. *The Week in Germany,* July 6, 2007. The court's decision is summarized at www.bundesregierung.de/nn_774/Content/DE/Artikel/2007/07/2007-07-03-urteil-bverfg-tornado-einsatz.html.

25. Thom Shanker, "Gates Says Anger Over Iraq Hurts Afghan Effort," *New York Times* online, February 9, 2008; "Bundesregierung widerspricht U.S.-Forderung," *Frankfurter Rundschau* online, February 1, 2008; Thorsten Knuf, "Eiszeit unter Freunden," ibid, February 1, 2008.

26. Stefan Hebestreit, "Afghanistan quält die SPD," *Frankfurter Rundschau* online, June 28, 2007; "Zweifel an Afghanistan-Einsatz wachsen," ibid, May 21, 2007.

27. A poll taken at about the same time for the television network ARD on September 16, 2006, showed that if further peace-keeping missions required more expenditures for the *Bundeswehr,* 63 percent would rather desist from further actions; 32 percent would pay more. Similarly, the decision to send 780 soldiers for a four-month EU mission to oversee elections in the Congo was regarded as "sensible" (*sinnvoll*) by only 37 percent, and "not sensible" by 59 percent of those polled. (Infrastest Dimap polling reported in "Kongo-Einsatz gebilligt," *Frankfurter Rundschau* online, June 2, 2006.)

28. These findings are part of a *Projekt Links* survey on a variety of political issues; see *Die Zeit* online, August 9, 2007.
29. See, for example, Geis (op cit.), and Münkler (op cit.).
30. For a cogent analysis of the operational and political difficulties, see Markus Kaim, "ISAF ausbauen—OEF beenden," SWP-Aktuell 43, *Stiftung Wissenschaftund Politik* online, July 2007; for the political difficulties as of summer 2007, see Judy Dempsey, "Keeping the Peace Abroad a Tough Sell in Germany," *International Herald Tribune,* August 9, 2007.
31. For some of the milder comments, as reported in the press, see Richard Bernstein, "The German Question," *New York Times Magazine,* May 2, 2004, 52–57, and Steven Erlanger, "U.S. Quietly Chides German for His Dissension on Iraq," *New York Times* online, August 17, 2002. A more balanced commentary by a U.S. diplomat with a long record of service in Germany is J. D. Bindnagel, "The Transatlantic Relationship in the Era of American Primacy," *American Institute for Contemporary German Studies* online, September 26, 2003. Ivo Daalder points out that Schröder's frank disagreements with the United States mirror what Colin Powell said earlier in 2002 about George W. Bush's style: that he states his views frankly and then goes ahead, hoping but not waiting for allied support. Ivo Daalder, "U.S.-German Relations after the Elections," *American Institute for Contemporary German Studies* online, October 25, 2002.
32. Jackson Janes, "The Change in Government and Transatlantic Relations," *German Politics and Society* 24, no. 1, issue 78 (Spring 2006): 121–124.
33. A sampling would include: on climate change, Helene Cooper and Andrew C. Revkin, "U.S. Rebuffs Germany on Greenhouse Gas Cuts," *New York Times* online, May 26, 2007; regarding multiparty support for Merkel's demand that the United States close the detention center at Guantanamo Bay, "Viel Beifall für Merkels Kritik," *Frankfurter Rundschau* online, January 9, 2006; and criticism from the CDU and SPD regarding Iran and Iraq and arms sales to Saudi Arabia: "Unverständnis in Berlin," *Frankfurter Rundschau* online, July 31, 2007, "Bushes Irakpolitik entsetzt Berlin," ibid, January 11, 2007, and "USA sollten Iranpolitik verändern," ibid, March 17, 2006.
34. For a discussion of German and French opposition to the Iraqi invasion, see M. Donald Hancock and Brandon Valeriano, "West European Responses to the Bush Doctrine," in Mary Buckley and Robert Singh, eds., *The Bush Doctrine and the War on Terrorism: Global Responses and Global Consequences* (London: Routledge, 2006).

35. The Rumsfeld-Fischer exchange at the February 2002 Munich strategy conference indicated the extent of the gulf between German and U.S. views. Speaking directly to Rumsfeld and breaking into English, Fischer declared, "Sorry, I am not convinced. You have to make your case. Sorry, you haven't convinced me." Paul Hockenos, *Joschka Fischer and the Making of the Berlin Republic: An Alternative History of Postwar Germany* (New York: Oxford University Press, 2008), 4–5.

36. At an election rally in Hannover on August 5, 2002, Schröder said, "It is true that we have set forth on our way, our German way [*unseren deutschen Weg*]" and later, discussing the danger of an Iraq War, he declared further that light-hearted war plans (*Spielerei mit Krieg*) would receive no support from his government. He charged that Kohl had evaded these difficult choices by refraining from military action but helping to finance them. But now, he continued, "this Germany, our Germany is a self-confident [*selbstbewusstes*] country." See http://berlin.spd.de/servlet/PB/show/1017816/btw 2002_0805schroeder_rede.pdf.

37. For example, see "Wir sind alle gegen diesen Krieg," [interview with Wolfgang Schäuble], *Die Zeit* online, no. 14 (2003); in 2005, Schäuble became interior minister in Merkel's government. Note that before the war began, Bush was able to disarm German suspicions, which may have fueled later disappointment; see his speech to the *Bundestag* and consultations with heads of party fractions in May 2002. See Bush's speech, "Wir verteidigen das gleiche Haus der Freiheit" (Beilage zur Wochenzietung *Das Parliament*) 52, nos. 22–23 (May 31–June 7, 2002): 17–18; Markus Feldenkirchen, "Freimütig und direct," *Der Tagesspiegel* online, May 24, 2002; and Steven Erlanger and Terence Neilan, "Bush Warns Germans on Terror: Has No Iraq 'War Plans on Desk'," *New York Times* online, May 23, 2002.

38. *Statistisches Jahrbuch der Bundesrepublik Deutschland 2006,* 470–473; "Rangfolge der Handelspartner im Außenhandel der Bundesrepublik Deutschland," Statistisches Bundesamt, 2007; Mark Landler, "Germany's Export-Led Economy Finds Global Niche," *New York Times* online, April 13, 2007.

39. More recently, Joschka Fischer has pointed out that while a post-Bush United States might be seen in a more favorable light in Germany, the strain between the United States on the one hand and the EU (and Germany in particular) on the other will remain, thanks to the disparity of power between them. Fischer therefore prescribes a range of close cooperative ventures to restore a harmonious Atlantic alliance. Joschka Fischer, "Wird alles wieder gut?" *Die Zeit* online, January 14, 2008.

40. Karen Donfried, "Germany on the Global Stage: The U.S.-German Relationship after Unification," in Carl Lankowski, ed, *Breakdown, Breakup, Breakthrough: Germany's Difficult Passage to Modernity* (New York: Berghahn Books, 1999), 51–76.

41. Robert G. Livingston, in "The Likable Germans," *Atlantic Times,* May 2007, 42. Livingston points to German embassy polling on Americans' attitudes toward Germany. The normal state is that Germany is considered an important international partner, mostly for trade reasons. The "normal" level of favorable ("high" or "good") about Germany is at a level of more than 40 percent; it rose very high (65 percent) after 9/11, dropped to 17 percent at the start of the Iraq War, and stands at 39 percent in the most recent survey.

42. These figures and related data in the following paragraph are taken from "Global Unease with Major World Powers," a forty-seven-nation survey presented June 27, 2007, "America's Image in the World: Findings from the Pew Global Attitudes Projects," [Congressional testimony by Andrew Kohut, President, Pew Research Center, March 14, 2007]. Both sources are at www.pewglobal.org.

43. "Botschafter wider Willen," *Der Spiegel* online, July 23, 2007, 30–31.

44. Paul Nolte, "Die unamerikanische Nation," *Die Zeit* online, no. 22 (May 28, 2002). A parallel analysis, but one critical of German attitudes, is Peter Schneider, "Zeit der Rechthaber," *Der Spiegel* online, no. 26 (June 23, 2003).

45. V.R. Berghahn, "German Americanism and Anti-Americanism in Historical Perspective," American Institute for Contemporary German Studies (online), December 20, 2002. Berghahn points out that European and German cultural suspicion of the United States, which dates back to the turn of the last century, was much stronger politically just after 1945 than at any time since. Survey data substantiates the view that any sharp rise in such views tends to be policy-related. For early postwar anti-Americanism in Western Europe, including West Germany, see Tony Judt, *Postwar: A History of Europe since 1945* (London: Penguin Books, 2005), 220–225.

46. For the background of current German-Russian relations see Angela E. Stent, *Russia and Germany Reborn: Unification, the Soviet Collapse, and the New Europe* (Princeton, N.J.: Princeton University Press, 1999). See especially 1–15 for a historical overview.

47. For some typical examples of Russian-German official goodwill, under both Schröder and Merkel, see Roger Cohen, "Putin Discovers a New Rapport with Germany," *New York Times,* June 13, 2000, 1; "Merkel will Beziehung zu Russland intensivieren," *Der Spiegel* online, January 16, 2006.

48. Roland Götz, "Deutschland und Russland—'strategische Partner'?" *Aus Politik und Zeitgeschichte* (Beilage zur Wochenzeitung *Das Parlament*) B 11 (March 13, 2006): 14–23.

49. Ibid, 14–15, and Tables 1 and 2.

50. Vladimir Milov, "Energy Relations of Europe, Germany and Russia in the Transatlantic Context," 17–26 of the AICGS Working Paper *The U.S.-German-Russian Triangle: German-Russian Relations and the Impact on the Transatlantic Agenda* (2007), at www.aicgs.org/analyses/publications. Milov assets further that while Germany is the largest consumer of Russian natural gas in Europe in absolute terms, this natural gas makes up less than 10 percent of Germany's total energy consumption. The main German incentive in using Russian natural gas is to offset declining production in the North Sea fields.

51. Upon leaving office, Schröder became a co-chair of the company that will operate this system, a move that aroused controversy within Germany. This also aroused intense Polish hostility. For some criticism, see "Schröder verrubelt seinen Ruf," *Der Spiegel* online, December 12, 2005; for Schröder's defense, see "Schröder wehrt sich gegen Vorwürfe," ibid, December 12, 2005, as well as in his interview a year later, "Für mich gibt es keine Rückkehr," ibid, October 23, 2006.

52. Angela Stent, "Berlin's Russia Challenge," *The National Interest* online, March 3, 2007. Stent places this issue in a broader EU-Russia framework.

53. See *Strategische Partnerschaft mit Russland,* April 26, 2006, at www.auswärtiges-amt.de.

54. Mark Landler, "Putin Prompts Split in German Coalition," *New York Times,* May 22, 2007. Merkel's aide for Russian affairs, Andreas Schockenhoff, has stressed that unlike Schröder, Merkel sees relations with Russia as having more than a trade dimension. However, he stressed that Germany is concerned not to single out Russia for political defects—he mentioned Guantanamo—and suggested Russian NGO presence at meetings to reflect Russian societal breadth. "Russland braucht keine verordneten Vereine," *Der Spiegel* online, July 10, 2006.

55. The subsequent "cyber attack" on Estonian computer networks during a dispute over a Word War II memorial, as well as the British controversy over the Litvinenko murder, have provided those suspicious of Moscow with added ammunition.

56. See the analysis by Angela Stent, *Russia and Germany Reborn,* 233–245, and Stent (note 46).

57. "Global Unease …," 73–74 [Pew poll, cited in note 42].

58. Florian Hassel, "Viele Russen halten Demokratie für schädlich," *Frankfurter Rundschau* online, March 13, 2007.

59. There is a voluminous literature on Germany' relationship to the ever-enlarging European community. For immediate background, see Banchoff, op cit., ch. 2; August Pradetto, "The Policy of German Foreign Policy: Changes since Unification," in Hans W. Maull, *Germany's Uncertain Power: Foreign Policy of the Berlin Republic* (New York: Palgrave Macmillan, 2006), 17–18.

60. "French Leader, in Berlin, Urges a Fast Track to Unity in Europe," *New York Times,* June 28, 2000. Chirac's Berlin speech reinvigorated close German-French EU cooperation. Nicolas Sarkozy's election as French president in May 2007, however, marked the onset of a new phase of "difficulty" in the Franco-German partnership. Sarkozy and Chancellor Merkel differ markedly in their leadership styles and personalities, and Sarkozy has sought to launch several EU ventures without prior consultation with the German government. A case in point was his 2008 initiative to create a Mediterranean Union consisting of European and North African nations, which riled Merkel because in her view it threatened to divide the EU. The two leaders subsequently patched up their differences. See "The Awkward Partners: The Franco-German Relationship," *The Economist,* March 15–21, 2008, 61.

61. Hans Stark, "The Franco-German Relationship, 1998–2005," in Maull, op cit., 109–121. The mutual importance of Germany and the larger European community for each other is a recurrent theme in Tony Judt's (op. cit., 153–160) history of postwar Europe.

62. For details on the growth and elaboration of the EU structures and practices, see Desmond Dinan, *Ever Closer Union: An Introduction to European Integration,* 3rd ed. (Boulder, Colo.: Lynne Rienner, Publishers, 2005); Roy H. Ginsburg, *Demystifying the European Union: The Enduring Logic of Regional Integration* (New York and London: Rowman and Littlefield, 2007); and Simon Hix, *The Political System of the European Union,* 2nd ed. (New York: Palgrave Macmillan, 2005). One of the authors of this volume provides an overview of the EU's development, institutions, and policies in M. Donald Hancock and Guy Peters, "The European Union," in Hancock, et al., *Politics in Europe,* 4th ed. (Washington, D.C.: CQ Press, 2007).

63. European Commission, *Eurobarometer 67* (Spring 2007) [German and English language versions], National Report: Germany. Issues Germans would like to see decided at the national level included: jobs, taxes, education, pensions, and health and social concerns.

64. As the data in Table 10.4 suggest, eastern Germans are less supportive of EU projects, perhaps reflecting their lower levels of trust in political institutions. See on this point Oscar W. Gabriel, Sonja Zmerlki, "Politisches Vertrauen: Deutschland in Europa?" *Aus*

Politik und Zeitgeschichte (Beilage zur Wochenzietung *Das Parliament*) nos. 30–31 (July 24, 2006): 8–15. It is noteworthy that the PDS (and now the Left Party) has always supported a European engagement, albeit with sharp policy differences from the major parties.

65. EU budget assessments are figured as a percentage of gross domestic product. However, a country such as Germany, although itself a major contributor, may receive structural aid funds for a part of its territory. Thus, in 2000–2006, Germany received almost €30 million for infrastructure and growth, furthering measures in the former East Germany. See www.bundesregierung.de/Europa/lexicon.

66. Alister Miskimmon and William E. Patterson, "Adapting to Europe? German Foreign Policy, Domestic Constraints, and the Limitations of Europeanization since Unification," in Maull, op cit., 29–46.

67. Sebastian Harnisch and Siegfried Schieder, "Germany's New European Policy: Weaker, Leaner, Meaner," ibid, 95–108.

68. The official title of the office is "High Representative for Foreign and Security Policy."

69. For some of the expansive press analysis, see Stephen Castle and Dan Bilefsky, "Leaders in Deal on Europe's Charter," *New York Times* online, June 23, 2007; former foreign minister Joschka Fischer, "Knapp am Totalschaden vorbei," *Sueddeutsche Zeitung* online, June 25, 2007; and "Merkel warnt vor Scheitern des EU-Verfassungsvertrags," *Frankfurter Rundschau* online, June 14, 2007.

Chapter 11 Notes

1. According to a recent poll by Harris Interactive for the *International Herald Tribune* and France24 television, 68 percent of French respondents considered Angela Merkel the leader of Europe, followed by 57 percent of Germans and Spaniards. Italians and the British divided their votes between Merkel and Gordon Brown, the British prime minister. Reflecting traditional attitudes about the "special relationship" between the United States and Britain, a majority of Americans viewed Brown as Europe's leader. "The leader of Europe? Answers an ocean apart," *International Herald Tribune,* April 4, 2008.

2. Laggard modernization characterizes a number of peripheral regions in Europe and elsewhere. Southern Italy and parts of northern England are prime examples. The Appalachian region of the United States is yet another.

3. Rainer Geißler, "Nachholende Modernisierung mit Widersprüchen. Eine Vereinigungsbilanz aus modernisierungstheoretischer Perspektive," *Aus Politik und Zeitgeschichte* (Beilage zur Wochenzeitung *Das Parlament*) no. B40 (2000): 21–29.

4. Between 1991 and 1998, net fiscal transfers from West to East Germany totaled approximately DM1215 billion. Ibid, 27.

5. "Verdienste in Deutschland," *Statistisches Jahrbuch 2007 für die Bundesrepublik Deutschland* (Wiesbaden: Statistisches Bundesamt, 2007), 523.

6. "Weniger Bevölkerung in neuen Ländern erwartet," *Frankfurter Rundschau* online, May 22, 2007.

7. "Tearing Itself Down: Depopulation in Eastern Germany," *The Economist,* April 12, 2008, 59–60.

8. Germans trod several different paths to contemporary modernity during the twentieth century. As Mitchell Ash has written, one might want to "consider the FRG and the GDR, perhaps even the Nazi regime, as different though not entirely incompatible structurings of modernity that existed not as yes or no opposites, but in definable historical relations with one another." Mitchell G. Ash, "Becoming Normal, Modern, and German (Again?)," in Michael Geyer, ed., *The Power of Intellectuals in Contemporary Germany* (Chicago: University of Chicago Press, 2001), 305.

9. Nicholas Kulisch, "Out of East Germany via Bulgaria," *New York Times,* March 25, 2008.

10. Ash, op cit., 267.

11. In what has been described as "one of the largest economic scandals ever in Germany's post–World War II history," government officials targeted 163 wealthy Germans for hiding more than €27 million in Liechtenstein bank accounts to avoid paying taxes at home. www.spiegel.de/international/business/0,1518,535768,00.html and www.transparency.org/publications/newsletter/2008/march_2008/i n_the_news/liechtenstein_bank_scandal.

12. See the polling data reported in Katharina Sperber, "Wo bleibt die Gerechtigkeit?" *Frankfurter Rundschau* online, April 4, 2008.

13. OECD, *Economic Surveys: Germany* (2006B-May 2006), 8.

14. In 2007–2008, the annual inflation rate averaged 2.7 percent in the euro zone, 3.3 percent in the United States, and 2.6 percent in Britain. Germany's unemployment rate during the same period was 7.8 percent compared to 7.1 percent in the euro area, 5.2 percent in Britain, and 5.1 percent in the United States. *The Economist,* April 12, 2008, 109. For performance indicators from 1982 to 2005, see Table 9.4 in chapter 9 of this text.

15. *Eurobarometer 68, Nationaler Bericht Deutschland* (Fall 2007), 7–8. Thirty-five percent of eastern Germans expected to be worse off in twelve months compared to 24 percent of western Germans expressing similar expectations.

16. In mid-April 2008 the euro was worth nearly $1.60, a significant increase in value since its introduction in January 2002 at nearly a 1:1 parity rate.

17. "Despite her popularity, Merkel has ceased to set the agenda," *International Herald Tribune,* April 16, 2008.
18. Ibid.
19. Franz Walter, "Im Sog der Ein-bisschen Gesellschaft," *Der Spiegel* online, March 23, 2008, www.spiegel.de/politik/deutschland/0. 1518.542979.00.html.
20. In a *Politbarometer* poll of April 2008, two-thirds of the general public and an astonishing 61 percent of SPD supporters did not want Beck to be the SPD's chancellor candidate in 2009. (Forschungsgruppe Wahlen, *Politbarometer,* April 1, 2008, KW 14).
21. The polling results described in this paragraph are taken from results of a *Infratest dimap* poll for the TV network ARD as reported in *Frankfurter Rundschau* online, March 11, 2008.
22. Michael Naumann, "Wohin treibt die SPD?" *Die Zeit* online, no. 14 (March 27, 2008), www.zeit.de/2008/14/SPD-Kurs.
23. It helped his argument that a newly elected Left Party Lower Saxony state legislator avowed her communist allegiance and approval of both the Stasi and the Berlin Wall.
24. Naumann, ibid.
25. Klaus Wowereit, "Meine Zeit wird kommen," *Cicero* online, April 2008, www.cicero.de/839.php?ausgabe=04/2008.
26. Ibid.
27. Wolfram Weimer, "Es war einmal ein Linksruck," *Cicero* online, April 2008, www.cicero.de/839.php?ausgabe=04/2008.
28. The decision by the Greens to enter into this coalition government is defended by their national co-chair, Renate Künast, in "Künast verteidigt Schwarz-Grün," *Frankfurter Rundschau* online, April 19, 2008, and analyzed further by Michael Schlieben, "Schwarz-Grün für Deutschland," *Die Zeit* online, April 18, 2008, www.zeit.de/online/2008/17/scharz-gruen-reaktionen.
29. The background for this section was detailed at greater length in chapter 1; among the important background sources noted there were, for Germany, Simon Green, *The Politics of Exclusion: Institutions and Immigration Policy in Contemporary Germany* (Manchester: Manchester University Press, 2004). For the broader west and east European context, see Kristen Ghodsee, "Headscarves in Homeroom: Women's Islamic Dress in the 'New' Europe," American Association for the Advancement of Slavic Studies, *NewsNet* 47, no. 4 (August 2007): 1–6 (on Bulgaria), and on western Europe but especially Great Britain, see the symposium "Engaging with Islamism in Britain and Europe," *Political Science & Politics* 41, no. 1 (January 2008): 11–42. See also the sources cited in chapter one: Timothy A. Byrnes and Peter J. Katzenstein, eds., *Religion in an Expanding Europe* (Cambridge: Cambridge University Press, 2006);

Jytte Klausen, *The Islamic Challenge: Politics and Religion in Western Europe* (Oxford: Oxford University Press, 2005).

30. Wolfgang Schäuble, "Der Islam ist Teil Deutschlands und Teil Europas" (Beilage zur Wochenzietung *Das Parliament*) 56, no. 40/41 (October 2/9, 2006): 15. This text is from *Bundestag* proceedings.

31. We have pointed to Akin's work in discussing political and general culture in chapter 4. For a more recent account of his social standing as a cultural intermediary, see Nicholas Kulisch, "A Hand That Links Germans and Turks," *New York Times,* January 6, 2008, MT9.

32. Of course, these are indeed real problems, and they involve real differences in values. One particular case of honor killings, for example, shook Berlin in 2006. It involved the murder of a Turkish (actually, Kurdish) woman who had fled from an arranged marriage in Turkey. She was killed by a brother (the family lived in Berlin) who was selected for the job because of his youth—so that he would fall under juvenile justice laws. German reaction to the relatively mild sentence of nine years was to press for deportation of the family. A leader of the Berlin Greens, in a typical reaction, declared that if the family refused to accept German values and legal norms, one should tell them to leave. The family applied for custodial care of the victim's son; Berlin child welfare officials objected that this would be contrary to the child's best interests. See "Das Verfahren," *Tagesspiegel* online, April 18, 2006; "Familie Sürücü soll gehen," *Berliner Zeitung* online, April 18, 2006; "Fall Sürücü kommt vor das Familiengericht," ibid. It is important to note that Turkish women activists denounced the light sentence: "Türkinnen halten die Strafe für zu milde," *Tagesspiegel* online, April 20, 2006.

33. Faruk Sen and Dirk Halm, "Wanted: The Chance to Become German," *Atlantic Times,* April 2008, 3.

34. In an interview Ertekin Özcan, head of Turkish-German PTA societies, stressed the role of parents' social background, not ethnicity, as a handicap to their children's education. "Mangelnde Bildung ist kein türkisches Phänomen," *Frankfurter Rundschau* online, May 3, 2006.

35. The German dimension of this is examined by Simon Green in "Rethinking Immigrant Integration in Germany," *AICGS Advisor* online, December 21, 2006. Karin L. Johnson, in "Religion and Politics: The European Debate," AICGS *Issue Brief* no. 15 online, May 2007, explores the larger European pattern.

36. Mark Landler, "Germans Split over a Mosque and the Role of Islam," *New York Times* online, July 5, 2007. What critics see as a symbol of a separatist minority, its proponents, including its German architect, see as a step toward integration. Paul Böhn, "Die Moschee steht für Toleranz," *Cicero* online, May 2006. www.cicero.de /97.php?ress_id=4&item=2152. For the parallel dispute in Munich,

see Mark Landler, "In Munich, Provocation in a Symbol of Foreign Faith," *New York Times* online, December 8, 2006.

37. See the interview with Ekin Deligöz in " 'Es ist ein Symbol der Unterdrückung'" (Beilage zur Wochenzietung *Das Parliament*) 56, no. 46 (November 13, 2006): 3. She was then the object of death threats. See Jörg Lau, "Die Macht der frechen Frauen," *Die Zeit* online, no. 4, 2006.

38. "Symbol der Unterdrückung," *Der Spiegel* online, October 15, 2006.

39. See the interview with an Iranian-born theologian, head of the Muslim Academy in Germany, Hamideh Mohaghegi, in "Wie Muslimas sich kleiden, sollen sie frei entscheiden dürfen," *Frankfurter Rundschau* online, November 4, 2006.

40. "Deutsche Schüler bekommen Islamunterricht," ibid, March 13, 2008.

41. Martina Fietz, "Fietz fragt: Lale Akgün, SPD-Bundestagsabgeordnete zur Islamkonferenz," *Cicero* online, March 2008, www.cicero.de/839.php?ausgabe=03/2008.

42. "Ministerin sucht Bündnis mit Christen," *Frankfurter Rundschau* online, April 20, 2006.

43. These and the data in the following paragraphs are taken from an extremely instructive series in *Die Zeit,* in which Germany's Turks were both polled and interviewed. Jörg Lau, "Wir wollen hier rein!" *Die Zeit* online, no. 12 (March 13, 2008), www.zeit.de/2008/12//Tuerken-Umfrage.

44. Data from the *Stastitisches Jahrbuch 2007*; see also "Zahl der Einwanderer sinkt unter 600 000," *Frankfurter Rundschau* online, July 7, 2006, and Vera Gaserow, "Weniger Zuwanderer," ibid, January 18, 2005. Gaserow points out that immigration from Turkey did *not* consist largely of wives in arranged marriages with Turkish-German men, a point often cited as a major obstacle to integration.

45. Ibid.

46. Mary Hampton, " 'The Past, Present, and the Perhaps': Is Germany a 'Normal Power'?" *Security Studies* 1 (2000): 179–202.

47. For an incisive analysis and survey of Germany's international position in the wake of Schröder's assertion of Germany's enhanced position, see Gunther Hellmann, "Von Gipfelstürmern und Gratwanderern: 'Deutsche Wege' in der Außenpolitik," *Aus Politik und Zeitgeschichte* (Beilage zur Wochenzeitung *Das Parliament*) no. 11 (March 8, 2004), online. Hellmann identified a number of useful projects wherein Germany could exert a due but not excessive measure of influence, such as the "Weimar Triangle" of France, Germany, and Poland, where Berlin could use its influence to bridge the supposed "old Europe"—"new Europe" divide.

48. Steven Erlanger and Steven Lee Myers, "Allies Upset as Bush Moves off NATO Script," *International Herald Tribune* online, April 3, 2008.

49. Charles S. Maier, "America among Empires? Imperial Analogues and Imperial Syndrome," *GHI Bulletin* no. 41 (Fall 2007): 25.

50. For pointed arguments—military, historical, economic, moral—against the Afghan deployment, see Wolfram Weimar, "Raus aus Afghanistan!" *Cicero* online, April 2008, www.cicero.de/839.php?ausgabe=04/2008. How widely these critics' views have penetrated the political establishment may be seen in a survey of *Bundestag* defense experts from all parties reported in Martina Fietz, "Raus aus Afghanistan, aber ... ," ibid. Note that a special Green Party congress called to decide the party's stand on reauthorizing the Afghanistan deployment voted against such approval, thereby overturning the recommendation of the party leadership and *Bundestag* faction. See "Klares Nein zu Afghanistan-Leitantrag," *Tagesschau.de* online, September 16, 2007.

51. The argument we offer here is drawn from James Sheehan's recent account of Europe's transformation from (following Harold Laswell) garrison states to civilian states. Sheehan traces this development from the rise of mass armies and public ideals of military heroism after 1815 to its replacement after 1945 by notions of economic and social security and individual achievement. See James Sheehan, *Where Have All the Soldiers Gone? The Transformation of Modern Europe* (Boston: Houghton Mifflin, 2008), especially chs. 8, 9, and the Epilogue.

52. Ibid, 200–201. Sheehan quotes then German president Richard von Weizsäcker as declaring—on the very occasion, October 3, 1990, when Germany celebrated recovery of full sovereignty in a unified country—that "Today sovereignty means participating in the international community."

53. This suggests that German-American relations will improve under another U.S. president and as the Iraq War winds down, although the era of unquestioning German acceptance of American leadership (if it ever existed!) will not reappear. Joschka Fischer makes these points in a recent essay, "Wird alles wieder gut?" *Die Zeit* online, January 14, 2008.

54. Sheehan, op cit., 223–224.

55. Nicholas Kulish, "Efforts to Restore Shine to Medal Tarnished by Nazis," *New York Times,* March 20, 2008. Kulish quotes Berlin political scientist Christoph Zürcher, who asserted, "In the German political culture, it is simply not possible to express esteem for young soldiers."

56. Sheehan, op cit., 180.

57. Robert Cooper, *The Breaking of Nations: Order and Chaos in the Twenty-First Century* (New York: Atlantic Monthly Press, 2003). Cooper was awarded the Orwell Prize (the preeminent annual British prize for political writing) for the book for his "distinguished contribution to honesty and clarity in public language."
58. Ibid, 16.
59. For example, conflicts in Chechnya in Russia and Northern Ireland in the United Kingdom.
60. Ibid, 22.
61. Ibid, 27.
62. Roger Cohen, "The Cold War as Ancient History," *New York Times,* February 4, 2008, and "Mauer? Welche Mauer?" *Frankfurter Rundschau* online, December 27, 2007.

Further Reading

Contextual

Black, C. E. *The Dynamics of Modernization*. New York: Harper and Row, 1966.

Dahrendorf, Ralf. *Society and Democracy in Germany*. New York: W. W. Norton, 1967.

Huntington, Samuel. *Political Order in Changing Societies*. New Haven: Yale University Press, 1968.

——. *The Third Wave: Democratization in the Late Twentieth Century*. Norman: University of Oklahoma Press, 1993.

Inglehart, Ronald. *The Silent Revolution: Changing Values and Political Styles*. Princeton: Princeton University Press, 1977.

——. *Culture Shift in Advanced Industrial Society*. Princeton: Princeton University Press, 1990.

——. *Modernization and Postmodernization Cultural, Economic and Political Change in 43 Societies*. Princeton: Princeton University Press, 1997.

Linz, Juan J., and Alfred Stepan. *Problems of Democratic Transition and Consolidation: Southern Europe, South America, and Post-Communist Europe*. Baltimore: Johns Hopkins Press, 1996.

Moore, Barrington, Jr. *Social Origins of Dictatorship and Democracy*. With a new foreword by Edward Friedman and James C. Scott. Boston: Beacon Press, 1993.

Rustow, Dankwart A. *A World of Nations*. Washington, D.C.: Brookings Institution, 1967.

Historical Background

Craig, Gordon. *The Politics of the Prussian Army, 1640–1945*. New York: Oxford University Press, 1956.

——. *Germany, 1866–1945*. New York: Oxford University Press, 1967.

Elon, Amos. *The Pity of It All: A History of Jews in Germany, 1743–1933*. New York: Metropolitan Books (Henry Holt), 2002.

Holborn, Hajo. *A History of Modern Germany: The Reformation*. New York: Alfred A. Knopf, 1961.

Jarausch, Konrad H., and Michael Geyer. *Shattered Past: Reconstructing German Histories*. Princeton: Princeton University Press, 2003.

Wende, Peter. *A History of Germany*. New York: Palgrave-Macmillan, 2005.

Winkler, Heinrich August. *Der lange Weg nach Westen*, 2 vols. Munich: C. H. Beck, 2000.

The Weimar and Nazi Eras, 1918–1945

Bracher, Karl Dietrich. *The German Dictatorship*. New York: Praeger, 1970.

——. *Die Auflösung der Weimarer Republic*. Stuttgart: Ring, 1977.

Evans, Richard J. *The Coming of the Third Reich*. London: Penguin Books, 2004.

Friedländer, Saul. *Nazi Germany and the Jews: The Years of Persecution 1933–1939*. New York: HarperCollins, 1997.

——. *The Years of Extermination: Nazi Germany and the Jews, 1939–1945*. New York: HarperCollins, 2008.

Gay, Peter. *Weimar Culture: The Outsider as Insider*. New York: Harper and Row, 1970.

——. *My German Question: Growing Up in Nazi Berlin*. New Haven: Yale University Press, 1998.

Kershaw, Ian. *Hitler: 1889–1936 Hubris* and *Hitler: 1936–1945 Nemesis*. New York: Norton, 2000.

MacMillan, Margaret. *Paris 1919: Six Months that Changed the World*. New York: Random House, 2002.

Mühlberger, Detlef. *The Social Bases of Nazism, 1919–1933*. Cambridge: Cambridge University Press, 2003.

Postwar Germany

Brandt, Willy. *In Exile: Essays, Reflections and Letters, 1933–1947*. Philadelphia: University of Pennsylvania Press, 1971.

Edinger, Lewis J. *Kurt Schumacher: A Study in Personality and Political Behavior.* Stanford: Stanford University Press, 1965.

Fulbrook, Mary. *The Divided Nation: A History of Germany, 1918–1990.* New York: Oxford University Press, 1992.

The Federal Republic, 1949–1990

Adenauer, Konrad. *Erinnerungen, 1955–1959.* Stuttgart: Deutsche Verlags-Anstalt, 1967.

Gunlicks, Arthur. *Local Government in the German Federal System.* Durham: Duke University Press, 1986.

Merkl, Peter H. *The Origin of the West German Republic.* New York: Oxford University Press, 1965.

———. *The Federal Republic at Fifty: The End of a Century of Turmoil.* London: Macmillan, 1999.

Smith, Gordon, et al., eds. *Developments in German Politics.* Durham: Duke University Press, 1990.

Smyser, W. R. *From Yalta to Berlin: The Cold War Struggle over Germany.* New York: St. Martin's Press, 1999.

Stern, Fritz. *Five Germanys I Have Known.* New York: Farrar, Strauss and Giroux, 2006.

German Democratic Republic

Dennis, Michael. *The German Democratic Republic.* London: Pintor Publishers, 1988.

Edwards, G. E. *GDR Society and Social Institutions: Facts and Figures.* London: Macmillan, 1985.

Fulbrook, Mary. *Anatomy of a Dictatorship: Inside the GDR, 1949–1989.* New York: Oxford University Press, 1995.

———. *The People's State: East German Society from Hitler to Honecker.* New Haven: Yale University Press, 2005.

Kopstein, Jeffrey. *The Politics of Economic Decline.* Chapel Hill: University of North Carolina Press, 1997.

Krisch, Henry. *German Politics under Soviet Occupation.* New York: Columbia University Press, 1974.

———. *The German Democratic Republic: The Search for Identity.* Boulder, Colo.: Westview Press, 1985.

McAdams, James. *East Germany and the West: Surviving Détente.* New York: Cambridge University Press, 1985.

——. *Germany Divided: From the Wall to Unification.* Princeton: Princeton University Press, 1993.

Plenzdorf, Ulrich, and Rüdiger Damann, *Ein Land, genannt die DDR.* Frankfurt am/Main: M. S. Fischer Verlag, 2005.

Rueschemeyer, Marilyn, and Christiane Leme, eds. *The Quality of Life in the German Democratic Republic.* New York: M. E. Sharpe, 1989.

Sandford, Gregory. *From Hitler to Ulbricht: The Communist Reconstruction of East Germany, 1945–1946.* Princeton: Princeton University Press, 1983.

Stern, Carola. *Ulbricht. Eine Politische Biographie.* Cologne: Kiepenheuer and Witsch, 1963.

Woods, Roger. *Opposition in the GDR under Honecker 1971–1985.* London: Macmillan, 1986.

Unification and Germany since 1990

Anderson, Christopher, Karl Kaltenthaler, and Wolfgang Luthardt, eds. *The Domestic Politics of German Unification.* Boulder, Colo.: Lynne Rienner, 1993.

Clay, Clemens, and William E. Paterson, eds. *The Kohl Chancellorship.* London: F. Cass, 1998.

Dennis, Mike, and Eva Kolinsky, eds. *United and Divided: Germany since 1990.* New York: Berghahn Books, 2004.

Fischer, Marc. *After the Wall: Germany, the Germans, and the Burdens of History.* New York: Simon and Schuster, 1995.

Glaessner, Gert-Joachim. *The Unification Process in Germany: From Dictatorship to Democracy.* London: Pinter Publishers, 1992.

Hampton, Mary N. *The Wilsonian Impulse: U.S. Foreign Policy, the Alliance and German Unification.* Westport, Conn.: Praeger, 1996.

Hampton, Mary N., and Christian Soe, eds. *Between Bonn and Berlin: German Politics Adrift?* Lanham, Md.: Rowman and Littlefield, 1999.

Hancock, M. Donald, and Helga A. Welsh, eds. *German Unification: Process and Outcomes.* Boulder, Colo.: Westview Press, 1994.

Huelshoff, Michael, Andrei Markovits, and Simon Reich, eds. *From Bundesrepublik to Deutschland: German Politics after Unification.* Ann Arbor: University of Michigan Press, 1993.

Kolinsky, Eva. *Women in Contemporary Germany: Life, Work and Politics,* 2nd revised ed. Providence, R.I.: Berg, 1993.

Ladd, Brian. *The Ghosts of Berlin: Confronting German History in the Urban Landscape.* Chicago: University of Chicago Press, 1997.

McAdams, James. *Judging the Past in Unified Germany.* New York: Cambridge University Press, 2001.

Merkl, Peter H. *German Unification in the European Context.* University Park: Pennsylvania State University Press, 1993.

Sinn, Gerlinde, and Hans-Wener Sinn. *Jumpstart: The Economic Unification of Germany.* Cambridge: MIT University Press, 1993.

Taylor, Frederick. *The Berlin Wall: A Word Divided, 1961–1989.* New York: HarperCollins, 2006.

Wise, Michael Z. *Capital Dilemma: Germany's Search for a New Architecture of Democracy.* New York: Princeton Architectural Press, 1998.

Political and Popular Culture

Almond, Gabriel, and Sidney Verba, *The Civic Culture: Political Attitudes and Democracy in Five Nations, An Analytical Study.* Boston: Little, Brown, 1965.

Baker, Kendall L., Russell J. Dalton, and Kai Hildebrandt. *Germany Transformed: Political Culture and the New Politics.* Cambridge: Harvard University Press, 1981.

Conradt, David P. "Changing German Political Culture." In *The Civic Culture Revisited,* Gabriel A. Almond and Sidney Verba, eds. Beverly Hills, Calif.: Sage Publications, 1989.

——. *The German Polity,* 8th ed. New York: Pearson-Longman, 2005.

Dalton, Russell J. *Citizen Politics: Public Opinion and Political Parties in Advanced Industrial Democracies,* 4th ed. Washington, D.C.: CQ Press, 2006.

Verba, Sidney. "The Remaking of German Political Culture." In *Political Culture and Political Development,* Lucian Pye and Sidney Verba, eds. Princeton: Princeton University Press, 1965.

Jarausch, Konrad H. *After Hitler: Recivilizing Germans, 1945–1955.* Translated by Brandon Hunziker. New York: Oxford University Press, 2006.

Ramet, Sabrina Petra. *Social Currents in Eastern Europe: The Sources and Consequences of the Great Transformation,* 2nd ed. Durham: Duke University Press, 1995.

Taberner, Stuart, and Frank Finlay, eds. *Recasting German Identity: Culture, Politics, and Literature in the Berlin Republic*. Rochester, N.Y.: Camden House, 2002.

Constitutional Principles, Political Institutions, and Decision Processes

Braunthal, Gerhard. *The West German Legislative Process*. Ithaca: Cornell University Press, 1972.

Green, Simon, and William E. Paterson, eds. *Governance in Contemporary Germany*. New York: Cambridge University Press, 2005.

Gunlicks, Arthur B. *Local Government in the German Federal System*. Durham: Duke University Press, 1986.

——. *The Länder and German Federalism*. Manchester, UK: Manchester University Press, 2003.

Klein, Hans, ed. *The German Chancellors*. Chicago: EditionQ, 1996.

Kommers, Donald. *Constitutional Jurisprudence in the Federal Republic of Germany*. Durham: Duke University Press, 1989.

——. *Judicial Politics in West Germany*. Beverly Hills, Calif.: Sage, 1976.

Loewenberg, Gerhard. *Parliament in the German Political System*. Ithaca: Cornell University Press, 1966.

Mayntz, Renate, and Fritz W. Scharpf. *Policy-Making in the German Federal Bureaucracy*. New York: Elsevier, 1965.

Rogowski, Ralf, and Thomas Gawron, eds. *Constitutional Courts in Comparison: The U.S. Supreme Court and the German Constitutional Court*. New York: Berghahn Publishers, 2002.

Political Parties, Interest Groups, and Social Movements

Braunthal, Gerhard. *The Federation of German Industry in Politics*. Ithaca: Cornell University Press, 1965.

——. *The West German Social Democrats, 1969–1982*. Boulder, Colo.: Westview Press, 1983.

——. *Parties and Politics in Modern Germany*. Boulder, Colo.: Westview Press, 1996.

Dalton, Russell J., ed. *The New Germany Votes: Unification and the Creation of a German Party System*. Providence, R.I.: Berg, 1993.

——. *Germans Divided: The 1994 Bundestag Elections and the Evolution of the German Party System.* Washington, D.C.: Berg, 1996.

Frankland, Gene E., and Donald Schoonmaker. *Between Protest and Power: The Green Party in Germany.* Boulder, Colo.: Westview Press, 1992.

Grebing, Helga. *The History of the German Labour Movement.* London: Oswald Wolff, 1969.

Heidenheimer, Arnold J. *Adenauer and the CDU.* The Hague: Martinus Nijhoff, 1960.

Hockenos, Paul. *Joschka Fischer and the Making of the Berlin Republic: An Alternative History of Postwar Germany.* Oxford: Oxford University Press, 2008.

Langenbacher, Erich, ed. *Launching the Grand Coalition: The 2005 Bundestag Elections and the Future of German Politics.* New York: Berghahn Books, 2006.

Lees, Charles. *The Red-Green Coalition in Germany: Politics, Personality and Power.* Manchester, UK: Manchester University Press, 2000.

Merkl, Peter, ed. *Western European Party Systems.* New York: Free Press, 1980.

Potthoff, Heinrich, and Susanne Miller. *The Social Democratic Party of Germany, 1848–2005.* Bonn: J. H. W. Dietz Nachf., 2006.

Wildenmann, Rudolf. *Partei und Fraktion.* Meisenheimer/Glan: Verlag Anton Hain, 1955.

Economic Policy

Katzenstein, Peter J., ed. *Between Power and Plenty: Foreign Economic Policies of Advanced Industrial States.* Madison: University of Wisconsin Press, 1978.

Lehmbruch, Gerhard, and Philippe C. Schmitter, eds. *Patterns of Corporatist Policy-Making.* Beverly Hills, Calif.: Sage, 1982.

Schmitter, Philippe C., and Gerhard Lehmbruch, eds. *Trends toward Corporatist Intermediation.* Beverly Hills, Calif.: Sage, 1979.

Siebert, Horst. *The German Economy: Beyond the Social Market.* Princeton: Princeton University Press, 2005.

Social Policy and Security

Byrnes, Timothy A., and Peter J. Katzenstein, eds. *Religion in an Expanding Europe.* Cambridge: Cambridge University Press, 2006.

Fetzer, Joel S., and J. Christopher Soper. *Muslims and the State in Britain, France and Germany*. Cambridge: Cambridge University Press, 2005.

Flora, Peter, and Arnold J. Heidenheimer, eds. *The Development of the Welfare State in Europe and America*. New Brunswick, N.J.: Transaction Books, 1981.

Green, Simon. *The Politics of Exclusion: Institutions and Immigration Policy in Contemporary Germany*. Manchester, UK: Manchester University Press, 2004.

Heidenheimer, Arnold J., Hugh Heclo, and Carolyn Teich Adams. *Comparative Public Policy: The Politics of Social Choice in America, Europe, and Japan*, 3rd ed. New York: St. Martin's Press, 1990.

Klausen, Jytte. *The Islamic Challenge: Politics and Religion in Western Europe*. Oxford: Oxford University Press, 2005.

Mattil, Birgit. *Pension Systems: Sustainability and Distributional Effects in Germany and the United Kingdom*. Heidelberg: Physica-Verlag, 2006.

Rein, Martin, and Winfried Schmähl, eds. *Rethinking the Welfare State. The Political Economy of Pension Reform*. Cheltenham, UK: Edward Elgar, 2004.

Taylor-Gooby, Peter, ed. *New Risks, New Welfare: The Transformation of the European Welfare State*. New York: Oxford University Press, 2004.

Foreign Policy and Military Security

Ash, Timothy G. *In Europe's Name: Germany and the Divided Continent*. New York: Random House, 1993.

Banchoff, Thomas. *The German Problem Transformed: Institutions, Politics and Foreign Policy, 1945–1995*. Ann Arbor: University of Michigan Press, 1999.

Clemens, Clay, ed. *NATO and the Quest for Post–Cold War Security*. New York: St. Martin's Press, 1997.

Hanrieder, Wolfram F. *West German Foreign Policy, 1949–1969*. Boulder, Colo.: Westview Press, 1980.

Katzenstein, Peter J., ed. *Tamed Power. Germany in Europe*. Ithaca: Cornell University Press, 1997.

Merkl, Peter H. *German Foreign Policies, East and West*. Santa Barbara, Calif.: ABC-Clio Press, 1977.

——. *The Distracted Eagle: The Rift between America and Old Europe*. New York: Routledge, 2005.

Pond, Elizabeth. *After the Wall: American Policy toward Germany.* Washington, D.C.: Brookings Institution, 1990.

Sheehan, James J. *Where Have All the Soldiers Gone? The Transformation of Modern Europe.* Boston: Houghton Mifflin, 2008.

Web Sites

Official Government Web sites

http://europa.eu: Official gateway to the European Union arranged by activities, institutions, documents, and services

www.bpb.de/wissen/Q01ETK,0,0,Das_Grundgesetz_f%FCr_die_Bundes republik_Deutschland.html: Article by article links to the Basic Law

www.bundesregierung.de: Useful gateway to ministries and other agencies

www.bundestag.de: Extensive information on legislative matters and party affairs, such as finances

www.bundeswahlleiter.de: Site includes all federal, state, and European election returns

www.destatis.de/jahrbuch/jahrbuch2006_downloads.htm: The annual *Statistical Yearbook,* which includes demographic, economic, social and other data

www.germany.info/relaunch/ politics/officials/officials.html: Official German government site

Parties

Each party has a Web site with a URL on this pattern:
www.spd.de (for the Left party, it is www.die-linke.de)

Press

Some important dailies:
Frankfurter Allgemeine Zeitung: www.faz.net.de
Frankfurter Rundschau: www.fr-online.de
Neues Deutschland: www.nd-online.de
Süddeutsche Zeitung: www.sueddeutsche.de
Important weeklies and monthlies:
Cicero: www.cicero.de
Der Spiegel: www.spiegel.de/international
Die Zeit: www.zeit.de

Index